D0983662

OXFORD EARLY CHRISTIAN STUDIES

General Editors
Gillian Clark   Andrew Louth

THE OXFORD EARLY CHRISTIAN STUDIES series includes scholarly volumes on the thought and history of the early Christian centuries. Covering a wide range of Greek, Latin, and Oriental sources, the books are of interest to theologians, ancient historians, and specialists in the classical and Jewish worlds.

Titles in the series include:

Evagrius of Pontus: The Greek Ascetic Corpus
Translation, Introduction, and Commentary
Robert E. Sinkewicz (2003)

Gregory of Nyssa and the Grasp of Faith
Union, Knowledge, and the Divine Presence
Martin Laird (2004)

The Suffering of the Impassible God
The Dialectics of Patristic Thought
Paul L. Gavrilyuk (2004)

Cyril of Alexandria and the Nestorian Controversy
The Making of a Saint and of a Heretic
Susan Wessel (2004)

The Byzantine Christ
Person, Nature, and Will in the Christology of St Maximus the Confessor
Demetrios Bathrellos (2004)

The Doctrine of Deification in the Greek Patristic Tradition
Norman Russell (2004)

The Body in St Maximus the Confessor
Holy Flesh, Wholly Deified
Adam G. Cooper (2005)

The Asketikon of St Basil the Great
Anna M. Silvas (2005)

Marius Victorinus' Commentary on Galatians
Stephen Andrew Cooper (2005)

Asceticism and Christological Controversy in Fifth-Century Palestine
The Career of Peter the Iberian
Cornelia B. Horn (2006)

Marcellus of Ancyra and the Lost Years of the Arian Controversy 325–345
Sara Parvis (2006)

The Irrational Augustine
Catherine Conybeare (2006)

Clement of Alexandria and the Beginnings of Christian Apophaticism
Henny Fiskå Hägg (2006)

The Christology of Theodoret of Cyrus
Antiochene Christology from the Council of Ephesus (431)
to the Council of Chalcedon (451)
Paul B. Clayton, Jr. (2006)

Ethnicity and Argument in Eusebius' *Praeparatio Evangelica*

AARON P. JOHNSON

OXFORD
UNIVERSITY PRESS

OXFORD
UNIVERSITY PRESS

Great Clarendon Street, Oxford OX2 6DP

Oxford University Press is a department of the University of Oxford.
It furthers the University's objective of excellence in research, scholarship,
and education by publishing worldwide in

Oxford New York

Auckland Cape Town Dar es Salaam Hong Kong Karachi
Kuala Lumpur Madrid Melbourne Mexico City Nairobi
New Delhi Shanghai Taipei Toronto

With offices in

Argentina Austria Brazil Chile Czech Republic France Greece
Guatemala Hungary Italy Japan Poland Portugal Singapore
South Korea Switzerland Thailand Turkey Ukraine Vietnam

Oxford is a registered trade mark of Oxford University Press
in the UK and in certain other countries

Published in the United States
by Oxford University Press Inc., New York

© Aaron P. Johnson 2006

British Library Cataloguing in Publication Data

Data available

Library of Congress Cataloging in Publication Data

Data available

Typeset by SPI Publisher Services, Pondicherry, India
Printed in Great Britain
on acid-free paper by
Biddles Ltd., King's Lynn, Norfolk

ISBN 0–19–929613–8   978–0–19–929613–2

1 3 5 7 9 10 8 6 4 2

For Heidi

Preface

Whether reading Herodotus on the ties that bound the Greeks together, Isocrates on the superiority of Greek *paideia*, Lucian's quibbles over the Attic purity of certain Greek words, or Julian the Apostate's declarations on the Greekness of pagan sacrificial practice, the modern reader is persistently struck by the Greeks' pervasive sense that they possessed a highly distinctive identity and had carved out for themselves a particular niche in a world of nations (*ethnē*). The concern to fortify, manipulate and reconfigure ethnic identities persisted among Greek authors from the classical to the early Byzantine periods. What was distinctively Greek about the Greeks, and what marked off non-Greeks—whether Scythians, Persians or Egyptians—from Greek identity, were topics brimming with significance and deserving of a great deal of literary industry and ingenuity. The apologetic literature produced by Jews and Christians joined the often heated conversation over ethnic identity and frequently developed its arguments within this ongoing Greek discourse on ethnicity. Eusebius' *Praeparatio Evangelica* (written between AD 313 and 324) stands as the most sustained and comprehensive work in this tradition, a monument to the literary battles fought over the contested field of identity in Greek antiquity.

Often misconstrued as nothing more than a repository of otherwise lost authors, the *Praeparatio* may yield more than just the verbatim quotations of missing works. The present discussion seeks to take seriously the representations of ethnicity in Eusebius' massive 15-book defence of Christianity. The role of ethnic identity in the argument against the Greeks and other nations has often been overlooked in attempts to delineate Eusebius' methodology, due in no small part to a focus on Christianity and its others as merely *religious* positions, extracted from their embodiment within the communal ways of life of particular peoples. I argue that a fuller appreciation of the argument of the *Praeparatio* is obtained by close analysis of the ethnic identities constructed by Eusebius within the text.

I refer to Eusebius' method as 'ethnic argumentation'—that is, the concern to strategically formulate ethnic identities as the basis for an apologetic argument. Assuming a discursive approach to ethnicity (one that recognizes the constructedness of such identities as a matter of boundary formation), I examine Eusebius' retelling of two narratives of descent: that of the Greeks and the Hebrews (as distinguished from the 'Jews', a later Egyptianized form of Hebrew identity). The former are represented as latecomers to history and dependent upon other nations for their ways of thinking and living (which are shown to be irrational and impious); the latter are shown to be the most ancient 'friends of God', whose way of life embodied piety and wisdom. By portraying Christians as a restoration of the ancient Hebrews, Eusebius legitimizes Christianity as rooted in antiquity and superior to other ethnic identities. Christians are a nation drawn from other nations (or, a 'Church out of the nations'). Eusebius thus blends universalism (people from any nation may join this restored Hebrew nation) and particularism (conversion involves the total rejection of one's ancestral ethnic customs for a new way of life) in his conception of Christian identity.

Throughout the course of my work on Eusebius, I have been continually surprised at the interest taken in my project and the kindness shown by a great number of people. I am grateful to members of the Classics community at the University of Colorado at Boulder, where this book had its beginnings as a doctoral thesis. Eckardt Schutrumpf, Christopher Shields, Susan Prince, Mark Benassi, John Gibert, and Peter Hunt, provided helpful suggestions, guidance and encouragement—whether as readers or as friends; Hal Drake, as a guest on my committee, offered a great deal of his time and good humour throughout every stage of its writing; Noel Lenski proved an insuperable adviser and friend, whose unstinting care and kindness I am most fortunate to have received. The dissertation was completed while I held a Junior Fellowship at Dumbarton Oaks Center for Byzantine Studies. I am grateful for the financial and academic support granted by the Trustees of Harvard University, and especially to Alice-Mary Talbot, who created an ideal environment in which my work could progress. While there, I received much helpful advice from its community of scholars and others whom I met during that year, including Scott Johnson, Kate Cooper, Kevin Osterloh, Evangelos Chrysos, Manolis Papoutsakis, and Christopher Jones. I also received warm hospitality from Greg Smith and Michael McCormick while a visiting fellow in Cambridge. I am indebted to the following for having read either a part or the whole of the manuscript as I was revising it for publication: Averil Cameron, David Olster, Andrew Jacobs, Peter Van Nuffelen, Kevin Van Bladel, and Michael Maas. Their suggestions and criticisms were invaluable; they certainly bear no burden for errors that remain. My family has provided the support without which I could not have finished. My children, Albian and Asher, have shown a great deal of patience and helped me to tell better the story of Eusebius, his library, and the ancient Greeks towards whom he focused his attention. My wife has shown unlimited goodwill, encouragement, and self-sacrifice. She provided the initial impetus to work on ethnicity in Eusebius. Heidi has been a true friend and faithful companion both intellectually and spiritually; it is to her that I dedicate this book. Finally, in addition to those humans who have given me so much, I should remark that this project has been sustained by the grace of a persistently caring God. I am grateful for the relentless care of the One who has carried me through these labours.

Contents

Abbreviations   xiii

1 Discourses of Ethnicity and Early Christian
  Apologetics: An Introduction   1

2 The Language of Ethnicity   25

3 Relocating Greekness: The Narrative of Greek Descent   55

4 Rewriting Hebrew History: The Descent
  of the Ancient Hebrews   94

5 Greek Descent Revisited   126

6 Rome Among the Nations: Eusebius'
  Praeparatio and the Unmaking of Greek Political Theology   153

7 The Church as Apologetic: Eusebius'
  Legitimation of Christianity   198

Appendix 1: The Structure of the *Praeparatio*   234

Appendix 2: The Concept of Progress in Eusebius   237

Select Bibliography   240

Index   259

Abbreviations

Journals and Reference Works

AJA	*American Journal of Archaeology*
AJP	*American Journal of Philology*
ANRW	series: *Aufstieg und Niedergang der Romischen Welt*, eds H. Temporini and W. Haase (Berlin and New York: Walter de Gruyter, 1972–)
BICS	*Bulletin for the Institute of Classical Studies*
CH	*Church History*
CJ	*Classical Journal*
C&M	*Classica et Mediaevalia*
CP	*Classical Philology*
CQ	*Classical Quarterly*
GCS	*Die Griechischen Christlichen Schrifsteller*
GRBS	*Greek, Roman and Byzantine Studies*
HSCP	*Harvard Studies in Classical Philology*
HTR	*Harvard Theological Review*
JEA	*Journal of Egyptian Archaeology*
JECS	*Journal of Early Christian Studies*
JRS	*Journal of Roman Studies*
JTS	*Journal of Theological Studies*
LSJ	*Liddel & Scott Greek-English Lexicon*, rev. H. Stuart Jones
NPNF	*Nicene and Post-Nicene Fathers Series*, ed. Ph. Schaff and H. Wace
PG	*Patrologiae Cursus, series Graeca*, ed. J.-P. Migne
P&P	*Past & Present*
PEQ	*Palestine Exploration Quarterly*
PCPS	*Proceedings of the Cambridge Philological Society*
RE	series: *Paulys Realencyclopadie der classischen altertumswissenschaft*, ed. G. Wissowa (Stuttgart J. B. Metzler, 1894–1963)
REA	*Revue d'etudes augustiniennes*
REG	*Revue d'etudes grecques*
RM	*Rheinisches Museum fur Philologie*

SCH	*Studies in Church History*
SO	*Symbolae Osloenses*
SP	*Studia Patristica*
TAPA	*Transactions of the American Philological Association*
TDNT	*Theological Dictionary of the New Testament*, ed. Gerhard Kittel, trans. G. W. Bromiley (Grand Rapids Eerdmans Publishing Co., 1964)
VC	*Vigiliae Christianae*
YCS	*Yale Classical Studies*
WS	*Wiener Studien*
ZKG	*Zeitschrift fur Kirchengeschichte*
ZNW	*Zeitschrift fur die Nuetestamentliche Wissenschaft*

Ancient Sources

Aeschylus	*Prom. Vinct. (Prometheus Vinctus)*
Anth. Pal.	*(Anthologia Palatina)*
Aristides (Apologist)	*Apol. (Apologia)*
Aristides (Sophist)	*Or. (Orationes)*
Aristotle	*EN (Ethica Nicomachea)*
	Pol. (Politica)
Athanasius	*C. Gent. (Contra Gentes)*
Athenagoras	*Leg. (Legatio)*
Augustine	*CD (De Civitate Dei)*
	Ep. (Epistulae)
Batrach.	*(Batrachomyomachia)*
Cicero	*Cael. (Pro Caelio)*
	Fin. (De Finibus)
	Rep. (De Re Publica)
	Tusc. Disp. (Tusculanae Disputationes)
Clearchus	*De Somn. (De Somniis)*
Clement of Alexandria	*Protr. (Protrepticus)*
	Strom. (Stromateis)
Ps.-Clement	*Hom. (Homiliae)*
	Rec. (Recognitiones)
Cyril of Jerusalem	*Cat. (Catecheses)*

Damascius	*Phil. Hist. (Philosophos Historia)*
Demosthenes	*De Cor. (De Corona)*
	Olynth. (Olynthiaca)
Dio Chrysostom	*Or. (Orationes)*
Diodorus Siculus	*Bibl. (Bibliotheke)*
Diogn.	*(Epistula ad Diognetum)*
Dionysius of Halicarnassus	*Thuc. (De Thucydide)*
Eusebius	*C. Hier. (Contra Hieroclem)*
	Chron. (Chronica)
	CI (Commentarius in Isaiam)
	C. Marc. (Contra Marcellum)
	Comm. Ps. (Commentaria in Psalmos)
	DE (Demonstratio Evangelica)
	HE (Historia Ecclesiastica)
	LC (Laus Constantini)
	Mart. Pal. (De martyribus Palaestinae)
	PE (Praeparatio Evangelica)
	Proph. Ecl. (Propheticae Eclogae)
	SC (De sepulchro Christi)
	Theoph. (De Theophania)
	VC (De Vita Constantini)
Firmicus Maternus	*Err. Prof. Rel. (De Errore Profanarum Religionum)*
George Syncellus	*Chron. (Ecloga chronographica)*
Gregory Nazianzenus	*Or. (Orationes)*
Gregory of Nyssa	*C. Fatum (Contra Fatum)*
Hermas	*Sim. (Similitudines)*
Hesiod	*Theog. (Theogonia)*
Hippolytus	*Comm. Dan. (Commentaria in Danielem)*
	Refut. (Refutatio omnium haeresium)
Homer	*Il. (Iliad)*
Ignatius of Antioch	*Magn. (Ad Magnesios)*
Irenaeus	*C. Haer. (Contra Haereses)*
Jerome	*Comm. Ezech. (Commentarii in Ezechielem)*
	Ep. (Epistulae)

Josephus	AJ (Antiquitates Judaicae)
	Ap. (Contra Apionem)
	BJ (Bellum Judaicum)
Julian	Or. (Orationes)
Justin Martyr	Apol. (Apologiae I & II)
	Dial. (Dialogus cum Tryphonem)
Lactantius	Div. Inst. (Divinae Institutae)
Lucian of Samosata	Anach. (Anacharsis)
	Fug. (De Fugitivis)
	Scyth. (Scytha)
Mart. Poly.	(Martyrium Polycarpi)
Maximus of Tyre	Dissert. (Dissertationes)
Melito of Sardis	Apol. (Apologia)
Methodius	Lepr. (De Lepra)
	Res. (De Resurrectione Mortuorum)
Minucius Felix	Oct. (Octavius)
Origen	C. Cels. (Contra Celsum)
	Comm. Gen. (Commentarii in Genesim)
	Comm. Iohann. (Comentarii in Iohannem)
	Comm. Matth. (Commentarium in Matthaeum)
	Hom. Num. (Homiliae in Numeros)
	Select. Genes. (Selecta in Genesim)
Philo of Alexandria	Abr. (De Abrahamo)
	Dec. (De Decalogo)
	De Migrat. Abr. (De migratione Abrahami)
	De Mut. (De mutatione nominum)
	De Spec. Leg. (De Specialibus Legibus)
	In Flacc. (In Flaccum)
	Leg. (Legatio ad Gaium)
	Praem. et Poen. (De praemiis et poenis)
	Provid. (De Providentia)
	Quis heres (Quis rerum divinarum heres sit)
	Quod Omnis (Quod Omnis Probus Liber Sit)
	V. Contempl. (Vita Contemplativa)

Philostratus	*VS (Vitae Sophistarum)*
Plato	*Leg. (Leges)*
	Phd. (Phaedo)
	Philb. (Philebus)
	Theaet. (Theaetetus)
Plotinus	*Enn. (Enneades)*
Plutarch	*De Def. Or. (De Defectu Oraculorum)*
	De Is. Et Os. (De Iside et Osiride)
	Erot. (Eroticos)
	V. Alex. (Vita Alexandri)
	V. Fab. Max. (Vita Fabii Maximi)
Porphyry	*Abst. (De Abstinentia)*
	Ad Marc. (Ad Marcellam)
	Phil. ex Orac. (Philosophia ex Oraculis)
	V. Pythag. (Vita Pythagorae)
Prudentius	*Symm. (Contra Symmachum)*
Sallust	*Cat. (Bellum Catilinae)*
Salvian	*Gub. Dei (De Gubernatione Dei)*
Scriptores Historiae Augustae (SHA)	*Hadr. (Hadrian)*
Sextus Empiricus	*Pyr. (Pyrrhoneioi hypotyposeis)*
Suetonius	*Nero*
SVF	*Stoicorum Veterum Fragmenta*, ed. H. von Arnim
Symmachus	*Rel. (Relationes)*
Tatian	*Or. (Oratio ad Graecos)*
Tertullian	*Ad Nat. (Ad Nationes)*
	Scorp. (Scorpiace)
Themistius	*Or. (Orationes)*
Theophilus	*Autol. (Ad Autolycum)*
Xenophon	*Mem. (Memorabilia)*

1

Discourses of Ethnicity and Early Christian Apologetics: An Introduction

THE CONTEXT OF CHRISTIAN APOLOGETICS

Early Christian apologetics, that is, the literary defence of particular visions of Christianity, was fundamentally about the formation of identity. The task of the apologists centred on defending a Christian 'us' against the hostile criticisms of a pagan or Jewish 'them'. A primary feature of apologetic literature involved the carefully crafted representation of a Christian social identity that stood in more or less sharp contrast to the identities of Christianity's others (be they Jews, Greeks, or Romans).[1] Positioned at the very borders of Christian discourse, the early apologist buttressed the bulwarks of Christian identity and strengthened the fortifications of the faith against the hostile assaults (real or imagined) of Jews or Greeks. The defender of the faith stood poised upon the battlements, reinforcing the weakened barriers and lobbing polemical missiles in the direction of anti-Christian assailants. The apologists' duty was twofold: the construction of a defensible and viable Christian identity, and the reconstrual of the identities of others to effectively weaken and unman their legitimacy. Scanning the enemy ranks marshalled in opposition, the apologist simultaneously kept an eye turned towards the enforcement of his own fortress: a Janus-faced sentinel in the struggle for identity. While not all apologists may have envisioned themselves in such a tense drama of combat and contestation

---

[1] For a fuller discussion of the issues surrounding the definition of 'apologetics', see the collection of essays in M. J. Edwards, M. Goodman, and S. Price (eds), *Apologetics in the Roman Empire* (Oxford: Oxford University Press, 1999), with the judicious review by A. Cameron, 'Apologetics in the Roman Empire—A Genre of Intolerance?', in *Humana Sapit: Études d'antiquité tardive offertes à Lellia Cracco Ruggini*, *L'Antiquité Tardive* 3 (2002), 219–27.

2 *Ethnicity and Argument*

over identity, Christian apologetics can nonetheless be described as a 'border discourse', that is, a discourse poised at the frontiers between rival identities.

The ways in which these various groups were represented within the world of the text could then function as the very basis for the defence of Christianity: Christians could be identified as a people who were more rational, pious, and wise (the exact opposite of what their accusers claimed), while the other peoples were characterized as irrational, impious, and prone to superstition. Answers to the questions 'Who are we? Where did we come from? Why are we the way we are?' and 'Who are they? Where did they come from? Why are they the way they are?' reverberate throughout the pages of apologetic texts from the second to the fourth centuries AD.[2] Arguments defending biblical prophecies, miracles or related issues are often subsidiary to, or couched within, a project of self-definition. Persuading the readers of the validity of one's description of Christians and others was the goal of the apologist in what can rightly be termed a battle over representation.

The sparring over identity that occurred in the pages of the polemical tracts of Christians and their rivals was conducted on a battlefield formed by the clash, confrontation, and even consumption of the cultures and peoples that inhabited the East Mediterranean world, making it such a cauldron of contrast and hostility in Hellenistic and Roman times. It was during the era after Alexander the Great that Hellenism as a hegemonic cultural force provoked sustained and vigorous responses from the native populations that had fallen under the net of Hellenistic, and later Roman, power. The historical works that came out of the very first generation following Alexander's death[3] offer early glimpses of the productive

---

[2] For the importance of identity in early Christian literature generally, see J. M. Lieu, *Christian Identity in the Jewish and Graeco-Roman World* (Oxford: Oxford University Press, 2004); eadem, *Neither Jew Nor Greek?* (Oxford: Oxford University Press, 2004).

[3] e.g. Hecataeus of Abdera, Megasthenes, Berossus, and Manetho. The standard edition of these authors' works is that of F. Jacoby, *Die Fragmente der Griechischen Historiker* (Leiden: Brill, 1958); Hecataeus (*FGrH* IIIA. 264); Megasthenes (*FGrH* IIIC. 715); Berossus (*FGrH* IIIC. 680); Manetho (*FGrH* IIIC. 609). Only Berossus and Manetho were recorded as being members by birth of the peoples about whom they wrote. Jacoby's collection of fragments should be used with caution, since much of what he attributes to Hecataeus in Diodorus Siculus has been convincingly questioned by K. Sacks, *Diodorus Siculus and the First Century* (Princeton: Princeton University Press, 1990). Other criticisms have been raised against Jacoby's methodology by G. Bowersock, 'Jacoby's Fragments and Two Greek Historians of Pre-Islamic Arabia', in G. Most (ed.), *Collecting Fragments* (Göttingen: Vandenhoeck & Ruprecht, 1997), 173–85.

activity by conquered nations affirming and fortifying their own identity against that of their rulers.[4] George Syncellus would later describe the work of these historians (in particular Manetho and Berossus) as embodying the desire 'to glorify their own nation (*ethnos*)'.[5] The early books of Diodorus' *Bibliothēkē* stand as a memorial to the competing claims of the respective nations to greater antiquity and greater progress in the arts and civilization.[6]

Jewish authors also laid claim to their own identity and history in this tradition of 'national(-ist) historiography'.[7] Abraham and Moses became the ancient heroes of the Jewish nation, liberally granting their own wisdom and inventions to allegedly less capable nations, such as the Phoenicians or Egyptians. Adapting the suggestion of Aristotle and earlier Greeks that primitive wisdom had originated among barbarian nations, Hellenistic Jews exhibited avidity and creativity in locating these origins in the Jewish nation itself. Eupolemus, for instance, found the origins of the alphabet in the person of Moses.[8] Artapanus, in turn, offered a tour de force against Manetho's disparaging narration of Jews under Egyptian rule by identifying Abraham as the discoverer of astrology, Joseph as the inventor of agricultural arts, and Moses as a wise man and cultural benefactor who even instituted the Egyptian religious system.[9] The Jewish apologists, with Artapanus among them, were followed by the monumental efforts of Josephus in his *Antiquitates*

---

[4] For a general survey of these authors, see E. J. Bickerman, 'Origenes gentium', *CP* 47 (1952), 65–81; S. K. Eddy, *The King is Dead: Studies in Near Eastern Resistance to Hellenism* (Lincoln: University of Nebraska Press, 1961); G. Sterling, *Historiography and Self-Definition* (Leiden: Brill, 1992), 55–136; D. Mendels, *Identity, Religion, Historiography* (Sheffield: Sheffield Academic Press, 1998), 139–57; 334–51; 357–64.

[5] George Syncellus, *Chron.* 29.8 (= *FGrH* 609. T11c).

[6] See Diodorus, *Bibl.* 1.9.3–4.

[7] See J. J. Collins, *Between Athens and Jerusalem: Jewish Identity in the Hellenistic Diaspora* (New York: Crossroads, 1983); D. Mendels, *The Rise and Fall of Jewish Nationalism* (Grand Rapids: Eerdmans Publishing Co., 1997); A. Droge, *Homer or Moses? Early Christian Interpretations of the History of Culture*, Hermeneutische Untersuchungen zur Theologie 26 (Tübingen: Mohr [Siebeck], 1989), 12–48; P. Pilhofer, *Presbyteron Kreitton. Der Altersbeweis der jüdischen und christlichen Apologeten und seine Vorgeschichte* (Tübingen: Mohr [Siebeck], 1990), 143–63, 193–206; Sterling, *Historiography and Self-Definition*; G. R. Boys-Stones, *Post-Hellenistic Philosophy* (Oxford: Oxford University Press, 2001), 60–90; L. H. Feldman and J. R. Levison (eds), *Josephus' Contra Apionem* (Leiden: Brill, 1996); M. Goodman, 'Josephus' Treatise *Against Apion*', in Edwards *et al.* (eds), *Apologetics in the Roman Empire*, 45–58.

[8] Cited at *PE* 9.26.1; cp. Clement, *Strom.* 1.153.4. Droge, *Homer or Moses*, 13–19.

[9] See Droge, *Homer or Moses*, 25–35.

Iudaicae and *Contra Apionem*, in what has been termed 'an oriental defense mechanism against Hellenism'.[10]

When political and military control of the Eastern Mediterranean fell into the hands of the Romans, even educated Greeks were left scrambling to assert their identity. This was manifested most fully in the literary circles of the so-called Second Sophistic,[11] and the Panhellenion, a league of city-states, formed under the auspices of the emperor Hadrian, whose exclusive membership depended upon the ability to trace historical descent from the mainland Greeks.[12] Yet, even as many Greek *poleis* sought to bolster their identity along racial lines of kinship and descent, there were many of 'barbarian' extraction who adopted Greekness (sometimes uneasily) through ostentatious shows of *paideia* and rhetorical finesse. As Favorinus, one of the most obvious examples of this self-conscious attempt at appropriating Greek identity, would openly claim, he had sought 'not only to seem but to be a Greek', and though a Roman he had been 'thoroughly transformed into a Greek (*aphellēnisthē*)' by emulating Attic speech and Spartan athletics.[13] In fact, Favorinus boasts, he had attained such a high level of philosophical achievement that he had become a role model (*paradeigma*) for the Greeks, showing that 'being cultured (*paideuthēnai*) differs not at all from birth (*phunai*) in outward bearing'.[14] The deliberate adoption, manipulation, and contestation over identity thus appears with rich clarity by one who was born Celtic, received Roman citizenship, and yet spoke and thought like a Greek.[15]

[10] Sterling, *Historiography and Self-Definition*, 163–4.

[11] See especially E. L. Bowie, 'Greeks and their Past in the Second Sophistic', in Moses Finley (ed.), *Studies in Ancient Society*, Past and Present Series (London: Routledge, 1974), 166–209; idem, 'Hellenes and Hellenism in Writers of the Early Second Sophistic', in S. Said (ed.), *ΕΛΛΗΝΙΣΜΟΣ. Quelques jalons pour une histoire de l'identité Grecque* (Leiden: Brill, 1991), 183–204; S. Swain, *Hellenism and Empire: Language, Classicism, and Power in the Greek World AD 50–250* (Oxford: Clarendon Press, 1996); S. Goldhill (ed.), *Being Greek Under Rome: Culture, Identity, the Second Sophistic and the Development of Empire* (Cambridge: Cambridge University Press, 2001); T. Whitmarsh, *Greek Literature and the Roman Empire: The Politics of Imitation* (Oxford: Oxford University Press, 2001).

[12] See variously, C. P. Jones, 'The Panhellenion', *Chiron* 26 (1996), 29–56; A. Spawforth, 'The Panhellenion Again', *Chiron* 29 (1999), 339–52; idem, 'Shades of Greekness', in I. Malkin (ed.), *Ancient Perceptions of Greek Ethnicity* (Cambridge: Harvard University Press, 2001), 375–400; I. Romeo, 'The Panhellenion and Ethnic Identity', *CP* 97 (2002), 21–40.

[13] Favorinus, *Corinthiaca* (= Ps.-Dio Chrysostom, *Or.* 37) 25–6; see Whitmarsh, *Greek Literature and the Roman Empire*.

[14] Ibid., 27.

[15] More complicated is the case of Lucian of Samosata who surpassed many in his facility and depth of Greek *paideia* (see e.g. *Somn.*), yet was unable (or unwilling) to ignore his Syrian (barbarian) roots; see esp. *Scyth., Anach.*

This was a world of contested identities and divided loyalties as members of subject nations manipulated and reformulated their representations of themselves and each other amidst the fray of competing claims to cultural, religious and historical superiority. Boundaries between the nations (*ethnē*) were redrawn, re-articulated, enforced, or even erased on the pages of animated and often polemical sophists, priests, and philosophers—if not also in the streets (or hills) of east Roman cities.[16] It was within the context of these nationalistic visions of the world, which articulated racial tension, interaction, and discombobulation, that the writings of the early Christian apologists and their interlocutors arose. In a world of more or less ancient nations, the non-Christian enquirer wanted to know where the Christians located themselves on the ethnic landscape. The asking and answering of this question became one of the most common features of the pagan–Christian debate. Both the anti-Christian assailants and the pro-Christian defenders of the faith cast their literary missiles from distinctively ethnic embattlements. It was within a discourse of ethnicity that the parrying of polemical blows and thrusting of counter-arguments, insults, and innuendo were fought.

Apologetic writings were defined, therefore, not so much by genre—as letters, dialogues, appeals to the emperor (or Senate), protreptic tracts, point-by-point refutations, and epideictic orations are incorporated under the apologetic rubric—but by shared concern, a *Tendenz* or strategy of identity formulation and world-construction.[17] The extant works of

---

[16] In varying degrees, ethnic identity was a salient feature of, if not a catalyst for, the Jewish revolts (see Josephus, *BJ*), the Alexandrian pogroms (see Philo of Alexandria, *Leg.*, *In Flacc.*; for discussion, see K. Goudriaan, 'Ethnical Strategies in Graeco-Roman Egypt', in Per Bilde *et al.* (eds), *Ethnicity in Hellenistic Egypt* [Aarhus: Aarhus University Press, 1992], 74–99; P. Borgen, 'Philo and the Jews', in idem, *Ethnicity in Hellenistic Egypt*, 122–38), Elegabalus' religious and cultural programme (see K. van Bladel, 'New Light on the Religious Background of Elegabalus, Aramaean Emperor of Rome', American Philological Association 2003 Annual Meeting, unpublished); Zenobia's Palmyrene Empire; the rebellion of the Saracens under Queen Mavia (the causes of which are uncertain, but the ethnic component is clear; see Sozomen 6.38; Socrates 4.36 (who notes Moses' ethnicity); for military and political background, see N. Lenski, *Failure of Empire: Valens and the Roman State in the Fourth Century A.D.* (Berkeley and Los Angeles: University of California Press, 2002), 196–210). Other native revolts may have been part of the process of Romanization under the late Republic and early empire; see S. Dyson, 'Native Revolts in the Roman Empire', *Historia* 20 (1971), 239–74.

[17] See A. Cameron, 'Apologetics in the Roman Empire—A Genre of Intolerance', esp. 223: 'In other words, apologetics is a strategy, not a genre. It is not a literary form practised by writers who have a clearcut and established set of views to contrast with another equally clearcut and established one. Rather, each "side" is in flux or under construction, and the nature and quality of the arguments put forward will determine what set of views is carried through to the next stage.'

the early apologists form a virtual museum of the remains of a vivid and dynamic discourse over identity.[18] Ethnic (or national) identity[19] played a fundamental role in the ways in which Christians argued and articulated their faith. When Christian apologists went about the task of defending themselves within this conceptual framework, the 'others' with whom they engaged were all seen as the representatives of distinct peoples, nations, or ethnicities. These apologists, therefore, defined Christianity as the way of life of a particular people whose strong roots in the distant past were superior to the other peoples from whom they marked themselves off.

In the earliest extant apology, Aristides the Athenian constructed his entire argument upon a portrayal of the world as consisting of particular nations or races,[20] which fell into three groups: the polytheist nations, the Jews, and the Christians. The polytheists embraced three sub-races: the Chaldaeans, the Greeks, and the Egyptians. He declared:

For it is clear to us that there are three races (*genē*) of humans in this world. These are the worshippers of those whom you call gods, the Jews and the Christians. And again, those who worship many gods are divided into three races: the Chaldaeans, the Greeks and the Egyptians. For these have become the founders and teachers of the veneration and worship of the many-named gods to the other nations (*ethnesin*).[21]

Aristides then offers a critique of each race and its national traits before showing how Christians, who 'trace their genealogy from Christ (*genealogountai*)', are superior to the others and stand, 'above all nations (*ethnē*)'.[22] This is significant in that Aristides bases his whole argument on an ethnic legitimation of Christianity. That is, his defence of Christianity rests upon a distinctively *ethnic* conceptualization of the Christians.

---

[18] See Droge, *Homer or Moses*; F. Young, 'Greek Apologists of the Second Century', in Edwards *et al.*, *Apologetics in the Roman Empire*, 81–104; Cameron, 'Apologetics in the Roman Empire'; Lieu, *Image and Reality*; eadem, *Christian Identity in the Jewish and Greco-Roman World*.

[19] On my use of the terms 'ethnic' and 'national', see Chapter 2.

[20] The terms *genos* and *ethnos* seem to be used interchangeably by Aristides in referring to the various peoples.

[21] *Apol.* 2.2; for text, see now B. Pouderon, *et al.*, *Aristide. Apologie*, SC 470 (Paris: Les Éditions du Cerf, 2003). For discussion, see D. Olster, 'Classical Ethnography and Early Christianity', in K. Free (ed.), *The Formulation of Christianity by Conflict through the Ages* (Lewiston: E. Mellen Press, 1995), 9–31.

[22] *Apol.* 15.1.

The bombastic criticisms of Tatian likewise rest upon a construal of ethnic identity in attacking the Greeks and defending the faith. His argument stays largely within the Greek–barbarian opposition (though he does not fail to acknowledge the characteristics of particular barbarian nations on occasion). He prefers to call Christianity 'barbarian wisdom',[23] to speak of Moses as the 'founder of all barbarian philosophy',[24] and his writings as 'barbarian books'.[25] This poses no problem for him, since he considers 'the barbarian nation' (he never calls them Jews) to be earlier and superior to the later Greeks.[26] As Josephus before him and Eusebius after him, the Greeks were borrowers and collectors of the inventions of other nations.[27] Most importantly, like Aristides, he constructed a Christian identity which was framed within ethnic categories. Though he claims to 'strike out on a new path',[28] Christianity was not represented as a *sui generis* identity that superceded racial identities, but was, rather, thoroughly ensconced within the ongoing discourses of ethnicity and race in the East Mediterranean world.

Much of the ethnic argumentation found in Clement of Alexandria's *Stromateis* is only a refined version of what had come before in Tatian. Clement elevated barbarian philosophy above Greek philosophy. He gave chronological superiority to the barbarian nations and pride of place to the Jewish race. To do so, he employed ethnographical sketches in two stages. The first provided an ethnographical doxography of the philosophies of the nations, including discussion of the ethnic background of the seven wise men (only two of whom were Greek).[29] The second ethnographic stage consisted of a delineation of the national origins of various arts.[30] The point of these ethnographies was to attack the high position that Greeks claimed for themselves during the Second Sophistic.[31] The Greeks were proven to be dependent upon the earlier barbarian nations, having tapped into these greater cultural traditions

---

[23] Tatian, *Or.* 12, 35, 42.

[24] Ibid., 31.

[25] Ibid., 29.

[26] Ibid., 1, 31, 40, *passim*.

[27] See Chapter 5.

[28] Tatian, *Or.* 35.

[29] Clement, *Strom.* 1.14; on the manipulation of the ethnic origins of the Seven Sages, see D. Richter, *Ethnography, Archaism, and Identity in the Early Roman Empire*, (Ph.D. dissertation, University of Chicago, 2000), 99–129.

[30] *Strom.* 1.16; cp. Tatian, *Or.* 1.

[31] See, e.g. Clement's criticism of the contemporary trend of Atticism in *Strom.* 1.3, 16.

through theft and plagiarism.[32] Clement utilized ethnic identity to legitimate the Christian (as barbarian) position and to delegitimate any presumed Greek superiority.

On the non-Christian side, Celsus, in his polemic against Christianity, would claim that Christians were merely a more erroneous and dysfunctional brand of Jewishness. For a portion of his *Alēthēs Logos*, Celsus created a Jewish character to raise criticisms against Christian neglect and misappropriation of Jewish heritage and way of life.[33] Interestingly, Origen responded by claiming that Celsus' Jew was not very Jewish at all; Celsus had constructed an unconvincing figure who was more representative of the Samaritans than the Jews.[34] The battle over Christian identity thus also involved skirmishes over the representation of Jewish identity. In this case however, Celsus had been motivated by the more far-ranging concern with the Christians' rejection of the ancestral customs of their forefathers—whether these belonged to the Jewish, Greek, or some other *ethnos*. Origen preserves his sentiment in a direct quotation, which I offer in full:

As the Jews, then, became a peculiar people, and enacted laws in keeping with the customs of their country, and maintain them up to the present time, and observe a mode of worship which, whatever be its nature, is yet derived from their fathers, they act in these respects like other men, because each nation retains its ancestral customs, whatever they are, if they happen to be established among them. And such an arrangement appears to be advantageous, not only because it has occurred to the mind of other nations to decide some things differently, but also because it is a duty to protect what has been established for the public advantage; and also because, in all probability, the various quarters of the earth were from the beginning allotted to different superintending spirits, and were thus distributed among certain governing powers, and in this manner the administration of the world is carried on. And whatever is done among each nation in this way would be rightly done, wherever it was agreeable to the wishes [of the superintending powers], while it would be an act of impiety to get rid of the institutions established from the beginning in the various places.[35]

This passage exhibits well the combination of notions of nationhood, racial ancestry, customs, and piety into a single integrated cluster of

---

[32] See D. Ridings, *The Attic Moses: The Dependency Theme in some Early Christian Writers* (Göteborg: Acta Universitatis Gothoburgensis, 1995); see also below, Chapter 5.

[33] For a summary statement, see Origen, *C. Cels.* 5.33.

[34] *C. Cels.* 1.48–9.

[35] *C. Cels.* 5.25 (trans. F. Crombie, *The Ante-Nicene Fathers* series, A. Roberts and J. Donaldson (eds), (New York: The Christian Literature Company, 1890), 4.553–4); see also, 1.1; 5.34–41; 8.2.

ideas that was so typical of the ancient world. Ethnicity and piety were united, and the rejection of both by early Christians was one of the central issues that caused concern among Greek polemicists such as Celsus.[36] Origen, for his part, may have only aggravated such concerns in his response, which detailed the active spurning of ancestral ways by Christians[37] and glorified their conversions as 'bidding farewell' to the unholy laws of their forefathers (and this, after slighting Celsus' approval of Pindar's statement that 'law is king of all').[38]

The above sketch is hopelessly cursory; but it is sufficient to make us aware that Christianity's others were always represented within the bounds of particular ethnic identities. Even religious and philosophical figures and their doctrines and teachings were couched within an ethnic, or national, framework; or they provided content for their respective ethnic identities, the members (or opponents) of which could claim them as exemplars, representative of the national character in question. Christianity was defended, therefore, within and against a world of nations; in other words, Christianity was conceived not merely as one among many separate religious positions, but, rather, was mapped into the imaginary and constructed national and ethnic landscape. And hence, Christians themselves were often represented as such.[39] Aristides had constructed a Christian identity in racial terms when he applied to

---

[36] See M. Frede, 'Celsus' Attack on the Christians', in J. Barnes and M. Griffin (eds), *Philosophia Togata II* (Oxford: Oxford University Press, 1997), 218–40. While not appreciating the nexus of piety, ethnicity and ancestry in the way I am laying out, the following studies remain valuable: A. Droge, *Homer or Moses*, 152–67; M. Frede, 'Origen's Treatise Against Celsus', in Edwards *et al.*, *Apologetics in the Roman Empire*, 131–56; Pilhofer, *Presbyteron Kreitton*, 285–9; Boys-Stones, *Post-Hellenistic Philosophy*, 105–7, 176–81.

[37] See, e.g. *C. Cels.* 1.1, 30, 46, 52; 2.1, 3–4; 3.11; 5.26–7, 36; 8.5–6, 47.

[38] *C. Cels.* 5.40. See Boys-Stones, *Post-Hellenistic Philosophy*, 195–200; D. Martin, *Inventing Superstition* (Cambridge: Harvard University Press, 2004), 161–4.

[39] See e.g. 1 Pet. 2: 9; *Diogn.* 1; *Kerygma Petri ap.* Clement, *Strom.* 6.5.41; *Mart. Poly.* 3.2; 14.1; 17.1; Hermas *Sim.* 9.17.5; 9.30.3; Justin *Dial.* 11.5; 110.4; 116.3; 119.3; 123.1; 138.2; 135.6; Tertullian, *Ad Nat.* 1.8; *Scorp.* 10; Melito, *Apol. ap.* Eusebius, *HE* 4.26.5; Seutonius *Nero* 16.2; for Aristides and Origen, see below; for Eusebius see *HE* 1.4.3; *DE* 1.1 (7); 2.3 (61cd, 83a); 10.3 (477a); 10.8 (510cd); *CI* 2.38 (Ziegler 322); 2.57 (Ziegler 402–3); *VC* 2.61.3; 2.63. A. von Harnack attempted to explain away the ethnic connotations of Christianity as a *genos* or *ethnos* ('The Tidings of the New People and of the Third Race', in idem, *The Mission and Expansion of Christianity in the First Three Centuries*, trans. J. Moffat [New York: Harper and Bros., 1962], 240–78); see now, Olster, 'Classical Ethnography and Early Christianity', 9–31; D. Kimber Buell, 'Rethinking the Relevance of Race for Early Christian Self-Definition', *HTR* 94 (2001), 449–76; eadem, 'Race and Universalism in Early Christianity', *JECS* 10 (2002), 429–68; eadem, *Why This New Race: Ethnic Reasoning in Early Christianity* (New York: Columbia University Press, 2005); Lieu, *Christian Identity in the Jewish and Graeco-Roman World*, 239–68.

them the terms *ethnos* and *genos* and claimed that Christians 'traced their genealogy from Christ'.[40] Origen had on numerous occasions referred to Christians as a nation. For instance, at *Contra Celsum* 2.51, he claimed that in the time of Moses and the time of Jesus respectively, two new nations were forged as a result of the performance of miracles.[41] And even Celsus had slandered the Christians as 'a cowardly race' and 'a flesh-loving race'.[42]

The identities represented and reformulated in the Christian–pagan disputes were thus much more than religious or philosophical positions; the doctrines defended and attacked were framed within the context of historically rooted races. And what matters for our analysis is not the accuracy of these representations and remembered histories; rather, their importance lies in the fact that such representations could be manipulated and deployed with so much force in polemical texts, and in the more basic fact that this was how authors on either side of the pagan–Christian divide imagined their identities and conceived of their task.

The present study thus seeks to isolate and analyse this sort of conceptualization as a foundational element of apologetic methodology. I have termed such a methodology 'ethnic argumentation', that is, the concern to formulate ethnic identities strategically as the basis for an apologetic argument.[43] The employment of ethnicity and racializing constructions obviously occurs in varying degrees in different apologetic texts. The apologies of Aristides and Tatian rely much more openly upon ethnic argumentation than those of Origen or Clement. Eusebius' *Praeparatio Evangelica* offers probably the clearest, and surely the lengthiest, example of ethnic argumentation.

---

[40] *Apol.* 15. For a similar expression, see Justin, *Dial.* 123.9 (see von Harnack, 'The Tidings of the New People and of the Third Race', 248; Lieu, *Image and Reality*, 136).

[41] See also *C. Cels.* 1.45; 2.78; 3.8; 4.42; 8.75; cp. Justin, *Dial.* 135.

[42] *C. Cels.* 7.39. Elsewhere, he considers Christians to be only renegades of the Jewish *ethnos* (see *C. Cels.* 5.33).

[43] What I call here 'ethnic argumentation' is similar to (though developed independently from) Kimber Buell's notion of 'ethnic reasoning' (see 'Rethinking the Relevance of Race for Early Christian Self-Definition', and 'Race and Universalism in Early Christianity'), and G. Byron's enquiry into 'ethno-political rhetoric' (*Symbolic Blackness and Ethnic Difference in Early Christian Literature* [New York: Routledge, 2002], 2).

ETHNICITY AND ARGUMENT IN EUSEBIUS'
PRAEPARATIO EVANGELICA

If the development of early apologetics is viewed along ethnic lines, then Eusebius can be viewed as part of an ongoing tradition of Christian engagement in discourses of ethnicity. The concern with matters of identity, especially ethnic identity, is in fact heightened in Eusebius' *Praeparatio Evangelica*, a work that can rightly be seen as the culmination (though by no means the end) of the apologetic tradition.[44] It stands at the threshold of a new era of Christian existence as ties between Church and Empire were in the process of being forged under Constantine following the horrific experiences of the 'Great Persecution'. The 15-book apology was begun about AD 313,[45] soon after Eusebius became bishop of Caesarea in Palestine.[46] The year before, Constantine had miraculously defeated Maxentius at the Battle of the Milvian Bridge after painting the sign of the cross on his soldiers' shields, supposedly under the guidance of a vision from Christ. In the period immediately following, Constantine had met his eastern counterpart, Licinius, in Milan to formulate an 'Edict of Toleration', which called for an end to the persecution of Christians and the restoration of their property. Shortly thereafter, Licinius defeated the last of the persecuting tetrarchs, Maximinus Daia.[47] Indeed, even the latter had already issued his own

[44] Eusebius, 'completes the system ... that his predecessors had begun' (A. Puech, *Histoire de la littérature grecque chrétienne* [Paris: Société d'Édition 'Les Belles Lettres', 1930], 3.187–8).

[45] J. Sirinelli and E. Des Places, give the time of composition as AD 313–325 (*Eusèbe de Césarée. La Préparation Évangélique, Livre I*, SC 206 [Paris: Les Éditions du Cerf, 1974], 8–14). See also, K. Mras, *Eusebius Werke VIII. Die Praeparatio Evangelica*, GCS 43.1–2 (Berlin: Akademie-Verlag, 1954), LIV-LV; E. Schwartz, 'Eusebios von Caesarea', *RE* 11.1390; H. Doergens, 'Eusebius von Cäsarea als Darsteller der phönizischen Religion', *Forschungen zur christlicher Literatur- und Dogmengeschichte* [Paderborn] 12.5 (1915), 4–6; J. B. Lightfoot, 'Eusebius of Caesarea', in W. Smith and H. Wace (eds), *A Dictionary of Christian Biography* (New York: AMS Press, 1967), 2. 330; T. D. Barnes, *Constantine and Eusebius*, 178; Ridings, *The Attic Moses: The Dependency Theme in some Early Christian Writers*, 141; A. Kofsky, *Eusebius of Caesarea Against the Pagans* (Leiden: Brill, 2000), 74–5.

[46] See T. D. Barnes, *Constantine and Eusebius*, 94.

[47] The so-called 'Edict of Milan' is preserved at Lactantius, *De Mortibus Persecutorum* 48; a Greek translation is offered at Eusebius, *HE* 10.5.1–14. O. Seeck, 'Das sogenannte Edikt von Mailand', *ZKG* 12 (1891), 381–6, first criticized the identification of these documents as an 'edict' issued at Milan ('First, it was not an edict; second, it was not at Milan; third, it was not by Constantine; fourth, it did not offer the entire Empire legal toleration, which Christians at that time already possessed for a long time—its contents were of a more limited importance,' 381). That the fall of the persecutor Maximinus Daia in AD 313 is the historical context for the *PE* is clear from the important passage at 4.2.10–11; see Chapter 6, below.

edicts of toleration: first, in accordance with the conference at Milan, though Christians had remained suspicious; second, following his defeat at the hands of Licinius and just before a fatal disease brought his end.[48]

The religious climate remained unclear in the eastern empire, however. Imperial statements calling for toleration and even restoration of Church property were quickly followed by Licinius' less friendly policies as tensions between himself and the western emperor soon erupted into war and intrigue.[49] It is doubtful whether the caricature of Eusebius' happily enfolding the distinct realms of Church and State together in his later writings (for instance, his panegyrical *Tricennial Oration*) is at all applicable to the writings of this period. We shall see that Eusebius was more cautious, even manipulative, in accepting Rome than is often allowed. Of course, the direct involvement of the Roman government in ecclesiastical affairs, which was already occurring in the West (the Council of Arles, AD 314), would soon be played out in the East as well (the Council of Nicaea, AD 325)[50] following Constantine's defeat of Licinius in AD 324. During the events leading up to Nicaea, Eusebius would become embroiled in the intense conflict over the relationship of God the Father and God the Son sparked by Arius at Alexandria.[51] From this point on, the Roman imperial government would remain heavily involved in ecclesiastical disputes, and the tendentious relationship of Church and State would play a vital role in the historical developments of both the Catholic West and the Byzantine East.

These were exciting, if uncertain, times for Christians in the Roman Empire, as Eusebius, an already established scholar in a number of fields ranging from chronography to apologetics and biblical scholarship, began to compose his magisterial defence of Christianity.[52] Together with its sister work, the *Demonstratio Evangelica* (originally comprising

[48] The first: *HE* 9.9a.1–9; the second: *HE* 9.10.7–11. See, R. M. Grant, 'The Religion of Maximin Daia', in J. Neusner (ed.), *Christianity, Judaism and Other Greco-Roman Cults* (Leiden: Brill, 1975), 4.143–166.

[49] See Eusebius, *VC* 1.49–2.5; T. D. Barnes, *Constantine and Eusebius*, 62–77.

[50] Aurelian had already intervened in ecclesiastical disputes at Antioch in AD 270; see Eusebius *HE* 7.30.6; F. Millar, 'Paul of Samosata, Zenobia and Aurelian: The Church, Local Culture and Political Allegiance in Third-Century Syria', *JRS* 61 (1971), 1–17. On Arles, see T. D. Barnes, *Constantine and Eusebius*, 53–61; H. A. Drake, *Constantine and the Bishops. The Politics of Intolerance* (Baltimore: Johns Hopkins University Press, 2000), 212–21.

[51] See especially, C. Luibheid, *Eusebius of Caesarea and the Arian Crisis* (Dublin: Irish Academic Press, 1978); and also, T. D. Barnes, *Constantine and Eusebius*, 208–23; Drake, *Constantine and the Bishops*, 250–7.

[52] See L. Perrone, 'Eusebius of Caesarea as a Christian Writer', in Avner Raban and Kenneth Holum (eds), *Caesarea Maritima: A Retrospective after Two Millennia* (Leiden: Brill, 1996), 515–30.

20 books), the librarian of Caesarea mounted a formidable assault against Christianity's most dangerous foes, the Greeks and the Jews. These two works stand as monuments to Eusebius' intellectual breadth, perspicuity and vigour.

Unfortunately, the *Praeparatio* has often been dismissed as unoriginal and tiresome by students of apologetics. According to one assessment, the *Praeparatio* 'is tedious and laborious reading, made up of extracts from many authors',[53] and, 'the reader lays [it] aside ... not without a sense of relief'.[54] His achievements as a thinker and author are impugned, while his only merit is that, 'at the least, he did not pretend to create a work of art'.[55] The fact that roughly 71 per cent of the work is direct quotation of earlier authors has, of course, contributed to the modern disfavour and neglect of the work.[56] While the quotations from otherwise lost works occasion great joy among scholars interested in those earlier authors, the importance of the *Praeparatio* as possessing its own unique literary integrity has often been dismissed. It is only the ponderous and awkward anthology of a dull and bookish 'archivist':[57] a 'literary storehouse' or *litterarum penus*,[58] or a 'vast catena of quotations'.[59] Eusebius is said to 'hardly speak with his own voice at all'.[60] According to this view, Eusebius lacks any originality as a thinker; his 'documentary anxiety'[61] has dragged him into a quagmire of quotations. Modern readers are overwhelmed by his apparently unwieldy use of sources. Indeed, Eusebius may have intended his exaggerated use of citations to make a similar onslaught on readers of his own time as well. According to J. -R. Laurin, Eusebius' erudition is 'the most powerful

---

[53] F. J. Foakes-Jackson, *Eusebius Pamphili, Bishop of Caesarea in Palestine and First Christian Historian: A Study of the Man and His Writings* (Cambridge: Heffers, 1933), 122.

[54] Ibid., 128.

[55] Puech, *Histoire de la littérature grecque chrétienne*, 3.219.

[56] For the percentage, see Laurin, *Orientations maitresses des apologistes chrétiens*, Analecta Gregoriana 61 (Rome: Pontificia Universita Gregoriana, 1954), 358.

[57] E. Schwartz: 'the great archivist of the early Church' ('Eusebios', 1371).

[58] G. Bounoure, 'Eusèbe citateur de Diodore', *REG* 95 (1982), 438. He borrows the phrase 'litterarum penus' from Aulus Gellius, *NA*, praef.2: Usi autem sumus ordine rerum fortuito, quem antea in excerpendo feceramus ... indistincte atque promisce annotabam eaque mihi ad subsidium memoriae quasi quoddam litterarum penus recondebam.

[59] D. S. Wallace-Hadrill, *Eusebius of Caesarea* (London: A. R. Mowbray & Co., Ltd., 1960), 138.

[60] Ibid., 140. See also E. H. Gifford, *Preparation for the Gospel* (Grand Rapids: Baker Book House, 1981) 1.xvii; Ridings, *The Attic Moses*, 147.

[61] Puech, *Histoire de la littérature grecque chrétienne*, 3.219: 'le souci du document', here used in a positive sense as a necessary quality of the historian.

argument of his entire apology'.[62] Its effect on readers today is often less appealing.

Purpose and Audience

Despite Eusebius' perceived prolixity and lack of originality, however, the work repays careful reading, for it contains a wealth of material that deepens our understanding of the late antique Christian mind, and offers the most sustained example of a Christian apologist who sets himself the task of answering the basic questions of identity, which I have claimed are central features of earlier Christian apologetics.[63] Tellingly, the very first lines openly stated 'I have wanted to present Christianity—whatever it is—to those who are ignorant...'[64] In particular, Eusebius intended his work to serve as a preparation for those who had recently converted to the faith, before advancing to the deeper studies of the Scriptures, which would receive treatment in the *Demonstratio*. 'For it seems to me that with this arrangement the discourse will proceed to the more perfect teaching of the *Demonstratio Evangelica* and towards the comprehension of deeper doctrines, if the material of the *Praeparatio* might be as a guide for us, taking the place of a primer and introduction (*stoicheiōseōs kai eisagōgēs*), being appropriate for those from the nations recently coming [to the faith].'[65] Works labelled 'introductions' were commonly used as tools in the curricula of

---

[62] Laurin, *Orientations maitresses des apologistes chrétiens*, 365. T. D. Barnes, *Constantine and Eusebius*, 178, sees 'a deliberate, even ostentatious, parade of erudition', while Gallagher, refers to Eusebius' 'profligate display of erudition' ('Piety and Polity: Eusebius' Defense of the Gospel', in J. Neusner, E. S. Frerichs and A. J. Levine (eds), *Religious Writings and Religious Systems* [Atlanta: Scholars Press, 1989], 154); see also, E. Schwartz, 'Eusebios', 1393.

[63] Attempts at better appreciating the *PE* have been made by, e.g., M. Frede, 'Eusebius' Apologetic Writings', in Edwards *et al.* (eds), *Apologetics in the Roman Empire*, 223–50; Gallagher, 'Piety and Polity: Eusebius' Defense of the Gospel', 2.139–55; idem, 'Eusebius the Apologist: The Evidence of the *Preparation* and the *Proof*, SP 26 (1993), 251–60; Kofsky, *Eusebius of Caesarea against the Pagans* (with the review of A. P. Johnson, *VC* [2005], 209–12); J. Ulrich, *Euseb von Caesarea und die Juden. Studien zur Rolle der Juden in der Theologie des Eusebius von Casarea* (Berlin and New York: Walter de Gruyter, 1999). Though dated, the following studies remain fundamental: J. Sirinelli, *Les vues historiques d'Eusèbe de Césarée durant la période prénicéene*, Faculté des Lettres et Sciences Humaines, Publications de la Section de Langues et Litteratures 10 (Dakar: Universite de Dakar, 1961), 142–57; D. König-Ockenfels, 'Christliche Deutung der Weltgeschichte bei Eusebs von Cäsarea', *Saeculum* 27 (1976), 348–65, esp. 356–7.

[64] 1.1.1. Τὸν χριστιανισμόν, ὅ τι ποτέ ἐστιν, ἡγούμενος τοῖς οὐκ εἰδόσι παραστήσασθαι....

[65] 1.1.12. See Ulrich, *Euseb von Caesarea und die Juden*, 39–40; A. P. Johnson, 'Eusebius' *Praeparatio Evangelica* as Literary Experiment', in J. George and S. Johnson (eds), *Greek Literature in Late Antiquity* (Aldershot: Ashgate, forthcoming).

late antique philosophical schools for those in the beginning stages of their education.[66] Eusebius himself had offered Christian students a *General Elementary Introduction* just a few years before (c.310).[67] This understudied treatise provided students with important passages from the Hebrew Scriptures, accompanied by comments to aid in developing a Christian interpretation of these texts. While the *Demonstratio* shared considerable similarities with the *Introduction*, the *Praeparatio* was unique among introductions. As an introduction for fledgling Christian students, the *Praeparatio* sought to inculcate a new vision of who they had now become, as well as a new understanding of the identities they had left behind and those that remained as threats.

Later in his prologue, Eusebius set out the basic question motivating the *Praeparatio*: 'For first of all someone might reasonably ask: who are we who have come forward to write, are we Greeks or barbarians? Or what can be between these? And who do we say that we are—not in title, for this is manifest to all—but in character and conduct of life?'[68] These questions set the tenor for his entire apologetic project. But what is interesting as we watch Eusebius tackle the problem of identity is that the great bulk of his energy is spent writing about Greek identity and reformulating an account of the historical origins of the Greeks. And second to them were, rather than the Christians, the Jews. For Eusebius, the answer to the question of Christian identity is essentially wrapped up in the issue of Greek, and then Jewish, identity. He made this point explicit at the outset: 'for we neither think like Greeks nor act like

---

[66] See J. Barnes, *Porphyry. Introduction* (Oxford: Oxford University Press, 2004), xiii–xvi; generally, J. Dillon, 'Philosophy as a Profession in Late Antiquity', in S. Swain and M. Edwards (eds), *Approaching Late Antiquity* (Oxford: Oxford University Press, 2004), 401–18.

[67] See T. D. Barnes, *Constantine and Eusebius*, 167–74; for date, see E. Schwartz, 'Eusebios', 1387.

[68] 1.2.1. πρῶτον μὲν γὰρ εἰκότως ἄν τις διαπορήσειεν, τίνες ὄντες ἐπὶ τὴν γραφὴν παρεληλύθαμεν, πότερον Ἕλληνες ἢ βάρβαροι, ἢ τί ἂν γένοιτο τούτων μέσον, καὶ τίνας ἑαυτοὺς εἶναί φαμεν, οὐ τὴν προσηγορίαν, ὅτι καὶ τοῖς πᾶσιν ἔκδηλος αὕτη, ἀλλὰ τὸν τρόπον καὶ τὴν προαίρεσιν τοῦ βίου. Since Willamowitz, scholars have unanimously attributed these and the following lines to Porphyry's *Contra Christianos* (U. Willamowitz-Moellendorf, 'Ein Bruchstück aus der Schrift des Porphyrius gegen die Christen', *ZNW* 1 (1900), 101–05); they appear as Frag. 1 in A. von Harnack, *Porphyrios, 'Gegen die Christen', 15 Bucher: Zeugnisse, Fragmente und Referate. Abhandlungen der königlichen preussischen Akademie der Wissenschaften*, Philosophisch-historische Klasse, Nr. 1 (Berlin, 1916). See also, E. Schwartz, 'Eusebios', 1391; Puech, *Histoire de la Littérature Grecque Chrétienne*, 3.194. The sentiments were common to critics of Christianity, however; see e.g., Celsus *ap.* Origen, *C. Cels.* 5.25 (cited above); Maximinus Daia *ap.* Eusebius, *HE* 9.7.3–14.

barbarians',[69] and 'we preserve neither the customs of the Greeks nor those of the Jews'.[70] Defining the corporate identity of the Christians inescapably involved defining the corporate identity of the others, both Greeks and Jews.[71] Hence, Eusebius argued at length for particular narratives of Greek (Books 1–3, 10–15) and Jewish (Books 7–9) descent.[72]

Whereas a number of discussions, ranging from his historiographical assumptions to his attitude to the Jews and his reception of Platonism, have made significant progress in our appreciation of Eusebius' *Praeparatio*,[73] the importance of identity, although often noted, has not yet sufficiently impacted modern approaches to the work.[74] Eusebius' identification of Christianity as the renewal of ancient Hebrew religion has received frequent attention in a number of important studies.[75] E. Gallagher, for instance, has correctly argued that it forms the basis

[69] *PE* 1.2.1. οὔτε γὰρ τὰ Ἑλλήνων φρονοῦντας . . . οὔτε τὰ βαρβάρων ἐπιτηδεύοντας.

[70] *PE* 1.2.4. For similar distinctions of Christians from the Greeks and Jews, see e.g. Rom. 10: 12; Gal. 3: 28; *Diogn.* 1; Aristides, *Apol.* 2; Clement, *Strom.* 6.41.6.

[71] The 'us' and 'them' distinctions are rarely as simple as a binary opposition (as Lieu, 'The Forging of Christian Identity', 81).

[72] For a more detailed schema, see Appendix 1.

[73] On the *PE*'s historiographical orientation, see Sirinelli, *Les vues historiques d'Eusèbe de Césarée*; G. Chesnut, *The First Christian Histories: Eusebius, Socrates, Sozomen, Theodoret, and Evagrius* (Macon: Mercer University Press, 1986), 33–110; König-Ockenfels, 'Christliche Deutung der Weltgeschichte bei Eusebs von Cäsarea', 348–65; Droge, *Homer or Moses*, 168–93; R. Mortley, *The Idea of Universal History from Hellenistic Philosophy to Early Christian Historiography* (Lewiston: Edwin Mellen Press, 1996), 151–99. On the *PE*'s response to anti-Christian polemic: T. D. Barnes, *Constantine and Eusebius*, 174–86; Kofsky, *Eusebius of Caesarea against the Pagans*, 74–75; Frede, 'Eusebius' Apologetic Writings', 223–50. On the *PE*'s treatment of Jews, see A. Kofsky, 'Eusebius of Caesarea and the Christian-Jewish Polemic', in O. Limor and G. Stroumsa, eds., *Contra Iudaeos. Ancient and Medieval Polemics between Christians and Jews* (Tübingen: Mohr [Siebeck], 1996), 59–83; Ulrich, *Euseb von Caesarea und die Juden*. Though still concentrated on Eusebius' sources, the following discussions should be mentioned: E. Des Places, *Eusèbe de Césarée commentateur: platonisme et écriture sainte* (Paris: Beauchesne, 1982); M. Smith, 'A Hidden Use of Porphyry's History of Philosophy in Eusebius' Preparatio Evangelica', *JTS* 39 (1988), 494–504; A. J. Carriker, 'Some Uses of Aristocles and Numenius in Eusebius' Praeparatio Evangelica', *JTS* 47 (1996), 543–9; idem, *The Library of Eusebius of Caesarea* (Leiden: Brill, 2003); P. Kalligas, 'Traces of Longinus' Library in Eusebius' Praeparatio Evangelica', *CQ* 51 (2001), 584–98.

[74] See however, Gallagher, 'Piety and Polity', 2.139–55; idem, 'Eusebius the Apologist: The Evidence of the *Preparation* and the *Proof*', 251–60.

[75] See T. D. Barnes, *Constantine and Eusebius*, 181; Kofsky, *Eusebius of Caesarea against the Pagans*, 101–14; Ulrich, *Euseb von Caesarea und die Juden*, 66–7; 113–16; Frede, 'Eusebius' Apologetic Writings', 249; Sirinelli, *Les vues historiques d'Eusèbe de Césarée*, 142–57; König-Ockenfels, 'Christliche Deutung der Weltgeschichte bei Eusebs von Cäsarea', 348–65, esp. 356–7.

of the entire work.[76] He claims that this identification is the 'fundamental assertion of Eusebius' apology'.[77] This insight demands a return to the questions of identity that have already been seen as integral to the apologetic projects of early Christians. Such a focus, however, will find a rather more complex and dynamic manipulation of identities than otherwise recognized. And we must squarely face the distinctively racial component of the identities under construction in the *Praeparatio's* argument. The Greeks of Eusebius' literary world have too often been deemed ciphers for 'pagans', while the Jews or Hebrews are 'monotheists'.[78] The Christians may be conceived as a 'third race', but, it is supposed, this is surely not meant to convey any ethnic baggage.[79] Only the Jews maintain their ethnic identification, rooted in biologically determined modes of identity.[80] Supposedly, Eusebius sought only to escape ethnicity, envisioning a Christian universalism that transcended racial particularity.

Yet, the language of nations, races, ancestral institutions, and communal ways of living and thinking, which are rife throughout the *Praeparatio*, call for a reading that attempts a greater sensitivity to the evocations and clusters of ideas that resonate from such language. Categories of religious identities—'paganism' or 'monotheism'—cannot sufficiently explain the formulations of identity produced in the *Praeparatio*.[81] The present study intends to examine the construction of identities in the *Praeparatio* through closer and more nuanced readings of the text, and hence to open the *ethnic* dimensions of these identities. A greater sense of the overall structure of the *Praeparatio*, as well as the contours of identities in Eusebius' literary world, can thus be gained.

---

[76] Gallagher, 'Piety and Polity', and idem, 'Eusebius the Apologist', 251–60.

[77] Gallagher, 'Eusebius the Apologist', 256.

[78] See e.g., J. B. Rives, 'Human Sacrifice among Pagans and Christians', *JRS* 85 (1995), 76; Ulrich, *Euseb von Caesarea und die Juden, passim*.

[79] For example, Sirinelli notes the conception of Christians as a new people, but quickly emphasizes that Eusebius is not concerned with a history of peoples but a history of the human conscience (*Les vues historiques d'Eusèbe de Césarée*, 136–8); see similarly, Kofsky, *Eusebius of Caesarea against the Pagans*, 100–01.

[80] Ulrich, *Euseb von Caesarea und die Juden*, 79.

[81] See, e.g., Laurin, *Orientations maitresses des apologistes chrétiens*, 348; Ulrich, *Euseb von Caesarea und die Juden*, 68–9 (on pagans); 80, *passim* (on monotheism). Ulrich's overemphasis on Jewish monotheism is a primary cause of his misconstrual of Eusebius' portrayal of the Jews; Eusebius may wave the monotheist banner in the face of polytheist antagonists, but such a bare theological position could not save the Jews from his consistently anti-Jewish criticisms (see Chapter 4 below).

Approaching the Praeparatio

How might one fruitfully engage the text of the *Praeparatio* in an attempt to better appreciate the richness of his articulations of identity? In the following pages I have attempted first to allow the text to stand as a unified and coherent argument, consisting of two master narratives (one of Greek descent, the other of Hebrew descent), rather than being caught up in the diversity and polemical play of citations by the master apologist. I have furthermore focused, except in the last two chapters, on the *Praeparatio* as an independent work standing apart from its sister and sequel, the *Demonstratio*. The *Praeparatio* possesses its own literary integrity. This is not meant to detract from the fact that Eusebius saw the *Praeparatio* and *Demonstratio* as a unified monolithic project. He explicitly stated that the *Praeparatio* was a 'preparation for the demonstration of the Gospel'.[82] However, there is no single book-length treatment of the *Praeparatio* as a single and self-standing argument (indeed, there is no book-length treatment of the *Praeparatio* as such).[83] The *Praeparatio* contains a wealth of material that deserves to be treated on its own terms. Prolonged reflection upon the *Praeparatio* has much to offer the student of early apologetics as a site for the production of early Christian identity. At the same time, completely neglecting the *Demonstratio* would impoverish this study. I have therefore turned to relevant passages from the *Demonstratio* in the discussions on Eusebius' 'political theology' and formulation of Christian identity in the last chapters, as the issues they deal with cannot be treated adequately without broadening the scope to his apologetic project as a whole. My treatment will pursue the following lines.

---

[82] *PE* 6.10.49. τὴν τῆς Εὐαγγελικῆς Ἀποδείξεως Προπαρασκευήν. See also the programmatic statements at 1.1.11–13. For discussion, see especially Ulrich, *Euseb von Caesarea und die Juden*, 30–1; and also, E. Schwartz, 'Eusebios', 1388–9; Kofsky, *Eusebius of Caesarea against the Pagans*, 74–85; T. D. Barnes, *Constantine and Eusebius*, 182; Laurin, *Orientations maitresses des apologistes chrétiens*, 345, 351.

[83] Important discussions limited to portions of the *PE* are: H. Doergens, 'Eusebius von Cäsarea als Darsteller der phönizischen Religion', 1–103, and idem, 'Eusebius von Cäsarea als Darsteller der griechische Religion', *Forschungen zur christlicher Literatur- und Dogmengeschichte* 14.3 (1922): 1–133, and the dissertation of S. L. Coggan 'Pandaemonia: A Study of Eusebius' Recasting of Plutarch's Story of the "Death of Great Pan"', (Syracuse University, 1992). The work of Ulrich, *Euseb von Caesarea und die Juden*, and Kofsky, *Eusebius of Caesarea Against the Pagans*, while not dedicated to the *PE* alone, have done much to fill this lacuna in the scholarship.

Since my analysis focuses upon how identities are *represented* within the world of a text—that is, how they are discursively constructed—I shall commence by attending to the insights offered by ethnicity theory before turning to Eusebius' terminology of ethnicity at its most basic levels. My examination compares his usage of certain key ethnic terms in the text, working out his 'philology of ethnicity'. *Genos* is often translated as 'race' and derives from the verb 'to be born'. *Ethnos* is often translated as 'nation' but carries a wide spectrum of applications to groups of people or animals. Often the two are conflated, but between them they can convey, at various points in the text, all the major characteristics of an ethnic group, especially those of a shared myth of descent and a sense of shared culture. A striking feature of Eusebius' use of both terms is his consistent connection of them to the notion of *politeia*, which can be variously translated as political constitution, citizenship, or more generally, communal way of life. The concept combined the cultural and religious elements of rituals, customs, teachings, legal institutions, and moral practices that were represented as having been established by a nation's forefathers. When used in the verbal form, *politeuō*, the term is always applied to legal contexts (meaning 'to establish laws'). Hence, an entire cluster of ideas were evoked through Eusebius' language of ethnicity, which should be emphasized before we turn to the various peoples whose identities Eusebius was carefully formulating in the *Praeparatio*.

Following this essentially philological discussion, I shall focus upon ethnicity in order to demonstrate the fundamental unity of a work sometimes construed as a hodge-podge of random arguments against disconnected anti-Christian accusations.[84] This approach reveals a coherence and unity to the argument that has not yet been recognized. I argue that Eusebius is concerned with two basic narratives of descent in each half of the *Praeparatio*. That is, Books 1–6 are dedicated to a narrative of descent for the Greeks; Books 7–9 seek to recast a narrative of descent of the ancient Hebrews; and Books 10–15 pick up the Greek narrative again, this time to show its connections (and disconnections) to that of the Hebrews.[85] Both narratives assume the superiority of the Hebrews, as forefathers of the Christians, over against the inferiority of the Greeks.

[84] See Johnson, review of Kofsky, *Eusebius of Caesarea Against the Pagans*, VC (2005), 209–12.
[85] See Appendix 1.

According to Eusebius' narrative of Greek descent, the Greeks derived their customs, theology, moral character, and way of life from the Phoenicians and Egyptians. Through quotations from Greek sources, Eusebius claims that the mythic figures of Cadmus and Orpheus were responsible for the importation into Greece of Phoenician and Egyptian customs, ways of life, and ways of thinking. Plato, on the other hand, represented a connection between the wisdom of the Hebrews and the wisdom of the Greeks, because of his borrowing from the latter during his travels to the East. These migrating figures marked significant stages in the Greeks' past and were portrayed as forging connections with other nations that defined Greek identity. The Greeks had contributed nothing of their own to the rise and progress of civilization; they were mere latecomers onto the field of history, dependent upon foreign 'barbarian' peoples for their cultural, religious and philosophical way of life. In a world that favoured the ancient as somehow more truthful and closer to the gods, while condemning the recent as lacking authority and even subversive, Eusebius' historical reconstruction of Greek descent was particularly damaging.

Eusebius recounts Hebrew descent as a narrative competing with that of the Greeks. The Hebrew forefathers were among the earliest nations and their antiquity was unquestioned. Unique among all other ancient nations, the Hebrews alone worshipped God as the Creator of all things. Their pursuit of things divine and practice of rigorous asceticism set them apart as a nation of 'friends of God'. Their lives, Eusebius writes in a fascinating passage, are to be images, or icons, for later readers to emulate.[86] Later, as a result of their sojourn in Egypt, the descendants of the Hebrews became corrupted in their way of life and effectively 'Egyptianized'. It was at this point, according to Eusebius, that the nation of the Hebrews devolved into the bastardized nation of the Jews. He writes:

Then the race (*genos*) of their descendants gave way to a multitude and the nation (*ethnos*) of the Jews was established out of them ... the ways of their forefathers, the friends of God, grew slack with them and were blunted in a short time, while the effects of their time spent among Egyptians prevailed so much over the multitude of whom I speak, that they came to forget the virtue of their forefathers, and their lives became entangled in customs like those of the

---

[86] *PE* 7.7.

Egyptians, so that their character seemed to differ in no way from the Egyptians.[87]

Moses, the great lawgiver of the Jews, described by Eusebius as a 'Hebrew of Hebrews', attempted to recall the people to their ancestral way of life. Because of their moral weakness, however, he could only institute a sort of halfway *politeia* between those of the Hebrews and the Egyptians, at least when his laws were taken in their literal sense. Interpreted allegorically, by contrast, his law code remained a source of Hebrew wisdom. Thus, a remnant of the true Hebrew *ethnos* persisted, resurfacing in personalities such as David, the prophets, and the Hellenistic Jewish authors Josephus and Philo of Alexandria.

As a result of the travels of Plato to the East, the Hebrew wisdom hidden in the writings of Moses was transmitted to the Greeks. Thus the narrative of Greek descent is picked up again as it connects, if briefly, with that of the Hebrews. According to Eusebius, Plato functioned as a 'translator' of Hebrew wisdom into Greek. He expends much effort quoting passages from the Hebrew Bible alongside passages from Plato's works that he believed were direct borrowings (Books 11–13). However, Eusebius takes great pains to show that Plato's successors quickly went astray by deviating from the truth he had borrowed from the Hebrews.

The primary emphasis of the narratives of descent is placed upon the Greeks, Hebrews and Jews; but the Romans, too, receive brief though revealing comments in the *Praeparatio*. It is important to give special attention to Eusebius' view of the Romans in this work since he has often been considered the architect of Byzantine political theology—that is, the conception of the earthly monarch as modelled upon (and hence legitimated by) the archetype of God, the heavenly monarch.[88] This sort of ideology, which tied so closely the Roman State with the Christian God, is universally accepted as having deep roots in Eusebius' thought. And it may, to some extent—if we focus exclusively on particular themes in a limited number of Eusebius' later works of the 330s, after

---

[87] *PE* 7.8.37.

[88] This notion of an earthly ruler modelled upon the heavenly ruler had become a prominent theme in Hellenistic and Roman political thought well before Eusebius; see E. R. Goodenough, 'The Political Philosophy of Hellenistic Kingship', *YCS* 1 (1928), 55–102; N. H. Baynes, 'Eusebius and the Christian Empire', *Annuaire de l'institut de philologie et d'histoire orientales* 2 (1933), 13–18; G. Chesnut, 'The Ruler and the Logos in Neo-pythagorean, Middle Platonic, and Late Stoic Political Philosophy', *ANRW* 2.16.2 (1978), 1310–32.

Constantine had become sole ruler, lavished imperial favour upon the Church, and called some very important Church councils. In the *Praeparatio*, however, a different vision of Rome arises than that which often receives disproportionate attention in the 'later' Eusebius. I offer close readings of certain key texts of the *Praeparatio* to show that his position towards Rome is more ambivalent than previously thought. Because my re-evaluation of this topic may seem startling, I combine my reading of these passages with some more explicit claims in the *Demonstratio*—one of which even claims that the prophecies of Daniel found in the Old Testament were encoded in riddles lest the Romans realize they were the targets of prophecy and so destroy the writings out of anger—and his later works.

The final theme of this study returns to the question 'who are the Christians?' expressed in the opening lines of Eusebius' *Praeparatio*. Clear and unmistakable claims that Christianity should be taken as an *ethnos* had been made by Eusebius in his great *Historia Ecclesiastica*.[89] Strikingly, however, the *Praeparatio*, a work more concerned with formulations of ethnic identity than any other extant work of Eusebius, labels Christianity an *ethnos* only once. The reason for this may be that Eusebius' central concern in the *Praeparatio* has been the identity of Christianity's others: both Greeks and Jews (as well as Phoenicians and Egyptians). In the second half of Eusebius' apologetic undertaking, the *Demonstratio*, he would turn much greater attention to Christian identity (especially in the first two books). Since Eusebius even claims later in the *Demonstratio* that it is in the first books of that work that he addressed the issue of Christian identity, I have incorporated the relevant passages from the *Demonstratio* into my discussion.

From both these works, the dominant conceptions for Christianity are 'the Church from the nations' and a 'nation (or people) out of the nations'. In either case, Eusebius represents Christianity as transgressive of older ethnic identities through the formation of a new identity. This

---

[89] *HE* 1.4.2. 'It is admitted that when in recent times the appearance of our Saviour Jesus Christ had become known to all men there immediately made its appearance a new nation (*ethnos*); a nation confessedly not small, and not dwelling in some corner of the earth, but the most numerous and pious of all nations, indestructible and unconquerable, because it always receives assistance from God. This nation, thus suddenly appearing at the time appointed by the inscrutable counsel of God, is the one which has been honoured by all with the name of Christ' (trans. A. C. McGiffert, NPNF series). See. M. R. Beggs, 'From Kingdom to Nation: The Transformation of a Metaphor in Eusebius' *Historia Ecclesiastica*', (Ph.D. dissertation, University of Notre Dame, 1998).

point is epitomized in the prologue to the *Praeparatio*. Here, Eusebius provides a brief 'ethnography of conversion'—that is, he describes the effects of conversion to Christianity upon members of various barbarian nations. Upon turning to Christianity, these individuals gave up their ancestral character and adopted the ways of Christ, characterized by piety, rationality and truth.

Persians who have become his disciples no longer marry their mothers, nor Scythians feed on human flesh, because of Christ's word which has come even unto them, nor other races (*genē*) of barbarians have incestuous union with daughters and sisters, nor do men madly lust after men and pursue unnatural pleasures, nor do those, whose practice it formerly was, now expose their dead kindred to dogs and birds, nor strangle the aged, as they did formerly, nor according to their ancient custom do they feast on the flesh of their dearest friends when dead, nor like the ancients offer human sacrifices to the daemons as to gods, nor slaughter their dearest friends and think it piety.[90]

Eusebius employs such ethnographic topoi here in an attempt to formulate an answer to the questions of Christian identity and Christian legitimacy, or rather, superiority. Christians are represented as members of various *ethnē* who have rejected their ancestral way of life. But the 'new' way of life adopted by Christians is actually the most ancient way of life—that of the Hebrews. Eusebius' apologetic is based, therefore, upon a negative portrayal of the ancestors of the other nations, and a positive portrayal of the Hebrew ancestors, whom the Christians make their own—not through biological connectedness, but through a shared character and way of life. In any case, the Church's identity is, for Eusebius, its own apologetic.

Eusebius' 'ethnography of conversion' exhibits well the way in which one could write apologetics within the broader conceptual framework of defining the 'national character' of various nations. Conversion was seen as radically affecting ethnic identity. Likewise, the two master narratives of descent could be strategically retold to defend rejection of other national options for a Church that was drawn out of the nations. The purpose of these narratives was to show how the two primary national identities offered by the Greeks and the Jews failed in certain fundamental ways (whether historical lateness, dependency on other nations for a way of life that they would only contaminate, or possession of depraved and superstitious character as portrayed in the lives of the forefathers).

[90] *PE* 1.4.6.

Meanwhile, the Hebrews (and by extension their Christian 'descendants') exhibited superiority on all counts.

CONCLUSIONS

Within a tradition of Christian apologetics that actively engaged with the ongoing discourses of national historiography and rhetorical representations of Greeks and others, Eusebius' defence of Christianity would make a substantial and sustained contribution. The present attempt to take seriously the *Praeparatio*'s nations and the narratives that shape their identities hopes to provoke renewed analysis of early Christian apologetics and the world the apologists thought they inhabited. Categories of 'religion' and 'culture' may be less helpful in such enquiries, for early Christians constructed their identity and argued its legitimation within a discourse of ethnicity. There are no 'pagans' in Eusebius' *Praeparatio*, only Greeks, Phoenicians and others. Christians were to be identified as a nation or a Church whose members were drawn from all nations, a restoration of the nation of the Hebrews, the most ancient and most wise 'friends of God'.

The fruitfulness of an examination of Eusebius' 'ethnic argumentation' in the *Praeparatio* is not limited to our understanding of this singular text. Such an approach to the *Praeparatio* might also offer fresh insight into central elements of Eusebius' thought that have received substantial attention among Eusebian scholars. Eusebius' accommodation to Greek philosophy must be viewed against the backdrop of his polemical retelling of Greek national history. His views of Judaism should be contextualized within his historical understanding of the rise and fall of nations, and his 'political theology' reformulated within the conceptual framework that he himself was developing, that is, the articulation of Christianity as a counter-theology to Greek *polis* theology. Finally, assessments of Eusebius' conception of Christian identity and ecclesiology should certainly benefit from careful examination of his language of ethnicity and his construction of a Christian ethnic identity in distinction from other ethnicities.

2

The Language of Ethnicity

INTRODUCTION: 'NATION', 'RACE', AND ETHNICITY THEORY

Racial identities are, at the very outset, dependent on ways of speaking. The identifications by which we make sense of ourselves and others, and by which we organize our social worlds, are fundamentally derived from particular vocabularies and their attendant conceptual categories. Already, I have used the term 'race' to translate the Greek *genos*; and I have preferred 'nation' for *ethnos*, and in general, use it to refer to the collectivities of the Egyptians, Greeks, Jews, and others. The applicability of either 'race' or 'nation' to ancient peoples may, however, seem questionable. To make matters worse, I employ the terms 'ethnicity' and 'ethnic' alongside of, and almost synonymously with, the terms 'nation' and 'national'. The issue is a vexed one, and I will not attempt to solve it here (indeed, I am convinced it cannot be solved). The problem rests, quite simply, upon the diversity of application of the vocabulary of *genos* and *ethnos* in ancient texts, and the similar diversity in the use of the terms 'nation', 'race', and 'ethnic group' in modern texts.

Walker Connor, in an often-cited essay entitled 'A Nation Is a Nation, Is a State, Is an Ethnic Group, Is a …', complained that the terms state, nation, nation-state and nationalism are 'shrouded in ambiguity' and are caught in a 'linguistic jungle'.[1] The use of the word ethnicity is worse: it is 'more definitionally chameleonic than nation'.[2] He then proceeded to offer his own definitional distinctions between these troubled terms, thus adding his own account (insightful as it is) to the jungle of

---

[1] W. Connor, 'A Nation Is a Nation, Is a State, Is an Ethnic Group, Is a …', *Ethnic and Racial Studies* 1 (1978), 378.
[2] Ibid., 386.

disparate meanings that he sought to overcome. Positivist approaches that seek to define collective identities in such a way that all rational observers of the phenomena can agree are rendered hopeless by the plethora of rhetorical manipulations of the relevant terms, by nationalists and theorists alike, in legitimating particular visions of the world and its peoples. Each term is like a many-headed hydra whose multiplicity of necks has become entangled among the necks of its neighbouring term.[3] In the following remarks, I cannot possibly bring order to the imbroglio of terminological disparity among theorists and commentators on ethnicity, nationality and race; I only wish to clarify my own use of the terms, as well as some theoretical assumptions that I have found helpful. I will first offer comments on defining ethnicity, then turn to my use of 'nation' in dealing with the ancient *ethnos* and ethnicity, before detailing Eusebius' use of the relevant terms.

The study of ethnicity was, in some sense, rooted in a desire to speak about biologically defined people groups without the negative connotations or assumptions that clouded the category of 'race' framed in the eighteenth and nineteenth centuries.[4] The very term 'ethnicity' may have come into fashion as an antidote to the term 'race' following the horrors of racist ideology enacted in Nazi Germany (after all, the term 'ethnicity' dates to the 1940s or '50s).[5] As Jonathan Hall writes, 'the basic conceptual apparatus of "race" had remained, despite a change in terminology'.[6] Even so, emphasis could be diverted away from biological traits to other characteristics of ethnic identity. One of the now-standard treatments of ethnicity and nationalism, Anthony D. Smith's *The Ethnic Origins of Nations*, presents six characteristics of ethnic identity that distinguish it from other forms of group identity: a collective name; a common myth of descent; a shared history; a distinctive shared culture;

---

[3] Contrary to Connor's attempt at ordering the multiplicity of uses, J. A. Armstrong, *Nations Before Nationalism* (Chapel Hill: University of North Carolina Press, 1981), 6, claims there is no 'purely definitional way of distinguishing ethnicity from other types of identity'. For Eusebius' use of the metaphor of the hydra, see *PE* 7.2.5.

[4] On the possible influence of ancient conceptions on modern notions of 'race', see now B. Isaac, *The Invention of Racism in Classical Antiquity* (Princeton: Princeton University Press, 2004).

[5] For the date 1953: J. Hall, *Ethnic Identity in Greek Antiquity* (Cambridge: Cambridge University Press, 1997), 34. For the date 1942: I. Malkin, 'Introduction', in idem, ed., *Ancient Perceptions of Greek Ethnicity*, 15, citing M. Banks, *Ethnicity: Anthropological Constructions* (New York: Routledge, 1996), 4, 9–10.

[6] Ibid., 19. See also, G. Baumann, *The Multicultural Riddle: Rethinking National, Ethnic, and Religious Identities* (New York: Routledge, 1999), 20.

an association with a specific territory; and a sense of communal solidarity.[7] What is important to note about such a list is that the focus has turned away from the notions of blood connections, biological necessity and genetic essentialism that dominated the earlier discourse on 'race'. Biological kinship seems to be confined to only one of his six factors, and even here there is recognition of the fictive and constructed quality to the stories of descent told by a people.

While notions of racial particularity persist most obviously in a common myth of descent, conceptions of race cannot be so easily limited to such myths. The other five characteristics of ethnic identity can often be claimed as deriving from assumptions, however fictive, about racial descent. Ethnonyms often stem from the name of the people's mythic progenitor.[8] A group's territorial claims are often rooted in narratives of ancient conquest, colonization or autochthony on the part of their legendary ancestors.[9] The shared history of a people is merely the continued story of the descendants of the original progenitor. Shared cultural features and a sense of communal solidarity depend upon the experiences and practices related in both the myth of descent and the ongoing shared history of the group. Ethnicity, then, seems unable to escape from conceptions of race.[10]

What is arresting in this schema is the thoroughgoing prevalence of the deployment of narratives of racial descent in carrying explanatory value for other (cultural, territorial) elements of a communal identity. It is in this way that we can begin to see the constructedness and manipulability of racial identity. Biological or genetic relatedness, as 'real' as it may be, is never a given of racial or ethnic identity.[11] On the contrary, it is always formulated in the context of particular situations and under particular pressures.

Recent developments in the area of ethnicity theory have now seen a shift of focus away from the *content* of ethnicity to the *boundaries* of ethnic identities.[12] What matters now is not what features are necessary

---

[7] A. D. Smith, *The Ethnic Origins of Nations* (Oxford: Blackwell, 1986), 22–31. Compare with G. Baumann, *The Multicultural Riddle*, 31. More recently, Smith has slightly modified his list of characteristics of ethnic identity by lessening the role of territory; see A. D. Smith, *The Antiquity of Nations* (Cambridge: Polity Press, 2004), 18.

[8] See *PE* 7.6.2; 10.14.2; 11.6.39; for discussion, see Chapter 4.

[9] See Philo of Byblos, *ap. PE* 1.10.9, 20, 55; Diodorus, *ap. PE* 2.1.6, 9–13.

[10] See Kimber Buell, 'Rethinking the Relevance of Race for Early Christian Self-Definition', 449–76; D. Olster, 'Classical Ethnography and Early Christianity', 9–31.

[11] See now, Kimber Buell, *Why This New Race*.

[12] This also assumes a rejection of the 'primordialist' model of ethnicity, which I will not discuss here as the topic has been adequately, and repeatedly, treated by other classical scholars. See e.g., Hall, *Ethnic Identity in Greek Antiquity*, and Malkin, 'Introduction'.

to define ethnicity in general, but rather, how any of the features are put to work in concrete social situations to distinguish 'us' from 'them'. All Smith's characteristics (and any others that might be added, such as language, religion, or physical appearance) need not be present in every articulation of ethnic identity; and furthermore, one or more features may replace others as social situations change, develop, or even disappear.[13] What is important is the way in which a given feature is manipulated to mark off difference between groups. In other words, the features are made to work within the formulation, maintenance or alteration of boundaries. As F. Barth wrote in his seminal essay, 'The critical focus of investigation ... becomes the ethnic *boundary* that defines the group, not the cultural stuff that it encloses.'[14]

The focus on boundaries has led theorists to grapple with an important point about the nature of ethnicity: it is a discursively constructed identity. This means that ethnic or racial identity is formed and maintained within a discourse that makes certain markers of difference definitive for the identity of one's own group, while other markers are made distinctive of other groups' identities.[15] To assert the discursive nature of ethnic identity is not to deny the reality of those markers, but rather to recognize the non-necessary relationship between such markers and the (constructed) identity. Ethnicity, then, is constituted in the dynamic ebb and flow of social interaction, from which boundaries are constructed between 'us' and 'them' in particular and changing social situations.

Such theoretical assumptions allow the student of early apologetics to appreciate more fully the ways in which ethnicity and race function within textual arguments. The mechanisms of constructing identities within texts can thus be better analysed, and the shifts from some markers of difference to others can be delineated. Rather than resulting in sloppy scholarship and slipshod philology, the theoretical grounding

[13] On the problem of such shifts in situation, see M. Moerman, 'Ethnic Identification in a Complex Civilization: Who are the Lue', *American Anthropologist* 67 (1965), 1222–3.

[14] F. Barth, 'Introduction', in F. Barth, *Ethnic Groups and Boundaries: The Social Organization of Culture Difference* (Boston: Little, Brown and Co., 1969), 15; or differently: '[An ethnic group] cannot be identified—cannot, in a sense, be said to exist—in isolation' (M. Moerman, 'Ethnic identification in a complex civilization', 1216). See also, K. Goudriaan, 'Ethnical Strategies in Graeco-Roman Egypt', in Per Bilde *et al.*, (eds), *Ethnicity in Hellenistic Egypt*, 76; Lieu, *Christian Identity in the Jewish and Graeco-Roman World*, 98–146.

[15] See especially, S. Hall, 'Race: The Floating Signifier', videorecording (Northampton, MA: Media Education Foundation, 1996); but also K. Goudriaan, *Ethnicity in Ptolemaic Egypt* (Amsterdam: J. C. Gieben, 1988), 8–13; and idem, 'Ethnical Strategies', 74–99.

(that is, the recognition of ethnicity as a discursive phenomenon) beckons us to engage in close readings of the relevant texts in their original languages to locate the driving forces of identity construction and the manipulation of language in describing self and others.

This emphasis upon the rhetoric and the representation of identities within texts, combined with the recognition that the markers of ethnic difference are not all necessary in every occurrence of ethnic identity formation, is also important for the study of ancient ethnicities because it allows us to adapt our modern understandings to the ancient conceptions of peoplehood. We need not force the ancient articulations into an anachronistic modern framework; nor need we neglect evidence that does not quite fit within rigid classifications. In other words, a discursive approach to ethnicity allows for sensitivity to the ancient literary phenomena.

Jonathan Hall's illuminating work on Greek ethnicity called attention to the value of these trends in ethnicity theory, although he claimed that, of Smith's six characteristics (noted above), common territory and a myth of shared descent were, in some sense, non-negotiable for determining ancient ethnicities.[16] Shaye Cohen had similarly recognized the importance of a discursive approach to ethnicity, yet (paradoxically) maintained the necessity of biological connectedness for ancient Jewish ethnic identity.[17] Both Hall and Cohen have been criticized for this tension within their treatments of ancient Greek and Jewish ethnic identity.[18] Hall responded to his critics, claiming that a 'polythetic' approach (one that did not hold on to territory and myths of descent, or some other characteristic, as necessary for defining ethnicity) would be too open-ended and vacuous: it would cease 'to possess any heuristic power as an analytical concept'.[19] This may not necessarily be so, however: if the markers of ethnic difference can change or be adapted over time within a discourse of ethnicity, then all that is necessary is the ancient authors' claims for peoplehood. It is sufficient that a people are

[16] Hall, *Ethnic Identity in Greek Antiquity*, 25–6.
[17] S. Cohen, *The Beginnings of Jewishness: Boundaries, Varieties, Uncertainties* (Berkeley and Los Angeles: University of California Press, 1999).
[18] On Hall, see D. Konstan, 'Defining Ancient Greek Ethnicity', *Diaspora* 6 (1997), 97–110; and R. Just, 'The History of Ethnicity', *Cambridge Archaeological Journal* 8 (1998), 277–9; and now, Kimber Buell, *Why This New Race*, 40. On Cohen, see D. Kimber Buell, 'Ethnicity and Religion in Mediterranean Antiquity and Beyond', *Religious Studies Review* 26 (2000), 243–9.
[19] J. Hall, 'Discourse and Praxis: Ethnicity and Culture in Ancient Greece', *Cambridge Archaeological Journal* 8 (1998), 268.

said to constitute an *ethnos*—whatever the markers of difference that are employed to distinguish them from other peoples.[20] Far from 'blunt[-ing] the analytical utility of the concept [of ethnicity]',[21] an approach that allows itself to remain polythetic, without making certain elements necessary, can be sensitive to the ancient authors' conceptualizations of the corporate identity of an *ethnos*.

This having been said, my approach will nonetheless still emphasize the importance of myths of shared descent. But this is not as a definitional sine qua non for all ancient ethnicities; rather, I am attempting to stress Eusebius' own focus in the *Praeparatio*. As later chapters will show, two narratives of descent provide the organizational structure for the entire *Praeparatio*. At the same time, other markers of ethnic difference, such as language and territory, do play a role in Eusebius' conception of ethnicity (as will be noted below). Hence, in assessing ethnic identity in Eusebius' *Praeparatio*, the following characteristics will be in play (for at least some of the *ethnē*): a collective name (ethnonym), a narrative of descent (with fictive notions of biological kinship), a shared history, a distinctive shared culture (including religious practices, theology, language, etc.), communal solidarity and sense of homogeneity, a collective character, and territorial association.

An important additional feature of Eusebius' portrayal of ethnic identity involves the legislative aspects of identity. The narratives of descent allot much significance to the role of certain key ancestors who acted as legislators for the people. Their legal codes and the way of life prescribed in their laws defined the communal activity and customs throughout the shared history of the *ethnos*. Furthermore, this implied some degree of political autonomy, at least at some point in their shared history.[22] This legal and political element to an *ethnos* is not conveyed as well by the terms 'ethnicity' or 'race'. Hence, I have

[20] Similarly, see Moerman, 'Ethnic identification in a complex civilization', 1220: '[The ethnographer] must not assume that any single "objective" difference or similarity—of language, polity, phenotype, or religion—is significant to all groups, and in the same ways, and to the same degrees.'

[21] J. Hall, 'Discourse and Praxis', 266.

[22] Even under Roman domination, many peoples were allowed to maintain their paternal customs and local legal traditions. In fact, it could be considered a stabilizing element in the security of the far-flung empire; see A. Lintott, *Imperium Romanum* (New York: Routledge, 1993), 18–21, 54–9, 129–53. For the impact of Christianity on civic legal autonomy, see M. Maas, '*Mores et Moenia*: Ethnography and the Decline in Urban Constitutional Autonomy in Late Antiquity', in W. Pohl and M. Diesenberger (eds), *Integration und Herrschaft: Ethnische Identitäten und soziale Organisation im Frühmittelalter* (Vienna: Verlag der Österreichischen Akademie der Wissenschaften, 2002), 25–35.

wanted to maintain the application of the term 'nation' when referring to an ancient *ethnos*, especially when Eusebius has emphasized the role of law-givers and the paternal laws in marking out an ethnic identity.[23] My adoption of 'nation' is not meant to obscure or deny the racial elements, but to conjoin notions that, in ancient texts, were often inseparable.

Of course, there is always the danger of confusion with the modern nation-state. However, the danger is often overstated, especially by those who wish to privilege the modern phenomena by claiming that nations are a product of historical developments (whether industrialism or print capitalism) in the modern era, particularly (if not exclusively) in Western Europe—this is the so-called 'modernist' approach to nations and nationalism.[24] While my primary reason for employing the term 'nation' is to convey the legal-political element of *ethnos* just noted, I will offer here some additional remarks on the issue. To begin with, some manifestations of the ancient *ethnos* may not be so different from some manifestations of the modern nation. Some classicists have identified what may be termed an *ethnos*-state;[25] while some students of the modern nation-state have identified what they label an 'ethnic nation'.[26]

[23] Numerous scholars have discussed ancient nations, and even nationalism, but rarely have they offered more than the most cursory remarks regarding the identification of the ancient *ethnos* with the term 'nation'. See e.g. F. W. Walbank, 'The Problem of Greek Nationality', *Phoenix* 5 (1951), 41–60; and idem, 'Nationality as a Factor in Roman History', *HSCP* 76 (1972), 145–68; M. Hadas, 'Nationalist Survival under Hellenistic and Roman Imperialism', *Journal for the History of Ideas* 11 (1950), 131–40; R. MacMullen, 'Tertullian and "National" Gods', *JTS* 26 (1975), 405–10; M. Finley, *The Use and Abuse of Ancient History* (London: Hogarth Press, 1986); R. A. Oden, 'Philo of Byblos and Hellenistic Historiography', *PEQ* 110 (1978), 115–26; E. Bickerman, 'Origenes gentium', 65–81; Sterling, *Historiography and Self-Definition*; E. Cohen, *The Athenian Nation* (Princeton: Princeton University Press, 2000).

[24] Among modernists, the foremost examples are E. Gellner, *Nations and Nationalism* (Oxford: Blackwell, 1983); B. Anderson, *Imagined Communities: Reflections on the Origins and Spread of Nationalism* (London: Verso, 1983); E. Hobsbawm, *Nations and Nationalism since 1780: Programme, Myth, Reality* (Cambridge: Cambridge University Press, 1990). Some scholars of antiquity have adopted modernist assumptions in their treatments of ancient nations; see F. Walbank, 'The Problem of Greek Nationality'; Mendels, *The Rise and Fall of Jewish Nationalism*.

[25] See C. Morgan, 'Ethnicity and Early Greek States', *PCPS* 37 (1991), 131–63; and more briefly, 'Ethnicity', in S. Hornblower and A. H. Spawforth (eds), *Oxford Classical Dictionary*, 3rd edn, (Oxford: Oxford University Press, 1996), 558–9.

[26] See A. D. Smith, *The Ethnic Origins of Nations*, 140–4; R. Brubaker, 'Civic and Ethnic Nations in France and Germany', in J. Hutchinson and A. D. Smith (eds), *Ethnicity* (Oxford: Oxford University Press, 1996), 168–73; A. Dawisha, 'Nation and Nationalism: Historical Antecedents to Contemporary Debates', *International Studies Review* 4 (2002), 3–22. For criticisms of the civic/ethnic distinction, see M. Billig, *Banal Nationalism* (London: Sage, 1995), 47–8; A. D. Smith, *The Antiquity of Nations*, 42.

The model of the 'ethnic nation' exhibits an important feature of the discourse on nations and ethnic groups today. An ethnic group is often seen as a potential nation, a nation in embryonic form. Once an ethnic group obtains political autonomy or statehood, then it becomes a nation.[27] Yet, this formulation equates nation with nation-state. Alternately, a nation without a state is often labelled instead an ethnic group. This shows a slippage in the employment of nation, in the first case with a state, in the second case with an ethnic group. The slippage can be accounted for in a number of ways. On the one hand, a state can be labelled a 'nation-state' or just 'a nation' in order to legitimate its existence. Political autonomy and statehood can be justified by claiming that they are (at least mostly) coterminous with the limits of a people, who, as a people, deserve certain rights to the control of land, laws, and way of life (a modern rendering of ancient myths of autochthony, where birth and land were intimately connected).[28] Thus, a modern state apparatus can be legitimized by the employment of terminology in this way: to believe that a state 'belongs' to an ethnic people validates its existence and its exercise of power. The language of nationhood does nothing less than to authorize the violence and brutality inherent in the performance of the modern nation-state.[29]

On the other hand, the slippage in the opposite direction, the application of nation to an ethnic group, at least partly lies in the history of the term in the English language.[30] The Old English 'nacioun' derived principally from the Latin use of *natio* (deriving from *nascor*, 'to be born') in the Vulgate. There it had been employed to render the Greek *ethnos* (in particular, the frequent occurrences in the plural) of the Septuagint.[31] Hence, the introduction into English of 'nacioun' carried much of the pre-modern (even if not always Greek) cluster of ideas surrounding the ancient *ethnos*. From these origins in English, the term nation carried, and still can carry, broader notions of peoplehood and

---

[27] See especially A. D. Smith, *The Antiquity of Nations*, 18–20, *passim*.

[28] Billig, *Banal Nationalism*, 24–8.

[29] Ibid., 28: 'The struggle for the nation-state is a struggle for the monopoly of the means of violence.' Or as E. Renan declared, national unity 'is always effected by means of brutality' (cited in Billig, *Banal Nationalism*, 38).

[30] See A. Hastings, *The Construction of Nationhood: Ethnicity, Religion and Nationalism* (Cambridge: Cambridge University Press, 1997), 14–19; A. D. Smith, *The Antiquity of Nations*, 134; less helpful is G. Zernatto, 'Nation: The History of a Word', *Review of Politics* 6 (1944), 351–66.

[31] On the Septuagint use of *ta ethnē*, see below.

racial identity that stretch beyond its more limited application to states or nation-states.

It remains to be seen how long the limited modernist definition of nation will last. Even as we supposedly move into a new era beyond the 'age of nations' (an interpretation of the world that may only arise from wishful thinking),[32] the modernist model of the rise of nations is being put to the question, especially by post-colonial critics, who are questioning the West European focus of the modernists.[33] The rejection of all pre-modern, pre-industrial, and non-Western societies as being incapable of supporting nations and nationalism may be myopic. Future developments in nationality and ethnicity theory, combined with changes in international politics and the global economy, will continue to offer new (if not always better) ways of conceptualizing peoplehood and of analysing the history of peoples. Given the constantly changing nature of the contemporary discourse on nations, ethnicity and race as well as the past and present disparity of definitions and conceptions, I feel that to leave *ethnos* untranslated would only be to avoid the ever-present task of translating the ancient world. My use of 'ethnicity', 'race', and 'nation' mark an attempt to grapple with the issues while recognizing the complexity of the case.

TERMS OF ETHNICITY

If ethnic identity is a discursive construct, formulated within contexts of social differentiation and demarcation, then special attention must be given to the words used to represent particular peoples. In other words, an enquiry into the 'philology of ethnicity' is required—and it must go beyond the analysis of a 'rhetoric of representation' of the ethnic self in

[32] The end of modern nationalism has been heralded, for instance, by R. Poole, *Nation and Identity* (New York: Routledge, 1999). For the opposite view, see M. Mann, 'Nation-states in Europe and Other Continents: Diversifying, Developing, Not Dying', *Daedalus* 122 (1993), 115–40; Billig, *Banal Nationalism*; A. D. Smith, *The Antiquity of Nations*, 1–2, *passim*.

[33] See esp. P. Duara, 'Historicizing National Identity, or Who Imagines What and When', in G. Eley and Ronald G. Suny (eds), *Becoming National* (Oxford: Oxford University Press, 1996), 151–77; P. Chatterjee, *The Nation and its Fragments* (Princeton: Princeton University Press, 1993); K. Davis, 'National Writing in the Ninth Century: A Reminder for Postcolonial Thinking about the Nation', *Journal of Medieval and Early Modern Studies* 28 (1998), 611–37; A. D. Smith, *The Antiquity of Nations*, 15–17.

contrast to the ethnic others. The enquiry must also direct itself towards the more basic level of the language of social groupings and the assumptions that underlie the representation of specific ethnic groups (that is, the assumption that people can validly be grouped according to 'ethnicity'). In English, for instance, there exists a vocabulary of race and even a taxonomy (or at least a definitional categorization) of generic terms for collective identities, so that, for example, the activity of constructing and differentiating 'blacks' and 'whites' in America is made sense of, and even validated by, a more basic prior assumption of the legitimacy of a category called 'race'.[34]

In ancient Greek texts, this generic vocabulary of ethnicity primarily consists of terms such as *ethnos, genos,* and *laos.* Without the assumptions that humans can be legitimately grouped under such a rubric of peoplehood, no further construction of specific identities such as Greeks, Egyptians, or Jews would be possible. Hence, analysis of these basic terms of ethnic identities is an important prerequisite for the study of particular identities. Yet, relatively few treatments of ethnicity in the ancient world offer sustained discussions of the precise terminology and corresponding definitions of these key words for corporate identities in Greek literature.[35] The remarks on the philology of ethnicity offered here will show the necessity of such examination into the workings of ethnic language for fully grasping ancient conceptualizations of 'race' and 'nation'.

The following analysis concerns itself only with Eusebius' own words in the *Praeparatio.* While Eusebius is often in agreement with his sources, and they definitely form at least a portion of his conceptual world, establishing his precise relationship to each of his sources would be an immense and incredibly complex task. Allowing his sources to speak in their own words does not necessarily entail any firm basis for determining the extent of his agreement with their terminology. Limit-

---

[34] See Billig, *Banal Nationalism,* 63.

[35] *Pace* Buell, 'Race and Universalism in Early Christianity', 432. Exceptions to this relative neglect of the philology of ethnicity are: J. K. Ward, '*Ethnos* in the *Politics*: Aristotle and Race', in J. Ward and T. Lott (eds), *Philosophers on Race* (Oxford: Blackwell, 2002), 14–37; C. P. Jones, '*ἔθνος* and *γένος* in Herodotus', *CQ* 46 (1996), 315–20; E. Cohen, *The Athenian Nation.* Both Jones and Cohen reject the attempt to define these terms by some objective criteria, and instead turn their attention to how the words were used by particular authors. Despite Cohen's critical note on Jones (25–6), I see them as largely adopting the same approach to ancient texts: Cohen's contention that 'The meaning [of *ethnos*] derives from contrast with [its] cognitive complements' (25) is equivalent to Jones' search for the 'intension' of ethnic language within a given author.

ing my enquiry to Eusebius' own words thus makes philological analysis more manageable, as well as safer.

I begin with considerations of *genos* ('race'[36]) since this carries the broadest range of meanings—only some of which are racial (that is, referring to a people's corporate identity). *Ethnos* ('nation') on the other hand, will be shown always to be confined to racial referents. Discussion of the terms in isolation can then be followed by reflection on their conjoined use within the same sentence or passage. At issue will be the cluster of notions that each term conveyed and the particular nuances one might carry in contrast to the other.[37]

Genos

The use of *genos* exhibits the general trend of the semantic profusion typical of *genos* in post-classical literature. Deriving from *gignomai* and hence bearing notions of biological connection between parent and child, *genos* signified familial relatedness.[38] Such a meaning could then easily develop from 'family' to any group (or 'class') of things sharing some set of common attributes. All these meanings are present in the *Praeparatio*'s use of *genos*.

On the one hand, *genos* refers to a class or category of things or people joined by one or more common attributes. In the broadest sense, *genos* is applied to the 'human race' as a category of beings distinct from animals, plants or divinities.[39] More narrowly, Eusebius can use the term to refer to 'the class of slaves' (*to oiketikon genos*), that is, slaves

---

[36] On the issue of translating *genos* as 'race', see Kimber Buell, 'Rethinking the Relevance of Race for Early Christian Self-Definition'; Olster, 'Classical Ethnography and Early Christianity'.

[37] I omit discussion of *laos* ('people') here since all its three occurrences in the *Praeparatio* vaguely denote the population of the Jews (though never explicitly stated as such) in relation to a particular leader: Samuel (10.14.4); Jeremiah (12.3.2); Moses (12.9.1). Eusebius will refer to the Christians as a *laos* at *DE* 1.1 (7); 2.3 (61cd, 83a); 10.3 (477a); 10.8 (510cd); see Chapter 7. Eusebius' favouring of *ethnos* over *laos* in the *PE* may follow the similar phenomenon in Philo of Alexandria; see Goudriaan, 'Ethnical Strategies', 81–2. Likewise, *phylē* ('tribe' or 'people') plays no major role in an exploration into the vocabulary of ethnicity in the *Praeparatio* since it occurs only twice, both in reference to the breakdown of the Jews into 12 tribes: either the tribe of Judah in particular (7.6.2), or all 12 tribes in general (12.47.title). Both cases represent a clear hierarchical categorization in relation to the Jewish nation. A *phylē* is always a division of a larger whole.

[38] See Jones, 'ἔθνος and γένος in Herodotus', 316–17.

[39] *PE* 1.4.1; 1.4.11, etc.

as a social category or even caste.[40] *Genos* can also comprise gender categories: the 'race' of men and the 'race' of women.[41] The term can also be applied to non-human categories as well: the classes of plants and animals,[42] of beings (*hekastōi genei tōn ontōn*) in the order of the created world,[43] or the 'tribes' (*phulai*) and orders of stars and heavenly powers.[44]

References to the 'races of gods/daemons' occur frequently.[45] Despite the fact that the gods are said to be connected by genealogical relationships at numerous places,[46] the application of *genos* to groups of divinities should be taken in the generic sense of 'class' and probably not in the sense of a quasi-familial connection in most of these occurrences. For instance, the four *genē* of divine beings classified at 4.5.1 puts the supreme God, 'the father and king of all gods', in a *genos* of his own, while the *genos* of heroes is surely not to be taken as designating members of the same kin or familial group, but as a class of semi-divine beings.

Eusebius thus applies *genos* to a number of categories, from the social to the theological.[47] None of these is ethnic in sense; they all exhibit only the pervasiveness of the extended use of *genos*. When we turn our attention to the strictly ethnic usage of the term, two related senses are noticeable. The first emphasizes the biological or 'blood' relatedness of the members of a group. The second emphasizes more the ethical, religious or cultural affinities of members of a group. This latter sense connotes a shared character or way of life that is prevalent over, while not necessarily abrogating, notions of biological kinship.

[40] *PE* 1.1.6; see also, *SC* 17.6; cp. e.g., *Acts of the Apostles* 4.6 ('the race of priests'); Maximus of Tyre, *Dissert.* 8.8 ('race of translators').

[41] *PE* 6.6.71; 12.32.7; 13.3.44. I use the English 'race' to translate *genos* in these cases since this term can still be used to refer to broader 'classes' of things as well as the more typical usage for biologically or phenotypically grouped collectivities of humans. The Oxford English Dictionary (1989) cites Spenser's *Fairie Quene*: 'In gentle Ladies breste and bounteous race/ Of women kind ...' with other examples, for the application of race to gender categories.

[42] *PE* 7.10.2.

[43] *PE* 6.6.24.

[44] *PE* 7.15.12.

[45] *PE* 4.5.1 (compare with Plutarch's statement cited at 5.4.1), 5.17.13; 7.16.7; 13.15.1, 4 and 7.

[46] *PE* 2.6.24; 2.7.4; 3.10.26; 10.9.23; 13.14.6.

[47] Cp. R. Kamtekar, 'Distinction without a Difference? Race and *Genos* in Plato', in J. Ward and T. Lott (eds), *Philosophers on Race*, 4–5.

The first emphasis (the purely biological) is most clearly marked in phrases denoting an individual's connections to a group of people through birth to a member of that group. It takes the form of 'so-and-so, a Syrian (or Egyptian, Greek, etc.) by birth'.[48] Such instances unambiguously evoke the sense of a kin group, and usually (if not always) occur in contexts where Eusebius wants to highlight racial identity. This is especially the case in the mention of Bardesanes the Syrian. Attention is drawn to Bardesanes' Syrian birth since the context concerns astrology, and Syrians were both geographically and conceptually closer to the Chaldaean experts on such matters (this is made clear in the passage: 'he is a Syrian by birth [*Syrou to genos*] and has pursued his enquiries to the highest point of Chaldaean science').[49] Also, at 3.10.20, Zeus is said to be 'the child of Kronos, a mortal born from a mortal, a Phoenician by race (*to genos*)'. Here, Eusebius' broader argument rests on a euhemeristic foundation in which gods are actually mortals deified after their deaths.[50] Emphasizing that Zeus was a Phoenician by race is thus a significant part of this project.

Beyond the attribution of this term to individuals, Eusebius applies the term to particular peoples such as the Jews,[51] Hebrews,[52] and barbarian races.[53] An interesting feature in the occurrences of *genos* joined with a particular ethnonym is its limitation to the Hebrews and Jews.[54] This centring of the use of *genos* upon the Jews and Hebrews

[48] Here *to genos* appears as an accusative of respect (literally: 'a Syrian with respect to race/birth'). The following ethnonyms appear in this construction in the *Praeparatio*: Greek (1.5.10); Phoenician (3.10.20; 10.5.1); Syrian (6.9.32); Jew (7.7.2, 'not foreigners by race from the Hebrews'); Hebrew (8.8.56); Milesian (10.14.11); and Eleatic (14.3.9; cf. Plato's reference to the 'Eleatic *ethnos*', 'Ελεατικὸν ἔθνος, cited at 14.4.8). Cp. S. Cohen, '*Ioudaios to genos* and Related Expressions in Josephus', in F. Parente and J. Sievers (eds), *Josephus and the History of the Greco-Roman Period: Essays in Memory of Morton Smith*, (Leiden: E. J. Brill, 1994), 23–38.

[49] *PE* 6.9.32.

[50] See Chapter 3.

[51] *PE* 7.6.1; 7.8.29; 7.8.30; 8.10.19.

[52] *PE* 1.9.15; 7.8.37; 9.10.1.

[53] *PE* 1.4.6 (where the Persians and Scythians are given as explicit examples); 14.10.11. In each of these occurrences the name of the people is given in the genitive plural (e.g. *to Ioudaiōn genos*, 7.6.1) or *muria ... genē barbarōn* (14.10.11). Specific ethnonyms are never given in adjectival form to modify *genos* (that is, there are no occurrences of *to Hellēnikon genos*, or *to Hebraïkon genos*, for example). Throughout the current discussion, I use the phrase 'the Jewish race (or nation, etc.)' for smoother reading, though a precise translation of these phrases should be 'the race of the Jews' or 'the race of the Hebrews'.

[54] The only exceptions are the two cases of barbarian *genē* (and even here, the generic 'barbarian' does not carry the sort of specificity that 'Hebrew' or 'Jew' does).

deserves some consideration, for it will illuminate the function of *genos* in an ethnic sense in the *Praeparatio*. A brief compilation of relevant examples will provide the basis for discussion.

At 7.6.1, Eusebius distinguishes the Hebrews from the Jews saying that the ancient Hebrews were the 'forefathers' of the Jews, but the *genos* of the Jews had not yet been established. In the account of Jacob (or Israel), at 7.8.29, Eusebius claims that it was from him that the '12-tribed *genos* of the *ethnos* of the Jews' arose.[55] Job is said not to have belonged to the *genos* of the Jews, but nevertheless to have been included in the Scriptures as a Hebrew for his right conduct of piety.[56] At 1.9.15, the other ancient *ethnē* are said to have been allotted the veneration of astral phenomena, while the *genos* of the Hebrews alone worshipped the creator of the stars. In his discussion of the rise of the Jews from the Hebrews who were in Egypt, Eusebius claims that 'the race (*genos*) of [the Hebrews'] descendants gave way to overpopulation (*poluanthrōpian*) and the nation (*ethnos*) of the Jews was now established from them'.[57]

I should include one more particularly striking example: at 8.10.18, Eusebius introduces an important division within the Jewish *ethnos*. 'The whole Jewish nation (*ethnos*) is divided into two sections (*tmēmata*).' The majority of Jews follow the literal interpretation of Mosaic Law; while a second group (now called a *tagma*) follows the allegorical, or more philosophical, interpretation of the Law. This second group is 'the race (*genos*) of Jewish philosophers'.[58] The succession of vocabulary from *tmēma* to *tagma* to *genos* would seem to point towards the sense of 'class' (as a category of people or things) rather than 'race' (as a kinship group)—and yet, the context is thoroughly racial. The appellation of 'race of philosophers' had been employed by earlier authors. Theophrastus had considered the Syrians and Jews as a race of philosophers.[59] Similarly Clearchus had averred that the Jews were descendants of philosophers in India.[60] In these instances, the philosophical life was seen as intimately tied to one's familial heritage.[61] Here (at 8.10.19), Eusebius seems however to limit the *genos* of Jewish

---

[55] The conjunction of *genos* and *ethnos* here will be treated below.

[56] *PE* 7.8.30. On the account of Job within the narrative of Hebrew descent, see Chapter 4.

[57] *PE* 7.8.37.

[58] *PE* 8.10.19.

[59] 'Being philosophers by birth' (*philosophoi to genos ontes*, quoted via Porphyry at 9.2.1). See Pilhofer, *Presbyteron Kreitton*, 73–5.

[60] Quoted from Josephus at 9.5.6.

[61] Philosophers could often be given a collective identity under terms such as *phulê*, *genos* or *ethnos*. See, for example, Lucian, *Fug.* 6 (the 'race of Brahmans') and 10 (the 'tribe of sophists').

philosophers to only an elite portion of the larger Jewish *ethnos*. *Genos* may thus be seen here in a taxonomic relationship to *ethnos*, the former term denoting a part of the whole.

Significant features of Eusebius' conceptualization of *genos* become apparent from these occurrences. In each of these cases, reference is made to a kin group, but only some of the time does their kinship as such play an important role in the passages in which they are located. On the one hand, the emphasis on forefathers and familial connectedness may be explicit.[62] The example of Job presumes the sense of kinship attached to *genos* in order to highlight the priority of piety and virtue in his life over his biological connections ('though he did not belong to the Jewish *genos*'). On the other hand, the biological kinship of the *genos* of the Hebrews may be left unexpressed.[63] In contrast to Eusebius' declarations about Job, these instances emphasize the way of life of a *genos*, not its connectedness by birth. Focus is centred on the possession of truth and virtue by the people as a whole, not the internal biological connectedness within the group (though kinship remains presumed).

Similarly, references to the *genē* of the barbarians neglect to represent kinship explicitly as an important element of identity. Rather, customs, moral behaviour, religious practices, or teachings are the sole focus in these cases. For instance, Eusebius' mention of the 'races of barbarians' at 1.4.6, in an ethnographical discussion including Persians and Scythians, is solely concerned with the immoral and abominable practices exhibited among each of them (such as incest, homoeroticism and killing of the elderly). Elsewhere, other *genē* of barbarians are noted for their philosophical teachings and sensible way of life.[64] In either case, the customs and way of life are determinative for his conception of a *genos*.

This ethnic conceptualization of *genos* thus exhibits two primary functions within the *Praeparatio*: it denotes either a people internally connected by biological kinship, or a people who have a particular external relationship to piety and truth—who are connected by way of life rather than blood. The former sense, as already noted, finds explicit expression only with reference to the Hebrews and Jews. But even here, character is what matters most for Eusebius. His goal is to show the evolution of a kin group from one sort of people (Hebrews) into another (Jews). They thus highlight the importance of character to the racial identity of a given people: the Jews are from the *genos* of the Hebrews but no longer

[62] *PE* 7.6.1, 7.8.29 and 7.8.37.
[63] *PE* 1.9.15 and 9.10.1.
[64] *PE* 14.10.11.

share the name because they no longer share the character of their fore-fathers.[65] The example of Job further highlights the importance of charac-ter, and thus serves as a bridge between the biological sense of *genos* and its religious and ethical sense. Although Job had no share in the biological *genos* of the Jews, he was nonetheless included within the narrative of Hebrew descent because of his way of life. Eusebius' treatment of Job shows a clear preference for the latter ethical sense over the biological relation.[66]

Ethnos

The connotations of the term *ethnos* and its relationship to *genos* further illuminate the workings of the representations of ethnicity and people-hood in the *Praeparatio*. *Ethnos* usually signified a 'nation' or a 'people' in classical literature, though it could bear a rather broad range of applications in marking collective identity—swarms of bees and flocks of birds,[67] the gender categories of men and women (in classical times), the vocational grouping of heralds, butchers, bakers, prostitutes, or farmers (in Hellenistic times), and even the designation of *provinciae* (in the Roman era).[68] In Eusebius' *Praeparatio*, the term *ethnos* is limited to its designation of racially distinct peoples.[69]

[65] This point will receive much further consideration in Chapter 4.

[66] In this, Eusebius' treatment parallels other patristic interpretations of Job; see J. Baskin, *Pharaoh's Counsellors: Job, Jethro and Balaam* (Chico: Scholars Press, 1983), 32–43.

[67] In apologetic literature, note the occurrence of the '*ethnos* of conies' at Origen, *C. Cels.* 4.87 (commenting on Proverbs 24.59 ff).

[68] See the entry in *LSJ* for a listing of classical sources. The vocational applications of *ethnos* in Hellenistic Egypt are discussed by D. Thompson, 'Ethnê, taxes and administrative geography in early Ptolemaic Egypt', in I. Andorlini *et al.* (eds), *Atti del XXII Congresso Internazionale di Papirologia* (Florence: Istituto Papirologico 'G. Vitelli', 2001), 2.1255–1263. For its application to *provinciae* during Roman times, see S. Mitchell, 'Ethnicity, Acculturation and Empire in Roman and Late Roman Asia Minor', in Stephen Mitchell and Geoffrey Greatrex (eds), *Ethnicity and Culture in Late Antiquity* (London: Duckworth, 2000), 117–50; B. Isaac, 'Ethnic Groups in Judaea Under Roman Rule', in idem, *The Near East under Roman Rule* (Leiden: E. J. Brill, 1998), 265; A. N. Sherwin-White, *The Roman Citizenship* (Oxford: Clarendon Press, 1973), 437–44; H. J. Mason, *Greek Terms for Roman Institutions, American Studies in Papyrology* 13 (Toronto: Hakkert, 1974), *ad loc*; R. MacMullen, 'Tertullian and "National" Gods', 409. Its first application to a province is apparently Josephus, *AJ* 18.1 (see Sherwin-White, *The Roman Citizenship*, 440 n. 3). For general discussion, see J. Hall, *Ethnic Identity in Greek Antiquity*, 35; Jones, 'ἔθνος and γένος in Herodotus', 316–17; A. D. Smith, *The Ethnic Origins of Nations*, 21.

[69] Though he often used it in the sense of *provincia* elsewhere; see e.g. *C. Marc.* 1.1.1; *CI* 78 (Ziegler 137); 91 (Ziegler 177); *LC* 7.7; 9.15; *SC* 11.2; *VC* 1.15, 19; 2.20.1; 2.23.1; 3.6; *et al.*

In its broadest and most generic sense, *ethnos* appears in the plural to function as a sweeping reference to 'the nations' (*ta ethnē*).[70] This is clearly a borrowing from the Septuagint application of the term to mark off the Jews from everybody else along racial lines. That Eusebius has just such allusions in mind is made abundantly clear by his quotations of significant passages from the LXX at programmatic places in the *Praeparatio*, especially the prologue. On the fulfilment of the prophecies that members of all the *ethnē* would convert to Christianity, Eusebius quotes Psalms 22: 28–29. 'All the ends of the earth shall remember and turn unto the Lord, and all the fatherlands of the nations (*ethnōn*) shall worship before him; for the kingdom is the Lord's, and he is the ruler over the nations.'[71] This is immediately followed by a quotation from Psalms 96: 10 ('Tell it out among the nations that the Lord is king') and Zephaniah 2: 11 ('The Lord will appear among them and will utterly destroy all the gods of the nations of the earth').[72]

These generic uses of the plural *ta ethnē* occur predominantly in passages where Eusebius is dedicated to representing Christians as a people who are spreading among all the nations, or a people whose membership consists of members of all nations.[73] In these contexts, the notion recurs in such phrases as 'Greeks and barbarians, in every place, city and land, to all nations under the sun',[74] 'every nation and city',[75] 'not in a part of a land, nor in the corner of one nation',[76] 'all nations, throughout the cities and country districts'.[77] *Ta ethnē* thus provides a fairly generic and all-encompassing tag.[78] Its importance lies in the way

---

[70] It should go without saying that *ethnē* is a neuter plural, rather than a feminine singular; *pace* N. Denzey, 'The Limits of Ethnic Categories', in A. Blasi *et al.*, *Handbook of Early Christianity* (New York: Altamira Press, 2002), 494–5, who constructs an emic-etic distinction upon a supposed gender distinction between masculine and feminine forms of *ethnos*.

[71] *PE* 1.1.9.

[72] See also the quotations of LXX passages at 1.3.15; 4.16.20; 11.26.8.

[73] For more detailed discussion, see Chapter 7.

[74] *PE* 1.4.11.

[75] *PE* 1.2.2.

[76] *PE* 2.5.2.

[77] *PE* 4.17.10; see also 5.1.1, 5, and 7; 10.4.6; 14.9.5. For a similar phrase (and similar argument), see Aristides, *Or.* 1.325. The phrase 'city and nation' was common in second- and third-century Greek authors; see Sherwin-White, *The Roman Citizenship*, 440–1; Walbank, 'Nationality as a Factor in Roman History', 147; MacMullen, 'Tertullian and "National" Gods', 409 n. 4; E. Cohen, *The Athenian Nation*, 24.

[78] Though in one instance 'all the nations' refers specifically to the Phoenicians, Egyptians, and Greeks (14.16.12).

it functions within an argument for Christianity's superiority and expansion among all peoples.

While the plural form of *ethnos* is often translated as 'gentiles', 'heathen' or 'pagans',[79] these may not provide the best sense for *ta ethnē*. *Gentilis* is of course the Latin translation of *ethnikos* (a word that does not occur in the *Praeparatio*).[80] However, in the current English usage, the meaning of 'gentile' is not always clear. As an oppositional term to the Jews, 'gentiles' may be taken in a racial or cultural or religious sense, depending on the speaker's conception of Jewish identity as particularly racial, cultural, or religious.[81] The terms 'heathen' and 'pagan' scarcely convey a religious identity at all, limiting themselves instead to the religious.[82] However, both in the Septuagint and early Christian authors, *ta ethnē* carried connotations of racial and political elements along with the religious.[83] As will be argued throughout this study, religious customs and practices, and theological doctrines and teachings, are always to be understood as integrally woven into a racial way of life and as characteristic of a particular people's collective *ethos*.[84]

Eusebius does not use *ta ethnē* to refer to 'the heathen' or 'pagans', but to peoples who have a shared history rooted in stories of their ancestors, possess distinctive social and religious customs, and define themselves

[79] See, for instance, Gifford's translation of the Ps.96: 10 passage quoted above. Also, *Oxford English Dictionary*, 2nd edition, *ad loc.*

[80] On which, see Schmidt, 'ἐθνικός', in *TDNT*, 372.

[81] While 'the nations' refers to non-Jewish peoples in the LXX, it can even incorporate the Jews into its broad parameters in Eusebius; see 10.4.3.

[82] See G. Bowersock, *Hellenism in Late Antiquity* (Ann Arbor: University of Michigan Press, 1990), 10–11.

[83] *Pace* G. Bertram, 'ἔθνος. People and Peoples in the LXX', in *TDNT*, 367, and Schmidt, 'ἔθνος in the New Testament', in *TDNT*, 370.

[84] *Ethnos* is applied to the following particular peoples: Persians and Scythians (1.4.6); Greeks and others (7.8.20); Egyptians, Phoenicians and others (7.9.2); Egyptians, Chaldaeans and 'other barbarian nations' (10.1.7); Hebrews, Phoenicians, and Egyptians (10.4.3); Phoenicians, Egyptians, and Greeks (14.16.12); Hebrews (7.8.22; 11.6.39; 12.47.title; 12.47.1); Christians (12.33.title, see Chapter 7 below); and Jews (1.2.7; 1.3.13; 7.8.29; 7.8.37; 7.9.1; 7.11.10; 8.1.1; 8.6.10; 8.10.18; 8.12.20; 9.1.title; 9.6.title; 9.42.title; 10.9.2; 10.14.3; 10.14.7 and 16; 12.17.3). The Jews receive the clear majority of references. As with *genos*, each of these cases takes the ethnonym in the genitive plural form (i.e. *to Hebraiōn ethnos* or *to Hellēnōn ethnos*). The ethnonym is never put in an adjectival form (i.e. *to Hebraikon ethnos* or *to Hellēnikon ethnos*). According to the entries of both *LSJ* and Lampe, there is no reference to a *Hellēnikon ethnos* from Roman imperial times on. However, these dictionaries overlook its occurrence at Eusebius' *CI* 26 (Ziegler 16.19) which contains the phrase πάντα τὰ ἔθνη Ἑλληνικά τε καὶ βάρβαρα. Eusebius does use the adjectival forms elsewhere; see e.g., *CI* 63 (Ziegler 89.6); 77 (Ziegler 136.22); 2.28 (Ziegler 294.15).

by certain legal formulations, morality and national character. The appearance of *ethnos* comes in contexts dealing with a number of features that are significant for the articulation and formation of ethnic identity. For instance, remarks regarding ancestry and the forefathers of a people often occur in discussions of an *ethnos*. An especially clear example of this is at 7.8.22, where Abraham is named the *genarchos* of 'the nation of the Hebrews'. The broader context is Eusebius' narration of the descent of the Hebrews and construction of moral portraits of the Hebrew forefathers.[85] More generally, *ethnos* can occur in discussions of events of a shared history of the people. For example, the exile and enslavement of 'the nation of the Jews' is related at 10.14.7 and 16.

Ethnos also appears in contexts that are principally concerned with describing customs (*ta nomima*) and communal ways of life.[86] Reference to the customs of an *ethnos* could also be broadened to incorporate the teachings and collective wisdom of a people. Hence, at one point, Eusebius argues for the transmission of the knowledge and teachings of one nation (*ta tōn ethnōn nomima te kai mathēmata*) to other nations, specifically in the areas of philosophy, literacy, inventions, and arts.[87] These ways of thinking and living are practised by particularly located peoples in the geographical landscape of the Mediterranean world. While not prominent, notions of territoriality are often assumed in discussions of particular *ethnē*. For instance, reference is made to the 'native lands' of the Phoenicians, Egyptians, and Greeks.[88] Christianity is said to have filled all Greece and the barbarian lands.[89] Jews are assumed to dwell primarily in Judaea.[90] Even Christians have a land which they will inhabit in the next life.[91] Jerusalem is named the 'royal metropolis' of the children of the Hebrews.[92]

Language is also occasionally joined to the identity of a given *ethnos*. Thus, Philo of Byblos translated the text of Sanchouniathon from 'the Phoenician tongue' into 'the Greek language'.[93] 'The Greek tongue'[94] and 'the language of the Greeks'[95] occur in contexts that make clear that

---

[85] See Chapter 4.
[86] E.g., *PE* 1.4.6.
[87] *PE* 10.4.3.
[88] *PE* 8.1.4.
[89] *PE* 14.3.4.
[90] *PE* 8.1.2.
[91] *PE* 11.36.2.
[92] *PE* 12.48.1.
[93] *PE* 1.9.20.
[94] *PE* 8.1.5.
[95] *PE* 11.6.16.

Eusebius takes language to be part of ethnic identity, and not an entity separate from the corporate life of a people. Both these cases appear in a larger argument for Greek dependence upon barbarian nations (particularly the Hebrews) for knowledge and wisdom. Words in the Greek language still bear hints, according to Eusebius, of an earlier borrowing from barbarians. Hence, these elements of the Greek language are indicative of a people's shared history—a history marked by lateness, dependency and cultural and philosophical immaturity.[96]

Hebrew is said to be 'the paternal tongue' of the Hebrews[97] or 'the native tongue'.[98] Similarly, particular words or names of things are called 'Hebraic names'.[99] The alphabet is expressly Phoenician: *Phoinikēia ta grammata*.[100] Likewise, texts that are somehow characteristic of, sacred to, or in the possession of a given people are often labelled with the ethnonym in adjectival form: the 'Judaic books';[101] the 'Judaic writings';[102] the 'Hebraic writings',[103] the 'oracles of the Hebrews'.[104] The point should be clear: language, letters, and texts are seen as belonging to, and indicative of, particular ethnic identities.

Each ethnicity also possesses a distinctive cluster of religious customs, beliefs, and expressions—a 'theology'—that is central to the identity of that *ethnos*. Hence, reference is made to the 'theology of the Phoenicians',[105] the 'theology of the Egyptians'[106] and so on. Even gods could be labelled by their associations to an ethnic identity: 'the Hellenic gods'.[107] Rather than appearing as a category of beliefs that we might label 'religion', these theologies are rooted in the ancient past of the nations and were instituted by the nations' forefathers. Their repeated practice and embodiment in the regularized social life of a community had become an integral element of each community's identity as a people. These ancient theologies should not be relegated to the realm of mere beliefs about the existence and nature of the gods, but encompass a

[96] See Chapter 4.
[97] *PE* 8.1.6.
[98] *PE* 11.5.2. See also, 11.6.19 ('the tongue [*glōssa*] of the Hebrews'); 11.6.39 ('the tongue [*glōtta*] of the Hebrews' and 'the language [*phōnē*] of the Hebrews').
[99] *PE* 11.6.14 and 41.
[100] *PE* 10.5.1.
[101] *PE* 1.5.10.
[102] *PE* 1.4.12; 8.1.8.
[103] *PE* 1.3.13; 11.9.4; 11.20.1; 11.21.1.
[104] See e.g., *PE* 11.6.16, 41.
[105] E.g., *PE* 1.9.5; 2.praef.1.
[106] E.g., *PE* 2.praef.6; 2.1.53.
[107] *PE* 2.1.56; 13.2.2.

range of cultural phenomena including a communal way of life, and a set of shared practices that provided expressions of collective identity in relation to the world and the gods.[108] Religious or theological elements were parts of a larger conglomerate of notions that made up Eusebius' conceptualization of ethnicity.

Theological teachings might be joined with philosophy, education, and collective wisdom. For example, the 70 translators of the Hebrew Scriptures into Greek (the Septuagint) were represented as being distinguished in 'understanding and paternal education'.[109] Reference could also be made to 'Hellenic wisdom';[110] teachings could be considered native or foreign to members of an *ethnos*.[111] The language applied in these contexts is often strongly evocative of kinship and communal continuity. Eusebius calls attention to the activity of transmission, as the teachings, customs, and way of life were 'handed down'.[112] The ethnic way of life was inherited over successive generations, 'from father to son'.[113] The regularity in Eusebius' phrasing of the transmission of an ethnic heritage from generation to generation is striking. It becomes clear that the identities of Greeks, Christians, Jews and others must not be limited to modern categories of 'religion' or 'culture'.[114] Although boundaries between *ethnē* remain somewhat permeable and are rarely strictly demarcated according to biological kinship alone, these considerations nonetheless show a formulation of ethnicity that is relatively stable and continuous over long periods of time, from the era of the ancient forefathers at the dawn of national history to the times of Eusebius.

The set of doctrines and teachings of a particular people could be supplemented by legislative features that included not only particular laws and codes of conduct, but accounts of particular forefathers of the *ethnos* who had served as lawmakers (*nomothētai*). Of course, Moses is the most notable and important example of this.[115] And likewise, Christ was represented as legislating true laws.[116] This legal element in

---

[108] This will be seen more clearly in Chapter 3.

[109] *PE* 8.1.7.

[110] e.g. *PE* 14.2.7.

[111] e.g. *PE* 14.4.14. In this context, it is of interest to note that, after Plato, the Academy became 'foreign' (*xenēn*, 14.4.15) as it deviated from the original teachings of Plato.

[112] *Paradidōmi* and its cognates; see e.g. *PE* 11.5.1–3; 14.3.4.

[113] See e.g. *PE* 1.6.2; 4.2.13; 14.3.1.

[114] See Chapter 7.

[115] e.g. *PE* 7.8.38.

[116] *PE* 4.1.5; 7.8.40. See M. Hollerich, 'Religion and Politics in the Writings of Eusebius: Reassessing the First "Court Theologian" ', *CH* 59 (1990), 318 for references in other works.

Eusebius' conception of *ethnos* raises the importance of *politeia* and related terms as part of the cluster of notions surrounding *ethnos*. The terms *politeia* or *politeuma* often encompassed legislative features of an ethnic identity within the overarching representation of communal ways of life.[117] For instance, the way of life organized around the legal code of Moses that shaped the collective life of the Jews was called 'the *politeuma* of the legislation of Moses',[118] or again, 'a *politeia* from the laws of Moses for the Jewish *ethnos*'.[119] The legal code was seen as the promotion of a particular way of life that could characterize the people's identity in moral, religious, and social terms. Eusebius even went so far as to claim: '*politeiai* cannot be established apart from laws'.[120]

The verbal form of *politeuō* marks the close relationship between *politeia* and legislation. It can be translated as 'to administer' or 'to establish' laws, and functions almost synonymously with 'to legislate'. For instance, at 2.6.15, Eusebius describes the life of the ancient nations as one in which 'laws had not yet been established (*politeuomenōn*)'. Likewise, Plato 'was not ignorant that his legislation had been established (*politeuesthai*) among certain barbarians'.[121] In fact, it may be Plato's own use of *politeuō* that has influenced Eusebius' application of the term.[122]

Politeuō and its related substantival forms were not, however, limited to the legal sphere. The verb could be applied to the establishment of the various theologies of the nations. Eusebius thus declares that 'nothing

[117] The classical treatment of both terms is found at Aristotle, *Pol.* 3.1278bff. For general discussions on *politeia* and *politeuma* in antiquity, see W. Ruppel, 'Politeuma. Bedeutungs-geschichte eines staatsrechtlichen Terminus,' *Philologus* 82 (1927), 268–312, 434–54; J. De Romilly, *The Rise and Fall of States According to Greek Authors* (Ann Arbor: University of Michigan Press, 1977), 30–40; G. Luderitz, 'What is the Politeuma?' in Jan W. Van Henten and Pieter W. Van der Horst (eds), *Studies in Early Jewish Epigraphy* (Leiden: E.J. Brill, 1994), 183–225; S. Cohen, *The Beginnings of Jewishness*, 99 n. 95; 126–7. A useful discussion of the terms in the works of Philo and Josephus is contained in A. Kasher, *The Jews in Hellenistic and Roman Egypt* (Tübingen: Mohr [Siebeck], 1985) 358–64. For a discussion of these terms within the context of Eusebius' thought (in particular, the *CI*), see the discussion of M. Hollerich, *Eusebius of Caesarea's Commentary on Isaiah* (Oxford: Clarendon Press), 116–30.

[118] *PE* 8.5.11.

[119] *PE* 8.6.10; see also 12.16.1; 14.3.2. That *politeia* is roughly synonymous with *politeuma* is evident from their alternation, apparently only to avoid repetition, in the list of chapter headings for Book 8, chapters 1 (*tou kata Mōsea theosebous politeumatos*), 7 (*tēs kata Mōsea theosebous politeias*) and 8 (*tou kata Mōsea politeumatos*).

[120] *PE* 7.3.3.

[121] *PE* 12.26.title.

[122] See, e.g. the quotation from Plato's *Crito* at 13.8.1–2.

more than the error-ridden theology of Phoenicians and Egyptians was established (*epoliteueto*) among the Greeks'.[123] The *politeia* of the Greeks occurs at 10.4.25 within a discussion of the implementation of wisdom and learning into life at a societal level. Notions regarding the life of virtue and piety (or their opposites) as embodied in the communal organization and regularized interaction of a people could thus be signified through the term *politeia*.[124] This is especially the case in his references to the *politeia* of the ancient Hebrews who lived before the Jews: 'the *politeia* of the Hebrew friends of God'.[125] Links are made between the *politeia* and the philosophical life of *askēsis* in remarks about the Essenes (though even here reference is made to 'the divine laws' of these people).[126] At the broadest level, Eusebius could employ *politeia* to refer vaguely to humanity's social existence and nothing more.[127]

Both *politeia* and *politeuma* are also applied to the communal life of Christians.[128] Tatian had already been quoted as referring to 'the *politeia* according to us' along with 'the history of our laws'.[129] Eusebius structured his conception of Christian conversion around this notion. At 15.61.12, he asked rhetorically:

Do you not think therefore that with judgement and reason we have justly kept aloof from the unprofitable and erroneous and vain labor (*mataioponias*)[130] of them all, and do not busy ourselves at all about the said subjects ... but cling solely to piety towards God the creator of all things, and by a life of temperance (*sōphronos biou*), and a different God-loving *politeia* according to virtue, strive to live in a manner pleasing to him who is God over all?

Such an expression of Christianity as a *politeia* involves the notions of piety and virtuous living in the corporate existence of its members.

All the applications of *politeia* and related terms in the *Praeparatio* are, to my mind, solidly embedded within a racial context and refer to

---

[123] *PE* 10.4.5.

[124] See *PE* 2.5.4; 2.6.22; 8.1.1.

[125] *PE* 12.15.1, using nearly identical language to 12.15.6.

[126] *PE* 8.12.20.

[127] *PE* 6.6.39.

[128] *PE* 12.33.3; 15.61.12; see Chapter 7. *Prutaneuomai*, a term similar to *politeuō*, was also applied to the Christian manner of life: 'the evangelic teaching was established (*prutaneutheisēs*) for us' (2.5.1). More generally, Eusebius could refer to the 'conduct (*anagōgēn*) for our manner of life' (14.3.4).

[129] *PE* 10.11.26.

[130] Cp. Clement, *Strom.* 1.8.41.2; 4.7.51.1; Theophilus, *Autol.* 2.1, 7, 12, 35; 3.26; Hippolytus, *Refut.* 6.43.5; Sextus, Empiricus, *Pyr.* 2.206.

the corporate way of life characteristic of the identities of the various *ethnē*. Extracting *politeia* from its racial, or even collective, conceptualization is to misrepresent the imaginary world of the *Praeparatio*. Those who practise a *politeia* of virtue and asceticism are never portrayed as individuals qua individuals, but rather as members of, and representative of, a particular *ethnos* and its national character. Eusebius emphasizes the connections between a particular kind of *politeia* and its *ethnos*. The character embodied in a *politeia* is a collective and racially particular character.

This survey of the uses of *ethnos* in the *Praeparatio* covers many of the characteristics considered distinctive of ethnic identity. In a previous section, the following features were noted as potential markers of ethnic difference: a collective name; a common myth of descent; a shared history; a distinctive shared culture; an association with a specific territory; a sense of communal solidarity; a common language; shared religious beliefs, practices, and traditions; and physical appearance. All but the last of these features have been found in the *Praeparatio*.[131] Furthermore, the legal elements of *politeia* and similar words exhibit salient aspects of Eusebius' conception of ethnic identity.

Specificity and Difference Between Ethnos and Genos

In its ethnic senses, *genos* has been shown to carry more meanings than merely those relating to birth or biological connections. It also carries notions of traditional customs performed by a community, a sense of shared history, and is especially evocative of a particular moral character and relationship to truth, piety, and the divine. Hence, while *genos* could bear the sense of genetic kinship, it often embraced a much broader corporate identity centred around a common way of life and national character. This broader signification of *genos* seems to be, at least partially, synonymous with the cluster of ideas produced by *ethnos*. In general, *ethnos* referred to a people who possessed a shared history, ancestry, customs, religious practices, theologies, and an overarching *politeia*. Two examples suffice here. The first occurs in Eusebius' narration of Jacob, whose name is changed to Israel, at 7.8.29: 'Such is the

---

[131] Physical appearance becomes important for Eusebius elsewhere, however; see *Theoph.* 1.38; *Comm. Ps.* 73.12–18.864AB (where he counters the racist interpretation of Origen, at e.g. *Select. Genes.* [*PG* 12.100]).

man from whom the 12-tribed race (*genos*) of the nation (*ethnos*) of the Jews was established.' The clear reference is to the descendants of his 12 sons ('the 12 tribes of Israel'), and thus carries the notion of a biologically related kin group. He could have simplified his language by merely referring to 'the race of the Jews'; the inclusion of the term *ethnos* does not seem to add significantly to the meaning. Nor does it bear any clear reference to broader cultural or religious features of the Jews as a people. The second occurrence comes soon after this one, at 7.8.37, where Eusebius mentions growth in population of 'the race of [the Hebrews'] descendants' and 'the Jewish nation'. Again, the reference is clearly to biological kinship, and the employment of *ethnos* does not bear any clear signification of something else, whether cultural, religious, ethical or whatever.[132] These examples seem to show the conflation of *ethnos* and *genos*. Together they both bear a strong signification of kinship, and any distinction between the one and the other (if it exists) can only be guessed at by speculation.

Although the two terms usually seem roughly synonymous, as in the examples just given, there are times when we may find differing levels of specificity between the two terms. A brief overview of the relevant passages makes this apparent. At 1.9.15, Eusebius claims that astral religion was allotted to 'the nations' while worship of the true God was allotted to 'the race of the Hebrews'. Here, *genos* appears as a particular people who are given special attention over against the other roughly equivalent peoples—equivalent, that is, in the sense of a people with particular common characteristics and relationship to the divine. Similarly, at 9.10.1, the 'race of the Hebrews' is mentioned along with 'other nations' who have been noteworthy for the possession of wisdom. In both these cases, *genos* marks out a specific people in the singular, whereas, *ethnos* is used in the plural and only refers to the other peoples in a vague and sweeping appellation. It is not a distinction between a kin group and a cultural group; nor is it a difference between a synchronic and a diachronic intension.[133] Hence, while the manipulation of the two terms does show a stylistic concern on Eusebius' part to

---

[132] Another instance of the application of *ethnos* in a clearly biological usage occurs at 7.8.22, where Abraham is named the '*genarchos* of the whole nation (*ethnos*)'.

[133] Jones, 'ἔθνος and γένος in Herodotus', has argued convincingly for such a distinction between the two terms in Herodotus. That this is not the case in Eusebius only confirms Jones' suggestion that the connotations of *ethnos* and *genos* are determined by the 'idiolect' of the particular author.

avoid repetition of the same words in a given sentence or passage,[134] it also evinces differing levels of specificity. *Genos* is applied to the more specific, *ethnē* to the less specific. This point is of course obvious merely from the shift from a singular noun to a plural noun. However, Eusebius never differentiates one particular *ethnos* from numerous generic *genē*; rather, *genos* marks particularity and *ethnos* generality in these cases.

These examples of the conjunction of *ethnos* and *genos* do not, however, exhaust all the relevant instances. The others show a more complicated picture. At least one case carries a clear distinction between a specifically kin-related people and broader ethnic groups. In a pro-grammatic sentence, Eusebius writes: 'Being Greeks by birth (*to genos*) and having the mindset of the Greeks, we have been gathered together out of the manifold nations (*ethnōn*) like the chosen men of a newly enlisted army….'.[135] Here, *genos* takes the unambiguously biological notion, while *ethnē* remains a vague and generic appellation for all peoples, without clear presumption of genetic connections.

In summary, *genos* could connote both biological and broader ethnic meanings when used alone. When joined with *ethnos* in the same sentence or passage, it could either mark a more particular level of specificity, or the two could be conflated, bearing a signification of biological kinship, but with no clear difference between them. Racial descent is presumed as basic and uncontroversial. While other elements of ethnicity, such as national character and *politeia*, remain Eusebius' primary concern, kinship relations play a pivotal role in the argument of the *Praeparatio*. Character traits, theology, religious practices, and relation to the divine are always based within a sense of shared history and ancestry. Such ways of life and ways of thinking about the world and the gods/God were transmitted from one generation to the next, and received as an inheritance from father to child. Familial descent (albeit occasionally metaphoric) remains an indisputable part of ethnic identity in the *Praeparatio*. This is especially the case in his narration of the historical development of the Hebrew nation as it declined into the nation of the Jews. In such a context, both *ethnos* and *genos* could be conflated and bear a sense of biological kinship. For Eusebius, one's

---

[134] On the style of the *PE*, see the brief notes of Mras, *Eusebius Werke VIII. Die Praeparatio Evangelica* 588–9. For general comments on Eusebian style, see E. Fritze, *Beiträge zur sprachlich-stilistischen Würdigung des Eusebios* (Borna-Leipzig: Robert Noske, 1910); S. Gero, 'The True Image of Christ: Eusebius' Letter to Constantia Reconsidered', *JTS* 32 (1981), 460–70.

[135] *PE* 1.5.10. τὸ γένος Ἕλληνες ὄντες καὶ τὰ Ἑλλήνων φρονοῦντες ἐκ παντοίων τε ἐθνῶν ὡς ἂν νεολέκτου στρατιᾶς λογάδες συνειλεγμένοι….

identity by birth (*to genos*) is important, especially in conceiving one's pre-Christian identity. It carried with it, of course, a particular way of life and character, but these were all part of one's paternal baggage that was rejected upon conversion. However, these cultural and ethical elements of ethnic identity remained relatively stable over long periods of time, transmitted to later generations in a familial continuity.

CONSTRUCTING BOUNDARIES: TERMS BETWEEN ETHNICITIES

In addition to the vocabulary of peoplehood centring upon the terms *genos* and *ethnos* noted above, Eusebius employs language that articulates boundaries between particular ethnic identities. The distinctive ways in which Eusebius separates or joins the various nations that are important for his argument will be the subject of the following chapters. Here, I merely want to call attention to the basic vocabulary he had at his disposal in any of these acts of boundary construction or manipulation.

Boundary-making is an essential task in the creation, maintenance and transformation of ethnic identity. Since identity rests upon a conceptualization of 'us vs. them', boundaries must be formulated to mark 'us' off as separate and superior from 'them'. While this boundary construction employs very specific markers of ethnic difference (for example, 'they' practise customs *x*, *y*, and *z*, while 'we' exhibit customs *a*, *b*, and *c*; or, 'we' speak the language *a*, while 'they' speak the unintelligible and barbarous language *b*), it often rests upon a more generic vocabulary of difference: they habitually enact 'strange' practices, their ways are 'foreign' to our own. Eusebius' *Praeparatio* consistently utilizes the language of foreignness and of being 'outside' in a way that is simultaneously delimiting and evaluative.[136] Use of such language was a traditional means of undergirding ethnic boundary formation.

The application of such language occurs most frequently in the *Praeparatio* when setting off either the Greeks from barbarians, or the Christians from everybody else (but especially the Greeks).[137] This latter use is most common in Eusebius' choice of sources. He claims that, to

---

[136] Reference to outsiders came early into Christian discourse; see e.g. Paul's use of *hoi exō* at I Cor. 5: 12–13; I Thess. 4: 12; Col. 4: 5.

[137] In addition to these two applications, the chapter heading for 7.6 sets the Hebrews apart from (*ektos*) the Jews.

avoid accusations of using biased sources, he will use the sources produced by the subjects about whom he is concerned at any given time.[138]
None of the sources will come from his own (*oikothen*) Christian
writings, but he 'will make use of testimonies from those who are
outside (*exōthen*)'.[139] Similarly, the Hebrew Scriptures are distinguished
from the writings 'of those outside' (*tōn exōthen*).[140] When speaking of
the 'race of Jewish philosophers',[141] Eusebius claims that many 'of
those outside' (*tōn exōthen*) marvelled at their asceticism, adding that
Josephus and Philo were 'the most renowned of their own [people]
(*tōn oikeiōn*)' to have commemorated their lives in writing.[142]

In marking off the Greeks from the other barbarian nations, Eusebius
forcefully states: 'The Greeks introduced nothing of their own (*oikothen*)
[literally: "from their home"] in their own (*oikeiais*) writings, but fell
into the mythologies of those outside (*tōn exōthen*).'[143] Employing the
starkly oppositional language of what is 'at home' (*oikeios, oikothen*)
with one ethnic identity and what belongs to 'outside' (*exōthen*) identities highlights a crucial feature of Eusebius' ethnic argumentation: the
displacement of Greeks from a position of ethnic superiority.[144] This
emphasis on the inferior relationship of the Greeks to the other nations
is again articulated in the same language in a fascinating discussion at
10.4.[145] The Greeks had to resort to 'foreign (*othneia*) and barbarous
teachings' for wisdom, since they were like someone 'naked and bereft
of their own (*oikeiōn*) reasonings and learning'.[146] The Greeks 'dwelt
together' or literally 'were at home with each other' (*sunoikountōn*) in
their 'poverty and lack of wisdom'.[147] Pythagoras 'became the source of
learning to the Greeks of the things he had acquired from those outside
(*exōthen*)'.[148] Hence, the polarization of those inside against those outside a given ethnicity provides an important mechanism for legitimizing
and sharpening the textual boundaries that Eusebius forges between
nations.

[138] See *PE* 1.6.8.
[139] *PE* 4.6.1.
[140] *PE* 6.10.49. See also 8.14.72; 9.11.title; 9.16.1; 11.praef.1.
[141] On which, see Chapter 4.
[142] *PE* 8.10.19.
[143] *PE* 2.1.54. For discussion of this passage, see Chapter 3.
[144] See Chapter 3.
[145] See Chapter 4.
[146] *PE* 10.4.9.
[147] *PE* 10.4.15. Note the contrast to Aristotle's civilizing use of *sunoikeō* at *Pol.* 1.
[148] *PE* 10.4.16.

The 'familiar' or 'native' (*oikeios*) occurs a number of times in these inside/outside representations. The term can also be placed in opposition to 'foreign' (*othneios*), as already seen above.[149] When Eusebius summarizes the objections of anti-Christian polemicists, who suppose that the Christians deserve punishment for their rejection of the 'paternal gods',[150] he writes: 'And to what kind of punishments would they not justly be subjected, who deserting the [customs] of their forefathers have become zealots for the foreign (*otheneiōn*) mythologies of the Jews, which are slandered by everybody? And must it not be a proof of extreme wickedness and levity lightly to put aside the customs of their own (*oikeiōn*) [people] ...'.[151] The paternal (*patria*) and familiar (*oikeia*) is thus clearly marked off from the foreign (*othneia*).

Eusebius continues his characterization of the arguments raised by anti-Christian opponents, this time the Jews: 'But the sons of the Hebrews also would find fault with us, that being foreigners (*allophuloi*) and aliens (*allogeneis*) we misuse their books, which do not belong to us at all ... and we thrust out the true family (*oikeious*) and kindred (*engeneis*) from their own paternal (*patriōn*) [possessions].'[152] The addition of other terms of foreignness and nativity unmistakably impress the stark and rigid boundaries that his Jewish opponents wanted to maintain in their formulation of anti-Christian argument.

This passage, then, clearly exhibits the conceptual world in which Eusebius develops his defence of Christianity. The attacks against Christianity centred upon its place within a particular ethnic landscape. Its foreignness invalidated it in the native and 'at-home' context of distinct peoples—Greeks and Jews.[153] Eusebius, in like manner, conceived of Christianity in ethnic terms and formed a defence of Christianity by providing an ethnic location (an 'at-homeness') that functioned to legitimate its existence and even asserted its superiority in relation to the other nations.

Importantly, Eusebius was unable, or rather unwilling, to extricate himself from the Greco-Roman discourse of ethnicity in making his apology. Any attempts to see Eusebius as a proponent of Christian 'universalism' must face this evidence. As will be discussed in a later

---

[149] *PE* 10.4.9.

[150] *PE* 1.2.2.

[151] *PE* 1.2.3–4. For a similar sentiment, put in the mouths of Ethiopians, see Diodorus 2.55.4.

[152] *PE* 1.2.5.

[153] See Origen *C. Cels.* 1.1; 5.25, 33–41; 8.2.

chapter, Eusebius constructs an image of Christian identity that is situated in the tension between inclusivism (members of all nations are welcomed by Christianity) and ethnic particularism.[154] Eusebius was convinced that his retelling of the histories of the nations would provide a powerful apology for Christianity. Furthermore, he did not conceptualize the identities of the Greeks, Phoenicians, Egyptians, Jews, and others as purely religious positions. These were communal identities rooted in the ancestors and defined by traditions and customs that exhibited the national character. The language of foreignness and ethnic difference were unavoidable for this very reason.

CONCLUSIONS

The primary purpose of this chapter has been to investigate the uses of the key terms of ethnicity in the *Praeparatio*. I have shown that both *genos* and *ethnos* bear a broad range of ethnic features that reflect a conception that sees these identities as fundamentally historically continuous, despite the ability to cross ethnic boundaries by the adoption of a new lifestyle and character. In so doing, the considerations offered here have shown the difficulty in untangling the supposedly separate categories of 'religion', 'culture', 'philosophy', and 'ethnicity'. For Eusebius, all these are facets of what it means to be 'Greek', 'Jew', or some other ethnicity. Each nation possesses a shared history of common ancestors, whose lives instantiate a particular way of life, or *politeia*, which embodies a particular character and is rooted in a particular philosophical and theological way of looking at the world, its peoples, and the gods.

This investigation into Eusebius' conceptualization of ethnicity has attempted to draw on a large number of passages scattered throughout the *Praeparatio*. This has already been sufficient to indicate the importance of the *ethnē* for Eusebius. However, these considerations only show the beginnings of the central role that nations and their ways of life play in the *Praeparatio*: this vocabulary provides, we might say, the scaffolding from which Eusebius could paint his picture of the history of nations. The delineation of the ways in which Eusebius' portrayal of the nations provided the driving mechanisms of his argument throughout the *Praeparatio* remains the task of the chapters that follow.

[154] See Chapter 7.

3

Relocating Greekness: The Narrative of Greek Descent

INTRODUCTION

Narratives of descent are a critical feature in the formation of ethnic identity. Strictly speaking, one cannot talk about ethnic identity in ahistorical terms. An understanding of the synchronic markers that distinguish one *ethnos* from another must be joined to, or rather, founded upon, the diachronic elements of its historical roots.[1] The articulation of ethnic identity in the present requires a story of national ancestors and a particular way of life depicting their national character. An ethnic past,

helps to teach us 'who we are', to impart the sense of being a link in a chain which stretches back over the generations to bind us to our ancestors and our descendants. It is also important, because it teaches us 'where we are' and 'who we should be', if we are to 'recover ourselves'. By conveying the atmosphere and drama of past epochs in the life of the community, we 're-live' the lives and times of our forbears and make ourselves part of a 'community of fate'.[2]

How members of an *ethnos* tell this story is both determined by and also determinative for the sorts of historically rooted claims they make.[3] A story recounting the lives of ancient national progenitors thus tells us more about the narrators than about the historical figures of the narrative. J. Hall writes: 'Ethnic genealogies were the instrument by which whole social collectivities could situate themselves in space and

---

[1] I use the terms 'synchronic' and 'diachronic' in the manner of Jones, '$\ἔθνος$ and $\gamma\ένος$ in Herodotus', 315–20.

[2] A. D. Smith, *The Ethnic Origins of Nations*, 180.

[3] See Gallagher, 'Piety and Polity', 2.152; idem, 'Eusebius the Apologist', 254; more generally, see Lieu, *Christian Identity in the Jewish and Graeco-Roman World*, 62–97.

time, reaffirming their identity by appeals to eponymous ancestors ... who were at the same time the retrojected constructions of such identity.'[4]

Furthermore, narratives of descent function not only as a primary way that members of a given *ethnos* define themselves; they can also define the distinctive features of the other *ethnē*. Our identification of 'us' contains (or presupposes) our identification of 'them'.[5] This is what F. Barth was attempting to elucidate in his now classic introductory essay on the construction and maintenance of ethnic boundaries.[6] Applied to narratives of descent, the emphasis on boundaries highlights the mechanisms by which a narrative contains some peoples to the exclusion of others. In fact, the narrative justifies such boundaries even as it constructs them. 'Your' ancestors are not included among 'our' ancestors, who were heroes of great renown for their civilizing deeds, upright way of life and wisdom (unlike the other ancient peoples, 'yours' included); hence, 'you' are marked by a national character and way of life that is imperfect and inferior, while 'ours' is superior and 'civilized'. Any other markers of ethnic difference can be grounded historically in the narrative: language, religious practices and festivals, cult sites, territory, as well as genealogical connections.[7] Such narratives function, then, as loci of ethnic gravity and expressions of identity-forming significance.

In this and the following chapters, I want to argue that Eusebius develops his apologetic argument through two basic ethnic narratives of descent. Roughly the first half of the *Praeparatio* concerns the account of the Greeks' descent from the Phoenicians and Egyptians; the second half deals with the narrative beginning with the ancient Hebrews and its dispersal into two separate trajectories: one among the Jews, the other among the Greeks. In the present chapter I argue that Eusebius tells the

---

[4] Hall, *Ethnic Identity in Greek Antiquity*, 41.

[5] P. du Preez, *The Politics of Identity: Ideology and the Human Image* (New York: St Martin's Press, 1980), 2: 'Identity is not maintained in isolation. Identities exist in systems of relations ... which maintain each other.' Also: 'Collective identity is as difficult to describe as individual identity for a very good reason. It emerges in context. "Who are you?" makes little sense until we know the context of the question: in relation to whom? doing what? when? Then out of the resources of shared history the appearance is fashioned' (13). See also E. Gruen, 'Jewish Perspectives on Greek Culture and Ethnicity', in Malkin (ed), *Ancient Perceptions of Greek Ethnicity*, 348, and S. Cohen, *The Beginnings of Jewishness: Boundaries, Varieties, Uncertainties* (Berkeley and Los Angeles: University of California Press, 1999), 1–2.

[6] See Chapter 2.

[7] See A. D. Smith, *The Ethnic Origins of Nations*, 22–31, and my remarks offered in Chapter 2.

narrative of Greek descent in such a way as to fit his apologetic needs, and then defends his way of telling the story against rival interpretations.[8] First, I survey the narrative of descent that Eusebius constructs from the quotations of others in 1.9.19–2.8.13, and point out its polemical force for Eusebius' overall argument in the *Praeparatio*. Next, I discuss the importance of the narrative in constructing the connections between nations, in particular the dependency of the Greeks upon the Phoenicians and Egyptians. Eusebius' rebuttal of rival interpretations of that narrative of descent—especially allegorical interpretations (3.1.1–3.17.3)—must also be considered. Then, I turn to the importance of narrative for portraying national character, both as it is manifested in the lives of the forefathers and as it is manifested in contemporary religious practices (or Greek 'political theology'; 4.1.1–5.36.5) localized at shrines and cult sites of the Hellenized Roman world (as well as the assumptions upon which the cults rest, namely, notions of Fate; 6.1.1–6.11.83). All these other issues (allegory, oracle cults, and Fate), I would argue, arise from his polemical telling of the narrative of Greek descent. Hence, one begins to see the first six books of the *Praeparatio* as unified around the theme of Greek descent, not as a collection of disjunctive, self-standing attacks against various elements of 'pagan religion'.[9]

THE NARRATIVE OF DESCENT

In the first half of the *Praeparatio* (1.6.1–6.11.83), Eusebius develops a narrative of descent that embraces in a single unified story the Phoenician, Egyptian, and Greek nations.[10] This first narrative of descent will provide a contrast to his narrative of descent of the Hebrew nation. After a preliminary discussion of accounts of cosmogony, he puts forth an account of the Phoenicians as an original nation characterized by impiety, sacrifice of animals, and the folly of treating mere humans as gods. The Egyptians, he claims, then borrowed the Phoenician

---

[8] The argument offered here appears in a modified form in A. P. Johnson, 'Identity, Descent and Polemic: Ethnic Argumentation in Eusebius' *Praeparatio Evangelica*', *JECS* 12 (2004), 23–56.

[9] For such an approach, see e.g., Kofsky, *Eusebius of Caesarea against the Pagans*, with review by A. P. Johnson, *VC* 59 (2005), 209–12.

[10] For Eusebius' own outline of his argument, see 1.6.5, and Appendix 1.

theology, worshipping humans, and practising impiety (such as veneration of the god Phallus). Even worse, the Egyptians engaged in full-scale
deification and veneration of animals (whereas the Phoenicians limited
their deification to the serpent). Finally, as Eusebius' narrative shows,
the Greeks adopted these impious practices and doctrines from the
earlier nations through the travels of Cadmus from Phoenicia and
Orpheus from Egypt. Rather than simply narrating the history of the
Greeks, Eusebius' account is complicated by his adoption of a tripartite
theological schema, comprising a mythological theology, a physical
theology, and a political theology.[11] In an incisive turn, he historicizes
the mythological branch of theology, transforming myth into history.
Hence, the material under this rubric can fall within the narrative of
descent proper, along with those of the Phoenicians and Egyptians. His
historical interpretation is essential to his argument, but it is not an
uncontroversial move. A vigorous assault against the rival interpretations of physical (allegorical) theology validates his historical narrative,
while a sustained critique of Greek political theology rounds out his
argument with a disparaging assessment of the contemporary oracular
practices that are rooted in that narrative. These points will receive
attention below, as they allow us to see the entire first half of the
Praeparatio as a coherent, unified argument.

Eusebius expends most of his efforts on aspects of Greek theology, for
it is the Greeks who are its primary target. But, despite the brief
treatment of the Phoenicians and Egyptians, their importance in forming a narrative of descent that historically grounds and explains the
theologies and practices of the Greeks must not be overlooked. Without
the narratives of these two nations, the role of the remaining account
of the Greek nation would be severely crippled in its function in the
argument. For, as will become clear, the narrative including these
nations provides the 'proof' for two crucial polemical points: Greek
dependency upon more ancient, more culturally advanced barbarian
nations; and the irrational and impious character of these nations.

Eusebius' narrative of descent provides his readers with a way of
making sense of the nations of the world and their interrelationships.
And, of course, this way of understanding the nations undermines their
potential validity as alternative ways of life to Christianity. The emphasis
upon the late and derivative nature of the theology of the Greeks is part
of this task. All that the Greeks maintain in their various branches of

theology is historically rooted in something foreign. The following discussion will detail the ways in which Eusebius' narrative of descent is a sustained polemic against Greek claims to chronological or cultural primacy. On the contrary, the narrative will lay down the lateness and relative unimportance of the Greek nation in ancient times. Thus, the historical impact of nations upon each other and the nature of their relationships is a central element of Eusebius' argument supplied by the narrative of descent.

Furthermore, by providing a single narrative of descent for these three nations, Eusebius brings into focus the similarity and shared nature of the national characters of their theologies. What he sees as similarities between the ways of worshipping and thinking about the world, which are contained in the theologies of the three nations, are made understandable and given coherence through this narrative. Eusebius then uses the narrative to highlight the negative qualities of each of the nations, both individually and collectively. He is explicit on this point: 'The history of all these [nations] we must necessarily recall, so that by comparison (*parathesis*) of the doctrines which have been admired in each the test of the truth may be exhibited, and it may become manifest to our readers from what opinions we have departed, and what that truth is which we have chosen.'[12] The story of these nations will either justify or refute them through the narration of the character and way of life of their founders and the customs and religious practices implemented by them. Hence, Eusebius is not attacking, one by one, a series of disconnected flaws in 'pagan religion', rather, his telling of the story (and treatment of the issues it raises) is firmly entrenched within a unified apologetic project.[13]

The Greeks on Cosmogony and Primitive Theology

If narratives of Phoenician, Egyptian, and Greek origins comprise the narrative of descent proper (1.9.19–2.8.13), Eusebius' preliminary cosmogonic material (1.6.1–1.9.18) and his subsequent arguments

---

[12] *PE* 1.6.7; see also 7.2–4.

[13] See Gallagher, 'Piety and Polity', 148. Hence, I stand in fundamental disagreement to the assertions of Kofsky, *Eusebius of Caesarea against the Pagans*, 130–1: 'A general theory on the development of pagan polytheism was not fully consolidated in his work. Details emerge from brief statements in different parts of the *PE* and the *DE*, and these have to be combined into a single picture.'

against physical and political theology (3.1.1–6.11.83) are still couched within a broad conception of the narrative of descent. This broad conception begins with the very origins of the world (according to Greek authors), goes through the ancient theologies, and continues up to contemporary practices and theologies of the Greeks (namely, political theology or oracles). Taken in these broad terms, it can fulfil the function typical of narratives of descent: it offers a unified and coherent explanation of what sort of world we inhabit, where we have come from, why we do the things we do, and the like. For Eusebius, the narrative of Greek descent is not concerned so much with the 'we' as with the 'they'—this narrative articulates the identity of the other nations. It will capitalize on the negative traits of the other nations' ancestors and highlight the lateness of one of these nations (the Greeks).

One of the fascinating features of this narrative is its use of the national histories of others. This was a bold stroke for Eusebius and should not be taken as merely a show of erudition by the master-librarian of Caesarea; rather, he performs what de Certeau has called 'poaching'. In this case, 'the reader invents in texts something different from what they "intended"'.[14] This is precisely what Eusebius does when quoting verbatim from non-Christian authors. The narratives previously told by members of the nations in order to portray their own greatness and construct a positive identity for themselves are now turned on their heads to portray their inferiority, irrationality and impiety within the constraints of a now-negative identity. The national way of life and identity are invalidated by a retelling of their own national histories. Greek voices are being used against their own Greek identity.[15]

Eusebius was not the first to employ such ethnic-polemical citations. He had been preceded by Clement of Alexandria[16] and

---

[14] M. de Certeau, *The Practice of Everyday Life* (Berkeley and Los Angeles: University of California Press, 1988), 24; cited in J. Levinson, 'Bodies and Bo(a)rders: Emerging Fictions of Identity in Late Antiquity', *HTR* 93 (2000), 366. This activity may be more broadly conceived as not only disregarding authorial intent, but also as a recontextualizing of the texts. The 'poaching' of another author's words thus involves their reappropriation within a new context, answering a new set of questions, and aiming towards new overall ends.

[15] See König-Ockenfels, 'Christliche Deutung der Weltgeschichte bei Eusebs von Cäsarea', 355.

[16] *Protr.*, 2.39.1. 'Do you imagine from what source these details have been quoted? Only such as are furnished by yourselves are here adduced; and you do not seem to recognize your own writers, whom I call as witnesses against your unbelief' (trans. W. Wilson, *The Ante-Nicene Fathers* series, A. Roberts and J. Donaldson (eds), [New York: The Christian Literature Company, 1890], 2.182).

others,[17] especially his contemporary Marcellus of Ancyra.[18] But Eusebius was the first to provide a sustained and coherent argument in the form of a retelling of narratives of descent based upon selective citation of the other nations' own accounts. The extent and assiduity in organizing his citations was prompted by his dual purpose of offering both an apology to meet external criticisms and an introductory preparation for the internal need of educating converts.[19]

After making explicit this citational methodology, Eusebius embarks upon the preliminary phase of the narrative, beginning with an account of the cosmogonies (1.6–8) and primitive theology of humankind (1.9) that are put forth by the Greeks (Diodorus, Plutarch, Xenophon, Plato, Porphyry). This starting point was most likely prompted by the model of Diodorus, who also began his record of the histories of the nations with a survey of cosmogonic theories.[20] Eusebius' treatment of the Greek account of cosmogony and primitive theology contains two significant points that flesh out the above considerations: a) that the Greeks offer discordant accounts of cosmic origins that agree only in the absence of God, and hence are untenable; and, b) that the early astral religion that made up the primitive theology of each of the three nations was at least better than the degenerate forms of superstitious polytheism of later generations.

Plutarch provided Eusebius with a doxographical account of the various doctrines of the first principles (*archē*) of the world: from Thales' doctrine of water to Diogenes of Apollonia's doctrine of air. Eusebius concludes: 'Such is the judgment of the all-wise Greeks, those

---

[17] See also Josephus, *Ap.* 1.13, 14, 15, *passim*; Tatian 31; Clement, *Strom.* 6.4.3; Lactantius *Div. Inst.* 1.5.

[18] Marcellus (=Ps.-Justin), *Cohortatio ad Graecos*, 9 (=*PG* 6.257). ('For I do not propose to prove these things only from our own divine histories, which as yet you are unwilling to credit on account of the inveterate error of your forefathers, but also from your own histories, and such, too, as have no reference to our worship, that you may know that, of all your teachers, whether sages, poets, historians, philosophers, or lawgivers, by far the oldest, as the Greek histories show us, was Moses, who was our first religious teacher' (trans. M. Dods, *The Ante-Nicene Fathers* series, Roberts and Donaldson (eds), [New York: The Christian Literature Company, 1890], 1.277). That this is the work of Marcellus has been convincingly argued by Christoph Riedweg, *Ps.-Justin (Markell von Ankyra?), Ad Graecos de vera religione (bisher 'Cohortatio ad Graecos')*. *Einleitung und Kommentar* (Basel: F. Reinhardt, 1994), 1, 167–82, upon philological-stylistic similarities. It should be noted that the only Greek historian whom this author actually quotes is Diodorus; see references at 9, 14, 25.

[19] See Johnson, 'Eusebius' *Praeparatio Evangelica* as Literary Experiment'.

[20] Diodorus, *Bibl.* 1.6–8.

... [who] did not assume any creator or maker of the universe .... So great also is their mutual opposition; for in no point have they agreed one with another, but have filled the whole subject with strife and discord.'[21] Through the doxography of Plutarch, the Greeks are shown to be both impious (in not attributing the world to a divine creator) and constantly divided and unharmonious in their cosmological theories.[22]

Eusebius clinches his criticism with two quotations about Socrates, asserting that he had no interest in these sorts of cosmological speculations.[23] Eusebius comments: 'So said Socrates, that very man so celebrated by all the Greeks. When, therefore, even this great philosopher had such an opinion of the physiological doctrines of those whom I have mentioned, I think that we too have with good reason deprecated the atheism of them all.'[24] Eusebius uses Socrates as an effective counter-witness to the views recorded in Plutarch's doxography.[25] This practice of 'poaching' from the authors of the Greeks, of using their own voices against them, remained a consistent practice throughout the *Praeparatio*. Furthermore, this poaching is always described in ethnic terms: the voices are from those 'outside' (*exōthen*) the Christian *ethnos*, 'from their very own' (*oikeion*), 'from the native' (*oikothen*) Greek, Phoenician, or Jewish authors.[26] Thus, the representatives of the nations are pitted against each other and are often made to turn traitor to their own nation by the controlling arrangement and critical commentary of Eusebius.

The second interesting feature of these preliminary portions of the broad narrative of descent has to do with the primitive theology of the nations concerned (these turn out to be just the nations that will become prominent later in the narrative: the Phoenicians, the Egyptians, the Greeks and even the Hebrews). Here Eusebius presents the notion that the early nations practised only a form of astral cult, worshipping the sun, moon, stars, and planets. A quotation from Diodorus[27] shows

---

[21] *PE* 1.8.13–14.

[22] On the use of the argument from disagreement in the rise of Platonist discourse, see Boys-Stones, *Post-Hellenistic Philosophy*, 123–50; with the review at Johnson, *CJ* 99 (2004), 362–5. The issue will become prominent in the last books of the *PE*; see Chapter 4.

[23] *PE* 1.8.15–18, from Xenophon, *Mem.* 1.1.11, 13 and Plato, *Phaedo* 96a–c.

[24] *PE* 1.8.19.

[25] On Eusebius' use and evaluation of Socrates in the *PE*, see A.–M. Malingrey, 'Le Personnage de Socrate chez Quelques Auteurs Chrétiens du IVe Siècle', in *Forma Futuri. Studi in Onore del Cardinale Michele Pellegrino* (Turin: Bottega d'Erasmo, 1975), 159–68.

[26] See also, *PE* 1.6.8; 1.9.14.

[27] Diodorus *Bibl.* 1.11.1–5, *ap. PE* 1.9.1–4.

that, 'the Egyptians, when they looked up to the cosmos, and were struck with astonishment and admiration at the nature of the universe, supposed that the sun and moon were two eternal and primal gods, one of whom they named Osiris, and the other Isis'. After all, Osiris could be translated into Greek as 'many-eyed' resembling the rays of the sun cast in all directions; and Isis could be translated as 'ancient', an appropriate epithet for the moon's 'eternal and ancient genesis'.[28] This attribution of astral worship to the ancient Egyptians was bolstered by a citation of Theophrastus (*ap.* Porphyry, *De Abstinetia* 2.5) that claimed that the Egyptians, 'the most rational race (*genos*) of all', made sacrifices of spices and plants to the heavenly gods.[29]

Similar things could be claimed for the other nations: the earliest of the Phoenicians and Greeks worshipped only astral deities, knowing, 'no other gods than the sun, the moon, and besides these the planets, the elements also, and the things connected with them'.[30]

This original astral theology of the ancient nations, while being a form of polytheism based upon ignorance, was nonetheless a somewhat innocent, less superstitious, and non-threatening manifestation of the polytheistic error.[31] Eusebius comments:

But I think it must be evident to every one on consideration that the first and most ancient of mankind did not apply themselves either to building temples or to setting up statues, since at that time no art of painting, or modelling, or carving, or statuary had yet been discovered nor, indeed, were building or architecture as yet established. Nor was there any mention ... of those who have since been denominated gods and heroes, nor had they any Zeus, nor Kronos, Poseidon, Apollo [etc.] ... nor any daemon good or bad reverenced among men, but only the visible stars of heaven ... received the title of gods, and even those were not worshipped with animal sacrifices and the honours afterwards superstitiously invented.[32]

---

[28] *PE* 1.9.4.   [29] *PE* 1.9.7.

[30] *PE* 1.9.5. Likewise, the Greeks originally worshipped astral gods; see Plato, *Cratylus* 397c, *ap. PE* 1.9.12.

[31] König-Ockenfels, 'Christliche Deutung der Weltgeschichte bei Eusebs von Cäsarea', 355, goes so far as to speak of this astral religion as that, 'original religion of humanity, which obtained for them a certain nearness to God'. She notes also Aristides, *Apology* 4–7.

[32] *PE* 1.9.13. Theophrastus, in Eusebius' quotation from Porphyry's *Abst.*, had revealed similar sentiments when he noted that later generations had applied the term *thusia* (originally meant for plant sacrifices) to the 'so-called worship through [the sacrifice of] animals ... But when the beginnings of sacrifices were carried by men to a great pitch of disorder, the adoption of the most dreadful offerings, full of cruelty, was introduced; so that the curses formerly pronounced against us seemed now to have received fulfillment, as men slaughtered victims and bloodied the altars' (*ap. PE* 1.9.9,11).

The primitive theology of the ancient nations represented for Eusebius a higher form of polytheism. Foreshadowing his narrative of descent of the Hebrew nation, Eusebius notes that this idea of a primitive astral theology is part of his own Christian conception of the earliest theological developments.

This is what our holy Scriptures also teach, in which it is contained, that in the beginning the worship of the visible luminaries had been assigned to all the nations, and that to the Hebrew race (*genos*) alone had been entrusted the full initiation (*epopteia*) into the knowledge of God, the Maker and Artificer of the universe, and of true piety towards Him. So then among the oldest of mankind there was no mention of a Theogony, either Greek or barbarian, nor any erection of lifeless statues, nor all the silly talk that there is now about the naming of the gods both male and female.[33]

Astral polytheism, then, was closer to the truth and less tainted by impiety than later more superstitious variants (and in fact was 'assigned' to the nations apparently by God himself).[34] Since ancient times, humankind had slipped into degenerate forms of polytheism: the use of idols, the personalizing of the gods as men and women, belief in daemons, and animal sacrifices. This disintegration of all vestiges of piety would be told in the remainder of the narrative of descent, from the Phoenicians to the Egyptians, and eventually to the Greeks.[35]

The Phoenicians

The narrative of descent proper (1.9.19–2.8.13) contains the history of the downward plunge into superstitious idolatry and irrational beliefs. The sources of this theological collapse are rooted in the histories of three nations. 'In fact,' Eusebius explains, 'the polytheistic error of all the nations appeared a great time later [than the primitive astral theology], having taken its beginning from the Phoenicians and Egyptians and passed over from them to the other nations even as far as the Greeks

---

[33] *PE* 1.9.15–16.

[34] For discussion of this point within the context of a theology of early 'angels of nations' (borrowed from Origen), see Chesnut, *The First Christian Histories*, 69. See also, *DE* 4.6–9.

[35] It may be of interest to note that Diodorus, on the other hand, had offered a narrative of humanity's progress from harsh and brutal beginnings. See Sacks, *Diodorus Siculus and the First Century*, 55–82. See also, *SC* 13.16; Athanasius, *C. Gent.* 3–11 (esp. 9). For discussion, König-Ockenfels, 'Christliche Deutung der Weltgeschichte bei Eusebs von Cäsarea', 354–8; and Appendix 2.

themselves.'[36] The history of moral and religious deterioration is a distinctively national history. It relates the transmission of ways of knowing certain gods and ways of acting towards those gods that originate in one nation (the Phoenicians) and are transferred to another nation (the Egyptians). Then these two nations provide a double source of theological knowledge, which migrates through certain key figures to a third nation (the Greeks).

A narrative of descent such as this one carried explanatory value for the understanding of the (imagined) relationships between the ways of life and religious thought of various nations. Also, as in the case now under consideration, such a narrative of descent could wield polemical force in relating the theologies of one nation (the Greeks) to those of other nations (the Phoenicians and Egyptians), which are excoriated as characteristically barbarian, irrational, and full of confused superstition. Some Greek authors had attempted to make barbarian wisdom innocuous by sifting it through what has been called an *interpretatio Graeca*. Plutarch's *De Defectu Oraculorum* and *De Iside et Osiride*[37] and Porphyry's *Philosophia ex Oraculis*[38]—all of which are cited in the *Praeparatio*—are good examples of this integration of barbarian wisdom into a completely Hellenic framework. Eusebius' rereading of the narrative of descent, however, runs directly counter to such interpretive attempts.

The history of the Phoenicians is recounted through the *Phoenician History* (*Phoinikikē Historia*) of Philo of Byblos, who had, in the time of Hadrian,[39] supposedly made a translation into Greek of Sanchouniathon's history of the Phoenicians.[40] Much scholarly concern has been aimed

---

[36] *PE* 1.9.19.

[37] See especially the passage cited from *De Def. Or.* (*ap.* 5.4.1). The Hellenocentrism of such passages is discussed by D. Richter, 'Plutarch on Isis and Osiris: Text, Cult, and Cultural Appropriation', *TAPA* 131 (2001), 191–216. Also of interest for Plutarch's construction of Greek identity vis-à-vis the barbarians is the study of T. Whitmarsh, 'Alexander's Hellenism and Plutarch's Textualism', *CQ* 52 (2002), 174–92; though dated, see Hadas, 'Nationalist Survival Under Hellenistic and Roman Imperialism', 135.

[38] See especially the quotation found at *PE* 9.10.2–4.

[39] The Suda asserts that he was born during the time of Nero and lived after the reign of Hadrian at least long enough to write a work entitled *On the Reign of Hadrian*. For discussion of the difficulties involved in the Suda's evidence for dating Philo, see A. Gudeman, 'Herrenius Philon von Byblos', *RE* 8 (1913): cols. 650–1; A. Baumgarten, *The Phoenician History of Philo of Byblos* (Leiden: Brill, 1983), 32–5. Testimonia and fragments of Philo are collected in F. Jacoby, *FGrH* III.C. 802–24.

[40] *PE* 1.9.20–1. Even Sanchouniathon, who was a contemporary of Semiramus (and hence before or simultaneous with the Trojan Wars), had worked from venerable temple records older than himself.

at determining whether or not Philo's account accorded with the actual myths and theology of the ancient Phoenicians (or rather Canaanites).[41] When the texts from Ras Shamra-Ugarit were discovered, dating to the second millennium BC, it appeared to many that Philo was in fact indebted to very ancient sources.[42] W. F. Albright concluded that it was 'certain that the work attributed to him is a rich source of authentic Phoenician data and is not a forgery of early Roman times'.[43] Nautin, Barr, and others[44] were less optimistic about the antiquity of Philo's sources. Especially damaging for assertions of antiquity was Philo's blatant euhemerism (discussed below).[45]

Interesting though the issue might be, a more promising approach may avoid such source-related questions. R. A. Oden,[46] and later M. J. Edwards,[47] have put investigation of Philo of Byblos on to a level that is more relevant for the present enquiry. Both claim that issues relating to the veracity of Philo's history cannot ultimately be proven (as Barr had shown). Instead, the significance of the *Phoenician History* rests on the Hellenistic context of writing national histories. Philo's *Phoenician History* is, according to Oden, 'a most typical specimen of Hellenistic historiography, particularly as such histories were composed by those living in lands subjected to the full force of Hellenism'.[48] More strongly still, Philo's work is, for Edwards, 'a Hellenistic imposture, though many

[41] See O. Eissfeldt, *Taautos und Sanchunjaton. Sitzungsberichte der deutschen Akademie der Wissenschaften zu Berlin*, Klasse fur Sprachen, Literatur und Kunst, 1 (Berlin, 1952); and idem 'Art und Aufbau der phonizischen Geschichte des Philo von Byblos', *Syria* 33 (1956), 88–96.

[42] For a narrative account of the discoveries made at Ras Shamra, see A. Kapelrud, *The Ras Shamra Discoveries and the Old Testament* (Norman: University of Oklahoma Press, 1963).

[43] W. Albright, 'Neglected Factors in the Greek Intellectual Revolution', *Proceedings of the American Philosophical Society* 116 (1972), 239, cited in R. A. Oden, 'Philo of Byblos and Hellenistic Historiography', *PEQ* 110 (1978), 116.

[44] P. Nautin, 'Sanchuniathon chez Philon de Byblos et chez Porphyre', *Revue Biblique* 56 (1949): 259–73; and ibid., 'La Valeur documentaire de l'histoire Phenicienne', *Revue Biblique* 56 (1949), 573–8; J. Barr, 'Philo of Byblos and his "Phoenician History"', *Bulletin of the John Rylands Library* 57 (1974–5), 17–68; and also, Baumgarten, *The Phoenician History of Philo of Byblos*.

[45] Baumgarten, *The Phoenician History of Philo of Byblos*, 80–82 and 92 n. 94, argues for direct literary dependence upon Euhemerus' account of the Panchaeans. A more cautious claim is made by T. Brown, 'Euhemerus and the Historians', *HTR* 39 (1946), 272–4.

[46] Oden, 'Philo of Byblos and Hellenistic Historiography', 115–26.

[47] M. J. Edwards, 'Philo or Sanchuniathon? A Phoenician Cosmogony', *CQ* 41 (1991), 213–20.

[48] Oden, 'Philo of Byblos and Hellenistic Historiography', 118.

of the ingredients employed must antedate its present form'.[49] Corollaries between Philo and other Hellenistic historians allow us to appreciate the force of Philo's project:[50] especially euhemerism (or the deification of mortals who have advanced civilization by their cultural benefactions, inventions or discoveries); 'nationalistic' sentiments[51] or the impulse towards a patriotic cultural history;[52] anti-Hellenism or anti-Judaism;[53] and the claim to ancient and reliable sources such as temple records.[54]

With these considerations in mind, there is actually much in common between what Eusebius is attempting to do in the *Praeparatio* and what Philo was attempting to do in the *Phoenician History*. Eusebius positions himself firmly within the euhemeristic approach to interpreting the polytheistic myths. Eusebius, too, claims the true benefactors of civilization to be the ancestors of one particular nation, the Hebrews. On this score, he provides a 'patriotic' narrative that stands in opposition to Hellenism. And lastly, Eusebius frames his argument upon the ancient and reliable sources, so as not to be accused of biased selection and alteration of the 'facts'. Both authors are nationalistic in Oden's sense: the *Phoenician History* is pro-Phoenician, while the *Praeparatio* is anti-Phoenician and pro-Hebrew. Having noted these general tendencies in Philo and their closeness to Eusebius, it is necessary to note the particularities and features that will be significant for Eusebius' first narrative of descent.

---

[49] Edwards, 'Philo or Sanchuniathon? A Phoenician Cosmogony', 219.

[50] Compare with the three points noted by Edwards, 'Philo or Sanchuniathon? A Phoenician Cosmogony', 214–16: euhemerism, use of sources available to other historians (especially temple records), and anti-Jewish polemic (similar to Manetho, *et al.*).

[51] So also Edwards, 'Philo or Sanchuniathon? A Phoenician Cosmogony', 214, '... antiquity was the proof of national virtue. The conquests of Alexander had annexed to the Greek world a number of ancient kingdoms, whose usurping potentates were soon at war. Nation was thus induced to compete with nation, and the works of such men as Berossus, Manetho and Hecataeus of Abdera are the progeny of cultures with long histories which had suffered the eclipse of political power.' See also, Baumgarten, *The Phoenician History of Philo of Byblos*, 267–8.

[52] Oden: 'This patriotism was the natural reaction of the subject peoples of the Hellenistic era, as they searched for self-esteem in the face of these new and mighty and clever rulers' ('Philo of Byblos and Hellenistic Historiography', 120).

[53] Ibid., 121.

[54] On this last point, Oden refers to the discussion in M. Hengel, *Judaism and Hellenism* (Philadelphia: Fortress Press, 1974), I.242. Here (and in the accompanying notes), Hengel cites the examples of Berossus, Ps.-Manetho, Josephus, *et al.*: 'One of the favorite "forms of revelation" in the Hellenistic Roman period was the discovery of scrolls, inscriptions or pillars from primeval times. Both the secret Egyptian hieroglyphic inscriptions and the Babylonian cuneiform monuments supported the spread of this frequent theme.'

The fragments of Philo's preface contextualize his purpose in translating Sanchouniathon as part of an argument against those who want to
read the Phoenician myths as allegories of natural phenomena. Here his
statements function as part of his own ethnic argumentation: the Greeks
are targeted for their ignominious misappropriations of the original true
histories of the Phoenicians.[55] He explicitly rejects the 'matter' (*hulē*) of
the Greeks, stating that he made discoveries from that of the Phoenicians
instead.[56] In fact, because of the disharmony among the accounts of the
Greeks, Philo had written another work entitled *Paradoxical History*
(*Paradoxos Historia*), which exposed their falsehoods.[57] Later, after
fragments of Sanchouniathon's cosmogony are given, Philo asserts
again that it is because of later Greek misinterpretations (*parekdochas*)
that he has had to provide the Phoenician account.[58] The idea that the
Greeks were dependent upon the Phoenicians for their stories is boldly
stated with explicit mention of Hesiod and others.

But the Greeks, surpassing all in genius, appropriated most of the earliest stories,
and then variously decked them out with ornaments of tragic phrase and
adorned them in every way, with the purpose of charming by the pleasant fables.
Hence Hesiod and the celebrated Cyclic poets framed their own theogonies,
and battles of the giants, and battles of Titans, and castrations; and making
adaptations to them, they conquered and drove out the truth.[59]

His criticism of the Greeks centres on two issues: the derivation of Greek
stories from Phoenician originals, and the subsequent misinterpretation
of those stories in physical allegoresis. His claims that it was Phoenician
hierophants who introduced the allegorical interpretations further support his claims against the Greeks. For not only are the Greeks dependent on the Phoenicians for the ancient stories, but they are also
dependent upon them for the allegorical method that they exploited
to pervert them.

---

[55] Though some Phoenician priests aided in the development of allegory: Thabion, a
hierophant of the Phoenicians, first gave an allegorical interpretation to the Phoenician
stories (1.10.39); Epeïs, 'a supreme hierophant and sacred scribe', provided an allegory of
the serpent deity (1.10.49).

[56] *PE* 1.9.27.

[57] *PE* 1.9.28. See Baumgarten, *The Phoenician History of Philo of Byblos*, 82–3. This
critique will be echoed later in the fragments of Philo's contemporary, Numenius (*On the
Revolt of the Academics Against Plato*, cited at *PE* 14.5–9). For a general account of the
argument from disagreement see Boys-Stones, *Post-Hellenistic Philosophy*, 123–50.

[58] *PE* 1.10.8.

[59] *PE* 1.10.40.

The allegorists have 'introduced much ambiguity into [the myths], so that one cannot easily see altogether the things that have truly happened'.[60] What really happened is that, 'the most ancient of the barbarians, especially the Phoenicians and Egyptians, from whom the rest of humankind received their traditions, considered those ones to be the greatest gods who discovered the necessaries of life, or in some way had done good to the nations. Esteeming these as benefactors and authors of many blessings, they worshipped them also as gods after their death.'[61] After these great men died, shrines and festivals were dedicated to them, and their names would be given to the heavenly elements.

Instead of understanding the myths of the gods as referring either to real divine (though anthropomorphic) beings or to allegories of physical and astronomical phenomena, Philo offers a euhemeristic account of the gods. This is not to do away with physicalist theories entirely, but to limit them to the astronomical realm. Some of the gods are astral entities and others are human benefactors. The last sentence of the previously quoted fragment contains the claim that the early Phoenicians 'knew no other gods than those of nature, sun, and moon, and the rest of the wandering stars, and the elements and things connected with them, *so that some of their gods were mortal and some immortal*'.[62] Euhemeristic and astral elements are equally present in the origins of Phoenician theology.[63] In the fragment at 1.10.7, the first mortals who will become divinized for their benefaction to humanity also worship the sun, 'for they regard the lord of heaven alone as god, calling him Beelsamen, which is among the Phoenicians the Lord of Heaven, but among the Greeks Zeus'. The solar theology and the euhemerism need not be mutually exclusive.[64] The sun, moon and other heavenly phenomena

---

[60] *PE* 1.9.26. G. Zanker, 'Enargeia in Ancient Criticism of Poetry', *RM* 124 (1981), 297–311, offers a useful survey of the poetics of *enargeia* in antiquity that was contrasted to such ambiguity as Eusebius is here attacking.

[61] *PE* 1.9.29.

[62] *PE* 1.9.29.

[63] See J. Sirinelli and E. Des Places, *Eusèbe de Césarée. La Préparation Évangélique*, 309–10.

[64] Diodorus' introduction to the fragment of Euhemerus in his lost sixth book says as much: 'With regard then to gods the ancient humans have handed down two notions to later generations.' First, the astral deities, 'for each of these has an eternal generation and persistence'. Second were 'earthly (*epigeious*) deities, having obtained immortal honour and glory through their benefactions to humanity, such as Heracles, Dionysus, Aristaeus, and the other similar ones' (*ap. PE* 2.2.53). See also, Brown, 'Euhemerus and the Historians', 263.

are first principles (*archē*) and are not the focus of euhemerist theories; rather, it is the myths of 'gods, male and female' and their names that are ascribed to human origins in euhemeristic interpretations.[65]

The astral theology is in fact the subject of the first fragments of Sanchouniathon's history, which Eusebius cites from Philo in 1.10.1–6.[66] The first principles, he says, were Air and Chaos.[67] When Wind fell in love with these principles, Mot was produced,[68] from whom animals and the heavenly elements were created. The first humans were Aeon and Proto-gonus, born from Wind and Night. The offspring of Aeon and Protogonus became the first inhabitants of Phoenicia.[69] As mentioned above, these first mortals worshipped the sun as the Lord of Heaven (Beelsamen).

Following the Phoenician cosmology, Philo records the narrative of the generations of ancient mortals and their contributions to humankind, mentioning also their subsequent divinization and the origins of their worship and honours.[70] The narrative includes the discoveries of fire,[71] reed huts,[72] sea navigation,[73] the arts of hunting and fishing, iron, oratory, and magic[74]—all these and more had been contributions made by the Phoenician progenitors. And these great men and women had been duly apotheosized upon their death. Monuments to their achievements had been erected which still stood as memorials even in the time of Philo. For instance, Agrotes, inventor of brick walls, received a statue and shrine that were still venerated in Phoenicia in Philo's day, and he was called the greatest of the gods by Philo's fellow-Byblians.[75]

The entrance of Elioun (called the 'Most High', *Hupsistos*)[76] and his wife Beryth, who both dwell in ancient Byblos, marks the beginning of

---

[65] See *PE* 1.9.16. Throughout the passages cited from the *Phoenician History*, Philo will indiscriminately refer to the characters of the story as men/women and as gods/goddesses.

[66] Barr, 'Philo of Byblos and his "Phoenician History"', 22–3, labels this section of Philo's narrative the 'cosmogony' for obvious reasons.

[67] Edwards, 'Philo or Sanchuniathon? A Phoenician Cosmogony', 218, sees this element of the cosmogony as parallel to Gnostic formulations and hence another indication of its Hellenistic milieu.

[68] On Mot as an ancient Ugaritic daemon, see Baumgarten, *The Phoenician History of Philo of Byblos*, 111–12. Alternatively, Barr, 'Philo of Byblos and his "Phoenician History"', 23 n. 2, asserts the possibility of a connection to the Hebrew for 'heavenly lights'.

[69] *PE* 1.10.7.

[70] Barr, 'Philo of Byblos and his "Phoenician History"', 23, labels this section of Philo's work the 'technogony'. A table of the genealogy of this section is provided at 62–3.

[71] *PE* 1.10.9.   [72] *PE* 1.10.10.   [73] *PE* 1.10.10.

[74] *PE* 1.10.11.   [75] *PE* 1.10.12.

[76] Barr, 'Philo of Byblos and his "Phoenician History"', 53, draws the connection to El Elyon of the Old Testament, though no equivalent has yet been found at Ugarit.

what J. Barr has aptly called the 'theogony' for its obvious parallels with the eponymous work by Hesiod. This couple and their family enact a story that sounds remarkably similar to Greek myths (even the names are the same).[77] Ouranos and Gē were born from this pair, and then deified their father, Elioun, after he was killed by wild animals. Ouranos married his sister and had numerous children by her, most notably Kronos.[78] Kronos drove his father from power and founded the first city—none other than Byblos in Phoenicia. The remaining story of Kronos is typified by familial bloodshed and incestuous marriages. Ouranos was later castrated by his son, and subsequently deified. Kronos would sacrifice his only son to Ouranos and circumcise himself.[79] The offspring of Ouranos and Kronos are a mix of men and women with the names of many traditional Greek and Phoenician deities:[80] Astarte, Rhea, Dione, Eimarmene, Hora, Dagon (= Zeus Arotrios[81]), Suduc, Asclepius, Apollo, Zeus Belus, Melcathrus (= Heracles), Muth (= Thanatos), and others. The offspring of the Dioscuri developed nautical sciences, Dagon made agricultural advances, and Sidon invented musical song.

The story of the offspring of Elioun and Beryth notes the benefactions to humanity on the part of its characters, even while relating the scandals and strife of the reigns of Ouranos and Kronos. Importantly, it also forges connections to traditional Greek mythology. By providing Phoenician names and slight alterations to otherwise well-known episodes of Greek mythology, Philo effectively claims the stories for the Phoenicians. In effect, Philo is saying: 'What you Greeks thought was yours, is really ours.' It is good to keep in mind the remarks already quoted above, that the Greeks originally borrowed Phoenician stories and dressed them in tragic style: 'making adaptations to them, they conquered and drove out the truth'.[82]

---

[77] *PE* 1.10.14–29. Barr, 'Philo of Byblos and his "Phoenician History"', 25. He adds: 'Philo does not call it by this name, but it is closely parallel to such theogonies as that of Hesiod, and modern scholars will regard it as a theogony even if Philo himself did not.' Barr provides a table of the genealogy of this section on page 64.

[78] For parallels to a Kronos, son of Ouranos and Gē, in *Sibylline Oracles* 3.110ff, see Barr, 'Philo of Byblos and his "Phoenician History"', 60.

[79] The story is repeated later with additional details, such as the son's name, Ieud (1.10.44).

[80] *PE* 1.10.21–9.

[81] I provide the Greek equivalent given by Philo himself, both here, with respect to Dagon, and with the other names for which Philo has offered the Greek equivalent.

[82] *PE* 1.10.40. See Baumgarten, *The Phoenician History of Philo of Byblos*, 236–7.

In addition to the history of the founders of Phoenician customs and religious practices, Philo offers an account of the Phoenician origins of the deification of animals (specifically the serpent). According to Philo's *Phoenician History*, Taautos was the first to introduce the notion that serpents were divine, albeit from an allegorizing theological standpoint.[83] Because the serpent is especially full of breath and fiery, and also because of its swiftness, ability to take on any shape, and immortality, this animal had been divinized by the Phoenicians and called the Good Daemon. Philo[84] summarizes: 'Everyone gave physical explanations [of the serpent god], taking their impulse from Taautos ... and having built temples, they consecrated in the shrines the primary elements represented by serpents, and performed festivals, sacrifices and mysteries to them, considering them the greatest gods and the founders (*archēgous*) of all things.'[85]

This account of the Phoenician divinization of the serpent will find a parallel later in the report on Egyptian animal worship that Eusebius cites from Diodorus. In each case, Eusebius has had to draw on later material from the respective author, Philo or Diodorus,[86] in order to include their descriptions of the animal worship of the two nations. Hence, the inclusion of such material should not be taken as a failure on Eusebius' part to end a quotation once it has got going, but rather as a conscious decision to include material that is significant for his apologetic purposes. In this case, he can capitalize on the superstitious and impious elements of Phoenician and Egyptian national character as it is embodied in the historical cult practices. Eusebius has crafted the narrative, even by employing their 'native' sources, to emphasize this aspect of their national character. By placing reports of animal worship at the end of the segment regarding each nation, he shows the depth to which their national theologies and religious practices had sunk. This arrangement of the material inscribes in no uncertain terms a narrative

---

[83] *PE* 1.10.46–8.

[84] I am following the suggestion of Mras, *Eusebius Werke VIII. Die Praeparatio Evangelica*, in the apparatus criticus of his edition (*ad loc.*), that the sentence here given is still part of Philo's fr. 9 Müller, even though Müller ends the quotation just before, at 1.10.52. Jacoby, fr. 4 follows Mras. Baumgarten's commentary (*The Phoenician History of Philo of Byblos*, 259) neglects the issue.

[85] *PE* 1.10.53.

[86] Eusebius adds Philo's discussion of Phoenician serpent divinization after giving a citation from an entirely different work of Philo (*On the Jews*) at 1.42–44; in the case of Diodorus, Eusebius will jump in his citations from 1.27 to 1.86 of the *Bibliothēkē* in order to obtain a record of Egyptian animal worship.

of decline onto the histories of the Phoenician and Egyptian ancestors. While the culture heroes of each nation may have made contributions towards the advance of the arts and 'civilization', the attendant apotheosis of humans and, even worse, of animals had brought them to a markedly depraved, mindless depth of superstition.

If we pause to consider the elements crucial for ethnic argumentation, two key features have become readily apparent in the narrative of Phoenician descent. First of all, the importance of the euhemerist interpretation of Philo must not be ignored. The historicity of the figures of ancient mythology is essential for the argument of the *Praeparatio*. Once these figures are recognized as mortal humans of ancient history, they can be understood as founders of a particular nation and as representative of an ethnic way of life. To deny the historicity of these figures through allegoresis would disperse any force they may have as mechanisms of ethnic identity. An *ethnos* cannot establish its existence in a shared history of its people if its own ancestors are relegated to the status of symbols for astral and other physical phenomena. Philo recognized this fact and so made explicit his historicizing aims. Eusebius adopted this approach from Philo, but turned it to his own ends for a new kind of national polemic within a distinctively ethnicizing apologetic methodology.

Secondly, the related issue of national character hinges upon a historically rooted way of life. The story of the ancient Phoenicians portrays a particular national character grounded in the ancestral customs and practices founded by the progenitors of the *ethnos*. This character is, for Eusebius, an abomination in comparison to the national character of the Hebrew 'friends of God' (exhibited later in Book 7, but already noted at 1.9.15). Whereas the ancient Hebrews comprehended the true invisible God behind the visible phenomena of the cosmos, the Phoenicians had deified mortals and animals—even the most debased kind, the serpent. This delusion of the Phoenician forefathers had to be highlighted for Eusebius' defence of Christianity to carry much weight. Eusebius must offer a valid rationale for the Christians' rejection of the ethnic way of life of their fathers, and this rationale is the point of the narrative.

After the account of the ancient Phoenicians, a second segment of the narrative of descent takes up the origins of the Egyptians. The figures of their stories would also be shown as mortal humans, and a national character quite similar to that of the Phoenicians would also be portrayed. In fact, according to Eusebius, they sank to even deeper levels of impiety in their sexual immorality and deification of animals. It is to this ancient Egyptian account of history and theology that we now turn.

The Egyptians

While no sustained treatment of the subject was offered, Philo had given hints in his narrative of a direct borrowing of features of Phoenician theology by the Egyptians. Taautos, a Phoenician, had given the Egyptians the knowledge of letters. He was known by them as Thoüth, or by the Alexandrians as Thoth, and by the Greeks as Hermes.[87] Kronos had given Egypt to Taautos as his kingdom.[88] The latter had also instituted the deification and veneration of the serpent.[89] Philo had claimed that Egyptians adopted the Phoenicians' own theta-like symbol of the deified serpent, the Good Daemon, to represent the cosmos.[90] Apart from these brief statements in Philo, the possible connection of Phoenicia and Egypt is never made explicit by Eusebius himself. As will be discussed later, the exact relationship between these two nations matters little to Eusebius. For him, the primary emphasis must be on the Greeks' dependence upon both of them (regardless of which came first or borrowed from the other). As Eusebius moves into this second phase of his narrative of descent, he allows Diodorus' statements that the first humans were Egyptians to stand without comment alongside the earlier claims of Philo for Phoenician chronological primacy. Eusebius' concern in his citations from Diodorus[91] on the Egyptians is primarily to describe the character of the early Egyptians and of their way of life and theology. Hence, as with the Phoenician stories, it matters a great deal that the figures of the story are human founding fathers and not allegorical representations of physical phenomena.

Diodorus begins: 'Accordingly the Egyptians say that the first humans arose in Egypt during the first creation of the universe because of the

---

[87] *PE* 1.10.14.   [88] *PE* 1.10.38.   [89] *PE* 1.10.46.   [90] *PE* 1.10.51.

[91] On the highly problematic nature of Eusebius' 'quotations' of Diodorus, see G. Bounoure, 'Eusèbe citateur de Diodore', 435–8, who names Eusebius' style of quoting Diodorus (as contrasted to the other authors quoted in the *PE* whose words we can verify by their extant writings) as 'le style abréviatif' (438), and claims that his Diodoran citations show 'the declining attention of the citationist and his growing indifference to details of the rationalist argumentation of the mythographer' (436). Bounoure also provides a list of the passages cited and their order (or disorder in the *PE* 2), see nn. 11, 15. For Diodorus' general attitude towards Egypt, see K. A. D. Smelik and E. A. Hemelrijk, 'Who Knows Not What Monsters Demented Egypt Worships?' *ANRW* 2.17.4 (1984), 1895–8.

temperate climate and the nature of the Nile.'[92] These first Egyptians worshipped mortal humans as gods, and 'they attained immortality because of their wisdom and public benefits to mankind'.[93] Some said Helios was the first king of Egypt, who also gave his name to a star; but others claimed that Hephaestus ruled first, since he was the discoverer of fire.[94] Kronos (or Osiris, according to others) ruled next, marrying his sister Rhea (or Isis). From this couple were born Osiris (= Dionysus), Isis (= Demeter), Typhon, Apollo, and Aphrodite. Osiris succeeded to the throne of his father (Kronos) and 'did many things for the benefaction of the populace'.[95] His accomplishments were religious and agricultural: first, he founded a temple dedicated to his parents, Zeus and Hera,[96] as well as other temples of gold to the other gods, especially Hermes; secondly, he discovered the vine and the art of farming.

After becoming the founder of Egyptian Thebes,[97] Osiris travelled over the whole world and founded numerous other cities. In Phoenicia he founded Busiris,[98] in Ethiopia and Libya he founded Antaios, in India he founded 'not a few cities'.[99] He went through Phrygia and into Europe, leaving one of his sons, Macedon, as king of Macedonia. He entrusted the arts of agriculture throughout Attica to Triptolemus. Diodorus remarks: 'And when every nation received him as a god because of his benefactions, Osiris left behind markers of himself everywhere' (2.1.12). His death by dismemberment and the subsequent retrieval of his body parts (except his *membrum virile*) by Isis was the basis for subsequent cult. The lost member was deified and its image

---

[92] *PE* 2.1.1.   [93] *PE* 2.1.2.   [94] *PE* 2.1.3.   [95] *PE* 2.1.5.

[96] The fact that there is a confusion of names here (since this Kronos/Osiris will have a son named Osiris, who will then establish temples to his parents, Zeus and Hera) need not concern us. Clearly there is a joining of separate traditions about Osiris here. What is significant for the purposes of the present analysis is how it functions within the larger narrative of descent that Eusebius is creating. This functional value of the episode of Osiris lies not in who Osiris' parents were, but in the fact that he was offering divine honours to his mortal parents. And furthermore, these mortals were native to the land of Egypt, not Greece. Osiris was the founder of the Thebes in Egypt, not the Hellenic Thebes.

[97] *PE* 2.1.6.

[98] This sort of Egyptocentric account of the founding of cities in other regions by an Egyptian is, of course, an oppositional story to such accounts as are found in Philo of Byblos. A similar account (other than that of Herodotus' second book), which greatly predates these Hellenistic renderings, may be found in an ancient attempt to establish kinship ties between Egypt and Phoenician Byblos: Rib-Abda, ruler of Byblos in 1370 BC, wrote to Pharaoh that Byblos was an Egyptian foundation (see J. Teixidor, *The Pagan God: Popular Religion in the Ancient Near East* [Princeton: Princeton University Press, 1977], 21). For such Hellenistic constructions, see Bickerman, 'Origenes gentium', 74ff.

[99] *PE* 2.1.9–13.

represented in temples, and initiations and sacrifices were appropriated to it as 'honours equal to the gods' (*timōn isotheōn*).[100] Isis was also the discoverer of the medicinal arts. Upon her death, she too was worshipped as a god. Horus, her son, was the last of the humans to become a god of Egypt for benefiting humanity through oracles and healings.[101]

Alongside the narrative of Osiris and Isis, the Egyptian deification of animals is given prominence.[102] The sacred bulls, Apis and Mnevis, were given divine honours for the aid they offered to the discoverers of wheat and agricultural arts.[103] Anubis received the attribute of a dog's head because of the dog's role as protector and guardian.[104] The quotation from Diodorus provided the possible sources for such deification of animals, though the topic remained a disputed one.[105] A discussion of contemporary treatment of animals (while alive and upon death) and the cities sacred to each complemented the review of the possible origins of Egyptian animal worship.[106]

The narrative of Egyptian descent thus developed elements that were fundamental for Eusebius' apologetic purposes. In a similar fashion to the Phoenician narrative, the Egyptian nation was shown to have mortal humans as their founders. These founders embodied a distinctively Egyptian way of life. The national character exhibited by these ancestors was such that Eusebius could denigrate them as despicable and irrational. While the progenitors of the Egyptian nation were said to be benefactors of humanity (by the Egyptians of Diodorus), they were in fact, as Eusebius would highlight, the sources of impiety. Their immorality, sacrificial practices, and deification of animals were all held up by Eusebius as representative of a national character that had reasonably and rightly been rejected by the Christians. Instead, Christians have opted for a way of life based upon ancestors who were models of virtue,

---

[100] *PE* 2.1.21.   [101] *PE* 2.1.31.

[102] On this subject, see the important study of Smelik and Hemelrijk, 'Who Knows Not What Monsters Demented Egypt Worships?' 1898–1903.

[103] *PE* 2.1.19.   [104] *PE* 2.1.35.

[105] Among the theories offered is one that locates their deification after certain gods used their shapes to escape the impiety of 'the earth-born men' (2.1.33). If this episode is derived from Greek myth (as I think it is, *pace* Smelik and Hemelrijk, 'Who Knows Not What Monsters Demented Egypt Worships?' 1904–5), the 'Gigantomachy' may be recalled; see Hesiod, *Theog.* 185; *Batrach.* 7; Sophocles, *Trachiniae* 1058; Aeschylus, *Prom.Vinct.* 351; Diodorus 1.26.7. See, W. K. C. Guthrie, *In the Beginning* (London: Methuen & Co. Ltd., 1957), 22–3 and notes. For a parallel story, see Josephus, *Ap.* 2.12. For the remaining sources on Egyptian animal deification, see *PE* 2.1.34–5.

[106] *PE* 2.1.4650.

reason, and friendship with God. But before Eusebius narrated the story of the ancient Hebrews, his argument reached a critical phase in the narrative of the Greeks.

The Greeks: Cadmus and Orpheus

By the time the narrative reaches the segment on the Greeks, Eusebius (or his sources) have already made some significant claims about the relationship of the Greek *ethnos* to the Phoenicians and the Egyptians. Philo asserted that Pherecydes had taken ideas of a serpent deity from the Phoenicians and brought it to Greece under the name Ophion.[107] According to Diodorus, Hermes had 'become the inventor of letters and ordained the sacrifices of the gods and discovered the lyre and taught the Greeks the explanation (*hermēneian*) of these things, and hence was called Hermes'.[108] Cadmus had brought the ways of the Phoenicians and instruction in their letters to the Greeks.[109] Orpheus had been responsible for the transmission of Egyptian mysteries.[110] It was these latter two wayfarers to whom Eusebius ascribed special importance in his overall scheme of the descent of the nations. Since Greek identity is one of the major ethnicities (besides that of the Jews) from which Eusebius wants to distinguish the Christian *ethnos*, the two figures of Cadmus and Orpheus play a pivotal role in the first narrative of descent. Eusebius remarks: 'The Phoenicians and then the Egyptians were the first authors of the delusion. For from them, it is said, Orpheus, son of Oeagrus, first brought over with him the mysteries of the Egyptians, and imparted them to the Greeks, just, in fact, as Cadmus also brought to them the Phoenician mysteries together with the knowledge of letters.'[111] Later in the *Praeparatio*, Eusebius asserts: 'Cadmus son of Agenor established the things about the gods from Phoenicia; Thracian Orpheus—or someone else Greek or barbarian—established the things about the gods from Egypt, or from wherever else, namely, the mysteries and initiations, and constructions of statues and hymns, and odes and epodes; both of these men becoming founders (*archēgoí*) of error.'[112]

---

[107] *PE* 1.10.50.   [108] *PE* 2.1.8.   [109] *PE* 2.2.1 ff.   [110] *PE* 2.1.22–9.
[111] *PE* 1.6.4.
[112] *PE* 10.4.4. These founding figures will appear elsewhere in the latter half of the *PE*, especially in the chronological discussions of Book 10. The most important later passages that discuss Cadmus and Orpheus are, for Cadmus: 10.5.1 (Cadmus, a Phoenician by race, introduced the letters of the alphabet), 10.12.21 (Cadmus came to Thebes and brought

Cadmus left Phoenicia searching for his sister, Europa, who had been abducted by Zeus disguised as a bull.[113] Not finding her, he stayed in Greece and founded Thebes in Boeotia. He married Harmonia and sired Semele, mother of Dionysus. Upon Semele's explosive death, Dionysus was brought up by nymphs in a secret cave halfway between Phoenicia and Egypt.[114] The subsequent narration covers a later individual also named Dionysus (or Sabazius), the band of Muses who accompanied Dionysus, Priapus the son of Dionysus and Aphrodite, and the legends of Heracles and Asclepius.[115] Eusebius appends, for further confirmation of the derivative status of the Greek stories, an account of the Atlantaean's ancient history,[116] the fragment of Euhemerus on the Panchaeans' ancient history (preserved only by Eusebius from Diodorus' lost sixth book),[117] and an extract from Clement's *Protrepticus* on the character of the mysteries founded by the ancient figures of the narrative.[118] Thus, this portion of the narrative of descent not only provides

Greek letters [quoting Clement]); for Orpheus: 5.4.1 (Orpheus could be Thracian, Egyptian or Phrygian [quoting Plutarch, *De Def. Or.*]), 9.27.4 (Moses is the teacher of Orpheus [quoting Artapanus]), 10.4.4 ('Thracian Orpheus, or someone else Greek or barbarian, established the things about the gods from Egypt, or from wherever else, namely, the mysteries and initiations, and constructions of statues and hymns, and odes and epodes; both of these men becoming founders [*archēgoi*] of error'), 10.4.5 (during the time of Orpheus, Linus and Musaios, nothing more was established than the error-ridden theology of the Phoenicians and Egyptians), 10.8.4–5 (Orpheus brought mystic initiations and orgies to Greeks [quoting Diodorus]), 10.11.22 (Musaios was a disciple of Orpheus [quoting Tatian]), 13.13.48–54 (Orpheus is in accord with Scriptures [quoting Clement]).

[113] *PE* 2.2.1 ff = Diodorus, 4.2.1ff.

[114] *PE* 2.2.3. An attractive hypothesis might claim that the location of this cave marked an attempt to reconcile Egyptian and Phoenician (Cadmean) claims to Dionysus.

[115] The inclusion of material on these latter two is somewhat puzzling, since they are not connected to the Cadmean saga. Two reasons for their inclusion are likely: first, to provide further demonstration of the Greek *tropos* and way of life; second, to show that important Greek 'gods' came after the time of Cadmus who postdated Moses. Eusebius had made this point explicit in the introduction to this segment of Diodoran quotations (2.1.55–6). An additional reason to include Heracles might be that, by joining it with material that has been borrowed from foreign nations, it is part of an underhanded attack upon Plutarch's claims to the contrary that Heracles was the distinctive possession of Greek prehistory. Plutarch's own assertions regarding Heracles were part of his critique of Herodotus' 'philobarbarism', in particular, Herodotus' remarks on an Egyptian *and* a Phoenician Heracles (Herodotus, 2.43–5); see Plutarch, *De Malignitate Herodoti*, 13–14.857d–f, as well as the excellent approach to this work by D. Richter, 'Plutarch on Isis and Osiris', 191–216, esp. 211.

[116] *PE* 2.2.35–51.   [117] *PE* 2.2.52–62.

[118] *PE* 2.3. That the quotation from Clement is meant only as an appendix to the narrative of descent is clear from Eusebius' introductory remarks: 'It is reasonable to append an account of the initiatory rites in the inner shrines of the same deities, and of their secret mysteries, and to observe whether they bear any becoming mark of a theology

explanation of the transmission of Phoenician letters to the Greeks via Cadmus, but also provides a narrative of descent of some crucial figures of what was claimed to be primitive Greek history, but was actually borrowed from other nations, as well as an exemplification of the sort of character being transmitted through religious practices to the Greeks. As Eusebius had remarked at the beginning of this section: 'That the Greek doctrines are mere fragments and misunderstandings of the [Phoenician and Egyptian theology] we have frequently stated already ... In their own records concerning the gods, they bring nothing forward from native sources, but fall into the fables of foreign nations.'[119]

The story of Orpheus adds a great deal of tension to this account. A digression found in Diodorus' passage on the Egyptians from the previous chapter,[120] narrates the travels of Orpheus from Thrace to Egypt. There he made some important discoveries before he was initiated into the mysteries of an *Egyptian* Dionysus. The Egyptians told a story that greatly contrasted with the Phoenician legend. They claimed Cadmus for themselves, saying that he was from Egyptian Thebes.[121] This Cadmus had a daughter named Semele, who bore a son named Osiris. Osiris was the equivalent of Dionysus (as Diodorus 1.96 says: 'For the rite of Osiris is the same as that of Dionysus; and that of Isis is very similar to that of Demeter, with only the change of names').[122] Hence, when Orpheus visited Egypt in search of wisdom and knowledge, he was initiated into the mysteries of Osiris/Dionysus, but wanting to make the Thebans of Greece happy, he changed the place of Dionysus' birth to Hellenic Thebes and then initiated the Thebans in the mysteries. This narrative shows that even those mysteries that the Greeks thought were peculiarly their own are in fact quite foreign and that they have been duped by a well-meaning traveller. Greek religious practices depend for their very existence upon the migrations of Cadmus and Orpheus from the nations of the barbarians.

---

that is truly divine, or arise from regions below out of long daemoniacal delusion, and are deserving of ridicule, or rather of shame....' (2.2.63).

[119] *PE* 2.1.53–4.

[120] *PE* 2.1. Though it might seem out of place to discuss Orpheus' story (found in 2.1) after Cadmus' story (found in 2.2), I do so because whenever Eusebius mentions both, Cadmus precedes Orpheus. See 1.9.19, etc.

[121] *PE* 2.1.22–3.

[122] Quoted at *PE* 10.8.4–5. This syncretism had been made as early as Herodotus (see 2.42.2; 2.144.2). See, Bickerman, 'Origenes gentium', 71–2.

Of course, the Egyptian Orpheus narrative obviously conflicts with the claims of the Phoenician account of Cadmus. According to the former, the only Cadmus of importance to the Greeks in ancient times was an Egyptian who never even came to Greece and never founded any cities, and whose offspring likewise lived and died in Egypt. Eusebius, however, does not comment on the competing claims of these stories (though he apparently wants to keep the Cadmus narrative as a serious option). Instead, without resolving the discrepancy, he allows both stories, the Phoenician and the Egyptian, to stand. For the *Praeparatio*'s argument, all that is necessary is that claims have been made for Greek dependency upon the nations of Phoenicia and Egypt, even by the Greek writings themselves. Hence, Eusebius' primary goal has been achieved. Through certain migrating figures who stand as founding fathers of the Greeks, connections of dependency were forged between the Phoenician and Egyptian nations and the Greek nation.

THE NARRATIVE OF DESCENT AND EUSEBIUS' ARGUMENT

The particular narrative developed by Eusebius through his sources formulates some fundamental themes that produce the driving force for his argument. Numerous remarks on the function of certain features of the narrative have already been made in the survey above. Here, they will be further delineated under two general headings: connections between nations, and portrayal of national character. These two themes provide the basis of Eusebius' argument in the first half of the *Praeparatio*. It is also these two themes that clarify the role of the sections that directly follow the narrative of descent: that is, Eusebius' treatment of 'physical theology', or the allegorical interpretations of that narrative (3.1.1–3.17.3); and 'political theology', or the current manifestations of the customs and practices rooted in that narrative (4.1.1–6.11.83).

Connections between nations

It had been emphasized at various points in the narrative that the figures being spoken of were not gods at all, but only humans who had been deified upon their death as a result of benefactions to humanity. This

method of interpreting the mythical stories was given clearest expression
by Euhemerus of Messene[123] (if not by Hecataeus of Abdera).[124] Its
adoption by Philo of Byblos has already been remarked. He asserted
that 'The most ancient of the barbarians, and especially the Phoenicians
and Egyptians, from whom the rest of mankind received their traditions,
regarded as the greatest gods those who had discovered the necessaries of
life, or in some way done good to the nations. Esteeming these as
benefactors and authors of many blessings, they worshipped them also
as gods after their death.'[125] His polemical motivation for writing his
Phoenician History rested on the fact that the Greeks had not only stolen
the history of the Phoenicians and claimed it as their own, but had also
adopted an improper way of understanding that history. The Greeks
had used allegory to integrate the stories of a barbarian *ethnos* into their
own hegemonic reading of foreign material—the so-called *interpretatio
Graeca*.[126] Hence, Philo attempts to return the Phoenician stories to
their proper place in the historical narrative of the early Phoenician
founding fathers. Diodorus held similar sentiments. He introduced his
narration of the Egyptians with the remark: 'The gods had been originally mortal humans, and obtained immortality because of wisdom and
public benefits to mankind, some of them also having become kings.'[127]

Eusebius may not always agree with his sources, but in this case he
fully concurs: 'It must be manifest that these are not fables and poets'
fictions containing some theory concealed in hidden meanings, but true
testimonies...'.[128] And again: 'We judged that it is an unholy and

---

[123] On the intellectual and historiographical context for Euhemerus' rationalism, see
Bickerman, 'Origenes gentium', 70. For Euhemerus' fate in the hands of earlier Christian
apologists, see F. Zucker, 'Euhemeros und seine *Hiera Anagraphe* bei den christlichen
Schriftstellern', *Philologus* 64 (1905), 465–72.

[124] For the position that Hecataeus of Abdera offered a 'euhemerist' interpretation
before Euhemerus and that he is the source of Diodorus' account of the ancient Egyptians
(so extensively cited by Eusebius), and furthermore that Euhemerus borrowed from
Hecataeus, see O. Murray, 'Hecataeus of Abdera and Pharaonic Kingship', *JEA* 56 (1970),
141–70, esp. 151. He had been preceded by F. Jacoby, 'Euemeros', *RE* 6 (1904), col. 958, and
Brown, 'Euhemerus and the Historians', 265. Murray's conclusions have been widely
accepted; but Sacks, *Diodorus Siculus and the First Century*, 56–9, has persuasively questioned this notion of Diodorus' slavish copying of sources, and shown the possible extent
of Diodoran ownership to the material in Book 1. For the historiographical context of
Hecataeus, see Bickerman, 'Origenes gentium', 74.

[125] *PE* 1.9.29.

[126] For a representative example of the use of allegory to appropriate foreign elements
into a Greek worldview, see Richter, 'Plutarch on Isis and Osiris'.

[127] *Ap.* 2.1.2.

[128] *PE* 1.10.55.

impious thing to honour with the adorable name of God those mortals who have long been lying among the dead, and have not even left a memorial of themselves as virtuous men, but have passed on examples of extreme incontinence and intemperance, and cruelty and madness, for those who come after them to follow.'[129] In fact, Eusebius' need for his sources to be euhemeristic is probably the reason he chose Diodorus.[130] This author of a voluminous universal history had offered a fully euhemeristic account of the early Egyptian 'gods'. In fact, Diodorus has been named 'the greatest euhmerist after Euhemerus',[131] and hence it was appropriate to choose him as a source. Later, Eusebius would assert:

The discoverers of the things supposed to be good and useful to the body, or certain rulers and kings, or even enchanters and magicians, though by nature mortal and subjected to the misfortunes of humanity, were called saviours and gods as the providers of good things, and men transferred the august conception which was implanted in them by nature to those whom they supposed to be benefactors.[132]

The historical rationalization that supports this sort of interpretation is fundamental to Eusebius' argument. That the mythic figures were in fact men and not gods deflated the power of traditional polytheism. Sirinelli noted that Eusebius' euhemerism is 'a rationalist history charged with reducing the objects of pagan faith to simple events'.[133] As mortal men and women, these individuals were considered the founders of nations and representatives of distinctively national ways of life. They were firmly embedded within a fully historical and ethnic context.[134] Eusebius' argument falls if the allegorists can successfully dehistoricize the mythical characters. Hence, he would offer a sustained polemic against this rival interpretation of the narrative. But, first, we should gain a

[129] *PE* 2.4.1. Cp. Lactantius *Div. Inst.* 1.18–11, 13–19, 22 (Ennius' translation of Euhemerus is quoted directly at 1.11).

[130] He explicitly states that he could have used the Egyptian Manetho as a source for Egyptian history (2.praef.5).

[131] Bounoure, 'Eusèbe citateur de Diodore', 433, citing J. P. Jacobsen, *Les Mânes* (Paris: E. Champion, 1924), 2.89.

[132] *PE* 2.6.13.

[133] J. Sirinelli, *Les vues historiques d'Eusèbe de Césarée durant la période prénicéene*, Faculté des Lettres et Sciences Humaines, Publications de la Section de Langues et Litteratures 10 (Dakar: Universite de Dakar, 1961), 186.

[134] In effect, Eusebius wants to destroy the myth–history distinction by asserting that the myth *is* history. In a way, he twists the myths just as much as he accuses the allegorists of doing, only in the opposite direction.

proper perspective of the nature of Eusebius' argument, for which his euhemeristic historicizing is so vital.

Establishing the humanity and historicity of the figures narrated in the early stories made it possible for Eusebius to connect the nations historically through an account of the travels of those figures. In Philo's narrative, Kronos, king of the first city, Byblos, had given Egypt to Taautos as his kingdom;[135] while Athena herself was seen as being Phoenician, since she was Kronos' daughter.[136] This sort of claim asserts Phoenician primacy over Egypt. In Diodorus' Egyptian narrative, however, the foundations of many contemporary cities are linked to the extensive travels of Osiris.[137] The myth thus maps out (literally) the primacy of Osiris and the indebtedness of the cities now found in other nations to this Egyptian king. These cities have connections rooted in Egyptian national history. In some sense, this relatedness of various cities to Egypt undermines any claims they might make to primal origins and their own national foundation myths. These narratives of descent offer competing stories of the way the world was, which nation's cities could claim the deepest roots in the history of the world, and also which nations could claim to be the source of benefactions to other nations.[138]

These sorts of remarks were made by Eusebius' sources, but for his own part, Eusebius seems to be unconcerned about who came first, the Phoenicians or the Egyptians. As mentioned above, he allows this kind of tension to stand between the Phoenician and Egyptian narratives. Of course, he does place the Phoenician account before the Egyptian account and so may have leanings towards Phoenician primacy. But in the overall scope of the narrative of descent, it does not matter which of these two nations and its distinctive theology came first. Before his quotation of Diodorus on the Egyptians, Eusebius makes an interesting observation: 'Of course, when the Egyptian and the Phoenician theology were thus run together in a mixed up manner, the superstition of ancient error naturally ruled among most of the nations.'[139] This highlights not only the negative nature of their impact upon other nations, but also the fact that the supremacy of either one over the other is irrelevant.

---

[135] *PE* 1.10.38.   [136] *PE* 1.10.18.   [137] *PE* 2.1.9–13.

[138] See Bickerman, 'Origenes gentium', 74.

[139] *PE* 2.1.52. The sentiment will come up again at 8.8.44 and 8.9.11. The statement here recalls the passage from Plato's *Laws* 3.692d–693a: 'all the *genê* of the Greeks would be mixed up with each other, barbarians with Greeks and Greeks with barbarians'. A somewhat interesting parallel is found at Plutarch, *V. Fab. Max.*, 21.2: 'War, mingling together all things, considers race least of all.' See also, Herodotus, 1.146 and Polybius, 2.7.6.

To grasp the importance of what Eusebius is doing, it may be helpful to compare his approach with that of Diodorus.[140] The first three books of Diodorus' *Bibliothēkē* contain the parallel stories of the rise of civilization transmitted by various nations. The stories of the Egyptians take up the bulk of the first book. Book 2 includes the accounts of the Assyrians, Medes, Indians, Scythians, and Amazons, and Book 3 contains those of Africans, Amazons, and Atlantaeans. Each of these nation's stories make claims to contributions towards the advancement of civilization and the birth of early culture heroes in their own country.[141] Diodorus allows these rival claims to stand without resolution. But the reason he does so is to grant a sort of ecumenical validity to each of the nations. For him, each people were able to make progress by their own benefactors to the point where they now all shared a sort of civilizational *koinē*. K. Sacks writes: 'As Diodorus carefully celebrates the accomplishments of all culture heroes, Greek and barbarian, necessity and individual benefactors work in harmony and emphasize his universalistic sympathies.'[142]

For Eusebius, however, the acceptance of the rival claims of the Phoenicians and the Egyptians, and the marginalization of any conflict between them,[143] serves to highlight the place of the Greek *ethnos* in ancient cultural history. The primary purpose of telling their stories is to show the ultimate late emergence and dependency of the Greeks upon them. The fact of the general similarities between the Phoenician and Egyptian theologies and religious practices, and the fact that they both greatly predate the Greeks is ample ammunition for Eusebius' apologetic project. As other nations had attempted to deride the claims of Hellenocentrism,[144] so also Eusebius is attempting to supplant the claims of the Greeks. Later, he will claim that it was the ancient Hebrews (not the

---

[140] In the following remarks, I am particularly indebted to the excellent treatment of Sacks, *Diodorus Siculus and the First Century*, 55–82.

[141] For example, the invention of letters is claimed by the Egyptians (1.69.4), the Ethiopians (3.3.4–5), and the Phoenicians (3.67.1), while the Etruscans claim to have perfected the alphabet (5.40.2).

[142] Sacks, *Diodorus Siculus and the First Century*, 68.

[143] The Phoenician narrative attempted to claim supremacy for itself by having Egypt be given to a Phoenician ruler. Likewise, the Egyptian narrative attempted to assert its own supremacy by having its own Osiris found cities in Phoenicia, Greece, India, and elsewhere. These claims are relegated to the sources which Eusebius is quoting; but he never affirms or denies the primacy of either nation.

[144] See especially, Bickerman, 'Origenes gentium'.

Phoenicians or Egyptians) who gave benefits to humankind.[145] The way of life that the Greeks derived from the other two nations does not (despite their own assertions) display benefactions so much as harmful and damaging customs and practices.

The sort of claim Eusebius is making places him within a tradition of anti-Hellenic historiography, which minimized the antiquity and bene-factions of the Greek *ethnos*.[146] 'We have often said before that the things of the Greeks are shreds and tidbits overheard (*parakousmata*) from those [Phoenicians and Egyptians] ..., introducing, on the one hand, nothing native in their own records concerning the gods, but falling into the mythologies of those from outside.'[147] Eusebius' repeated avowals of Greek lateness and dependency sought to disenfranchise the Greeks from any claims to chronological, technological, or religious and philo-sophical superiority based upon assertions of antiquity.

For this claim to be effective, however, Eusebius knew that he had to deal with rival interpretations of the narrative of descent, and in par-ticular, the allegorical interpretations (2.4–3.13).[148] Plutarch had pro-vided a taxonomy of interpretations of myth in a work known by Eusebius, the *De Iside et Osiride*, and had gone from the lower-level interpretation to the higher (which he preferred):

1. euhemerism (the characters are humans)
2. daemonological (the characters are great daemons)
3. Stoic physical allegoresis (the characters represent physical phenomena)
4. philosophical allegoresis (the characters represent metaphysical principles).[149]

---

[145] See Chapter 4.

[146] The bibliography is quite extensive on the accusations of Greek lateness; most importantly, see Pilhofer, *Presbyteron Kreitton*; Boys-Stones, *Post-Hellenistic Philosophy*, 176–202; Ridings, *The Attic Moses*.

[147] *PE* 2.1.53–4. Cp. Celsus *ap.* Origen, *C. Cels.* 3.16; 6.7; Tatian *Or.* 40.1. On the notion of shreds of ancient wisdom preserved in the poets, see Droge, *Homer or Moses?*, 77, 98; Boys-Stones, *Post-Hellenistic Philosophy*, 28–43. In addition to his accounts of Phoenicians and Egyptians, his treatment of Atlantaeans and Panchaeans (2.2.35) function in the same way.

[148] Lactantius seemed to have sensed a similar need in his own euhemeristic argument; see *Div. Inst.* 1.12, 17.

[149] Plutarch, *De Is. Et Os.*, 20.358*eff*; for useful discussion, see Richter, 'Plutarch on Isis and Osiris', 203–04, and P. Hardie, 'Plutarch and the Interpretation of Myth', *ANRW* II.33.6 (1992), 4761–75.

Philo of Byblos had been primarily concerned with physical allegory; Eusebius, however, gave attention to both physical and philosophical allegory.[150] He claimed that the allegorists were motivated by embarrassment over the stories handed down by their fathers. These allegorists, 'having woke up as it were from a deep slumber, and cleared the eye of the soul from an ancient film, became conscious of the deep folly of the error of their fathers . . .'. Some adopted atheism, Eusebius continues, 'while others, who shrank from the dogma of atheism, neither stood upon their old ways, nor withdrew from them altogether, but preferring to flatter and serve their native doctrine, they declared that the histories about those gods celebrated among them were true myths, having been fabricated by the poets, and said that physical theories were concealed in them'.[151] Again, the allegorists were eager 'to palliate the paternal error (*to patrikon hamartēma*)', Eusebius declares, and, 'as if ashamed of the theologies of their forefathers, which each found from their own [traditions], they contrived respectable explanations for the myths about the gods, as no one dared to disturb the customs of their fathers, but paid great honour to antiquity, and to the familiar training which had grown with them from their boyhood'.[152]

Eusebius therefore turns to a sustained criticism of allegory, which is, at the same time, a defence of the euhemeristic approach. A second extract from Clement's *Protrepticus* provides proof that the gods of mythology were actually mortals by systematically showing that certain renowned temples are actually tombs of the dead who were honoured there.[153] Examples from the allegorists' own writings are given in the extracts of Plutarch's (otherwise lost) *De Daedalis Plataeensibus*[154] and the extant *De Iside et Osiride*, and from Porphyry's *Epistola ad Anebonem*, *De Abstinentia*, and *De Statuis*. Eusebius finds problematic the fact that each of these authors offers numerous allegorical equivalences for each god or goddess: they give 'first one allegorical rendering and afterwards another'.[155] Furthermore, the very existence of statues, which

---

[150] See especially his distinction between the two kinds of allegory at 3.6.7; or also 2.6.17.

[151] *PE* 2.4.4–5.   [152] *PE* 2.6.17 and 19.   [153] *PE* 2.6.1–10.

[154] On the authenticity of the passages, see P. Decharme, 'Note sur un fragment des "Daedala" de Plutarque', in *Mélanges Henri Weil: Recueil de mémoires concernant l'histoire et la littérature grecques dédié à Henri Weil* (Paris: Thorin, 1898), 111–17, who claims (rightly) that they must be the thoughts of an interlocutor (because the defence of *physical* allegoresis is not Plutarchean) in a genuinely Plutarchean dialogue (based upon stylistic considerations).

[155] *PE* 3.3.12.

Porphyry attempts to defend in *De Statuis*, undermines the claims of the allegorists; for whom else do the statues represent than humans? And if they were meant to symbolize physical forces, human bodies are inappropriate corollaries. On the contrary, the existence of statues in religious cult supports the euhemerist interpretation.[156] Furthermore, even if the ancients actually did mean to represent physical phenomena in their stories, it is inappropriate to venerate irrational and lifeless elements rather than the Creator of those elements.[157]

Throughout his criticisms of allegory, Eusebius uses a distinctive terminology in describing such interpretations. At 1.9.25, he describes the allegorists whom Philo opposes as those who reduce 'forcibly (*bebiasmenōs*) and untruly ... the myths concerning the gods to allegories and physical interpretations and theories'. Again, at 2.praef.3, he refers to physical explanations as 'forced'. To see Demeter, Korē and Dionysus as symbolic of physical forces was to introduce 'a forced (*bebiasmenon*) and untrue embellishment of their myths'.[158] The Greek physical theories are 'strange and not beneficial, or rather forced (*bebiasmenas*) and incoherent'.[159] Or again, they contain nothing divine, but only 'a forced and deceptive physiology having a solemnity from outside'.[160] Such language represents the interpretive activity of the allegorists as something unnatural, which violates the simple meaning of the texts, wresting from them something that is otherwise not there. On the other hand, his own historical rendering appears (so he thinks) natural and effortless.[161]

Eusebius' critique of allegory is absolutely essential to the overall argument of the first half of the *Praeparatio*. If the allegorical approach is granted validity, then there will always be a way out of the barrage of Eusebius' criticisms regarding the impiety and irrationality exemplified by the narrative of descent. One can always respond (as Plutarch and Porphyry wanted to) that the myths were not meant to be taken literally, but were actually representative of a higher, more sublime truth. According to this view, the narrative did not depict historical events at all, but rather ahistorical and timeless realities. Not only would Eusebius' accusations of irrationality and shamefulness not stand up, his claims for

---

[156] *PE* 3.3.13–15.   [157] *PE* 3.4.4; 3.6.4 ff.   [158] *PE* 2.6.18.   [159] *PE* 2.7.9.

[160] *PE* 3.3.21. See also, e.g. 1.10.55; 4.1.6; 11.6.23. It is unfortunate that Mras' index offers only two references.

[161] See the characterization of his interpretation as unambiguous (*anamphilektōs*) at *Proph. Ecl.* 1.12 (*PG* 22.1068C).

the dependency and inferiority of the Greek nation would lose their force. Hence, Eusebius grasped the necessity of debunking the allegorists. His critique of allegory in the second and third books of the *Praeparatio* is not a disconnected attack upon a separate aspect of 'pagan religion'. Instead, it is part of a coherent presentation of one particular reading of the primitive stories as history because rival readings are shown to fail.

National character

The second driving theme of this narrative of descent is the distinctive character (*tropos*)[162] that is portrayed by the figures of the story, and so is representative of the nations of which they are the founders. Hence, the narrative of descent performs the function of providing an account of a people's identity: who are they? What sort of character do they bear, or what sort of people are they? And, why do they continue the practices that had become part of their communal life? The issue is one of national character and the traits or customs that make one nation distinct from others. In the present narrative of descent, it is the religious practices and customs that primarily establish these contours of national identity. This national identity is embodied in a way of life, religious customs, practices, and theological understanding of the forefathers of a nation. Theology and philosophy are both included as national character traits. Particular ways of thinking about the world and about the gods infuse the particular way of living in the world and relating to the gods that a given nation marks out as its own. Theology is embodied, therefore, in an ethnic way of life, and this is thoroughly rooted in the stories of a nation's past. Eusebius explicitly states that his purpose in giving the narrative of descent had been to portray what sort of character the Greek theology produced.

The character of [the Greek theology] is proved to be something of the kind which has been already made manifest by the words quoted from the Greek historians themselves. And this character we have with good reason set before our readers in the beginning of this our *Evangelic Preparation* for their judgement and decision, that both we and those who as yet have no experience of this subject, may learn for ourselves: what we were long ago and from what sort of

---

[162] Eusebius also uses the term *tropos* when referring to Christian ethnic identity at *HE* 1.4.4, 13.

forefathers we have sprung, by how great evils we were previously fettered, and in how great a stupor of impiety and ignorance of God our souls were buried.[163]

For Eusebius, the narrative of descent, whether in its Phoenician, Egyptian, or Greek stages, portrayed a theology and way of life that is irrational and superstitious. At best, the ancestors of those nations worshipped astral phenomena as gods and offered plant sacrifices to them. From this less daemonically fettered stage, the ancient astral theology soon slipped into more depraved theological forms. The ancients began to deify their parents as gods and even went a step further and established the deification of animals.[164] Furthermore, the sacrifices offered to these gods became more degraded: at first only animals were sacrificed, but then human sacrifice was instituted. Introducing the sacrifice of Kronos' only-begotten son, Philo is quoted: 'it was customary (*ethos ēn*)' for rulers to offer up children as sacrifices to wicked daemons in times of emergency.[165]

Such religious practices served as markers of the depth of depravity to which the religious customs of the nations sank. And, such depravity does not bode well in Eusebius' evaluation of the theology passed down from the Phoenician and Egyptian nations to the Greeks. He concludes his survey of Philo's writings with the following statement: 'Such then is the character (*tropon*) of the theology of the Phoenicians, from which the word of salvation in the gospel teaches us to flee with averted eyes, and earnestly to seek the remedy for this madness of the ancients.'[166] Following the selection from Diodorus on the Egyptian theology, Eusebius offers his own comments. The character (*tropos*) of Egyptian theology being such as it was, Eusebius claims that Christians have naturally 'spat out (*kataptusantes*) this theology—or rather, shameful atheism—of the Egyptians'.[167] The only redemption and freedom from 'such evils' is found in the evangelic teaching, which 'preaches the

---

[163] *PE* 2.5.1; cp. 6.11.83.

[164] See Athenagoras, *Leg.* 14. For a general survey of Christian views on Egyptian animal worship, see Smelik and Hemelrijk, 'Who Knows Not What Monsters Demented Egypt Worships?', 1981–96.

[165] *PE* 1.10.44. H. Doergens, 'Eusebius von Casarea als Darsteller der phönizischen Religion', *Forschungen zur christlicher Literatur- und Dogmengeschichte* 12.5 (1915), 11, summarizes: 'the lewd sins of incest, sodomy, marriage to mothers, the gruesome murder of burdensome family members, human sacrifice, desecration of corpses, and cannibalism'.

[166] *PE* 1.10.54.

[167] *PE* 2.1.51. Plutarch, *De Is. Et Os.*, 20.358e, cites Aeschylus (Mette, fr. 310b, pr 112), 'it is necessary to spit (ἀποπτύσαι) and cleanse the mouth' from the Egyptian, barbarizing accounts of Isis; the metaphor recurs at 2.4.5. See Richter, 'Plutarch on Isis and Osiris', 200.

recovery of sight to those who are blind in their minds'.[168] Eusebius
concluded the narrative of descent, stating: 'With good reason then do
we avow that we have been freed from all this and rescued from the long
and antiquated delusion as from some terrible and most grievous
disease.'[169] Thus, for Eusebius, the narrative of descent is fundamental
to his argument and is fraught with polemical weight, the significance of
which is not to be second-guessed.

Eusebius' attack on national character is not, however, limited to the
distant past. The ancient way of life had continued up to the time of
Eusebius in the practices subsumed under the heading of 'political
theology'—that is, the theology manifested in the local cult sites of the
poleis throughout the eastern Roman world.[170] Between the cult practices, as well as the Greek theology justifying these practices, and the
histories of national ancestry lay 'an unbroken tradition'[171] that infused
polis religion with significance and gravity. Contemporary cult was
firmly rooted in the ancient past.

Already, in the narrative of descent, connections have been made from
national antiquity up to the present, a cultic landscape has been mapped
for the present by being planted in the past.[172] The story is given
credibility in the physical existence of temples and statues and in
the continuation of religious customs from earlier times. Numerous
examples may be found in the segment on the ancient Phoenicians.
Many Phoenician place-names continue the memory of their eponymous mythological characters. The mountains of Cassius, Libanus,
Antilibanus and Brathy received their names from the grandsons of
Genos, whose huge size and stature were unsurpassed in the ancient
world.[173] The statue of Agrotes,[174] the temple founded by the Dioscuri on
Mt Cassius,[175] the *baetylia* devised by Ouranos,[176] or the temple of the

---

[168] *PE* 2.1.51.   [169] *PE* 2.4.1.

[170] See Chapter 6.

[171] Doergens, 'Eusebius von Casarea als Darsteller der griechische Religion', 12.

[172] This is what Mortley has aptly termed 'remythicization' (*The Idea of Universal History*, 95–6).

[173] *PE* 1.10.9. Mt Cas(s)ius received attention as a sacred locale throughout the Roman period; see the emperor Hadrian's poem to Zeus Casius (*Anth. Pal.* 6.332, with SHA, *Hadr.* 14.3); also, Ammianus Marcellinus, 22.14.

[174] *PE* 1.10.12.   [175] *PE* 1.10.20.

[176] *PE* 1.10.23; cp. Damascius, *Phil. Hist.* 72F, for *baitylia* on Mt Lebanon. On ancient *baitylia* generally, see G. F. Moore, 'Baetylia', *AJA* 7 (1903), 198–208; G. Zuntz, 'Baitylos and Bethel', *C&M* 8 (1945), 169–219; and F. Millar, *The Roman Near East. 31BC–AD337* (Cambridge: Harvard University Press, 1993), 13–15.

fallen star at Tyre founded by Astarte[177]—all these were claimed as still standing in Phoenicia. The spot where Ouranos was finally killed by Kronos and his blood dripped into the streams 'is still pointed out to this day'.[178] Hence, Philo's testimony contains 'things of earlier date than all poets and historians, and derives the credibility of [his] statements from the names and history of the gods still prevailing in the cities and villages of Phoenicia, and from the mysteries celebrated among each people'.[179]

The topographical and monumental features of the narrative of descent were present reminders of a traditional way of life that had continued since the times recounted in the story. The cultic activities performed at local shrines were steeped in antiquity; the present practices were rooted in the institutions of the ancients. Therefore, Eusebius provides abundant space for a polemic against these current practices under the rubric of 'political theology'. His critique covers three main areas: the prophetic messages delivered at the oracular cults (4.1–3), the impious practices at the cult sites, especially sacrifices (4.4–23 and Book 5), and the notion of Fate (Book 6), which was an essential presupposition for the belief in oracles as well as the practices revolving around human interaction with daemonic forces (that is magic as manipulation of the gods/daemons).[180]

I do not intend to offer a survey of his argument in the area of political theology here,[181] but rather to show its connection and coherence to the narrative of descent that has gone before it.[182] At the beginning of his treatment of oracles, Eusebius refers to the use of the general heading 'political theology' as that 'which is especially enforced by the laws, being both ancient and paternal'.[183] The submission to daemons localized at the cult sites is referred to as 'the error passed down from the fathers' (*tēs patroparadotou planēs*).[184] The temples are called 'antiquated (*pepalaiō-mena*) shrines of the error of all nations'.[185]

---

[177] *PE* 1.10.31.   [178] *PE* 1.10.29.   [179] *PE* 1.10.55.

[180] For a general survey of Eusebius' critique of Fate, see Chesnut, *The First Christian Histories*, 33–64.

[181] For further discussion, see Chapter 6.

[182] *Pace* Sirinelli, *Les vues historiques d'Eusèbe de Césarée*, 199–200, who claims that Eusebius has left history behind when he introduces the four categories of divinity: Supreme God, heavenly deities, daemons, heroes (at *PE* 4.5). While I agree that the fourfold division seems to be purely theological, it is nonetheless introduced to understand the *historical* activity centred around oracle sites.

[183] *PE* 4.1.2; cp. Julian, *Or.* 11.152d.   [184] *PE* 4.4.1.   [185] *PE* 4.4.1.

In his argument in Book 5 on the failure of the oracles and their daemons,[186] Eusebius only vaguely draws a line between the ancient past and the present. The reader is never sure whether the events and practices under discussion are current ones or those of long ago (though he confidently asserts that the oracles have sunk into obscurity as a result of Christ's victory over daemons).[187] This is because the cult sites of the present are steeped in, and manifestations of, their ancient beginnings. Eusebius quotes Plutarch's *De Defectu Oraculorum* that current religious practices, 'the sacrifices, initiations and mythologies, though scattered about, often save and preserve traces and indications' of the distinctions of virtue among men and daemons of long ago.[188] Later, to show that it is daemons who preside over the oracle cults, Eusebius says that he must examine 'the oracles most ancient in time, being celebrated in the mouths of all the Greeks and passed down in the schools throughout the cities to those attending for their education'.[189] Then he offers the otherwise lost work of Oenomaus, 'who refutes the most ancient oracles...'.[190] Ambiguous oracular responses have been foolishly followed by rulers, according to Eusebius, 'from ancient times to our own'.[191]

The ancient character (*tropos*) attacked by Eusebius was of continuing relevance in his own day.[192] Hence, the contemporary cult practices are the continuation of those begun in ancient times. For Eusebius and his readers, the past was not 'a foreign country', but grew out of the stories that made sense of the present and infused the present with meaning and

[186] For a useful survey of the waning of the principal oracle sites (Delphi, Didyma, Claros, and Trophonius) and discussion of the related views of Plutarch, Porphyry and Oenomaus, see S. Levin, 'The Old Greek Oracles in Decline', *ANRW* 2.18.2 (1989), 1599–1649. For a general overview of the decline of oracles during the third century followed by renewal in the early fourth, based especially upon epigraphic evidence, see J. Geffcken, *The Last Days of Greco-Roman Paganism*, trans. S. MacCormack (Amsterdam: North-Holland Publishing Co., 1978), 25–34. The continuing importance of sacrifice and ritual during late antiquity is treated well by K. W. Harl, 'Sacrifice and Pagan Belief in Fifth- and Sixth-Century Byzantium', *P&P* 128 (1990), 7–27.

[187] See especially 4.4. One is never sure whether the daemons who are castigated in *PE* 5 are identical with the deified mortals of the historical narrative of descent. Dionysus the mortal man from Book 2 is now Dionysus the daemon. Part of the reason for this 'discrepancy' may be that he is drawing heavily upon Plutarch's *De Iside et Osiride* and *De Defectu Oraculorum*, where one of Plutarch's main characters defends a 'daemono-logical' interpretation of the myths (for instance, 5.5). However, that Eusebius is not just going along with his sources is shown by the fact that he draws the parallel between the daemons discussed in Plutarch with the 'sons of God' from Genesis 6 (*PE* 5.4.9).

[188] *PE* 5.4.3.   [189] *PE* 5.18.1.   [190] *PE* 5.23.4.   [191] *PE* 5.27.5.

[192] In fact, he claims that his description of oracles and their daemons in Book 5 has offered a portrayal of the 'character (*tropos*) of the oracles' (6.praef.1).

significance. The narrative of descent, while describing events long past, nonetheless lived on, embodied in the customs and religious habits of the present. Persistent threads and traces of the past shaped the current way of life and practices of those who saw in the oracular shrines sites of hoary antiquity and the deep traditions of their forefathers.

CONCLUSIONS

I have here claimed that the most fruitful way of understanding the unified argument of the first six books of the *Praeparatio* is to see Eusebius' primary aim as the presentation of a narrative of the earliest times and a polemic against the issues arising from that narrative. His narrative draws connections between the nations (showing especially the dependency of the Greeks upon the others) and exhibits the distinctive *tropos* embodied in their shared way of life (along with its continuing manifestations). Even while Eusebius defends the historicity of the narrative, he attacks the way of life embodied in that narrative. In this way, he can defend the withdrawal and apostasy of Christians from the paternal way of life. Assertions that Eusebius is concerned with 'pagan religion' misrepresent the argument of the *Praeparatio* by ignoring its concern with matters of historic, ethnic identity. The 'pagans' are members of peoples who attempt to claim through a narrative of descent ancient origins and benefactions for themselves, but whose very claims, in Eusebius' construal, fatally undermine their position. Thus the *Praeparatio*'s apologetic is grounded in constructions of an ethnic past and an ongoing ethnic identity.

4

Rewriting Hebrew History: The Descent of the Ancient Hebrews

INTRODUCTION

In the first six books of the *Praeparatio*, Eusebius had aimed to construct a narrative of national descent that emphasized the recent arrival of the Greeks on the historical scene and the depraved and irrational nature of the national character, which was typified in the ancestral way of life of their nation. In Book 7, he turns to the account of a nation whose superiority over the nations of the first narrative he wants to emphasize. This second narrative centres upon the lives of the ancient Hebrews. Whereas the Greeks were shown as latecomers to the history of civilization and were dependent for their customs, religious practices, and theologies upon older nations, Eusebius depicts the Hebrews as the most ancient *ethnos*. Furthermore, while the nations of the Phoenicians, Egyptians, and Greeks were represented as possessing depraved and irrational characteristics, the Hebrews would exhibit piety, true rationality, and closeness to the divine.

The narrative of Hebrew descent would also provide an explanation for why Christians did not adopt the way of life of the Jews. The Jewish *ethnos*, Eusebius emphatically declares, arose as a corrupted form of the Hebrew *ethnos* as a result of Egyptianization before the exodus of the people under Moses. Eusebius can thus undergird an essentially anti-Jewish sentiment by retelling Jewish history as a deviation from the larger story of the ancient Hebrews. After the Jews, Eusebius can also pick up a second line of the narrative of Greek descent to explain why some Greeks (especially Plato) did in fact possess a mostly rational form of philosophy. For it was through the travels of Plato and other philosophers to the land of Palestine that one of the most important 'migrations of knowledge' occurred. These philosophers had found nothing worthy of the name of philosophy in Greece and hence had been forced to borrow, or 'plagiarize', from the Hebrew wisdom encapsulated in the writings of Moses.

This narrative of the second half of the *Praeparatio* is clearly central to Eusebius' argument, and contains much that is of interest for a variety of discussions on different aspects of Eusebius' thought. Here one can see the roots of the hagiographical impulse,[1] the theorization of asceticism, the notion of a holy man's life as an icon, the Christian incorporation of, and interaction with, Platonism, and the continued adoption of the methodology of nationalistic historiography. All these will come into play in the following analysis of how the narrative of Hebrew descent functions within the ethnic argumentation of the *Praeparatio*.

Both this and the following chapter will treat *Praeparatio* 7–15 as a continuous, if convoluted, narrative of descent, drawing attention to certain salient metaphors that give force to the narrative. Both will attend to particular elements of the narrative that are central to the argumentative force of Eusebius' apologetic. One of these is the portrayal of the Hebrew forefathers as models of virtue; their lives are conceived as icons of national character typified by friendship with God. Another is the employment of boundary-solidifying mechanisms such as ethnonymic distinctions and differing approaches to Moses' Law, which serve to demarcate firmly the division between Hebrew and Jewish identity. The degree to which the boundary nonetheless maintains some permeability will be examined subsequently. The delineation of boundaries and representations of identities in this portion of Eusebius' argument are complex since he is attempting to claim the ancient Scriptures as Christianity's own while simultaneously distancing themselves from the Jews as far as possible. Furthermore, Hellenistic Jewish authors who were influential on,[2] and carried considerable esteem with, the Christian apologist had

---

[1] For the phrase, see P. Cox Miller, 'Strategies of Representation in Collective Biography: Constructing the Subject as Holy', in T. Hägg and P. Rousseau (eds), *Greek Biography and Panegyric in Late Antiquity* (Berkeley: University of California Press, 2000), 222; A. P. Johnson, 'Ancestors as Icons: The Lives of Hebrew Saints in Eusebius' *Praeparatio Evangelica*', *GRBS* 44 (2004), 245–64.

[2] Josephus offered a model historical and apologetic approach, while Philo of Alexandria had developed a Logos theology, which would carry due weight in Eusebius' own formulations (see, e.g. the quotations from Philo at 7.13).

to be saved from the dismal portrayal of Jewish history and identity that Eusebius formulated.

THE NARRATIVE OF DESCENT

Eusebius makes a clear break from the narrative of Books 1–6 in his introduction to Book 7, and reiterates the main issues that his apology seeks to confront. With typical concern for order and arrangement, and in order to alert his reader to what his argument has accomplished thus far and what it will set out to do in the remainder of the work, he writes: 'Since it has been proven that our abandonment of the false theology of Greeks and barbarians alike has not been made without reason, but with well-judged and prudent consideration, it is now time to solve the second accusation by stating the cause of our claiming a share in the Hebrew doctrines.'[3]

Eusebius intends this second narrative to stand in marked contrast to the first. The portrait of a nation that can meet the standards of wisdom, piety, and truthfulness, which the Phoenicians, Egyptians, and Greeks had been found to fall so far short of, will emerge in his telling of the Hebrew past.[4] Whereas the other nations had fallen from astral theology to the deification of humans and animals, the Hebrews looked beyond astral phenomena to their Creator. And while the Greeks fell into the depraved superstition of oracles founded on the work of daemons, the ancient Hebrews had worshipped the one God with true spiritual devotion and escaped the tyranny of daemons. This contrast between the first and second narrative will be reiterated throughout the second half of the *Praeparatio*. In fact, the narrative of the Hebrew nation, in many respects, parallels the narrative of Greek descent in the first half of the *Praeparatio*: the character of the nation's forefathers (7.3–8); cosmogonical reflections (7.9–22);[5] Hebrew allegorists (8.9–10); the Hebrew notion of Providence (8.13–14).[6]

---

[3] *PE* 7.1.2. For the centrality of Book 7 to the entire *PE*, see König-Ockenfels, 'Christliche Deutung der Weltgeschichte bei Eusebs von Cäsarea', 356: 'The especial high point of the *PE* is the seventh book.'

[4] See G. Schroeder and E. Des Places, *Eusèbe de Césarée. La Préparation Évangélique, Livre VII*, SC 215 (Paris: Les Éditions du Cerf, 1975), 41–2.

[5] Note the explicit comparisons to Phoenician, Egyptian, and Greek cosmogonies at 7.9.2; 7.11.13; 7.12.1; 7.17.1.

[6] In marked contrast to the Greek notion of Fate criticized in Book 6.

Reformulation of National Decline

Eusebius begins the second half of the *Praeparatio* with a recapitulation of his general theory of national decline that had already arisen in the first half, especially at 1.9.13–19.[7] There, he had portrayed the history of the nations (explicitly excluding the Hebrews from this narrative, however) as moving from a less depraved, less superstitious form of polytheism to lower and more impious practices and doctrines. God had originally assigned astral polytheism to the nations, but they had quickly rejected it for the deification of humans and animals, the making of statues, sacrifices and enslavement to wicked daemons. Hence, he declares: 'So then among the oldest of mankind there was no mention of a Theogony, either Greek or barbarian, nor any erection of lifeless statues, nor all the silly talk that there is now about the naming of the gods both male and female.'[8] In this context, he had attempted to portray ancient theology in as good a light as he could allow. At least astral polytheism had not sunk as low as later forms of polytheism embodied by the Phoenicians, Egyptians, and Greeks.[9]

Now, at 7.2, as Eusebius goes back to briefly retell this narrative of decline, the image of the theology of the ancients darkens and takes on a bleaker tone. The movement is still one of downward corruption, but now the earliest stage is not one 'assigned by God' to the nations, nor is it merely a matter of ignorant and primitive failure to recognize the Creator of the stars. The depraved search for pleasure, and devotion to pleasure as a wicked daemon, is now the key factor in explaining the movement of the nations towards decline and corruption.[10] According to Eusebius, the roots of astral polytheism were embedded in the ancient supposition that pleasure came from the heavenly bodies. The deification of humans had resulted from their services in the pursuit of pleasure.[11] And finally, some philosophers resorted to atheism out of embarrassment for this state of affairs, while others (clearly the Epicureans) declared the life of philosophy to be bound up in pleasure.[12] 'And so in this way the whole

---

[7] *PE* 7.2.

[8] *PE* 1.9.16.

[9] Cp. Lactantius, *Div. Inst.* 2.14.

[10] For general discussion see Schroeder, *Eusèbe de Césarée*, 28–40.

[11] Cp. Eusebius, *Theoph.* 3.61.

[12] While the Epicureans may have been in Eusebius' sights in this passage, Socrates himself had referred to pleasure as a goddess at *Phileb.* 12B (which is misunderstood by Origen at *C. Cels.* 4.48, even though he seems to have taken it rightly at 1.25).

race of mankind has become enslaved to the goddess, or rather the foul
and licentious daemon, pleasure, as to a harsh and most cruel mistress,
and was involved in all kinds of miseries.'[13]

Dio Chrysostom had already denounced the Epicureans (without
explicitly naming them) for treating pleasure as a goddess: 'These
men, then, despise all things divine, and having set up the image of
one single female divinity, depraved and monstrous, representing a kind
of wantonness or self-indulgent ease and unrestrained lewdness,
to which they gave the name of Pleasure—an effeminate god in
truth—her they prefer in honor and worship....'[14] Dio's attack is
primarily against Epicureans or initiates of certain mystery religions,[15]
as he defends the idea that belief in a supreme god is natural and innate.
The polemic of Eusebius' description is brought into relief against
the backdrop of Dio's account. Eusebius is making a sweeping,
transnational, claim in his assertions about pleasure. The pursuit of
pleasure is the basis for the many manifestations of the theology of the
ancient (non-Hebrew) nations. Hence, Eusebius' brief overview of his
previous narrative offers a generalizing account of what had been
occurring in different ways among the different nations. Besides the
national connections that Eusebius drew in the first narrative, the
insidious daemon of Pleasure was at work among these nations.

Eusebius' vision of decline resonates with that of Romans I: 18–32.
Paul had here painted a picture of human history as one of successive
grades of impiety and depravity resulting from a rejection of the Creator
of all visible phenomena. For Paul, the downward slope issued from
humanity's refusal to give the Creator his due; instead they turned to the
worship of created things and hence were 'handed over' to ever deeper
levels of moral depravity. This way of thinking about decline is echoed
by Eusebius. After all, Eusebius cites *Sapientia* 14.12, 'The devising of
idols was the beginning of wickedness.' In fact, this same line is quoted
in Eusebius' account of decline at 1.9.18 (this is one more reason to
assume that Eusebius wants to recall his previous discussion). And,
in fact, he even quotes the lines of Paul on the deterioration from
heterosexual to same-sex activity that was not natural (*para phusin*).[16]

---

[13] *PE* 7.2.3.

[14] *Or.* 12.36. Translation by J. W. Cohoon, LCL (Cambridge: Harvard University Press,
1939).

[15] His description of worshipping pleasure with 'tinkling cymbals' probably refers to the
Magna Mater or Isis cult.

[16] Rom. 1: 26, quoted at *PE* 7.2.3; the terms 'heterosexual' and 'same-sex' are not meant
to accurately reflect ancient frameworks of sexual activity, see H. N. Parker, 'The Terato-

What distinguishes Eusebius' comments from Paul's is their national context. Paul had been addressing 'the impiety and injustice of humanity (*anthropōn*)' in general.[17] Eusebius, on the other hand, wants to offer a portrayal of decline that applies only to non-Hebrew nations. In order to highlight the greater piety and wisdom of the ancient Hebrews, he must lump all the other nations together under an overarching rubric of irrationality and impiety. His summary at 7.2 does not make the distinctions between Phoenician, Egyptian, and Greek in the way that the narrative of *Praeparatio* 1–6 had: here he merely refers to 'Greeks and barbarians'. But this is for the purpose of being able to castigate all of them collectively with blanket statements and so offer a holistic or universalizing account of national depravity.

At this point, Eusebius offers a striking metaphor: 'So great had been the manifold variety, to speak briefly, of the theology of the other nations, attached to impure and abominable pleasure as its one beginning, and like a hydra of many necks and many heads it is carried out into many various divisions and sections.'[18] This metaphor of pleasure as a many-headed hydra is, so far as I can tell, unique to Eusebius. The metaphorical use of a hydra could be evoked in a multiplicity of contexts from Plato[19] to a number of early Christian authors.[20] But it had not yet been applied to the pursuit of pleasure by the ancient nations. The image of a hydra offered a vivid metaphor of the ways in which a single daemon's activity branched out in various ways in the different nations. The hydra-like manifestations of impiety provide an incisive contrast to the nation of the Hebrews, the lives of whose ancestors Eusebius was about to narrate.

---

genic Grid', in J. P. Hallett and M. B. Skinner (eds), *Roman Sexualities* (Princeton: Princeton University Press, 1997), 47–65.

[17] Rom. 1.18.

[18] *PE* 7.2.5; cp. Eusebius' *Comm. Ps.* 73 (*PG* 23.864B), in reference to the devil working through his many daemons.

[19] *Euthydemus* 297C (referring to sophistical arguments) and *Republic* 3.426E (referring to the proliferation of wrong dealings in the polis under inadequate legal measures). See also, Lucian, *Anach.* 35 (the strength of a well-trained body is like a hydra); Numenius *ap. PE* 14.6.3 (Arcesilaus the academic divided himself in contrary arguments like a hydra).

[20] See, e.g. Irenaeus, *C. Haer.* 1.30.15; Justin, *Dial.* 2 (referring to the many schools of Greek philosophy); Methodius, *Lepr.* 6 (referring to envy) and *Res.* 1.62 (referring to the complexities of an argument); Ps.-Clement, *Hom.* 6.16 (referring to those whom the wise and philosophic person meets as '[Nemean] lions and multifarious hydras'); Macarius Magnes *Apocriticus* 3 (referring to the many anti-Christian arguments); Jerome, *Comm. Ezech.*, praef. (on the Origenist agenda of Rufinus). My collection of examples here expands that in Lampe's *Patristic Greek Dictionary*.

He concludes: 'Such then was the character (*tropos*) of the ancient nations, and of their false theology, as exhibited in the preceding books by the Greek historians and philosophers whom we have brought together.'[21] His aim is to paint a picture of the nations and their way of life, religious customs, and theologies as a stark contrast to the Hebrew character he is about to champion.

The Narrative of Hebrew Descent

In *Praeparatio* 7.3–8.14, Eusebius sets out to provide a coherent account of the ancient Hebrew *ethnos* that will provide valuable material for the apologetic task of defending Christianity's rejection of Greek ancestral ways and adopting that of the 'Jews' (the label used by his opponents). His narrative denies the validity of this criticism by first making a distinction between Hebrews and Jews, and then showing the chronological primacy and superior wisdom of the Hebrews to the Greeks. He even goes a step further, by asserting the direct dependence upon the Hebrews by the best of the Greeks—Plato.[22]

Eusebius begins the narrative by tracing the development of the distinctive way of thinking of the Hebrews from the beginnings of social existence. 'For of all mankind these were the first and sole people who from the very first foundation of social life devoted their thought to rational speculation, and set themselves to study the physical laws of the universe with piety.'[23] Their observation of the physical universe led them to search for the Creator of all these things, for they recognized that a lifeless principle could not be the cause of life, nor could an irrational principle be the cause of rational beings.[24] The physical universe could never have produced life and reason on its own. 'With these and similar thoughts, then, the fathers of Hebrew piety, with purified mind and clear-sighted eyes of the soul, learned from the grandeur and beauty of His creatures to worship God the Creator of all.'[25] Eusebius narrates a story of Hebrew beginnings that stood out against the deterioration of the other ancient nations. The bright eyes of the Hebrews shone out as a solitary light in the midst of the darkened minds of the ethnic landscape of earliest antiquity.

[21] *PE* 7.2.6.   [22] See Chapter 5.   [23] *PE* 7.3.2.
[24] *PE* 7.3.2.   [25] *PE* 7.3.3.

The subsequent narrative continues to follow the intellectual and spiritual progress of the Hebrews. The discovery of the soul, the doctrine of humanity's creation in the image of God, the control over bodily impulses and pleasures, and friendship with God as the 'consummation of all happiness', were all theological advances made by the earliest Hebrews.[26] As a result of their keen pursuit of truth, they were allowed ever greater revelations from God, which included visions of angels and knowledge of the future.[27]

Their pursuit of the Creator and practice of asceticism in striving after the life of the mind formed a special relationship between themselves and God. Eusebius offers a particularly interesting comment here: 'Having then been shown to be both lovers of God and beloved by him,[28] they were declared to be true worshippers and priests of the Most High God, or were deemed worthy to be called "a chosen race (*genos*) and a royal priesthood and holy nation (*ethnos*) of God", and have bequeathed to their descendants a seed of this true piety.'[29] The ascription of titles regarding race, priesthood and, nation to the Hebrews has its roots in the Hebrew Scriptures. Exodus 19: 5–6 (LXX) recorded the words of God to Moses regarding the Jewish people: 'If you heed my voice and observe my covenant, you will be for me a people peculiar from all the nations; for the whole earth is mine. You will be for me a kingly priesthood and a holy nation.'[30]

Allusions to this appellation from Exodus are rare in Jewish literature of the Hellenistic and Roman era.[31] Philo of Alexandria, however, had picked up the phrase in his *De Abrahamo*. After referring to the 'new race of humanity' (*kainou genous anthrōpōn*) established after the Deluge by Noah, he writes: 'The triad [Abraham, Isaac and Jacob] of the one form of the aforementioned race, which is most august and worth defending,

[26] *PE* 7.4. On the 'friends of God' appellation, see Ulrich, *Euseb von Caesarea und die Juden*, 59–60.

[27] *PE* 7.5.1.

[28] This phrase is clearly an allusion to Philo, *Abr.* 50; see also *Quod Omnis* 42. On the relationship of Eusebius to Philo in this passage, see A. P. Johnson, 'Philonic Allusions in Eusebius, *PE* 7.7–8', *CQ* 56 (2006: forthcoming).

[29] *PE* 7.4.6.

[30] Other biblical references to the people as a nation of priests are at Is. 61: 6; Rev. 1: 6; 5: 10; 20: 6.

[31] For a brief discussion and other references, see G. Harvey, *The True Israel: Uses of the Names Jew, Hebrew and Israel in Ancient Jewish and Early Christian Literature* (Leiden: Brill, 1996), 220–1; also, Johnson, 'Philonic Allusions in Eusebius'.

the oracles call "royal" and "priesthood" and holy nation.'[32] It may very well be this characterization by Philo that prompted the author of the New Testament epistle attributed to Peter to apply the appellation in a slightly different form to the Christians. 'You are a chosen race, a royal priesthood, a people for [God's] possession.'[33] The addition of 'chosen race' and 'people for possession' result from combining an allusion to Isaiah 43: 20–1[34] with the Exodus passage. The claim in the New Testament passage is specifically for Christians and made only a generation or so after Philo had written the *De Abrahamo*.[35]

The rather complex allusion to both Philo's *De Abrahamo* and I Peter produce a declaration rich in meaning for Eusebius' construction of both Hebrew and Christian identity. The parallel use by Philo and Eusebius of the Exodus passage to evoke the philosophic and virtuous character of the early Hebrews is striking. The fact that Eusebius' litany of appellations more closely echoes the New Testament passage (especially the use of *eklekton genos*), which definitively gives the appellation to the Christians, while Eusebius specifically speaks of the ancient Hebrews, serves to strengthen the later claim that Christians are merely the restored Hebrew nation.[36] This point will receive more attention at the proper time; for now it suffices to note the reversion of this text, after being appropriated by Christians in the New Testament (and other Christian authors) for themselves, to refer, in Eusebius, back to the Hebrew ancestors once more.

In short, this early portion of the narrative of Hebrew descent articulates a vision of early Hebrew life as one dedicated to the pursuit of the truth beyond the physical world, one that set them apart from the inclinations and ways of life of the other ancient nations. The Hebrews are thus a nation of friends of God—a chosen race, royal priesthood, and holy nation whose (constructed) affinities with later Christians are already being written into Eusebius' narrative.

---

[32] *Abr.* 12.56. Philo had elsewhere referred to the nation as fulfiling a priestly function; see *De Spec. Leg.* 2.163, and also 1.97

[33] I Peter 2: 9.

[34] See J. H. Elliott, *The Elect and the Holy* (Leiden: Brill, 1966), on the appellation of 'royal priesthood'; and for general discussion F. W. Beare, *The First Epistle of Peter* (Oxford: Blackwell, 1958), 100–5. Cp. Gregory Nazianzenus, *Or.* 4.35.

[35] See Beare, *The First Epistle of Peter*, 9–19.

[36] See also its application to the Hebrews by Origen, *C. Cels.* 4.32; 5.10, 43; cp. e.g., Clement, *Protr.* 4, where it is reserved for the Christians.

From here Eusebius begins a series of brief biographical sketches of some of the most distinguished of the Hebrew forefathers. Enos was the first of those 'who hoped to call upon the name of the Lord God'[37] in the period before the Deluge.[38] The Hebrew scriptures, 'accustomed to use names in their proper meaning',[39] called him Enos because the name meant 'true man'.[40] If they had wanted 'to denote the man of the common multitude and the race itself', they would have used the 'suitable and natural appellation' of Adam, meaning 'earth-born'.[41] Enos exhibited the proper use of reason in attaining knowledge of God and recognizing the proper worship due to him. In contrast to those early humans who were steeped in superstition and sought pleasure, like wild beasts casting themselves upon the ground 'in the manifold forms of wickedness',[42] Enos' life was an example of piety and knowledge of God.[43]

Enoch, who 'pleased the Lord and was not to be found, because God translated him',[44] is the second figure in the narrative. Commenting upon the fact that he cannot be found, Eusebius writes: 'It is difficult to find the one who is truly wise,'[45] for, unlike the multitude who frequent the market-place and law courts, the wise person cannot be found in this environment, but has been transferred by God to another world and become a 'friend of God'.[46] His avoidance of crowds and bustle of this ephemeral world marked Enoch as a wise man in the

<hr>

[37] *PE* 7.8.4, quoting from Gen. 4: 26.

[38] Philo's *Abr.* 46, 48 also demarcates the history of the ancient Hebrews into a pre-flood phase and post-flood phase (the first containing the 'trinity' of Enos, Enoch, and Noah, the second that of Abraham, Isaac, and Jacob).

[39] *PE* 7.8.6. κυριολεκτεῖν εἰθισμένη τὰς προσηγορίας.

[40] *PE* 7.8.5. Philo (*Abr.* 7–8), on the other hand, asserts that Enos was the Chaldean form of *anthrōpos*, which means 'lover of hope'. The giving of such a name to him was a favour since it was 'the common name of the [human] race'. Then Philo adds that he is 'only a man in accordance with truth', who expects goodness and has noble hopes. Eusebius may be distancing himself from Philo's account by firmly distinguishing Enos from *anthrōpos* and differentiating between this term for the race in general and the 'true man'. At the same time, however, Eusebius gives 'hope' a prominent place in his narrative of Enos (see 7.8.9,12).

[41] *PE* 7.8.8. See also 11.6.10–15.

[42] *PE* 7.8.6. In a similar manner, Philo had claimed that, since *anthrōpos* meant 'lover of hope', the one who was without hope was not a human but a 'beast in human shape' (*Abr.* 8).

[43] *PE* 7.8.9.

[44] *PE* 7.8.13. The phrase is from Gen. 5: 24, and is also central to Philo's treatment of Enoch (*Abr.* 17).

[45] *PE* 7.8.13.

[46] *PE* 7.8.14; cp. Philo, *Abr.* 19–20; *Quod Omnis* 63, 76; *De Mut.* 34–8.

Platonic tradition. The Socrates of the *Theaetetus* had declared that true philosophers 'do not know the path to the market-place, nor where the courtroom, the council-chamber, or any other meeting-place of the city is. And they neither see nor hear the decrees—whether spoken or written. Rivalries of factions for office, meetings, banquets, and revels with flute-girls never occur to them to do, even in a dream.'[47] Already echoed by Philo, this sentiment of the wise man's withdrawal from worldly matters was now applied to an ancient Hebrew wise man by a Christian apologist.[48] Because of his otherworldly focus, Eusebius notes, the Hebrews gave him the name Enoch, meaning 'the grace of God'.[49]

Noah was the third of the Hebrew forefathers who lived before the flood. While the rest of humanity had fallen into a 'great foulness and darkness of indescribable wickedness', and the giants warred against God,[50] and the arts of witchcraft and sorcery were introduced, Noah stood apart as 'a righteous man in his generation'.[51] As a 'friend of God' he and his family were preserved from the flood sent by God against the wickedness of humanity.[52]

Following the flood,[53] Abraham is introduced as 'the progenitor of the whole nation', and as such is in some sense given a higher position than the other ancestors who had come before.[54] Eusebius briefly recounts the claims made by God regarding Abraham, that he would be 'a father of many nations' and that 'all the nations and all the tribes on earth shall be blessed' through him.[55] These claims by God were taken by Eusebius to be prophecies of contemporary events ('things fulfilled in our time'). The emphasis upon this episode from the biblical Abraham story is echoed throughout the *Praeparatio* and is an important component of Eusebius' ethnic argumentation, to which I will return.

[47] Plato, *Theaet.* 173CD; Eusebius will quote this passage *in extenso* at 12.29.2–21, and more briefly at 13.13.20 (within a citation from Clement's *Strom.* 5). See also in Plato, e.g., *Rep.* 3.405B; 5.476B; 6.492B, 503D; 7.517D; 8.549D.

[48] See Philo, *Abr.* 20; cf. *Dec.* 2–13; *Praem. et Poen.* 20–1.

[49] PE 7.8.15. Philo similarly gives the etymology of the name as κεχαρισμένος (*Abr.* 17).

[50] For a similar combination of the biblical and Greek accounts regarding the 'sons of God' and the giants, see Josephus, *AJ* 1.73.

[51] PE 7.8.16; the phrase is from Gen. 6: 9. See also, Philo, *Abr.* 27.

[52] PE 7.8.17.

[53] Eusebius gives a sidelong glance to Melchizadek at 7.8.19 between his accounts of Noah and Abraham. On Philo's and Eusebius' slight allusions to this mysterious king, see Schroeder and Des Places, *Eusèbe de Césarée*, 66.

[54] ὁ βοώμενος τοῦ παντὸς ἔθνους γενάρχης (7.8.22). See Philo, *Quis heres* 279, for this appellation.

[55] PE 7.8.23. See 11.6.25–26.

A striking feature of the segment on Abraham is Eusebius' effort to separate Abraham's act of circumcision from the later 'Jewish' practice under Mosaic Law.[56] Abraham's circumcision and the transmission of this ritual act to his descendants, according to Eusebius, may have been for the purpose of later being able to show by a physical sign the fulfilment of the prophecy that Abraham's offspring would be numerous; or it was to be a reminder to his offspring of the virtuous life of their forefather.[57] But in any case, Eusebius says, 'we do not have leisure to needlessly busy ourselves with the causes [for his circumcision] at the present time'. And whatever the reasons may be, this practice of circumcision must not be confused with Jewish practice: 'the Law of Moses was not yet in existence'.[58]

A portrait of the lives of Abraham's descendants fills out Eusebius' biographical overview of the ancient Hebrews. Isaac was 'a successor to his father's knowledge of God and friendship with God'.[59] His self-control was so strong that he had marital intercourse only once, which resulted in twins. One of these twins was Jacob, whose name meant 'one in training' or 'athlete'.[60] Jacob would later receive the name of Israel, as 'one who sees and contemplates',[61] for he would advance from mere training to the true life of contemplation. These men's lives were lives of 'philosophic endurance and discipline, some things viewed literally, and some in allegorical suggestions'.[62]

Breaking the continuity of the lineage of Abraham's descendants, Eusebius slips in a brief mention of Job, before proceeding to Joseph. He writes that Job was a 'blameless, true, just, and devout' man who 'abstained from every evil thing'.[63] The reasons for including Job in the middle of the family line is that he did 'not belong at all to the race of the Jews'.[64] In effect, Eusebius wants to detract from any notion of biological connections as a necessary component

---

[56] See Origen, *C. Cels.* 1.22 and 5.48, for earlier efforts to explain Abraham's circumcision.

[57] *PE* 7.8.24.

[58] *PE* 7.8.22.

[59] *PE* 7.8.25. For an etymology of Isaac, see 11.6.29.

[60] *PE* 7.8.26. See also, 11.6.30.

[61] *PE* 7.8.28. See 11.6.31.

[62] *PE* 7.8.29.

[63] *PE* 7.8.30, citing Job 1: 1.

[64] Patristic authors seem to be unanimous on Job's non-Jewish birth; see Baskin, *Pharaoh's Counsellors: Job, Jethro and Balaam*, 32. Rabbinic exegetes were less agreed on his birth; ibid., 8–32.

of Hebrew identity.[65] While he does not want to ignore this element altogether—after all, he consistently makes reference to the transmission of paternal ways from father to son—nevertheless, the biological relations of familial kinship must be subsumed under the more important category of character and way of life. It is these two latter elements that are essential for Eusebius' demarcation of the boundaries of collective identities. For Eusebius, familial connections are only important in so far as they foster the transmission of virtue.

Resuming the narrative with the children of Jacob, Eusebius writes: 'They cherished the knowledge of God and the piety inherited from their forefathers, and advanced the fame of the elder Hebrews to a high degree of glory, so that at length they annexed the government of all Egypt.'[66] This last comment is best seen in light of the historical revisionism of ethnic historiography in the Hellenistic and Roman periods.[67] Anti-Jewish historians (such as Apion) had asserted that the Jews were descendants of the Egyptians, the lower and despised 'unclean' classes of Egyptian society, or shepherd people who were driven out of Egypt. Such historical accounts attempted to place the Jews in an inferior and dependant relation to ancient Egypt. Josephus had combated these claims in his *Contra Apionem*. Eusebius continues the tradition of Josephus by providing a narrative of gradual expansion as a result of the virtue and wisdom displayed by the Hebrews.[68] Had he considered these people as Jews he surely would not have cared to paint a favourable picture of how they got into Egypt. These people were Hebrews; but, as will be seen, by the time they emerged from Egypt they had largely lost their Hebrew heritage.

Joseph figures last in Eusebius' narration of the ancient Hebrews. Because of his steadfast chastity he received from God the government of Egypt, even though he had begun his experiences in Egypt as a slave.[69]

[65] Ulrich, *Euseb von Caesarea und die Juden*, 63.

[66] *PE* 7.8.31.

[67] See in general, E. Bickerman, 'Origenes gentium', 65–81; J. Gager, *Moses in Greco-Roman Paganism* (Nashville: Abingdon Press, 1972), esp. 113–33; Sterling, *Historiography and Self-Definition*; A. J. Droge, 'Josephus Between Greeks and Barbarians', in L. H. Feldman and J. R. Levison, (eds), *Josephus' Contra Apionem* (Leiden: Brill, 1996), 115–42; Mendels, *The Rise and Fall of Jewish Nationalism*, 35–54; and Boys-Stones, *Post-Hellenistic Philosophy*, 60–95.

[68] On Eusebius' use of Josephus' *Ap.*, see M. Hardwick, *Josephus as an Historical Source in Patristic Literature Through Eusebius* (Atlanta: Scholar's Press, 1989), 90–4.

[69] *PE* 7.8.32.

But after withstanding the seductive advances of his master's wife, God 'crowned him as a victor with the rewards of virtue, and gave to him the royalty and governance over his masters and over Egypt itself.[70] Moreover', Eusebius adds, 'he has been received among the thrice-blessed and most highly favoured friends of God, since he was a Hebrew of Hebrews, and not a Jew (because the Jewish nation did not yet exist).'[71] Joseph's life and heroic act of self-control serve as a last ray of light from the life of the ancient Hebrews before the darkness of the Egyptians gradually snuffed it out, with only a few flickers remaining.

The Rise of the Jews

Eusebius concludes his series of biographical notes on the Hebrew forefathers with a description of the national decline into the Jewish nation during their stay in Egypt. 'The race of their ancestors', he writes, 'gave way to a great multitude and the nation of the Jews was established out of these.'[72] Unlike their forefather, Joseph, who had withstood the temptations of the Egyptian seductress, these descendants fell into the practices of the Egyptians.

The influence of the pious conduct of their godly forefathers of old began little by little to be weakened and blunted, while the effects of their association with Egyptians gained so much strength over the multitude of whom I speak, that they forgot the virtue of their forefathers, and came round in their modes of living to customs like (*homoiotropia tous bious*) those of the Egyptians, so that their character seemed to differ in no way from the Egyptians.[73]

The effects were so bad that when God sent Moses as a 'leader and lawgiver',[74] he was not able to fully restore to them the national character of their ancestors. Their weakness in the face of pleasure and susceptibility to vice constrained them from following the example of the ancient Hebrews. They were 'sick in the soul', and hence Moses gave them 'a polity that corresponded to their condition, ordaining some things openly and clearly, and implying others enigmatically, by suggesting symbols and

---

[70] Compare with Josephus' account at *AJ* 2.41–90.

[71] *PE* 7.8.36.

[72] *PE* 7.8.37.

[73] *PE* 7.8.37; cp. the Syriac version of Aristides *Apol.* 2.5; see Lieu, *Image and Reality*, 169–70.

[74] 7.8.38.

shadows, but not the naked truth, for them to keep and observe'.[75] To take Moses as representing a high point in religious history[76] fails to give this point adequate weight. Likewise, if we extract the Jews from their ethnic location within a narrative of descent from Hebrew ancestors and instead assume them to represent a theological category (in so far as they represent an Urmonotheismus), we fail to recognize the secondary level of Moses' Law because of the people's deplorable moral status that resulted from the inordinate influence of the Egyptians.[77]

Mosaic Law was 'God's will' only in so far as it was a measure leading back towards the life of virtue of the Jews' Hebrew ancestors. Moses' polity was meant to function as a remedial form of legislation until the coming of Christ. For Eusebius, the monotheism of the Jews was insufficient to obtain the noble name of their Hebrew forefathers. He sought to emphasize the disconnection between the Jews, on the one side, and the Hebrews and Christians, on the other. Christ's 'customs and ordinances' were to replace those of Moses.[78] Christ established a new covenant for all nations.[79]

This effort to create a boundary between the Hebrew and Jewish nations, despite their biological connectedness,[80] is a systematic and consistent feature of Eusebius' *Praeparatio* (he had asserted the difference as early as 1.6.6). In several places throughout his account of the ancient Hebrews, Eusebius had been careful to distinguish the subjects of his narrative from the Jews. He ignores the historical reasons for the use of *Ioudaios* as an appellation for the Jews resulting from the extension of the term from the children of the tribe of Judah to the territory, then to the entire nation following Babylonian exile, which had become prominent in Hellenistic times.[81] Instead, he opts for a clear distinction between Hebrews and Jews, which arose during their Egyptian sojourn. There

---

[75] 7.8.39.

[76] Ulrich, *Euseb von Caesarea und die Juden*, 62.

[77] Ibid., 80, where Ulrich claims that, 'Insofar as the Jews followed the Mosaic Law, they followed the will of Moses' highest God … The Jews stood clearly and unequivocally in the line of the ancient original monotheism (represented by the ancient Hebrews).'

[78] *PE* 7.8.40.

[79] *PE* 7.8.40.

[80] That he does not ignore the biological relationship is clear from 7.7.2, where the Hebrews are depicted as not being foreign with respect to race from the Jews.

[81] See S. Cohen, 'Religion, Ethnicity and Hellenism in the Emergence of Jewish Identity in Maccabean Palestine', in Per Bilde *et al.* (eds), *Religion and Religious Practice in the Seleucid Kingdom* 204–23; idem, *The Beginnings of Jewishness*, 14; Harvey, *The True Israel* 11–61; A. Arazy, *The Appellations of the Jews (Ioudaios, Hebraios, Israel) in the Literature*

were no Jews before the Egyptian era, nor were there many Hebrews left after it. Of the earlier period, he claims: 'The ones of whom I speak were Hebrews alike by name and in character, and as yet neither were, nor were called, Jews.'[82] Egypt was a watershed of national deterioration—in fact, in Eusebius' scheme, it constituted a period of ethnogenesis for the nation of the Jews, and of near extinction for the Hebrews.

FROM HEBREWS TO JEWS: ASPECTS OF ETHNIC ARGUMENTATION IN *PRAEPARATIO* 7–8

In the present discussion, I have attempted to delineate the overall direction and aims of the argument that Eusebius constructs in Books 7–8. However, certain central features of his argument need to be reiterated and singled out for particular attention as to their function and force within his apologetic project. As in the previous chapter, I aim to note the ways in which Eusebius' narration provides a picture of national character and national connections (or in this case, disconnections) that support his ethnic argumentation in the *Praeparatio* as a whole. His narration of the ancient Hebrews and the later rise of the Jewish *ethnos* is fraught with no little significance for grasping his apologetic argument and for illuminating his conceptualization of Jews and Jewishness in general.[83] The following remarks are meant to highlight the particular salience of the character of the Hebrew holy men, the boundary-forging mechanisms employed to mark off Jews from Hebrews, and the ways in which that boundary could be manipulated for other ends when needed.

Ancestors as Icons: National Character in the Narrative of Hebrew Descent

As in the first, so now in the second half of the *Praeparatio*, Eusebius is concerned to exhibit through his narrative the *tropos*, or character,

---

from Alexander to Justinian (Ph.D. dissertation, New York University, 1977) 1.33–71. Compare with Josephus, *AJ* 11.173.

[82] *PE* 7.6.1.

[83] See J. Parkes, 'Jews and Christians in the Constantinian Empire', *SCH* 1 (1964), 69–79; A. Kofsky, 'Eusebius of Caesarea and the Christian-Jewish Polemic', in Limor and Stroumsa, (eds), *Contra Iudaeos*, 59–83.

embodied in the way of life of each of the nations. The character of the ancient Hebrews is represented as entirely different from that of the other nations.[84] The national character of the Phoenicians, Egyptians, and Greeks had been shown in *Praeparatio* 1–6 as steeped in polytheistic error, irrationality, and impiety. At 7.3, Eusebius makes the following remarks on the degradation of their character:

When therefore they had entrenched themselves in so great an error, naturally in their service of the goddess and evil daemon, pleasure, evils upon evils gathered round them, while they defiled the whole of life with mad passions for women and outrages on men, and had surpassed in their excess of wickedness the character (*tropos*) of the ancient nations, and of their false theology, as exhibited in the preceding books by the Greek historians and philosophers whom we have brought together.[85]

This declaration of national decline, of the increase in manifestations of the immorality and impiety attached to the life of pleasure like the multiplication of the heads of a hydra, stands as the last remark on the character of the other nations before Eusebius embarked on the narrative of virtue and simplicity displayed by the ancient Hebrews. The contrast could not be greater.

The life of the ancient Hebrews was marked by rational reflection upon the universe: the minds of the Hebrews were pure, the eyes of their souls clear-sighted.[86] Hence, they avoided the error of the other nations, whose decline had begun with astral theology. Instead, they looked beyond the stars to their maker and diligently sought the creator of all. In this way, they were led on towards friendship with God as 'the consummation of all happiness' (*telos hapasēs eudaimonias*).[87] This, coupled with the discovery of the soul as separate from the body, resulted in the disciplining of the body through asceticism.[88] For Eusebius, the character of Hebrew theology (namely, their rationality) was thus inseparable from their virtuous lives. In fact, Eusebius refers to their distinctive way of thinking about God and the world as the character of their doctrine (*dogmatikon tropon*) or rational character (*logikon tropon*), as distinct from the character of their piety (*eusebeias charactēra*).[89]

The character of the Hebrews was both rational and virtuous. At the same time, they did not need legislation such as Moses had established

---

[84] Johnson, 'Ancestors as Icons'.   [85] *PE* 7.2.6.   [86] *PE* 7.3.3.
[87] *PE* 7.4.4.   [88] See especially *PE* 7.4.2–4.   [89] See *PE* 7.8.41, 11.5.1.

for the Jews. 'They enjoyed a free and unfettered mode (*tropon*) of piety, being regulated by the manner of life which is in accordance with nature, so that they had no need of laws to rule them, because of the extreme freedom of their soul from passions, but had received true knowledge of the doctrines concerning God.'[90] They were Hebrews, as opposed to Jews, in 'both name and character'.[91]

One of the most significant aspects of Eusebius' conception of Hebrew character is the particular way in which he describes the exemplary quality of their way of life. He writes that Moses had described the lives of the ancient Hebrews as a 'preface' to his laws.[92] Moses had done so because he wanted to remind the Jews, for whom he was legislating, of the greatness and virtue of their Hebrew ancestors. The lives of these Hebrews were meant not only as reminders but as models to follow.

At this point, Eusebius adopts the language of painted images to provide a striking metaphor of Moses' biographical method.[93] Eusebius explains that Moses 'was handing down their ancestors' portraits (*eikonas*) to those who were being instructed in the things of God, recounting the lives of the men of old, and delineating as in painted likenesses the peculiar virtue of each one'.[94] This description vividly exhibits Moses' literary activity as the presentation of ancestors as models to be emulated. Like a painter, Moses creates a picture that highlights with bright colours the particular virtue of each individual.[95]

Eusebius had been preceded in seeing ancestors as images or icons. Plutarch's preface to the *Vita Alexandri* is the most well-known example of the metaphor of biographical sketches as painted images. Plutarch claims in the *Vita* that he is writing lives not histories, and hence will

[90] *PE* 7.6.4.

[91] *PE* 7.6.1.

[92] *PE* 7.7.1–4; see below.

[93] See, Johnson, 'Ancestors as Icons', 245–64; for discussion of the importance of the visual in late antique literature, see A. Cameron, *Christianity and the Rhetoric of Empire* (Berkeley and Los Angeles: University of California Press 1991), 141–54; J. Francis, 'Living Icons: Tracing a Motif in Verbal and Visual Representation from the Second to Fourth Centuries C.E.', *AJP* 124 (2003), 575–600; P. Cox Miller, 'Visceral Seeing: The Holy Body in Late Ancient Christianity', *JECS* 12 (2004), 391–411.

[94] *PE* 7.7.4.

[95] On the metaphor, see Francis, 'Living Icons'; Johnson, 'Ancestors as Icons'; D. Krueger, 'Typological Figuration in Theodoret of Cyrrhus's *Religious History* and the Art of Postbiblical Narrative', *JECS* 5 (1997), 413–19; P. Canivet and A. Leroy-Molinghen, *Théodoret de Cyr. Histoire des moines de Syrie*, SC 234 and 257 (Paris: Les Éditions du Cerf, 1977), 1.149–50.

focus upon those features that emphasize the individual's character.[96] 'Therefore, just as painters pick out the likenesses from the face and the forms of his appearance, those things in which character is manifest, caring least for the other parts of the body, so we must be granted to undertake rather the signs of the soul and to portray each one's life through these, leaving to others the great deeds and struggles.'[97]

No doubt, it is Plutarch's programmatic statement here that is the model for Eusebius' methodological reflections in the *Vita Constantini*, where he claims that he will 'record with words the image (*eikona*) of the God-beloved [emperor] in remembrance, in imitation of mortal portraiture (*skiagraphias*)'.[98] And, just as Plutarch claimed to disregard the great battles and achievements of his subject, so also Eusebius there states that he 'will pass over most of the deeds of the thrice-blessed [emperor]'.[99] Instead, he 'will speak and write only those things pertaining to [Constantine's] God-beloved life'.[100]

This is obviously quite similar to the image of Moses' portrait-making given by Eusebius at *Praeparatio* 7.7.4. However, Eusebius would have been familiar with other occurrences of the metaphor. At the beginning of his *De Abrahamo*, Philo draws out the relationship between the Hebrew forefathers who lived before Mosaic Law and the Law itself. In an illuminating comment, Philo remarks that particular laws of Moses' legislation are, in fact, copies (*eikonōn*) of mortal Hebrew archetypes (*archetupous*), 'such men as lived blameless and good lives, whose virtues are inscribed in the most sacred books, and this is not only for their praise, but also so that the readers will be encouraged to emulate the same'.[101] Literally, Philo says that the laws are *icons* of the Hebrew *archetypes*. Just as in Eusebius' account of Moses' lives, these Hebrew models are to serve a protreptic function for the reader. For Eusebius, Moses' laws were to be 'as an encouragement (*protropēn*) for the life of the pious'.[102]

Following these programmatic statements on the lives of the Hebrew saints, the metaphor of a holy life as an image recurs frequently throughout Eusebius' treatment of Hebrew descent.[103] For instance, Eusebius claims that a man of such character as Enos is worthy of emulation, and that Christians have attempted to seek God 'in a manner

---

[96] Plutarch, *V. Alex.* 1.2.   [97] Plutarch, *V. Alex.* 1.3.   [98] *VC* 1.10.
[99] *VC* 1.11.   [100] *VC* 1.11.   [101] Philo, *Abr.* 3–4.
[102] *PE* 7.7.1. εἰς προτροπὴν τοῦ τῶν εὐσεβῶν βίου. Cp. Clement, *Strom.* 4.5.3–4; Johnson, 'Ancestors as Icons', 258–9.
[103] Ibid., 259–61.

equal to the image of [Enos]'.[104] In his report of Enoch, Eusebius adds: 'We considered it a blessed thing to emulate the life of this image.'[105]

The most significant example of this metaphoric understanding of the ancestor as an image is his assertion following the account of Noah: 'This man, then, also would be an archetype, a living and breathing image, who had given an example to his posterity of the character that is pleasing to God.'[106] This statement raises some important issues. For Philo, in the passage noted above, the Hebrews were archetypes, while the laws were images of the men. Eusebius, however, seems here to conflate both archetype and image to refer to the ancient Hebrews. A similar conflation occurs later in Book 7 when he describes the Logos as being an 'archetype and true image of the God of all'.[107] He then follows this by saying that the human mind is created in the image of the Logos, and as such is 'an image of an image'.[108] The passage on Noah reflects a distinctively moral focus in its use of the term 'image'. At 7.7.4, Eusebius had used 'image' to refer to the biographical sketches (the *bioi*) of Hebrews contained in Moses' writings. But now, Eusebius is making the additional claim that the 'images' are to serve as models (as *hupodeigmata*).[109] The character represented in the biographical sketches functions as an image to be observed and so incorporated into the moral lives of the readers. The picture painted through the words of the narrative summons the viewer (reader) to emulate its distinctive model for virtuous living.[110]

The character of the Hebrew ancestors stands not only as a positive contrast to the character of the other nations delineated in Books 1–6 but also places a certain obligation upon the reader. The narrative account of Hebrew character beckons the reader to the life characterized by friendship with God. The character of the Greeks and other peoples had only elicited Eusebius' aversion to such impiety and superstition. There was no iconic quality to the accounts of the Greek forefathers. But in Eusebius' treatment of the biographical sketches of Hebrew

---

104 *PE* 7.8.12.

105 *PE* 7.8.15.

106 *PE* 7.8.18. γένοιτο δ' ἂν καὶ οὗτος ἀρχέτυπος εἰκὼν ζῶσα καὶ ἔμψυχος τοῖς ἐξ αὐτοῦ γεγενημένοις ὑπόδειγμα τρόπου θεοφιλοῦς παρεσχημένους.

107 *PE* 7.10.12. εἶναι δὲ ἀρχέτυπον καὶ ἀληθῆ τοῦ θεοῦ τῶν ὅλων εἰκόνα τὸν αὐτοῦ λόγον.

108 εἰκόνα δὲ εἰκόνος τὸν ἀνθρώπειον νοῦν.

109 Cp. Clement, *Strom.* 4.5.3–4; Origen, *C. Cels.* 1.68; 3.66.

110 On the notion of verbal images carrying an iconic function, see V. E. F. Harrison, 'Word as Icon in Greek Patristic Theology', *Sobornost* 10 (1988), 38–49.

ancestors, a sort of moral response by the reader was encouraged. And in this way, the Hebrew lives were icons.[111]

Separating Jews from Hebrews

Two boundary-making mechanisms are pertinent for the present discussion regarding Eusebius' Hebrew–Jew distinction. First, an important means of making the distinction was through the conscious manipulation and use of separate ethnonyms.[112] The difference in ethnonyms, according to Eusebius, lay not only in a difference of character but also in the fact that they went back to two different founders: Heber for the Hebrews and Judah for the Jews. 'The difference between the Hebrews and Jews you may know in this way: the latter assumed their name from Judah, from whose tribe the kingdom of Judah was long ages afterwards established, but the former from Heber, who was the forefather of Abraham. And that the Hebrews were earlier than the Jews, we are taught by the sacred writings.'[113]

The two eponymous forefathers were somewhat awkwardly drawn from biblical references. At Genesis 10: 21, Heber is mentioned as an ancestor of Shem.[114] This is somewhat late for him to be eponymous for the Hebrews before the flood, since Shem's father was Noah. Yet, Josephus had already made this connection between Heber and the Hebrews.[115] In fact, however, the name may not go back to any one individual, but refer rather to 'slaves' or some lower social

[111] My account here should be read in light of Eusebius' letter to Constantia (*PG* 20.1545–50), which offers one of the earliest expressions of iconoclastic sentiment. Hence, while he is opposed to the use of visual icons in the letter, he is here (and in the *VC*) promoting the use of verbal icons. On the authenticity of the letter, see Gero, 'The True Image of Christ: Eusebius' Letter to Constantia Reconsidered', 460–70. The best treatment of Eusebius' views on art remains, C. Murray, 'Art in the Early Church', *JTS* 28 (1977), 303–45. Attempts to explain the iconoclastic ideas of the letter by Eusebius' Origenism (so G. Florovsky, 'Origen, Eusebius, and the Iconoclastic Controversy', *CH* 19 [1950], 77–96) or Arianism (a 'shrinking from the historical Jesus', Mortley, *The Idea of Universal History*, 151–3) are less convincing. For a general account of the rise of iconism, see Cameron, *Christianity and the Rhetoric of Empire*, 189–221.

[112] See Ulrich, *Euseb von Caesarea und die Juden*, 57–131 for general discussion.

[113] *PE* 7.6.2. See also 10.14.2; 11.6.39; cp. Justin *Apol.* 1.32.3, 14.

[114] See also Gen. 10: 24–5; 11: 15–16.

[115] *AJ* 1.146.

category.[116] Furthermore, Judah had given his name to one of the 12 tribes of Israel, but the use of *Ioudaioi* would not be extended to all Jews collectively until at least post-exilic or even Hellenistic times. Even Josephus had noted this fact when he wrote: 'They are called by this name from the tribe of Judah, since the time when they returned from Babylon.'[117] The fact that both titles are somewhat tendentiously connected to Heber and Judah draws attention to the importance of collective names for the identities of peoples in antiquity. Eusebius shares with Josephus the need to attach particular peoples to ancient roots, however disingenuous such connections might be. Despite the fact (or even because of the fact) that Heber is a fairly hazy figure in the biblical books, he makes an excellent person to be remembered as a founding father. He is a source for the Hebrews' collective name, and reserves a space in the faded mists of earliest time in which an identity can be historically planted.

The ethnonymic distinction between Hebrews and Jews is supplemented later, when Eusebius sums up the narrative of the Hebrews before the flood. He remarks:

[They were neither Jews nor Greeks,] but they would be more properly called Hebrews, either because of Heber, or rather because of the interpretation of the name. For by interpretation they are a kind of 'passengers', who have set out on their journey from this world to pass to the contemplation of the God of the universe. For they are recorded to have travelled the straight path of virtue aright by natural reasoning and by unwritten laws, and to have passed beyond carnal pleasures to the life of perfect wisdom and piety.[118]

This etymology of Hebrews from 'passengers' was based on the biblical passage of Genesis 14: 13 and had already been pointed out by Philo. For reasons similar to Eusebius, Philo adopts the etymology: the Hebrews were these who passed over from the things of this world to pursue the truth found in contemplation of the divine.[119]

---

[116] See G. von Rad, 'Israel, Judah and Hebrews in the Old Testament', in *TDNT*, 358–9. Contrast Eusebius' citation on the Mosaic injunction prohibiting Hebrews from owning Hebrew slaves (12.37.1).

[117] *AJ* 11.173; see also, Origen *C. Cels.* 1.53. Later, at *DE* 3.2 (95d), Eusebius will adopt this same idea.

[118] *PE* 7.8.20–1. For the same meaning, though rendered in a slightly different manner, see *PE* 11.6.39.

[119] *De Migrat. Abr.* 20. See Harvey, *The True Israel*, 121–2 for discussion. The etymology was brought into Christian discourse by Origen in his *Comm. Gen.* 14.13, *Comm. Matth.* 11.5 and *Hom. Num.* 19.4, as well as in Julius Africanus' *Chronicon* 8. See Harvey, *The True Israel*, 139.

The conjunction of the two explanations for the ethnonym—the one resorting to ancestry, the other to etymology—well illustrates the extent of Eusebius' boundary-forming project. Not only do the Hebrews trace their lineage to a different legendary founder than the Jews, but their character as contemplative ascetics, or 'passengers', through this present life, contrasts with the weak and corrupted character of the Jews.

A second means of emphasizing the boundary that Eusebius had constructed between the Hebrews and Jews centred upon Mosaic Law.[120] Eusebius repeatedly stressed that the virtuous lives of his Hebrews were based upon living according to nature, right use of reason (*orthos logismos*) and unwritten laws.[121] At 7.6.4, he described them as having nothing to do with Mosaic Law or with the sorts of regulations it required:

But the Hebrews who were earlier in time than Moses having never heard of all the Mosaic legislation, enjoyed a free and unfettered mode of piety, being regulated by the manner of life which is in accordance with nature, so that they had no need of laws to rule them, because of the extreme freedom of their soul from passions, but had received true knowledge of the doctrines concerning God.[122]

Again, before Moses' 'own written laws, [the Hebrew] forefathers by right use of reason had already been honourably distinguished for excellence in reverence for God'.[123] Hence, the mere fact of chronology, for Eusebius, pre-empts any connection between the way of life of the Hebrews and the way of life legislated in the Law of Moses. Anyone who wanted to treat the Hebrew patriarchs as part of the Jewish *ethnos* was thus confronted by Eusebius' contention that the defining and formative factor of Jewish identity centred upon the legislation of Moses to those descendants of Abraham who had Egyptianized and could no longer fully participate in the ancestral life of virtue. This defining moment of Jewishness had not yet occurred, was chronologically later than the lives of the Hebrew forefathers, and as such could not be used to define Hebrew identity.

Circumcision is a central issue in Eusebius' claims that the Hebrews did not follow Mosaic Law. Among the Hebrews before the flood, Eusebius asserts 'there was not a single word about bodily circumcision,

---

[120] See Ulrich, *Euseb von Caesarea und die Juden*, 63–4.
[121] These are also central features in Philo's description of the ancient Hebrews; see *Abr.* 6.
[122] *PE* 7.6.4.
[123] *PE* 7.7.2.

nor of the Judaic pronouncements of Moses'.[124] Circumcision stood as a semiotic marker of ethnic difference between the Hebrews and Jews. It should be remembered that Eusebius named the Jewish opponents to Christianity to whom his *Praeparatio* was addressed as 'those of the circumcision'.[125] Since this is the case, it was an especially troubling fact in the biblical story of Abraham that he had himself been circumcised in his old age upon a command from God. Eusebius attempted to explain this away as meaning something other than the circumcision of the Jews: possibly it was to remind later generations that they were to walk in the ways of their ancestor, Abraham; or it was performed in order to keep track of his numerous descendants, who could, by this bodily sign, be differentiated from other peoples. But realizing that these answers may not be good enough to separate Abraham's circumcision from Mosaic Law, Eusebius adds the line cited above: 'Or for some other reason, whatever it is, which we do not now have leisure to busy ourselves with.'[126] Even if Eusebius felt uneasy about the possible reasons he had given, he was clearly eager to explain away the circumcision of Abraham.

The apologist's primary goal in these considerations was to make a clear demarcation, to fortify the boundary, between Hebrews and Jews. Unless the deeper meaning or kernel of Hebrew wisdom could be located through allegorical techniques, Moses' legislation scarcely represented what Eusebius would consider a rational and pious way of life. What elevated Moses to the rank of 'Hebrew of Hebrews' was not the fact of his legislation for the Jews, but rather his concealing of Hebrew wisdom within it. Before moving on, it may be instructive to compare the *Praeparatio*'s portrayal of Moses with that of a slightly earlier work.

The *General Elementary Introduction* had been composed in about 310 while the Great Persecution was still wreaking havoc on the Church's sense of security in the Roman world.[127] The remaining four books of this work (going under the title *Prophetic Eclogues*)[128] exhibit its importance in a number of areas, from its development of a Logos

---

[124] *PE* 7.8.20.

[125] *PE* 1.1.11, 13; see also 4.16.20 and 15.62.18.

[126] *PE* 7.8.24.

[127] For date, see E. Schwartz, 'Eusebios von Caesarea', col. 1387; for an excellent overview of the work, see T. D. Barnes, *Constantine and Eusebius*, 167–74.

[128] See above, Chapter 1; Johnson, 'Eusebius' *Praeparatio Evangelica* as Literary Experiment'. For the possibility that the *Introduction*'s tenth book survives in the form of Eusebius' *Commentary on Luke*, see D. S. Wallace-Hadrill, 'Eusebius of Caesarea's *Commentary on Luke*: Its Origin and Early History', *HTR* 67 (1974), 55–63.

theology to its method of scriptural interpretation, its contribution to Christian education, and its relevance for anti-Jewish polemic.

In a discussion of manifestations of the Logos to key figures of the biblical narrative, Eusebius gives due consideration to what he claims is a noticeable change in the way the second person of the Trinity appeared to the ancients. God did not appear at random to humans, but restricted his being seen to Abraham, Isaac, and Jacob.[129] Moses himself was not allowed to see God:[130] even when the biblical text describes his encounter with God on Mount Sinai, Moses only saw his back.[131] When God spoke with Moses, it was only dimly, 'visage to visage (*enōpios enōpiōi*)' rather than 'face to face (*prosōpon pros prosōpon*)' as God had done with the Hebrew patriarchs.[132]

Eusebius' interpretive tactics (which may seem to verge on sophistry to the modern reader) artfully manipulate the details of the Bible's narrative. God's revelations to Moses and the people under his leadership are consistently portrayed with evaluative terms that inscribe a shift from the earlier revelations to the Hebrew patriarchs. Divine manifestations to Moses and the Jews were clothed in some sort of form (*eidos*),[133] either fire or cloud, that was fleshly and indirect, since they were 'babies in their souls and wicked; and the divine things were riddled through symbols to them in types (*tupikōs*) and images (*eikonikōs*), nor in this was it a more mystical and spiritual teaching such as [the Hebrew patriarchs] received, since it was to children who had changed their accustomed way of life for the character of Egyptians'.[134] Even the monotheism of the Hebrews could scarcely be grasped by the foolish Jews: 'they were yet without an elementary introduction (*stoicheiōdous eisagōgēs*) of the monarchy regarding God'.[135] 'The Law of Moses,' Eusebius baldly declares, 'could not see the face of God since it was human and rather fleshly.'[136] This was in sharp contrast to God's clear,

---

[129] *PG* 22.1041C

[130] *PG* 22.1049B–1053A, esp. 1052A.

[131] *PG* 22.1065Aff.

[132] *PG* 22.1060D–1061B. Later, Eusebius notes that God spoke to Moses 'mouth to mouth' (*PG* 22.1064B–the inconsistency in his use of *prosōpon pros prosōpon* with the previous passages should be noted).

[133] *PG* 22.1061B–C.

[134] *PG* 22.1052B.

[135] *PG* 22.1068B. *Pace* Ulrich, who claims that monotheism was a common denominator for Jews and Hebrews (*Euseb von Caesarea und die Juden*, 80–3).

[136] *PG* 22.1069A; see also, 1053C; and also 1057C–D, where Moses' Law is referred to as slavery.

unmediated and open (literally, 'naked' [*gumnōs*]) appearances to the Hebrew holy men who had lived before Moses and the rise of the Jewish nation.[137]

While Eusebius' concerns in the *General Elementary Introduction* are different from those in the *Praeparatio*, his attempt to distinguish the ancient Hebrews and their way of life from Moses and his legislation remains consistently clear. As a result of the Jews' moral deterioration while they lived among the Egyptians, a new identity with a new ethnonym, different laws, and lower levels of spiritual and intellectual perceptiveness came into existence. The ethnogenesis of the Jewish nation drew on chronological, legal, moral, and religious elements that highlighted its difference from the Hebrew friends of God.

Hebrews After Moses

After the Egyptian sojourn and the formation of the Jewish *ethnos* under Mosaic legislation, a small remnant of Hebrews remained. This considerably complicates Eusebius' conception of the development of ethnic history. But in order to grasp what Eusebius is doing in his construction and manipulation of ethnic boundaries, it is critical that those whom Eusebius names Hebrews after the rise of the Jews be given proper consideration.[138]

The issue begins with the identity of Moses. Moses is a central figure in the ethnogenesis of the Jews. It is his legislation that guarantees their status as a distinct people.[139] Whenever Eusebius refers to the origins of the Jewish nation, Moses' name is almost never absent.[140] His legislation is referred to as 'Judaic proclamations'.[141] Yet, Moses is hailed as 'the great theologian, a Hebrew of Hebrews if there ever was one'.[142]

---

137 *PG* 22.1053C; 1061B.
138 See Ulrich, *Euseb von Caesarea und die Juden*, 64–8.
139 See Sirinelli, *Les vues historiques d'Eusèbe de Césarée*, 157–8.
140 See *PE* 7.6.1, 3; 7.8.38, 40; 7.9.1; 8.5.11; 8.8.56; etc.
141 *PE* 7.8.20: ἰουδαικῶν παραγγελμάτων.
142 *PE* 7.7.1. Moses is called a theologian at 7.9.1, as well. The naming of Moses as a 'Hebrew of Hebrews' makes inexplicable Sirinelli's bold claim that 'Moses is not a Hebrew' (*Les vues historiques d'Eusèbe de Césarée*, 157). Ulrich, *Euseb von Caesarea und die Juden*, 62 n. 19, rightly questioned Sirinelli's statement, but then comes dangerously close to equating the Hebrews and the Jews (despite his disavowal of such a move at 81; just after he has stated that, at *PE* 9.10.6, Eusebius 'uses both conceptions [Jews and Hebrews] nearly interchangeably'). As I argue here, the favourable statements towards the Jews in the *PE* are

Furthermore, he is called 'all-wise'.[143] The reason for this double role is that although he established a legislation that was at a lower level than the way of life practised by the earlier Hebrews and in this respect was crucial for the rise of the Jews, he was nonetheless wise in the traditions of his Hebrew forebears. Therefore when he set himself to write up a legal code for the Jews in their morally weakened state, he provided it with a preface that, according to Eusebius, contained crucial elements of Hebrew wisdom.[144] There were two of these in the preambles to Moses' Law, and they are given abundant space in *Praeparatio* 7. First, Moses recognized the necessity of including the lives of the ancestral Hebrews to serve as models and sources of inspiration to virtuous living for the Jews. At 7.7.1–4, a central passage in Book 7 and one to which we will return again, Eusebius writes:

[Moses], understanding well the customs of his forefathers, by way of preface (*en prooimiois*) to the sacred laws has committed to indelible records (*mnēmais anexaleiptois*) the lives of the forefathers of the Hebrews, and the blessings which God vouchsafed to them ... because he thought that this would be a needful lesson for those who were to be taught his laws. ... [It was necessary for those who] were by birth descendants of righteous men beloved of God, to show themselves emulous of the piety of their forefathers, and to be eager to obtain from God equal blessings with those who had begotten them.

Hence, according to Eusebius, the very fact that Moses included the narrative of the lives of the Hebrew ancestors showed that Moses knew quite well that his Law was only meant as a middle ground for the morally handicapped Jews. Moses' privileging of the Hebrews and their way of life exhibited for Eusebius his true Hebrew identity—even as 'a Hebrew of Hebrews'.

Moses had also made space in the preambles of his legislation for philosophic reflections on the nature of God, the creation of the world, the nature of humans, and the nature and activity of evil forces such as daemons. When Eusebius introduces what he calls the 'theology of the Hebrews',[145] later called the 'philosophy of the Hebrews',[146] or even the

only in the context of an allegorical approach to the Law so as to discover the Hebrew truths embedded within, which complement the project which he sets himself in the *DE* (attacking Judaism based upon a literal reading of the Law).

[143] *PE* 7.12.10.

[144] For the importance of prefaces for Eusebius and Plato, see Johnson, 'Ancestors as Icons', 248–51.

[145] *PE* 7.9.2; see also 7.11.4, 13, etc.

[146] *PE* 7.11.14.

'dogmatic character of the Hebrews',[147] he adds this statement regarding Moses' preambles:

In founding by his own writing a polity (*politeia*) in accordance with piety for the Jewish people, [he] did not think it fit to employ the common and trite preambles (*prooimiois*) to his books; but after he had collected every law enjoining what ought to be done and forbidding what ought not to be done, and the public and civic arrangements concerning their mutual contracts, he thought it right to make his teaching begin with their ancestral theology, because he considered no other instruction to be proper to laws pertaining to piety than that theology which had come down to him from their forefathers.[148]

What follows then is an exposition of the theology to be gleaned from the account of the creation of the world found in Genesis. Much of this contains highly significant material for analysing Eusebius' 'Logos theology' (especially 7.12–15).[149] For our purposes, however, it is important to notice that Eusebius is attributing this theology to the ancient Hebrews. Moses, then, is a preserver of the knowledge of God possessed by the earlier Hebrews.

Besides the emphasis on what Eusebius considers to be the distinctively Hebrew features to Moses' preambles, Eusebius claims that Moses is a Hebrew for another, even more striking, reason. In the *Demonstratio Evangelica*, Eusebius would dedicate himself to the task of responding to the accusation that Christians had misappropriated the Jewish Scriptures for themselves, while not adhering to their legal pronouncements. Eusebius will there take special pains to show that the Law of Moses was only meant to apply for a limited time to a limited group of people in a limited geographical area (see especially *DE* 1–2). By way of foreshadowing this discussion in the *Demonstratio*, Eusebius writes: 'For we shall prove at the proper opportunity that the institutions of Moses were suited to Jews alone, and not to the other nations of the world, nor were possible to be observed by all men, I mean by those who dwelt at a distance from the land of Judaea, whether Greeks or barbarians.'[150]

---

[147] *PE* 7.8.41.

[148] *PE* 7.9.1.

[149] See F. Ricken, 'Die Logoslehre des Eusebios von Caesarea und der Mittelplatonismus', *Theologie und Philosophie* 42 (1967), 341–58; A. Dempf, *Der Platonismus des Eusebius, Victorinus, und Pseudo-Dionysius*. Sitzungsberichte der Bayerische Akademie der Wissenschaften, phil.-hist. Klasse 3 (Munich: Beck, 1962), 3–8; J. R. Lyman, *Christology and Cosmology: Models of Divine Activity in Origen, Eusebius and Athanasius* (Oxford: Clarendon Press, 1993), 106–23.

[150] *PE* 8.1.2.

However, here in the *Praeparatio*, he offers a way of understanding the Law that is in harmony with Hebrew theology, without slipping into an espousal of Jewish religious practices and way of life. The way out from under the Jewishness of the Law is through employment of the allegorical approach. The 'multitude' of Jews followed the literal sense since they were morally and theologically incapable of deeper interpretation. However, some Jews, who were known as the 'race of Jewish philosophers' among the Greeks, interpreted the Law allegorically and led a life of asceticism and virtue.[151] After providing sources on the transmission of Moses' writings into Greek (that is the Septuagint),[152] an overview of the polity prescribed in fairly literal terms (according to quotations from Philo and Josephus),[153] and then some examples of the allegorical meaning symbolized in the legal endorsements (from Aristeas and Aristobulus),[154] Eusebius distinguishes between the two types of Jews:

The whole Jewish nation is divided into two sections. And while the lawgiver [Moses] meant to lead the multitude on gently by the precepts of the laws as enjoined according to the literal sense, the other class, consisting of those who had acquired a habit of virtue, he meant to exempt from this sense, and required them to give attention to a philosophy of a diviner kind too highly exalted for the multitude, and to contemplation of the things signified in the meaning of the laws.[155]

As an example of this second class of Jews, in 8.11–12 Eusebius adds descriptions of the way of life of the ascetic Essenes. He is unclear if this second class of allegorizing Jews is to be identified with the Hebrews or not. He may merely be seeking an explanation for the admirable life of such groups as the Essenes in his division of the Jewish *ethnos*. While no sure conclusion can be reached, the first possibility is substantiated by the fact that Philo, who is otherwise named a Hebrew (see below), is here given the appellation of a 'wise Jew'.[156] In this case, Eusebius has just concluded his extracts on the Essenes and wants to introduce 'contemporary' Hebrew theology on the subject of Providence (no doubt to provide a Hebrew alternative to the Greek notions of Fate attacked in Book 6). He writes: 'Let us closely examine the thoughts of the wise men

---

[151] *PE* 8.10.19. Eusebius no doubt has in mind the mention of the Jews as a race of philosophers in Porphyry, *Abst.* 2.26, which he cites at 9.2.1; see also Clearchus' *De Somn.*, cited at 9.5.6.

[152] *PE* 8.2–5.   [153] *PE* 8.6–8.

[154] *PE* 8.9–10.   [155] *PE* 8.10.18.   [156] *PE* 8.12.22.

among the Jews, that we may learn what qualities the Hebrews have shown both in theology and in excellence of speech.'[157] If this statement is determinative, it closely identifies the wise Jews with the Hebrews, at least as conduits for Hebrew wisdom.[158]

It should be remembered that in the *HE*, Eusebius had taken the Therapeutae, an ascetic group in Egypt described by Philo in *De Vita Contemplativa*, to be Christians and 'apostolic men from the Hebrews' although they 'observed the customs of the ancients in the manner of Jews'.[159] They were, however, open to both Greeks and barbarians.[160] And, most importantly, they devoted themselves to the allegorical interpretation of the Scriptures, 'since they consider the writings to be hidden meanings of nature which are revealed in secret notions'.[161] This passage remains unclear as to how the Jewishness of their observation of ancient customs fits in with their identity as Hebrews, since as such they now incorporate Greeks and barbarians, and they pursue allegorical interpretive techniques. The fact that the Therapeutae are specifically named Hebrews, and that they are familiar with asceticism and allegory in the same way that the Essenes are described, seems to point towards the identification of the philosophical Jews with the Hebrews. Clearly, Eusebius allows for some manoeuvring between the boundary of Hebrews and Jews that he had constructed in the first part of *Praeparatio* 7. Not only was the legislator for the Jews himself a 'Hebrew of Hebrews', but his Jewish Law could be taken in a more philosophical, and hence less Jewish, way.

Eusebius' boundary, demarcating Hebrews from Jews, possessed some degree of permeability and allows for inclusion into the Hebrew *ethnos* of anyone Eusebius considers to be philosophical enough (that is, anyone

---

[157] *PE* 8.12.22. Compare with Eusebius' notion of two levels of Christians in *DE* 1–2; see M. Hollerich, 'Hebrews, Jews, and Christians: Eusebius of Caesarea on the Biblical Basis of the Two States of the Christian Life', in P. M. Blowers *et al.* (eds), *In Dominico Eloquio (In Lordly Eloquence): Essays on Patristic Exegesis in Honor of Robert Louis Wilken* (Grand Rapids: Eerdmans Publishing Co., 2002), 172–84.

[158] It may, however, only be the result of Eusebius' consistent attempt to have the opposition's own sources speak in his defence.

[159] *HE* 2.17.2. For an illuminating discussion of how this passage fits within the rise of Christian asceticism, see J. Goehring, 'The Origins of Monasticism', in Harold W. Attridge and Gohei Hata (eds), *Eusebius, Christianity and Judaism* (Detroit: Wayne State University Press, 1992), 235–55, esp. 236–8. For general discussion of Therapeutae, see J. Riaud, 'Les Thérapeutes d'Alexandrie dans la tradition et dans la recherche critique jusque'aux découvertes de Qumran', *ANRW* II.20.2 (1987), 1189–1295.

[160] *HE* 2.17.7.

[161] *HE* 2.17.10.

who can promote a reasonably similar form of ascetic idealism, a Logos theology, a doctrine of Providence, and so on). And therefore, those authors whom Eusebius finds congenial are identified as being Hebrews. They include the prophets after Moses, Josephus, Philo, Aristobulus, the High Priest Eleazar, and David.[162] These examples testify to Eusebius' desire to use exclusionary, boundary-forming mechanisms to mark off the Jews as other and (as will be the focus in the *Demonstratio*) illegitimate, while at the same time using a rhetoric of inclusion for those Jewish authors that can best support and legitimate his own form of Christianity.

CONCLUSIONS

It has often been assumed that *religious* positions (given the designations Jewish, Hebrew, Greek) are the subject of the *Praeparatio*, and that the titles given these positions are only incidentally connected with peoples, that is, with ethnic identity. This results from a great deal of abstraction from the concerns and formulations with which Eusebius himself works. I have attempted to show the importance of taking the ethnic terminology (of ethnonyms, ancestral character portraits, and so on) seriously. Hence, instead of a series of exemplars of a religious or theological category—an Urmonotheismus—I have shown the material of *Praeparatio* 7–8 as a narrative of descent, providing the stories of a nation's forefathers (the ancient Hebrews), their decline into a bastardized national identity (the Jews), and the persistence of a remnant of Hebrews until the time of Christianity. This picturing of the world, this inscribing of ethnic character and national demarcations, is absolutely crucial to Eusebius' apologetic methodology. One of the fundamental tasks of apologetics was not merely the criticism of doctrinal positions on a theological or philosophical level, but the formulation of a viable vision of the world in which Christianity makes sense and looks attractive. The *Praeparatio* is, then, concerned with painting a picture of the world of nations in such a way that the other nations are seen in a negative light,

---

[162] Post-Mosaic prophets: 7.11.9; 11.23.8–9; Josephus: 10.6.15; 10.12.31; Philo: 7.12.14; 7.17.4; 7.20.90; 11.14.10; 11.15.7; 11.23.12; Aristobulus: 7.13.7; 8.8.56; 13.11.3; Eleazar: 8.8.56 (in a quotation from Aristeas); David: 11.14.3; 11.23.12. For a partial listing of other post-Mosaic Hebrews in Eusebius' other writings, see Ulrich, *Euseb von Caesarea und die Juden*, 64–8.

while the nation of the Hebrews (and so of their descendants, the Christians) are depicted positively. Furthermore, Eusebius is concerned to build his argument on the basis of certain national 'facts'. This allows him to paint the Jews as a rejected nation, for they are only partly connected to the ancient Hebrews; their origins as Egyptianized and morally weak descendants of the Hebrews had placed a stain upon their continued national identity.

By reading the argument of the *Praeparatio* as fundamentally ethnic in nature, we are able better to appreciate its richness and intensity. To construe the argument as centred on religious positions impairs our understanding of the mechanisms of the *Praeparatio* and the world that Eusebius was creating through his narrative. For Eusebius, the argument was only a matter of 'religion' in so far as it was embedded within the lives and histories of the forefathers of the nations.

5

Greek Descent Revisited

INTRODUCTION

Much of the apologetic project of early Christians was dedicated to an appraisal of Greek philosophy, which resulted in either positive or negative evaluations of the foundational figures of Greek thought. The positive treatments of Justin Martyr and Clement of Alexandria, who sought to accommodate Greek philosophy favourably within a Christian framework, were balanced by the denigrating judgements of Tatian, Theophilus, and others. By the ninth book of the *Praeparatio*, it remained unclear as to which side the weight of Eusebius' magisterial apology would fall. His labours had been expended primarily upon the retelling of a historical narrative of the Greeks, with a defence of that narrative and its contemporary effects and manifestations. This narrative had been joined with a second narrative of Hebrews and Jews that served as a foil to the former.

A brief perusal of the remaining books of the *Praeparatio* exhibit the names of a number of seminal Greek philosophers, in particular Plato. Had Eusebius left history behind finally to pursue intellectual and philosophical themes in a manner more resonant with modern attempts to defend the faith? Such a suggestion might seem natural. Yet, even in these final books of the *Praeparatio*, Eusebius' vision of the world as comprised of more and less ancient nations, whose collective characters, connections and differences were fundamental for his apologetic argument, persists in his treatment of Greek philosophers. His narrative survey of the history of Greek philosophical developments is artfully grafted onto his narrative of Hebrew descent. After his account of the ancient Hebrews, their way of life and theology, and their distinction from the later Jews, Eusebius attempted to delineate a connection with the Greeks. Plato was the prime migrating figure to receive attention when Eusebius picks up this second phase of Greek descent. Plato had been known to have travelled to the East in search of wisdom. For Eusebius, then, Plato's writings had to be thoroughly searched for hints of his interaction with this ancient wisdom. Parallels between Moses' writings and Plato's works are drawn with great care in Books 11–13, since he needed to engage with Plato's thought at length for reasons that will become clearer in the course of the present discussion. First, he was obliged to account for the positive aspects of Greekness, which for him were embodied in Platonic thought. He was not so antagonistic to the Greeks as to attempt a rejection of Plato, but he emphatically set Plato in his historical and ethnical place: Plato was a repository of Hebrew wisdom, who, when located in his proper historical schema, could be shown to have exemplified the process of Greek borrowings from eastern nations. As the transmitter of Hebrew wisdom to the Greeks, Plato's authority was simultaneously invoked and undermined. The greatness of Plato's philosophy was allowed—but only because (and in so far as) it reflected its Hebrew source. Second, Eusebius wanted to depict Plato and the other philosophers who had borrowed Hebrew wisdom as models or precursors for Christian conversion. As he declared:

You may judge that not without sound reason have we given a secondary place to the doctrines of the Greek philosophy, and preferred the theology of the Hebrews, when you learn that even among the Greeks themselves those who have most of all treated philosophy correctly, and thought out something more and better than the vulgar talk about the gods, have discovered no other true doctrines than those which had received a previous sanction among the Hebrews.[1]

If the most philosophic and wise of the Greeks were forced to look elsewhere for truth, and they were now held in high esteem among the Greeks, why should Christians receive blame for rejecting the ancestral theology of the Greeks for that of the Hebrews? Christians were doing nothing less than following the same route as Greek philosophers, and in fact were surpassing them by more fully grasping Hebrew wisdom.

As in the previous chapter, I wish to note the ways in which Eusebius' narration provides a picture of national character that supports his ethnic argumentation in the *Praeparatio* as a whole. Second, the ways in which this narrative forges national connections (especially between

---

[1] *PE* 10.4.1.

the Hebrews, Jews, and Greeks) will be given due consideration. And third, I will provide analysis of how the 'argument from disagreement' (that is, the rejection of Greek philosophy because of the disagreement of Greek philosophers among themselves) offered in Books 14–15 functions within a distinctively ethnic context.

THE GREEKS AS PLAGIARISTS

Eusebius has so far exhibited a method of incorporating aspects of Jewishness into his defence of Christianity by marking off 'Jews' as 'Hebrews'. But this retelling of Jewish and Hebrew history can pull yet more apologetic weight by incorporating the best of the Greeks as well. He does so in four stages. First, he provides evidence, through copious citation, that the Greeks did in fact know who the Hebrews and Jews were (9.1–10), and even knew substantial portions of their history (9.11–42). Second, Eusebius offers proof that the Greeks were known to be thieves and plagiarizers of the labours of others, since they possessed neither any wisdom of their own nor any philosophers who lived early enough to contribute wisdom to the other nations (Book 10). He then offers an account of the various ways in which the Greeks had borrowed from the Hebrews, in particular through the travels of Plato (11.1–13.13). Finally, he enumerates the ways in which the Greeks fell short of the high standard of the Hebrews in wisdom and in virtue (13.14–15.62).

The Jews in Greek Texts

Josephus had set a precedent for Eusebius when he made a point of addressing the issue of Greek knowledge of the Jews in his *Contra Apionem*.[2] Criticisms had been levelled against the Jews as being latecomers upon the scene of the history of civilization and as being largely dependent upon other nations for cultural advances. On a very basic level, it could be argued that the Jews were excluded from the history of civilization and progress by the very fact that they were not

---

[2] A. J. Droge, 'Josephus Between Greeks and Barbarians', in Feldman and Levison (eds), *Josephus' Contra Apionem*, 42–3.

mentioned by those who were the primary movers of history, namely the
Greeks. Hence, it was imperative, Josephus thought, that such assertions
regarding the obscurity of the Jews among the Greeks be opposed.[3]

Josephus' *Contra Apionem* becomes a primary source from which
Eusebius quotes when he takes up the issue.[4] Beyond the sources quoted
by Josephus, Eusebius offers additional quotations from other Greek
sources on the Jews: Theophrastus,[5] Porphyry,[6] Clearchus, Megasthenes
and Aristobulus,[7] Numenius,[8] Abydenus,[9] and Alexander Polyhistor and
his sources.[10] The fact that these authors are all later than Josephus
(except for Theophrastus, and even he is found only in the work of the
later Porphyry), does not seem to bother Eusebius. In fact, his purpose
may be only to update Josephus with the sources from Clement and
Porphyry. After all, he claims that 'illustrious Greek philosophers, even
in our own day', bear witness to the Jews, or rather Hebrews.[11] In any
case, he only wants favourable mention of 'the Jews'—as his Greek
sources will name them, though they are now placed within his own
historical schema as 'Hebrews', not 'Jews'. Thus, he selects Greek
testimonies to the ascetic lifestyle and greatness of the ancient Hebrews.
For instance, Eusebius cites Alexander Polyhistor, who is in turn citing
Eupolemus, as praising Abraham as one who 'surpassed all men in
nobility and wisdom, who was also the inventor of astronomy and the
Chaldaic art, and pleased God well by his zeal for piety'.[12] The concern of

---

[3] See especially *Ap.* 1.1–5.

[4] Though he does so without acknowledgement: fragment of Hecataeus (9.4);
Clearchus (9.5); Choerilus (9.9); as well as from *AJ* at 9.11.15–16. Eusebius consistently
refers to the work as *On the Antiquity of the Jews* (see 8.7.21; 10.6.15; etc.); whereas his
Antiquities is named the *Archaeologia*. For discussion of the title(s) of the *Contra Apionem*
in antiquity, see H. Schreckenberg, 'Text, Überlieferung und Textkritik von *Contra Apionem*', in Feldman and Levison (eds), *Josephus' Contra Apionem*, 75–7. For Eusebius'
appropriation of Josephus' ideas and methods, see Hardwick, *Josephus as an Historical
Source*, 69–102, 119–25; and idem, '*Contra Apionem* and Christian Apologetics', in Feldman and Levison (eds), *Josephus' Contra Apionem*, 384–96.

[5] Cited from Porphyry's *Abst.* 2.26 at 9.2.

[6] *PE* 9.3, 10.

[7] All three cited from Clement's *Strom.* 1.15, 22 at 9.6.

[8] *PE* 9.7–9.

[9] *PE* 9.12, 14, and 41.

[10] *PE* 9.17.1–9.20.1; 9.21–37; 9.39. On Polyhistor, see J. Freudenthal, *Alexander Polyhistor
und die von ihm erhaltenen Reste jüdischer und samritanischer Geschictswerke*, Hellenistische
Studien I, II (Breslau: Skutsch, 1875); G. F. Unger, 'Die Blüthezeit des Alexander Polyhistor',
Philologus 47 (1889), 177–83; Sterling, *Historiography and Self-Definition*, 144–52.

[11] *PE* 9.1.4.

[12] *PE* 9.17.3.

the apologist in amassing such citations by Greek authors was to prove not only that Christians had aligned themselves with well-established nations, but also to show that the ancient Hebrews had received high marks in the assessment of at least some of the Greeks.

Beg, borrow, and steal: the Greeks as thieves

Once Eusebius has made the point that Greek authors have not only known the Hebrews and their deeds, but also esteemed them, he builds up the claim that the Greeks have had a propensity for borrowing what is not theirs, especially in the area of philosophical wisdom, since they had produced nothing of value in this regard on their own:[13] they had been forced by their own scarcity of native wisdom to look elsewhere. Eusebius marshals a number of different strategies with which to implement this portrayal of the Greeks. I will only focus on some of the more important ones, consideration of which will help us grasp the contours of his ethnic argumentation.

The first of these is the adoption of the rhetoric of plagiarism and theft to represent the Greek borrowing of ideas, arts, or skills from other nations (10.1–3).[14] Eusebius scarcely allows for the possibility that the Greeks discovered the idea of monotheism through natural conceptions (*phusikai ennoiai*).[15] Such a scenario would at any rate be favourable for Christians, Eusebius avers.[16] But, given the Greek propensity to steal what is not theirs, it is more likely that they also stole ideas of monotheism and other philosophical tenets from the Hebrews. Before giving a selection of citations as proof, he himself employs a terminology of theft and plagiarism. He writes: 'But you must not be surprised if we say that possibly the doctrines of the Hebrews have been plagiarized (*eskeuōrêsthai*) by them, since they are not only proved to have stolen (*aposulêsantes*) the other branches of learning from Egyptians and Chaldeans and the rest of the barbarous nations, but even to the present

---

[13] See Eusebius, *Theoph.* 2.19. On the theme of Greek borrowing from barbarian nations, especially the Hebrews, see W. Jaeger, 'Greeks and Jews: The First Records of Jewish Religion and Civilization', *Journal of Religion* 18 (1938), 127–43; N. Roth, 'The "Theft of Philosophy" by the Greeks from the Jews', *Classical Folia* 32 (1978), 53–67, which includes a survey of medieval sources.

[14] See also, e.g. Tatian, *Or.* 1; Clement, *Strom.* 1.16.

[15] See Ridings, *The Attic Moses*, 141–7.

[16] *PE* 10.1.5–6; cp. Dio Chrysostom *Or.* 12.27 ff, and 39.

day are detected in robbing one another of the honours gained in their own writings.'[17] Here, plagiarism becomes a provocative metaphor for the Greek activity of taking as their own something originating elsewhere. These acts of plagiarism can extend from lines of writing to whole 'branches of learning'. Eusebius seems to be concerned with both, for he adds: 'At all events one after another they surreptitiously steal (*hupoklepsas*) the phrases of their neighbours together with the thoughts and whole arrangement of treatises, and pride themselves as if upon their own labours.'[18] This theft (*klopē*) exhibits the character (*tropos*) of the Greeks.[19]

The vocabulary used in these descriptions of Greek acts of cultural and philosophical appropriation is loaded with pejorative connotations. The word often translated as 'plagiarist' in Gifford's translation is *kleptēs* or 'thief'.[20] This is not to be understood as innocent borrowing of wisdom from other nations, but rather within the stark terms of stealing and robbing (*aposulēsantes, aposterountes*, and *hupoklepsas*). The extracts from Clement would provide additional terms such as 'filching' (*huphairoumenoi*) and 'copying' (*apomimoumenoi*), and speak of the Greek 'style of plagiarism' (*to kleptikon eidos*). Eusebius also employs the (less negative?) term *eskeuōrēsthai*,[21] apparently occurring in this sense only in Diogenes Laertius 2.61, and Clement's *Stromateis* 6.2.27.[22]

The rhetoric of plagiarism offers a vivid picture of the relation of the Greeks to other nations. The members of the dominant culture are thereby put in an embarrassing and deplorable light. This manner of representing the Greeks adds much to the claim that the Greeks are later than and dependent on other nations. In fact, the language of theft and plagiarism provides an evaluative, even moral, framework for seeing the Greeks. Eusebius' adoption of such language not only indicates the tenor of his polemic, but also is an effective mechanism in his mapping of national connections. In defining the connection as one of deceptive theft and plagiarism, Eusebius represents Greekness within a moral

[17] *PE* 10.1.7.
[18] *PE* 10.1.8.
[19] *PE* 10.1.9.
[20] A. –H. Chroust, 'Charges of Philosophical Plagiarism in Greek Antiquity', *The Modern Schoolman* 38 (1961), 220 n. 1 contains a fairly comprehensive list of terms for plagiarism in Greek literature.
[21] 10.1.7 and 11.praef.1.
[22] The former occurrence is noted by LSJ, s.v.; the latter is noted by Chroust, 'Charges of Philosophical Plagiarism in Greek Antiquity', 220 n. 1 (Lampe's *Patristic Greek Dictionary* lacks an entry for *skeuōreomai*). Compare with Porphyry, *V. Pythag.* 53 (Nauck 46).

dimension that alienates the Greeks from the other nations, but especially from the Hebrews.

A second and more striking mode of portraying the Greeks lies in the tale of Philosophy personified as a female figure who looks in vain for wisdom among the Greeks (10.4.1–10). The story of the personification of Philosophy as a woman coming to the Greeks appears in a similar manner at Lucian's *De Fugitivis* 6–11. There, Lucian tells the story of how Philosophy, being sent by Zeus to bring wisdom to humankind, first goes to the barbarian nations under the assumption that it would be harder to instil wisdom among these peoples. Upon her establishment of wisdom in India (where an entire race of philosophers, the Brahmans, is formed),[23] Ethiopia, Egypt, Babylon (where the Chaldeans and Magi had arisen), Scythia and Thrace, Philosophy arrives in Greece after sending Eumolpus and Orpheus ahead.[24] In Greece, she is able to attach to herself the Seven Sages.[25] But after the Sophists obscure the truth, she nearly leaves, being persuaded to stay only by the pleas of the Cynics, Antisthenes and Diogenes, and later Crates and Menippus.[26] The story continues with the present mistreatment of Philosophy by the Greeks. Such a tale contains the major elements of Eusebius' account: the personified Philosophy, the openness of other nations to her guidance, and the recalcitrance of the Greeks to her teachings.

Dio Chrysostom had already related a similar tale in his twelfth oration at Olympia. Like the wise owl whose advice went unheeded by the other birds, Philosophy had given counsel to the ancient Greeks, but they 'were ignorant and dishonoured her'.[27] While not specifically saying she went to the other nations, Dio next claims that for his audience to find wisdom, they may have to search in Babylon, Bactra (in Bactria), Susa (in Persia) or Palibothra (in India). The rejection of the personified Philosophy by the Greeks of old had thus become an important topos in Roman times, even by authors who identified themselves with the Greeks, though in varying ways.[28]

This background further illuminates Eusebius' use and manipulation of the story. After the Greeks had borrowed the customs and religious practices revolving around polytheism from the other nations, Eusebius says that Philosophy arrived to instil her wisdom among them.

---

[23] Lucian, *Fug.* 6.   [24] Ibid., *Fug.* 8.
[25] Ibid., *Fug.* 9.   [26] Ibid., *Fug.* 11.   [27] Dio, *Or.* 12.9.
[28] For a different application of the personified Philosophy, see Themistius, *Or.* 17.213d–214a.

[She] found among their forefathers nothing that properly belonged to herself, but discovered that the sanctities and antiquities of the theology which had come to them from their fathers, and even the marvellous and universally famous divinities and oracles, were in reality superfluous and unprofitable. Wherefore she proceeded to put these back into a secondary place, as they could not be of any use to her for the discovery of things necessary and true: and thenceforth, as one naked and destitute of any reasonings or learning of her own, she went about examining the foreign and barbarous systems, and provided, collected, and borrowed what was useful to her from all sides, whatever she found among the several nations. For indeed she began to discover that not only the true theology was lacking to the Greeks, but also the most useful in daily life of all the other arts and sciences.[29]

Eusebius' account possesses distinctive elements of its own in contrast to the previous Philosophy stories. For him, even the ignorance and polytheism of the early Greeks had been borrowed from the barbarian nations, making it the more difficult for Philosophy to establish herself there. Also, Eusebius' Philosophy is a distinctly monotheistic entity, in contrast to the polytheism borrowed from the other nations before her arrival. Like Lucian (and in some sense Dio), Eusebius represents Philosophy as going to the other nations. Unlike Lucian and Dio, however, Eusebius has painted Philosophy as being herself somewhat impotent and in need of the wisdom that other nations could offer her. In other words, Eusebius turns the story of Philosophy's far-flung travels upon its head: rather than visiting the other nations to spread her wisdom, Philosophy goes in search of the wisdom she lacks. Eusebius' narrative of Philosophy attempts to effect a memorable and striking image of the state of affairs among the ancient Greeks. They were utterly destitute of all wisdom and beneficial knowledge; philosophy was not innate to the Greeks, but came from outside.

Shortly after the arrival of Philosophy, Eusebius asserts (in a manner similar to Lucian) that the Seven Sages arose and began to discover truth. Importantly, most of the Sages were not originally Greeks themselves, but were from other nations; or if they were Greeks, they had nonetheless gone to barbarian nations for their learning.[30] Pherecydes was a Syrian.[31] His student, Pythagoras, was from Samos or Tyrrhenia, Syria or Tyre, according to the divergent accounts, so that 'the first of the philosophers, celebrated in the mouth of all Greeks, was

---

[29] *PE* 10.4.8–10.
[30] See Richter, *Ethnography, Archaism, and Identity in the Early Roman Empire*, 99–129.
[31] *PE* 10.4.14.

not a Greek but a barbarian'.[32] But even more than his birth, Pythagoras
had sought wisdom from abroad, studying in Babylon, Egypt, and
Persia, and becoming a pupil of the Magi and then of Brahmans from
India.[33] Thales was a Phoenician, or Milesian according to variant
reports, and studied in Egypt.[34] Solon likewise studied in Egypt, Eusebius says, citing the passage from the *Timaeus* on the Greeks' historical
lateness: 'O Solon, Solon, you Greeks are always children, and there is
not one old man among the Greeks ..., nor is there among you any
learning grown hoary with time.'[35] Plato, too, had gone abroad in his
search for truth, travelling first to Italy then to Egypt.[36] After noting
Democritus' travels to Babylon and Egypt, Eusebius calls off his enumeration of migrating philosophers and claims that the point has been
sufficiently made that the Greeks had been 'left for long ages very poor,
and devoid of all learning'.[37]

It is in this context that Eusebius offers a rather remarkable 'proof' of
the dependency of Greek learning upon the other nations, namely the
transmission of the alphabet. Beginning with the story of Cadmus, who
had transmitted Phoenician letters to the Greeks, Eusebius claims that
the geographical label 'Phoenicia' needs to be properly understood.
For the land in which the Hebrews lived was in ancient times called
Phoenicia, only later becoming Judaea and then Palestine.[38] Then to
clinch the argument, Eusebius systematically goes through each letter of
the Hebrew alphabet and gives the special meaning for which each
stands. He writes: 'Each letter among the Hebrews has its name from
some significant idea, a circumstance which it is not possible to trace
among the Greeks: on which account especially it is admitted that the
letters are not originally Greek.'[39] For example, the first five letters of
the Hebrew alphabet, standing together, mean 'The learning of a house,
this is the fullness of tablets',[40] since Aleph (in Eusebius, 'Alph') means

[32] *PE* 10.4.13.
[33] *PE* 10.4.15. For a survey of Pythagoras' travels to the East in earlier literature, see
P. Gorman, 'Pythagoras Palaestinus', *Philologus* 127 (1983), 30–42.
[34] *PE* 10.4.18.
[35] *PE* 10.4.19 (from *Timaeus* 22B). See also, *PE* 7.18.11.
[36] *PE* 10.4.20.
[37] *PE* 10.4.25. ἡ παρ' Ἕλλησι πολιτεία τὸν μακρὸν αἰῶνα πτωχεύουσα καὶ γυμνὴ παντὸς
μαθήματος ἀπολειφθεῖσα.
[38] *PE* 10.5.1–2.
[39] *PE* 10.5.3.
[40] *PE* 10.5.4. μάθησις οἴκου, πλήρωσις δέλτων αὕτη.

'learning', Beth means 'of a house', and so on. (In fact, Aleph does mean 'learning' and Beth does mean 'house' in Hebrew.)

Whether or not it was Eusebius' idea to attempt to arrive at a coherent thought or phrase when reading them in order, this manipulation of alphabetic signification is highly important in the history of the alphabet in general, and in Jewish–Greek polemic in particular. Unfortunately, Eusebius' description of alphabetic meaning has not found its way into any scholarship on the history of the alphabet, as far as I can tell. In fact, Jerome's *Epistulae* 30, which has received scholarly attention,[41] is merely another example of Jerome's unacknowledged use of other authors, in particular Eusebius. While Eusebius' discussion seems to be without precedent, the argument for alphabetic superiority may have arisen within the context of the rabbinic schools or from a lost Jewish polemic against the Greeks.[42] Either way, this argument fits well within his overall argument for Greek dependency on barbarians and their lack of native wisdom.

So far, Eusebius' rhetoric of plagiarism and his use of Philosophy personified have been seen as driving mechanisms for his portrayal of Greek dependency. The third means of putting the Greeks in their proper place, both historically and culturally, is through a scholarly display of chronological erudition (10.9–14). In some sense, chronology offers a more sure-fire way of asserting Greek dependence, for if the founding fathers of Greek philosophy can be shown to have lived only after the philosophers of other nations, then any claim to their high position in cultural and philosophical history becomes indefensible. As Eusebius says:

This would be one of the most conclusive proofs for the argument before us, that before dealing with the learned men among the people we should first decide about their antiquity; in order that if the Greeks should be found to hold the same doctrines with the prophets and theologians of the Hebrews, you may no longer be in doubt who were likely to have borrowed from the others; whether the elder from the younger, Hebrews from Greeks, and barbarians from philosophers, whose language even they were not likely to understand;

---

[41] See J. Drucker, *The Alphabetic Labyrinth* (London: Thames and Hudson, 1995); J. N. D. Kelly suggested that Jerome's alphabetic lore was 'perhaps derived from Jewish advisers' (*Jerome: His Life, Writings, and Controversies* [London: Duckworth, 1975], 97).

[42] On the importance of symbolic language for cultural and/or ethnic identity, see S. Schwartz, 'Language, Power and Identity in Ancient Palestine', *P&P* 148 (1995), 3–47; M. Rubin, 'The Language of Creation or the Primordial Language: A Case of Cultural Polemics in Antiquity', *JJS* 49 (1998), 306–33.

or, what is more likely, that the younger borrowed from the elder, and that those Greeks who had most busily studied the history of the various nations were not unacquainted with the writings of the Hebrews.[43]

Eusebius follows this statement with a prolonged recounting of the dates for various figures from Hebrew history, contrasting these with the later dates of particular Greek figures. He supplements his own calculations with those enumerated by Julius Africanus,[44] Tatian,[45] Clement,[46] and Josephus.[47] The citations from these authors are sandwiched between Eusebius' own chronological considerations, which are at 10.9 (concerning the dates of those who lived until the time of Moses) and 10.14 (concerning those who lived after Moses). The latter chronology further drives home the recent arrival of Greek civilization: Solon, one of the Seven Sages, lived at the time of Cyrus, king of Persia.[48] Cyrus enters Jewish history, however, at a fairly late stage, even after most of the prophets, while Solon and the Seven Sages had already been marked out as the founders of Greek philosophy. The earliest Greek philosophers were thus shown to have lived embarrassingly later than the ancient Hebrews and Moses.

Eusebius had already laboured diligently in the field of chronological studies.[49] His *Chronicon* had set down the chronologies of the major nations in parallel columns to highlight the early or late development of each. This project was apologetic at its core: Eusebius' innovative use of parallel columns was a clear indicator of the relative lateness or antiquity of each nation.[50] However, its full apologetic utility was not realized until his chronological conclusions found their place within the *Praeparatio*'s argument. Combined with his employment of the rhetoric of plagiarism and his narrative of Philosophy's arrival among the Greeks, the chronological argument marshalled in Book 10 strikes a devastating blow to Greek claims for possessing the origins of philosophy and truth.

---

[43] *PE* 10.8.18.   [44] *PE* 10.10.   [45] *PE* 10.11.
[46] *PE* 10.12.   [47] *PE* 10.13.   [48] *PE* 10.14.9.

[49] See A. A. Mosshammer, *The Chronicle of Eusebius and the Greek Chronographic Tradition* (Lewisburg: Bucknell University Press, 1979); W. Adler, *Time Immemorial: Archaic History and its Sources in Christian Chronography from Julius Africanus to George Syncellus* (Washington, DC: Dumbarton Oaks, 1989), 15–71; and idem, 'Eusebius' *Chronicle* and Its Legacy', 467–91.

[50] See Frede, 'Eusebius' Apologetic Writings', 224; Kofsky, *Eusebius of Caesarea against the Pagans*, 38–40.

Plato: Traveller and Translator

Reference to Plato's travels was first made in the tenth book of the *Praeparatio*.[51] Here, Eusebius claimed that Plato had visited Italy, to study under the Pythagoreans, as well as Egypt.[52] He had also made favourable remarks on the ancient philosophy of the Syrians and Egyptians. Eusebius quotes the pseudonymous *Epinomis* 986E–987A, where the Syrians and Egyptians are said to have first acquired accurate knowledge of astronomical phenomena as a result of the 'beauty of the summer season … whence the knowledge has reached to all countries, including our own, after having been tested by thousands of years and time without end'.[53]

In the eleventh book of the *Praeparatio*, where Eusebius turns his full attention to Plato, he moderates his accusation of Greek 'theft' and makes the much milder claim that Plato is in agreement (*sumphōnia*, or even *homodoxa*) with the Hebrews,[54] or that they thought similar things (*ta homoia*).[55] The mass of parallels—from the tripartite division of philosophy into ethics, dialectic, and physics to the nature of God or the soul[56]—are meant to exhibit the conformity of Plato's thought with that of the Hebrews. Eusebius uses the language of agreement throughout, even using the metaphoric phrase 'like the harmony of a well-tuned lyre'.[57] Of course, he does not allow the reader to forget who came first.[58] The Hebrews began practising true philosophy 'before the Greeks had learned even the first letters'.[59]

The idea that Plato was actually dependent for his wisdom upon the Hebrews begins to crop up only gradually as Eusebius continues to compare Hebrew and Platonic thought. At 11.6.1, Eusebius begins

---

[51] *PE* 10.4.20.

[52] Cicero's *Rep.* 1.16 seems to be the earliest reference to Plato in Egypt (see also, Diodorus, 1.96.2); for travels elsewhere in the East, see also Cicero, *Fin.* 5.19.50; *Tusc. Disp.* 4.19.44; see A. Swift Riginos, *Platonica: The Anecdotes concerning the Life and Writings of Plato* (Leiden: Brill, 1976), 60–9; H. Dörrie, 'Platons Reisen zu fernen Völkern: Zur Geschichte eines Motivs der Platon-Legende und zu seiner Neuwendung durch Lactanz', in W. Den Boer *et al.*, (eds), *Romanitas et Christianitas* (Amsterdam: North-Holland, 1973), 99–118.

[53] *PE* 10.4.21.

[54] *PE* 11.praef.3; 11.3.10; 11.5.9; 11.28.18–19; 11.38.1.

[55] *PE* 11.1.1; 11.32.11; 11.33.4.

[56] Tripartite division of philosophy: 11.2–7; God: 11.12–22; soul: 11.27–8.

[57] *PE* 12.1.1.

[58] *PE* 11.3.10; 11.4.7; 11.6.1.

[59] *PE* 11.4.7; see also 7.18.11.

to assume the connection: 'Plato, following (*hepomenos*) [Moses], assents to these things.' *Hepomenos* allows for more than a mere chronological ordering, and includes the notion of imitating Moses' ideas. However, the statement is not strong, and is probably meant only to introduce the dependent relationship rather naturally.[60] The relationship is affirmed more clearly at 11.8.1, where Eusebius states that, 'the admirable Plato followed the all-wise Moses and the Hebrew prophets in regard also to the teaching and speculation about things incorporeal and seen only by the mind'.[61] However, the matter is quickly complicated in the remainder of the sentence:

Whether it were that he learned from hearsay which had reached him (since he is proved to have made his studies among the Egyptians at the very time when the Hebrews, having been driven the second time out of their own country, were in the habit of visiting Egypt during the Persian supremacy), or whether on his own he hit upon the true nature of things, or in whatever way, he was deemed worthy of this knowledge by God.[62]

This sort of waffling between dependency and natural knowledge on the part of Plato has already been seen in regard to the Greeks in general at 10.1.5–6.[63] While it seems to detract from Eusebius' case, it could show the initial caution with which Eusebius begins approaching the relationship between Plato and the Hebrews. On the other hand, he may only be putting on a show of mock objectivity and openness to other interpretations. For instance, he raises the issue in somewhat more disingenuous terms when he states: 'Whence these ideas came to Plato, I cannot explain.'[64] Of course, this is after he has made clear statements that Plato took them directly from the Hebrews, and hence it here appears to be more rhetorical flaunting than caution.

If it is caution, though, it is soon left behind when he asserts that Plato 'imitated not only the thought, but also the very expressions and words of the Hebrew scriptures', and so, 'appropriated' Hebrew dogma.[65] This description is further supplemented by the terminology of paraphrase and translation: 'Plato seems directly to paraphrase (*metaphrazein*) the

---

[60] See Frede, 'Eusebius' Apologetic Writings', 247, who nevertheless notes only the use of *epakolouthein*.

[61] See also *PE* 11.16.3; 11.26.1; 12.15.6. In earlier apologists, see e.g. Clement, *Protr.* 6; Origen *C. Cels.* 4.39; 6.19; 7.30.

[62] *PE* 11.8.1.

[63] See Ridings, *The Attic Moses*, 154.

[64] *PE* 11.26.4.

[65] *PE* 11.9.4.

oracle of Moses.'[66] Amelius, in interpreting Plato's thought, is said to 'paraphrase' the barbarian's theology (that is, of St John).[67] Plato writes 'as if having been taught by Moses'.[68] And again, Moses is named the 'teacher' of Plato's and Porphyry's doctrine of the soul.[69] In the *Symposium*, Plato is declared to be 'all but translating' (a phrase that reccurs) the words of Moses' account of Paradise, and uses allegory just as Moses had done.[70] Plato thus 'speaks in riddles like Moses'.[71] Plato's account of affairs before the flood 'makes use of [Moses'] archaeology'.[72] Or alternatively, Plato 'walks in the footsteps' of Moses.[73] At another place, Plato 'alters' (*metabalōn*) the words of David's Psalms.[74] More provocatively, Eusebius claims: 'you may find each of the philosopher's sayings stated word for word throughout the whole sacred writing of the Psalms'.[75] At 12.44.1, Eusebius straightforwardly claims that Plato translated (*diermēneuei*) Moses.

Under the barrage of Platonic and Hebrew parallels, Eusebius methodically pushes on from the milder claim that Plato may have been only moderately influenced by the Hebrews to the conviction that Plato was, in fact, the translator of Moses. Hence, Eusebius' treatment of Plato and Hebrew wisdom goes beyond drawing parallels between similar passages. He has, rather, strategically placed Plato into a position of subordination to the Hebrews, which allows him to create a certain critical distance between his own thought and that of Plato.[76] Eusebius himself may have inadvertently adopted a great deal of Platonic thought in his own theological and philosophical formulations—one thinks most readily of his Logos theology.[77] However, to claim that Eusebius is here attempting to reconcile Platonic and Hebrew wisdom in an 'assimilationist exercise',[78] and is forging a Christian—Platonic

---

[66] *PE* 11.26.8.   [67] *PE* 11.19.2.   [68] *PE* 11.27.4.
[69] *PE* 11.28.17.   [70] *PE* 12.11.1; see also, 12.13.1.   [71] *PE* 12.11.2.
[72] *PE* 12.14.2.   [73] *PE* 12.16.1.   [74] *PE* 12.21.6.
[75] *PE* 12.21.7. Incidentally, Eusebius never mentions Plato in his commentary on the Psalms.
[76] See E. Des Places, 'Eusèbe de Césarée juge de Platon dans la *Préparation Évangélique*', in *Mélanges de philosophie grecque offerts a Mgr. Dies* (Paris: Libraire Philosophique J. Vrin, 1956), 71.
[77] See Mortley, *The Idea of Universal History*, 151–99, esp. 167 ('Eusebius is one of the great Platonists of the late antique era'); Frede, 'Eusebius' Apologetic Writings', 223–50; M. J. Edwards, 'Pagan and Christian Monotheism in the Age of Constantine', in Swain and Edwards, *Approaching Late Antiquity*, 227–32.
[78] Mortley, *The Idea of Universal History*, 167. Despite my disagreement on this point, Mortley's treatment remains highly important for understanding the complexity of the traditions within, or against, which Eusebius is working.

synthesis, is to misconstrue Eusebius' aim. His argument for Plato's dependence upon earlier and wiser Hebrew thinkers attempts nothing less than to dismantle the authoritative status of this philosopher upon which so much later Greek thought, especially under the empire, rested. Authority in matters of truth and morality reside instead with a group of holy men in a barbarian nation.

Even more important for his ethnic argumentation, Eusebius has written Plato into an ethnic framework that highlights dependency on other nations and shows him to be constrained by the weakness of his own Greekness. As just noted, it could be argued that Eusebius is unwittingly putting Hebrew thought into Greek dress, and so Hellenizing Moses. And this would be a fair assessment. For Eusebius, after all, does claim a tripartite division of Hebrew philosophy into ethics, dialectic, and metaphysics that sounds remarkably Hellenistic. And while he insists that a theology, such as his own, which places important emphasis on the operation of divine reason (the Logos), is distinctively Hebrew, it nevertheless has a very strong resonance with Middle Platonic developments.[79] However, on the other hand, Eusebius has provided a paradigm for only selective accommodation of Plato's thought. And, in the end, what is at stake is not so much particular doctrines but a fundamental shift in ethnic and cultural vision—an overturning of the dominant Hellenocentric approach to evaluating cultural, philosophical, and religious truth. The truth, for Eusebius, does not lie in Greece but is scattered across the *oikoumenē*, wherever Hebrews live out their lives of asceticism, pursuit of wisdom, and friendship with God. And in place of picturing Greekness as a steady stream of development from earlier Greeks to later Greeks, from superstition to the rise of philosophy, Eusebius imagines a world of travelling thinkers criss-crossing the ancient world with cargoes of distinctive ideas taken from distinctive locations and peoples. It is not a world of steady development by a particular people, but one of transmission, alteration, paraphrase, and translation.

This is the framework for understanding Eusebius' Plato. For Eusebius, Plato is a transmitter, a translator. He is only the greatest of many who had sought the truth outside Greece. But, his philosophy could only be considered great in so far as his translations were accurate. Hence,

---

[79] Eusebius is more likely indebted to Philo of Alexandria and earlier Christian apologists than non-Christian middle Platonists; see, e.g. Athenagoras, *Leg.* 10; Tatian, *Or.* 5, 7; Theophilus, *Autol.* 2.10; Origen, *C. Cels.* 5.39.

Eusebius turns from those aspects of Plato's thought that were in harmony with Hebrew writings to the less faithful parts of his philosophy.[80]

Eusebius presented an attitude of deference and respect to the philosopher in 11.1.1–13.13.13. But at 13.14, he becomes hostile, claiming that Plato should be blamed for the continuation of polytheistic superstition among the Greeks.[81] Whereas Plato had 'followed' the Hebrews in the passages related in 11.1.1–13.13.13, Eusebius now brings to the reader's attention texts of Plato that have fallen away from Hebrew wisdom: Plato 'no longer follows them'.[82] Instead, Plato has turned, for example, to the Egyptians when he adopts the notion of metempsychosis: 'Plato is Egyptianizing (*aiguptiazōn*) in his doctrine.'[83] In comparison with Moses' legislation, Plato's prescriptions on common wives, pederasty, harsh punishment in legal cases, and more, do not stand up well.[84] After quoting from Plato's *Phaedrus* on pederasty, Eusebius asserts that 'Moses expressly legislated the opposite',[85] and then quotes the Levitical passages castigating the abominable nature of such practices.

Such an enumeration of Plato's weak points exhibits well Eusebius' critical approach to Plato.[86] These undesirable aspects of Plato's thought must be highlighted for Eusebius' apologetic programme to maintain its force. He himself had shown that the criticism might be raised that Christians had no need to go to the Hebrews for wisdom if Plato was shown to be in agreement with them. The Greek interlocutor might ask, Eusebius notes: 'Why ... if Moses and Plato have agreed so well in their philosophy, are we to follow the doctrines not of Plato but of Moses, when we ought to do the reverse, because, in addition to the equivalence of the doctrines, the Greek author would be more congenial to us as Greeks than the barbarian?'[87] Eusebius has anticipated the question with

---

[80] For a balanced treatment, see Ridings, *The Attic Moses*, 141–96; Des Places, 'Eusèbe de Césarée juge de Platon dans la *Préparation Évangélique*', 73–6 (though his conclusion that Eusebius valued Greek philosophy as a 'preparation for the Gospel' ignores Eusebius' aims).

[81] Although he retains some admiration for him at *PE* 13.18.17.

[82] *PE* 13.16.1.

[83] *PE* 13.16.12.

[84] Theophilus had earlier criticized Plato for wife-sharing (*Autol.* 3.6) and metempsychosis (3.7).

[85] 30.20.7. Gifford omits the entirety of Chapter 20 from his translation for the sake of his more sensitive readers.

[86] See Eusebius, *Theoph.* 2.30–46.

[87] *PE* 13.praef.

a response that highlights the limits of that agreement. Plato had not been able to turn fully from his Greekness; Hebrew wisdom held only partial sway over his thought. His writings evinced a mixture of barbarian wisdom and piety with Greek foolishness and impiety. Even if Plato had been able to embrace more completely the teachings and practices of the Hebrews, he nonetheless held only a secondary and belated position in comparison with the purity of original Hebrew wisdom. Eusebius concludes his discussion of the divergences between the Hebrews and Plato by noting: 'We gladly welcome all that is noble and excellent in him, and bid a long farewell to what is not of such a character.'[88]

This and similar statements in the *Praeparatio* have led many to misconstrue Eusebius' aim as an attempt to vindicate Christian doctrine by outlining its parallels with the best of Greek philosophy.[89] In effect, he may be doing just this. However, his explicit intention for offering the comparison between Platonic and biblical teaching is to convict Plato of dependence upon the Hebrews. Plato's value lies, for Eusebius, only in those areas in which he accurately conveyed Hebrew wisdom; for those areas in which he failed, he should be roundly condemned as a faulty translator. Contrary to the predominant view of Eusebius' attitude toward Greek philosophy, the *Praeparatio* eschews any claim that Greek thought provides a preparation for the Gospel. Instead, it is Hebrew philosophy that furnishes the preparation for Greek philosophy. Christians have no need to borrow from the best of Greek wisdom since that wisdom is only (mis-)appropriated from an original and pure form of Hebrew wisdom.

THE DISCORD OF THE GREEKS

The fourteenth and fifteenth books of the *Praeparatio* are primarily dedicated to showing the dissension among Greek philosophers on various doctrinal issues.[90] Eusebius says his primary purpose in doing this is to further establish his defence of the Christian rejection of such Greek thinking and Christianity's adoption of the way of life of the

---

[88] *PE* 13.21.14. See Origen, *C. Cels.* 5.40.

[89] See Lyman, *Christology and Cosmology*, 91–2.

[90] Philosophical discord had been an important theme in earlier apologists as well; see Tatian, *Or.* 3, 25–6; Theophilus, *Autol.* 2.4–5, 8; Origen, *C. Cels.* 2.12; 3.12–13.

Hebrews. Furthermore, he writes that he will draw attention to the discord of the Greeks, 'not at all as a hater of the Greeks or of reason, far from it, but to remove all cause of slanderous accusation, that we have preferred the Hebrew oracles from having been very little acquainted with Hellenic wisdom'.[91] Christian rejection of Greekness cannot be denigrated as stemming from ignorance or from a lack of reason. According to Eusebius, Christians know full well what it is they are rejecting (a late, derivative and discordant Greekness), as well as what it is they are accepting (an ancient, pure and rational Hebrew way of life). The opposition between Greek discord and Hebrew unity provides the main theme of the final books of the *Praeparatio*.

The final element of Eusebius' apologetic methodology that requires attention, then, is the manner in which the account of discord among Greek philosophers fits within the framework of ethnic argumentation. The purpose of Eusebius' argument from disagreement is to trace the corrosion and fragmentation of an original and unified body of wisdom possessed by the Hebrews alone. The force of the argument from disagreement lies in the assumption that if the complete and pure form of wisdom is possessed at any given time, then any change made to that body of truth must be a change for the worse.[92] In Eusebius' narration of the rise of Greek philosophy, the true wisdom of the ancient Hebrews is transferred to the Greeks under Plato. Some alterations, or rather deviations, are made at that time—alterations which are *ipso facto* for the worse. When Plato's successors then made further changes to the already faded wisdom that Plato had preserved, the truth quickly vanished.

Within Eusebius' ethnic argumentation, this discord is seen as distinctively Greek. The harmony of the Hebrews is, accordingly, a distinctively Hebrew trait. In other words, discord or harmony was part of the set of national character traits that were representative of each of the nations. The Hebrew way of life, characterized by rationality and unity, is fit to preserve true wisdom intact. The Greeks on the other hand, as superstitious and ignorant, could not possibly maintain the truth in its purified form.

Eusebius had already shown that the Greeks, destitute of any native wisdom, had become thieves and plagiarizers of barbarian wisdom. Even the greatest of Greek philosophers, Plato, had been forced to resort to

---

[91] *PE* 14.2.7. See also 15.1.7, 12.
[92] For its use in middle Platonism, see Boys-Stones, *Post-Hellenistic Philosophy*, 123–50.

barbarian (Hebrew) wisdom; his greatness was diminished in so far as he deviated from that wisdom. Now Eusebius wants to continue the narrative of Greek philosophy to show that Plato's successors quickly turned from his thought and fell further and further from the wisdom that had been embodied in the Hebrew philosophy and way of life. The contrast between the ancient Hebrews and the later Greek philosophers becomes more and more vividly highlighted.

Before embarking on his citational tour of Greek discord, Eusebius recalls the way of life exhibited by the ancient Hebrews that he had narrated in Book 7. This time, however, he wants to highlight one particular aspect of the Hebrews: the unity and consistency of life and doctrine among them. 'The Hebrews on their part from long time of old and, so to say, from the very first origin of humanity, having found the true and pious philosophy have carefully preserved this undefiled to succeeding generations, son from father having received and guarded a treasure of true doctrines, so that no one dared to take away from or add to what had been once for all determined.'[93] He adds that Moses, through his legislation and founding of the Jewish nation, nonetheless had left unchanged the true philosophy handed down from the Hebrews. His legislation was meant only to implement a 'certain moderate constitution' (*tinos mesēs politeias*) for the Jews, while he altered the 'dogmatic theology of his forefathers' not at all.[94] The prophets, likewise, never 'ventured to utter a word of discord (*diaphōnon*) either against each other, or against the opinions held by Moses and the elders beloved of God'.[95] The Christians, too, had preserved without alteration the wisdom of the Hebrews.[96] 'Our doctrines ... with one mind and one voice, confirm with unanimous vote the certainty of that which is both the true piety and philosophy, and are filling the whole world, and growing afresh and flourishing every day.'[97] Throughout Hebrew history there had been, according to Eusebius, no hint of deviation from the ancients, nor disharmony among its protagonists. Thus, the picture of Hebrew harmony and purity, in

---

[93] *PE* 14.3.1; cp. Eusebius, *Theoph.* 1.42; Clement, *Strom.* 1.11.3, with D. Kimber Buell, *Making Christians* (Princeton: Princeton University Press, 1999), 83–6.

[94] *PE* 14.3.2.

[95] *PE* 14.3.3; cp. Dionysius of Halicarnassus, *Thuc.* 5; Josephus, *Ap.* 1.8; *AJ* 1.17; *Revelation* 22: 18–19.

[96] *PE* 14.3.4–5.

[97] *PE* 14.3.5. See Clement, *Protr.* 9 ('a symphony following one choir leader'); 12. On the power of such rhetoric for unity, see Kimber Buell, *Making Christians*, 5–10.

thought and way of life, stands in stark contrast to the history of conflict and dissension among the Greeks that Eusebius is about to record.

Eusebius does not, however, limit himself to the philosophers who come after Plato. Instead, he steps back from his narrow focus upon Plato to take in a panoramic view of the history of Greek philosophy from the Presocratics to the Hellenistic schools.[98] The Greeks who had turned plagiarizers for not having any wisdom of their own, described in Book 10 before Plato had been introduced as a bringer of Hebrew wisdom, are brought back into the narrative of Greek philosophical development. Before, their lack of rationality and wisdom had been the focal point of Eusebius' argument; here it is their persistent discord and inability to attain any form of philosophical unity. If all truth is one, then their incessant disagreement proves the absence of it from their philosophical attempts.[99] The physiological doctrines of the philosophers before Plato were 'tottering about on short [evidence]',[100] and Plato himself was the foremost witness to their dissension, as quotations from the *Theaetetus* and *Sophist* exhibit.[101]

The central position of Plato, both for Greek philosophy and for Hebrew–Greek connections, marked a lull in the storm of opposing voices. However, the harmony (*sumphōnein*) that Plato represented was not one of agreement with his Greek predecessors, but with his Hebrew teachers. His successors in the Academy perpetuated the eristic vices of discord and verbal warfare that had characterized philosophers before him. Eusebius castigates Speusippus, Xenocrates and Polemon, the first successors to the Academy:

These ones began from his own hearth at once to undo the teaching of Plato, distorting what had been clear to the teacher by introducing foreign doctrines, so that you might expect the power of those marvellous dialogues to be extinguished at no distant time, and the transmission of the doctrines to come to an end at once on the founder's death; for a conflict and schism having hereupon begun from them, and never ceasing up to the present time, there are none who delight to emulate the doctrines that he loved, except perhaps one or two in our lifetime ... [102]

The philosophical project of the Greeks, when left to themselves (that is, apart from Hebrew teachers), was a deplorable failure.

Quotations from Numenius' *The Revolt of the Academics against Plato* provided a vivid witness of the fractured state of philosophical affairs in

---

[98] Cp. Eusebius, *Theoph.* 2.47–50.   [99] See Lactantius, *Div. Inst.* 3.4, 7, 15.
[100] *PE* 14.3.6.   [101] *PE* 14.4.1–11.   [102] *PE* 14.4.14.

Plato's school.[103] His metaphors for the disruption and dispute are striking and provocative. Like the ill-fated king torn apart by Maenads, Plato was 'now being torn in pieces more furiously than any Pentheus deserved, he suffers limb by limb'.[104] The Homeric language of warfare also provided a reservoir of metaphors for depicting philosophical disputatiousness.[105] Their verbal clashes resembled the violent combat of the *Iliad*. Arcesilaus' argumentative parries on both sides of an issue were like Diomedes, the son of Tydeus.[106] A number of Homeric texts are joined together in representing the conflict between Arcesilaus and Zeno, for whom arguments served as auxiliary forces (*sumpolemoun-tōn*).[107] 'Together they cast their shields, together the spears and spirits of the men with bronze breastplates; and their embossed shields met, and a great din had arisen. Shield pressed on shield, helmet on helmet, and man knocked against man.'[108] Instead of facing off against Arcesilaus, Zeno 'turned the mighty jaws of war' against Plato.[109] The language of war and conflict recur throughout Numenius' discussion of Plato's successors.[110] The picture is insistently one of discord, intellectual failure, and ineptitude.

Numenius furthermore set before the Academics the embarrassing fact that even the Epicureans had been able to maintain unity and concord with their philosophical master. 'The school of Epicurus', claims Numenius, 'is like some kind of true polity, without civil war, having one mind in common and one manner of thought.'[111] Despite the falsity of Epicurean philosophical tenets, the Epicureans' recognition

---

[103] *PE* 14.4.13–14.9.3; see Boys-Stones, *Post-Hellenistic Philosophy*, 138–41; R. Lamberton, *Homer the Theologian* (Berkeley: University of California Press, 1986), 54–77; and also, E. Des Places, 'Numenius et Eusèbe de Cesaree', *SP* 13 (1975), 19–28, reprinted in *Études Platoniciennes. 1929–1979* (Leiden: Brill, 1981), 316–25; idem, *Numenius. Fragments* (Paris: Société d'Édition 'Les Belles Lettres', 1973), 28–32.

[104] *PE* 14.5.8. Cp. Clement, *Strom.* 1.13.57.1–6; Origen, *C. Cels.* 2.34; Atticus *ap. PE* 11.2.2.

[105] See Lamberton, *Homer the Theologian*, 55–9; for the metaphysical implications behind this, see D. J. O'Meara, *Pythagoras Revived* (Oxford: Clarendon Press, 1989), 10–14. The vocabulary of wrestling had already been applied to verbal conflicts as early as the sophistic period in classical Greece; see M. Gagarin, *Antiphon the Athenian* (Austin: University of Texas Press, 2002), 19–20.

[106] *PE* 14.6.1, where *Il.* 5.85 is quoted.

[107] *PE* 14.6.7.

[108] Homer *Il.* 4.447–449 *ap. PE* 14.6.7.

[109] Homer *Il.* 10.8 *ap. PE* 14.6.11.

[110] *Stasis* and cognates: 14.5.4, 7; *machē, polemos* and cognates: 14.5.12; 14.6.8, 9, 10, 13; 14.8.1, 2; see also the descriptions of Carneades at 14.8.2, 5–6.

[111] *PE* 14.5.3; see Boys-Stones, *Post-Hellenistic Philosophy*, 138–9.

that divergence from their founder was to be guarded against was marked out as a single praiseworthy practice of the oft-criticized school. Epicurean unity in spite of philosophical inaccuracies made the discordant cacophony of the Academy the more embarrassing and Numenius' reprimand the more damaging.

If the successors of Plato in the Academy were so susceptible to accusations of disagreement and attack upon their master, the members of the other philosophical schools could hardly be expected to escape similar charges. The physical philosophers, treated as their own school, had been in perpetual discord because of the conjectural nature of their intellectual pursuits.[112] These philosophers boasted of their aptitude in astronomy, arithmetic, geometry, and music (disciplines not clearly heralded in Hebrew teachings);[113] yet their more scientific approach had not led them to the truth or virtue.[114] Their verbal battles (*logomachia*) and discord (*diaphōnia*) were proof of the erroneous path they pursued.[115] Similarly, the Sceptics (or Pyrrhonists),[116] Cyrenaics,[117] empiricists,[118] Epicureans,[119] Peripatetics,[120] and Stoics[121] were exposed for the disagreement within and between their rival schools.

Eusebius' treatment of these philosophical schools claims to be a direct criticism of the error of their various positions rather than explicitly a focus on their dissension. He consistently introduces and concludes the criticisms of each school or individual with a statement to the effect that 'these are the objections raised against these philosophers',[122] or, 'let us look at the arguments against them',[123] and so on. However, these criticisms not only show the irrationality of the doctrines of the various schools, but also highlight in no uncertain terms the radical divergence and incessant disagreement on all matters between them. The criticisms levelled against the different schools are

---

112 *PE* 14.9.4–14.13.9; cp. *Theoph.* 2.22.

113 *PE* 14.10.10.

114 *PE* 14.10.11.

115 *PE* 14.10.9. Their points of difference are enumerated at 14.14.1–14.16.13; and again at 15.22.68–15.32.8; and 15.32.9–15.52.17 (on cosmogonical doctrines).

116 *PE* 14.17.1–14.18.30.

117 *PE* 14.18.31–14.19.7.

118 *PE* 14.19.8–14.20.12.

119 *PE* 14.20.13–14.21.7; cp. *Theoph.* 2.19.

120 *PE* 15.2.1–15.13.5; cp. *Theoph.* 2.20.

121 *PE* 15.13.6–15.22.67; cp *Theoph.* 2.21.

122 *PE* 14.18.32.

123 *PE* 14.19.10.

not (except briefly) Eusebius' own; rather, they are the words of other Greeks—most prominently Aristocles and Atticus—both well-known exponents of their own schools (Peripatetic and Platonic respectively). Hence, Eusebius' argument from disagreement is most powerful through the criticisms of the combatants themselves.

Though Eusebius does not, in these cases, explicitly bring out the disagreement, they must be seen as part of that larger argument. Likewise, in the quotations from Plutarch on the cosmogonical theories of physical philosophers, to whom he returns after his treatment of the schools listed above, Eusebius claims that the material from Plutarch will prove that the physical philosophers worshipped astral phenomena as gods.[124] His claim, however, is hardly supported by the extensive quotation, which lists the ideas about various astral phenomena by the different philosophers. For example, the following doctrines on the moon are listed:

> Anaximander: ... it is like a chariot wheel ... and full of fire.
> Xenophanes: a cloud condensed.
> The Stoics: a mixture of fire and air.
> Plato: mostly of earth.
> Anaxagoras and Democritus: a fiery solid ...
> Heraclitus: earth surrounded with mist.
> Pythagoras: a mirror-like body.[125]

This sort of doxographical citation seems to support much better the general argument from disagreement than the claim that physical philosophers were actually formulating an astral theology. And in fact, Eusebius continues the quotations from Plutarch when he later explicitly shifts back to the argument from disagreement:[126] 'For since they stood in diametrical opposition to each other, and stirred up battles and wars against each other, and nothing better, each with jealous strife of words confuting their neighbours' opinions, must not every one admit that our hesitation (*epochēn*) on these subjects has been reasonable and secure?'[127]

---

[124] *PE* 15.22.68; cp. Clement, *Protr.* 5.

[125] *PE* 15.26.

[126] *PE* 15.32.9–15.52.17.

[127] *PE* 15.32.9. Eusebius' use of *epochēn*, or the withholding of judgement, is no doubt meant to play upon the doctrine favoured by a number of Academic philosophers, especially Arcesilaus and the 'second Academy' (see 14.4.15; with Numenius' criticisms at 14.6–9).

The argument from disagreement is clearly Eusebius' overriding concern. In addition to the dissension, of course, the particular positions of the various dissenting schools rarely, if ever, fall within what Eusebius takes to be the truth. On the one point where some philosophers do attain an approximation of truth (namely, monotheism), Eusebius is sure to put this philosophical advance in its proper place. I refer to his treatment of the doctrine put forth by Anaxagoras, Pythagoras, Plato, and Socrates on the notion of Mind as the supreme being. Anaxagoras had nearly been stoned to death by the Athenians for atheism when he had declared that 'not the sun but the maker of the sun was God',[128] and in any case, he did not 'preserve the doctrine intact'. Eusebius summarizes: 'Pythagoras, Anaxagoras, Plato and Socrates were the first who made mind and God preside over the world. These then are shown to have been in their times very children, as compared with the times at which the remotest events in Hebrew antiquity are fixed by history.'[129] The reference to these philosophers as children no doubt recalls the Egyptian declarations of the *Timaeus* (already quoted at 10.4.19).[130] Thus, even those developments in the history of Greek philosophy that Eusebius considers to be improvements are used to highlight the Greeks' late arrival and the unusual nature of these steps. For, according to Eusebius, only a few Greeks arrived at a monotheistic position, and when they did, they faced opposition, as in the case of Anaxagoras. It was the polytheistic theology of the Phoenicians and Egyptians that prevailed among the Greeks.[131]

NATIONAL CONNECTIONS REVISITED: THE CENTRALITY OF MOSES FOR THE GREEKS

Unlike the Hebrew holy men, the Greeks were unable to provide accounts of their ancestors that could carry any iconic weight—they were not images to be imitated. Nor could they offer even the more basic theological doctrine of humans as images of God, which the Hebrews

[128] *PE* 14.14.9–10.
[129] *PE* 14.16.11.
[130] See also, Herodotus 2.53.1–2; Plato *Leg.* 677d; Demosthenes *De Cor.* 130; Josephus *Ap.* 2.12, 14; Eusebius, *Theoph.* 5.28; for discussion of the topos in apologetic literature, see Droge, *Homer or Moses?*, 43.
[131] *PE* 14.16.12.

had recognized early on. Eusebius makes much of this point in providing additional contours to the map of national connections that he had already offered in the first half of the *Praeparatio*. There, he had elaborately shown how recent and dependent were Greek religious customs and ways of thinking on older barbarian nations. Now, he is concerned to plot the points of contact between Hebrews, Jews, and Greeks. After his enumeration of the Hebrew notion of humanity as made in the image of God, Eusebius writes: 'Such were the philosophic doctrines concerning man's nature taught by the Hebrews originally, before any Greeks had even come into the world: for these being of yesterday and quite newly sprung up from the earth, designed to steal away the doctrines of barbarians, and did not abstain from those of the Hebrews.'[132] The salient features of the national connections constructed in the second half of the *Praeparatio* are present in this statement. First, the language of Greek historical lateness and dependency upon others becomes much stronger than before. Second, the Hebrew nation is portrayed in the ethnic world of antiquity so as to carry explanatory value for the positive elements in Plato's philosophy and to account for what was worthy of adoption from Moses' or the prophets' writings.

The rhetoric of theft has already received sufficient attention. But it needs to be seen along with other examples of strong language as part of a rising tone of disparagement towards the Greeks. Echoing the *Timaeus* passage, Eusebius represents the Greeks as mere youths in relation to other nations.[133] In these passages, he focuses primarily upon the Greek philosophers. At 10.4.3, Eusebius states that they were 'younger in time, so to speak, than all men, not Hebrews only, nor yet Phoenicians and Egyptians only, but also than the ancient Greeks themselves'. The Greeks were already late in chronological terms in other cultural and religious developments; philosophical developments, however, where at least some level of progress was achieved over the previous superstition (thanks, of course, to Hebrew influence), were the last of all.

Alongside this damagingly recent position for Greek philosophy, Eusebius' account has fully sapped the Greeks of any ability to contribute to the discovery of truth by representing them as thieves of the other nations. The language of dependency and borrowing employed in the earlier books of the *Praeparatio* now gives way to the language of plagiarism and robbery. The use of this sort of vocabulary places them low on an evaluative and moral topography of nations. Hence, the

[132] *PE* 7.18.11.   [133] *PE* 7.18.11; 10.4.19; 14.16.11.

double force of a rhetoric of youth and of theft combine in Eusebius' ethnic representation of Greekness to condemn them to an inescapably inferior status.

In addition to his renewed assault upon the Greeks, Eusebius places the Hebrew and Jewish nations at the centrepoint of the ethnic makeup of the ancient world. Besides the fact that Eusebius can then connect Christians to the ancient Hebrews as part of his defence, he also manipulates, or rather creates, relations of dependency between the Greeks and Hebrews that will be important for his appraisal of Greek philosophy. In this regard, Plato functions as a hinge between the Hebrews and Greeks. His authoritative status among philosophers of late antiquity could not easily be dismissed. But it could be undermined; and this is what Eusebius attempts to do in *Praeparatio* 11.1–13.14. If Plato could effectively be transformed into a translator and epitomator of the Hebrew wisdom found in Moses' writings, his authoritative status could then be transferred back to the source from which he drew. This would help not only to explain why Plato's thought could resonate so closely with that of Eusebius' Christianity; at the same time, this displacement of Plato's authority left him vulnerable to criticism, and hence, Christians could feel safe in not accepting all Plato's philosophy. The Hebrew source of Plato's wisdom could thus be used as a standard by which to judge his thought and discern where he deviated from the purity of Hebrew philosophy. What needs to be remembered in these considerations is that the issue is not a merely philosophical one. It is, rather, an ethnic one—the choice is between philosophies distinctively represented by members of particular nations. The polemic is based, furthermore, upon the connections that are constructed between those nations.

CONCLUSIONS

Eusebius' second phase of the narrative of Greek descent was defined by the connections between Hebrews and Greeks and by the discordant character of the Greeks. On both counts the Greeks are found seriously wanting on the scales of chronological antiquity and cultural or philosophical contributions to the history of nations. Their dependency and discord undermined any claims to validity or superiority they would make. This most philosophical portion of

Eusebius' argument remains firmly embedded within his polemical retelling of the history of nations. The history of Greek philosophy is definitive in shaping Greek identity, against which Eusebius was concerned to defend Christian identity. The disharmony that crowded the narrative of Greek philosophical schools contrasted strongly with Eusebius' picture of the harmonious unity of Hebrew and Christian history. Even Plato, the greatest of Greek philosophers, had nothing to offer the sorry state of Greek philosophical affairs but the wisdom of barbarian others, imperfectly transmitted to the Greeks. Greek thought was not a 'preparation for the Gospel' in Eusebius' *Praeparatio*.[134]

In the literarily constructed world of the *Praeparatio*, ethnic identity encompassed religious positions, philosophical schools, cosmogonies, and moral and intellectual character. To recognize how these elements were embedded within strategies of national representation allows for a more coherent picture of the *Praeparatio* as a whole. When the theological doctrines and philosophical tenets that arise throughout the *Praeparatio*'s 15 books are read in isolation from this ethnic context, the coherence of Eusebius' argument suffers unduly. On an even higher level than his earlier *Chronicon*, Eusebius had produced a world historical apologetic argument like none before it.[135] The work evinces the firm command of sources, broad vision, indomitable imagination, and incisive perspicuity of the bishop of Caesarea.

---

[134] As the unfortunate rendering of the work's title (for instance in Gifford's translation) might lead one to believe. A more felicitous rendering might be *Gospel Preparation* (as A. S. Jacobs, *The Remains of the Jews: The Holy Land and Christian Empire in Late Antiquity* [Stanford: Stanford University Press, 2004], 26–36, *passim*). That the work is more properly conceived as a preparatory text for new converts, introducing them to the deeper truths of Christianity, has been shown in Chapter 1; see also, Johnson, 'Eusebius' *Praeparatio Evangelica* as Literary Experiment'.

[135] Its closest parallels in earlier apologetic literature are Josephus' *Contra Apionem* and Aristides' brief pamphlet.

6

Rome Among the Nations: Eusebius' *Praeparatio* and the Unmaking of Greek Political Theology

INTRODUCTION

Modern interest in Eusebius has often been caught up with his role as a political theologian, especially as this is manifested in his portrayal of Constantine in the final edition of his *HE*, the *VC*, and the *LC*.[1] Church historians and theologians have often seen Eusebius as a blithering panegyrist for the new Christian emperor, willing to subsume the Church into the State since the imperial office was a model on earth of divine rule in heaven. After all, in AD 335, Eusebius had openly declared that Constantine's earthly government imitated the cosmic government of the Logos, 'from whom and through whom the sovereign dear to God, bearing the image (*eikona*) of the higher kingdom and in imitation of the Higher Power, directs the helm and sets straight all things on earth'.[2] And his biographical work on Constantine, written soon after the emperor's death in AD 337, was surely flattering. Apparently,

---

[1] See, e.g. Baynes, 'Eusebius and the Christian Empire', 168–72; K. M. Setton, *The Christian Attitude Toward the Emperor in the Fourth Century* (New York: Columbia University Press, 1941), 40–56; J. R. Fears, 'Optimus princeps – Salus generis humani: The Origins of Christian Political Theology', in E. Chrysos (ed.), *Studien zur Geschichte der Römischen Spätantike* (Athens: A. A. Fourlas – S. D. Basilopoulos Co., 1989), 88–105; H. Ahrweiler, 'Eusebius of Caesarea and the Imperial Christian Idea', in Avner Raban and Kenneth Holum (eds), *Caesarea Maritima: A Retrospective After Two Millenia* (Leiden: E.J. Brill, 1996), 541–6; R. Farina, *L'Impero e l'imperatore cristiano in Eusebio di Cesarea* (Zurich: Pas Verlag, 1966).

[2] *LC* 1.6; translation adapted from H. A. Drake, *In Praise of Constantine: A Historical Study and New Translation of Eusebius Tricennial Orations*, University of California Publications: Classical Studies 15 (Berkeley: University of California Press, 1975), 85. For

Eusebius was making the most of the new-found imperial favour and capitalizing on the opportunity for ecclesiastical aggrandizement afforded by Constantine's assumption of sole rule over the empire and concern for the Church's affairs. It seems only natural, therefore, that Eusebius should be said to possess a 'convinced Romanitas',[3] or even 'a zeal for empire that one could attribute to a strong national pride'.[4] He has been labelled the 'hoftheologischen Friseur der kaiserlichen Perücke' (Overbeck), a 'political publicist' (Peterson, Eger), or the 'herald of Byzantinism' (Berkhof).[5] Gerhard Ruhbach referred to such indictments as part of a 'tradition of damnatio Eusebii', which declared Eusebius the 'prototype of a fatal liaison between Church and State'.[6] Despite the attempts of some to treat Eusebius' earlier works on their own terms, many scholars have imputed representations of his later views onto his earlier thought.[7] This has been especially true of the synchronism of Augustus and Christ in the first book of the *HE*, and key passages of the *Praeparatio* and *Demonstratio*.[8]

The present analysis of the *Praeparatio* has attempted to show the centrality of Eusebius' representation of certain important nations for his apologetic methodology. His portrayal of the nations requires us to reconsider his theology of Rome and his broader political theology in light of this project of national representation.[9] The Romans were part

---

discussion, see Baynes, 'Eusebius and the Christian Empire', 168–72, drawing on Goodenough, 'The Political Philosophy of Hellenistic Kingship', 55–102; Farina, *L'Impero e l'imperatore cristiano in Eusebio di Cesarea*, 107–27.

[3] Farina, *L'Impero e l'imperatore cristiano in Eusebio di Cesarea*, 139.

[4] J. Palm, *Rom, Römertum und Imperium in der griechischen Literatur der Kaiserzeit* (Lund: Reg. Societas Humaniorum Litterarum Lundensis, 1959), 121; cited at Farina, *L'Impero e l'imperatore cristiano in Eusebio di Cesarea*, 139.

[5] The authors cited here are taken from G. Ruhbach, 'Die politische Theologie Eusebs von Caesarea', in idem (ed.), *Die Kirche angesichts der konstantinischen Wende* (Darmstadt: Wissenschaftliche Buchgesellschaft, 1976), 238–9.

[6] Ibid., 238, 239.

[7] See however, Ruhbach, 'Die politische Theologie Eusebs von Caesarea'; Chesnut, *The First Christian Histories*, 111–40; A. Cameron, 'Eusebius and the Rethinking of History', in E. Gabba (ed.), *Tria Corda: Scritti in onore di Arnaldo Momigliano* (Como: Edizioni New Press, 1983), 71–88; M. Hollerich, 'Religion and Politics in the Writings of Eusebius: Reassessing the First "Court Theologian"', *CH* 59 (1990), 309–25.

[8] See, F. E. Cranz, 'Kingdom and Polity in Eusebius of Caesarea', *HTR* 45 (1952), 47–66; Sirinelli, *Les vues historiques d'Eusèbe de Césarée*, 388–411; F. Dvornik, *Early Christian and Byzantine Political Theology* (Washington DC: Dumbarton Oaks Center for Byzantine Studies, 1966), 2.614–622; Kofsky, *Eusebius of Caesarea against the Pagans*, 215–19, 286–7.

[9] See E. Peterson, 'Das Problem des Nationalismus im alten Christentum', in idem, *Fruhkirche, Judentum und Gnosis* (Freiburg: Herder, 1959), 51–63.

of the world of nations that Eusebius portrayed throughout his apologetic work. Like the Phoenicians or Greeks, they possessed a shared history based upon common ancestors, traditions, and ways of living and thinking. As in other instances, the city was representative of a (sometimes, though not always, larger) ethnic identity.[10] Eusebius (and his sources, such as Porphyry) would occasionally include cities within larger treatments of the character and practices of certain nations. So Athens and Rome, for example, are included in a list of nations which practise human sacrifice, alongside Africans, Thracians and Scythians.[11] Even as Eusebius moves to the level of the *polis* from the national level of Phoenicians, Egyptians, and Greeks in his narrative of descent, civic identity remains bound up with national identity.

Eusebius' representation of Rome and the Romans is framed within his larger concern for the identities of nations. *Polis* identity is enmeshed in the web of ethnic identity.[12] As in his portrayal of other nations, Eusebius constructs a history, a national character, and a set of boundaries for the Romans. To apprehend more readily what he is doing, Eusebius' political thought, or theology of Rome, will be examined within the context of his attack on Greek civic ('political') theology. Hence, the following questions will be treated in the course of the present chapter. First, I want to consider the question of how Eusebius' treatment of Greek 'political theology' in the *Praeparatio* 4–5, and his daemonology in general, bears upon his development of a distinctively Christian political theology. Second, I will look at the sorts of national connections (or disconnections) he draws between Rome and other nations. Here, I will consider the ways in which he constructs boundaries between Rome and the nations, which are more or less permeable, and assist him in the development of his ethnic argumentation. I will argue that this construction is more complex than is often acknowledged. Within the context of his ethnic argument, Rome appears less central a concern than it would later become when the first Christian emperor began to involve himself actively in ecclesiastical affairs. This background allows us to return to the Augustus–Christ synchronism from

[10] At least as early as Aristotle, a *polis* could be conceived of as coterminous with an *ethnos*; see E. Cohen, *The Athenian Nation*, 26, see nn. 101, 111.

[11] *PE* 4.17.3; see also the list at 4.17.4.

[12] For the larger effects of Christianity on *polis* identity, see M. Maas, ' "Delivered from Their Ancient Customs": Christianity and the Question of Cultural Change in Early Byzantine Ethnography', in K. Mills and A. Grafton (eds), *Conversion in Late Antiquity and the Early Middle Ages* (Rochester: University of Rochester Press, 2003), 152–88.

a new perspective. The question will be raised as to how Augustus fits within the mapping of nations offered in the *Praeparatio*, and furthermore, what role, if any, does Roman imperialism play in unifying the vast plethora of nations of the *oikoumenē*? Significant passages from the *Demonstratio* will be included to illuminate the issue.

Far from exhibiting the inclinations of a 'court theologian', Eusebius shows himself to be a fundamentally independent apologist with a complex vision of the Romans' place within a world of different nations. The ambivalent representation of the Great City and its rulers and inhabitants helps us better understand Eusebius' political thought as a whole as well as the force of his argument as an apologist. I will conclude with a sketch of how my reading of the *Praeparatio* and *Demonstratio* might alert us to the need for close readings of his later material as well. I am convinced that Eusebius maintained to the end a firm vision of Rome, which is only obscured under the disparaging titles of 'imperial panegyrist' or 'court theologian'.

POLITICAL THEOLOGY: EUSEBIUS AGAINST THE GREEKS

Any approach to Eusebius' political theology must confront fully two important facts. First, Eusebius never uses the term 'political theology' to refer to any set of Christian ideas on political subjects such as Rome or monarchy (that is, to any 'theology that, in its method and formal principle, is political, or even the religious–theological vision of the political, and the political vision of the religious').[13] There is no 'Christian political theology' as such in the *Praeparatio* or elsewhere. This is because of a second point: the term 'political theology' (*politikē theologia*) is only ever applied to a *Greek* set of doctrines about the nature and appropriate worship of the *polis* cult sites of the Eastern Mediterranean.[14] At 4.1.2, Eusebius reported a tripartite division of theology

---

[13] Farina, *L'Impero e l'imperatore cristiano in Eusebio di Cesarea*, 258.

[14] For general surveys of *polis* religion, see P. Atherton, 'The City in Ancient Religious Experience', in A. H. Armstrong (ed.), *Classical Mediterranean Spirituality* (London: Routledge & Kegan Paul, 1986), 314–36; S. Stowers, 'Greeks Who Sacrifice and Those Who Do Not: Toward an Anthropology of Greek Religion', in L. M. White and O. L. Yarbarough (eds), *The Social World of the First Christians. Essays in Honor of Wayne A. Meeks* (Minneapolis: Fortress Press, 1995), 293–333; R. Lane Fox, *Pagans and Christians*

made by the Greeks: the mythical (which he had classified as historical), the physical (containing the allegorical interpretations of philosophers), and the civic or 'political theology'. This last theological category was 'the one enforced by the laws and guarded in each city and region'.[15] Traditional religious customs and communal practices, and especially the theological ideas about the gods that supported them, were at the root of this *polis* theology. 'This is the one established throughout the cities and regions and called by them political; this one is also especially enforced by the laws, as ancient and paternal and revealing at once the virtue and the power of those who are given theological treatment.'[16]

Eusebius refers to his retelling of the account of Greek descent and his attack of allegorical interpretations of that account as corresponding to the first two branches of theology (the historical, 'which they call mythical', and the physical). Eusebius' attack on Greek political theology as historically rooted in an ancestral way of life would naturally follow from his historicizing of myths and disavowal of the legitimacy of allegorical approaches.[17] As we have seen, the narrative of descent of the ancient Greeks and the way of life embodied in that narrative was to be seen as manifesting itself in Eusebius' times in contemporary cultic activity and its attendant theological doctrines. These cults were maintained as communal customs central to the *poleis* of the eastern Roman Empire. They were seen by Eusebius as possessing a certain continuity with the ancient Greeks and their customs; there was, for Eusebius, no clear distinction between ancestral past and cultic present.

In general terms, therefore, 'political theology' denotes the attempted explanation of the origins and character of the gods and the religious

---

(New York: Knopf, 1987), 27–101; for classical precedents, see C. Sirvinou-Inwood, 'What is *Polis* Religion?', in R. Buxton (ed.), *Oxford Readings in Greek Religion* (Oxford: Oxford University Press, 2000), 13–37; originally published in O. Murray and S. Price (eds), *The Greek City From Homer to Alexander* (Oxford: Oxford University Press, 1990), 295–322; eadem, 'Further Aspects of *Polis* Religion', in Murray and Price, *The Greek City*, 38–55.

[15] Cp. Porphyry, *Ad Marc.* 25.

[16] *PE* 4.1.2. This tripartite structure of theology is found in Scaevola (*ap.* Augustine, *CD* 4.27: *tria genera tradita deorum: unum a poetis, alterum a philosophis, tertium a principibus civitatis*) and Varro (ibid., 6.5.1: *tria genera theologiae [Varro] dicit esse, id est rationis quae de diis explicatur, eorumque unum mythicon appellari, alterum physicon, tertium civile*), and was apparently of Stoic origin. See also, Tertullian, *Ad Nat.* 197; Plutarch, *Erot.* 18.753BC; Dio Chrysostom, *Or.* 12.39–40; with the discussion of J. Pepin, 'La théologie tripartite de Varron', *REA* 2 (1956), 265–94. For a survey of the scholarship, see G. Liebert, 'Die "theologia tripertita" in Forschung und Bezeugung', *ANRW* I.4 (1973), 63–115.

[17] See Chapter 3.

practices (with their procedures, paraphernalia and images) devoted to those gods by which the *polis* defined itself. It expressed the ways assumed to be appropriate for worshipping the gods within the context of the *polis* cult sites. Such cult activity was endorsed by the laws of the *polis* and supposed to be rooted in the ancient past. According to Eusebius, these cults were centres of daemonic activity steeped in superstition (*deisidaimonia*). If we are to get an adequate sense of how Eusebius' ethnic argumentation might fit within his political thought, it is necessary, then, to start with his treatment of this Greek political theology.

The theology in question was a distinctively Greek conception that offered an overarching framework for understanding activity at the civic level, whether in the *polis* of Rome or Delphi, or elsewhere. Often these cultic practices were mentioned as belonging to 'the nations' in general.[18] But the *theology* about these national cultic activities is consistently assumed to be Greek. Its categorization within a tripartite theology is a Greek theological move.[19] As we shall see, assertions that Eusebius has in mind something Roman when he uses the term 'political theology' fail to find any footing in the text of the *Praeparatio*.[20]

Eusebius does offer some hints (sparse though they are) that Rome is to be included within his overall critique of the role of daemons throughout the nations; but the theology about these cultic centres is distinctively Greek. Rome is firmly situated among those nations that this Greek political theology embraces. In what follows, I will first review those passages that do mention Rome, though in passing; then I will turn to Eusebius' overall critique of Greek political theology—since this, not Rome, is his central concern. I will postpone discussion of two central passages (Eusebius' comments on the quotation of Dionysius of Halicarnassus, and his Augustus–Christ synchronism) to the later sections of this chapter. Analysis of these passages would be misleading if

---

[18] e.g., *PE* 4.15.4; 4.15.9; 4.19.6; 5.1. *passim*; 5.3.10.

[19] Pepin, 'La théologie tripartite de Varron', 283–4, in a discussion of the origins of the tripartite theology, noted that Eusebius is the first source to label it as 'Greek theology'. See e.g. 3.17.2.

[20] 'If the Greek poets represent for him the agents of the diffusion of myths and the Greek philosophers with their successors represent the allegorists, the Romans in turn represent the upholders of political theology in its most characteristic form', Sirinelli, *Les vues historiques d'Eusèbe de Césarée*, 200; followed by Farina, *L'Impero e l'imperatore cristiano in Eusebio di Cesarea*, 78.

not first placed squarely within his apologetic diatribe against Greek political theology.

Consideration of the various mentions of Rome within the *Praeparatio*'s discussion of Greek political theology reveals no great emphasis upon this world power. Although the many cults that receive mention were located within the Roman Empire, Eusebius usually connects them to traditions older than Rome. For instance, he quotes a passage of Clement castigating Hadrian's deification of his lover, Antinöos.[21] But here, the cult is said to be located in Egypt, and is only meant to provide further proof that the 'gods of the Greeks' are merely dead mortals who have been deified. Again, Eusebius quotes Porphyry on the regular practice of human sacrifice at Rome: 'Even now, who does not know that a man is sacrificed in the Great City at the feast of Jupiter Latiarius?'[22] But this is part of a long list of the human sacrifices performed among the other nations.[23] Eusebius also cites Dionysius of Halicarnassus for evidence of human sacrifice, performed by the Pelasgian forerunners of the Romans in ancient Italy.[24]

For his own part, Eusebius mentions the burning of the Temple of Vesta (Hestia) and the Temple of Capitoline Jupiter in his own words.[25] Here again, his statements on Roman religion are part of a larger list, this time of examples of cult sites destroyed by natural disasters. These instances, combined with the reports of his sources noted above, are all that Eusebius says of Rome in the context of the civic theology of the cults of the various nations. The picture that arises, then, is one of Rome possessing the same sorts of cults that fall within the purview of Greek political theology, but with no particular emphasis on Rome. Expressions of Rome sharing in the political theology of the Greeks are firm; Rome exhibits similar character traits to the other nations (as exhibited

---

[21] *PE* 2.6.8. See also, Theophilus, *Autol.* 3.8; Tatian *Or.* 10; for a general discussion of Christian reactions to Antinöos, see P. Guyot, 'Antinous als Eunuch: Zur christlichen Polemik gegen das Heidentum', *Historia* 30 (1981), 250–4.

[22] *PE* 4.16.9.

[23] Eusebius will mention the human sacrifices at 'the Great City' later (4.17.3). The human sacrifices to Jupiter Latiaris at Rome were a recurrent subject among early Christians, especially apologists. See Justin, *II Apol.* 12; Theophilus, *Autol.* 3.8; Tatian, *Or.* 29.1; Lactantius, *Div. Inst.* 1.21.3; Athanasius, *C. Gent.* 25; Eusebius, *LC* 13.8; Firmicus Maternus, *Err. Prof. Rel.* 26.2; Prudentius, *Symm.* 1.39.6. For discussion, see H. J. Rose, 'De Iove Latiari', *Mnemosyne* 55 (1927), 273–79; Rives, 'Human Sacrifice among Pagans and Christians', 75–7.

[24] *PE* 4.16.15–17.

[25] *PE* 4.2.8; for the fire at the Temple of Vesta, see the *Chron.*'s entry for 242 BC; for the two fires at the Capitoline Temple, see the *Chron.*'s entries for 84 BC and AD 69.

in cultic activity)—Eusebius targets *both* the Greek understanding of Rome's (and others') civic religion and the sort of character embodied within their practices.[26] The general point seems to be clear: Eusebius had little concern for the Romans except in so far as their cultic activity fell under the rubric of Greek civic theology.

Oracular Fraud

Eusebius identifies and attacks the character exhibited in *polis* cults in two ways, both of which focus on the oracular activity conducted at these sites. The first is the argument from fraud, which, Eusebius notes, others have brought against the oracles.[27] This argument claims that there are no daemons or gods behind the oracles, but that the oracles are only the results of priestly trickery and deceit. They are uttered with such ambiguity that they can always be said to have been fulfilled, regardless of what happens in the future. 'For the poems and the compositions of the oracles, one might say, are fictions of men not without natural ability but extremely well furnished for deception, and are composed in an equivocal and ambiguous sense, and adapted, not without ingenuity, to either of the cases expected from the event.'[28] According to Eusebius, if events turn out as a prophecy foretold, the devotees of the cult focus all their attention on the one fulfilment, ignoring the vast majority that have failed.[29]

The argument about the fraud of oracular cults receives irrefutable proof from the very fact that their own prophets and priests have admitted their deception. Eusebius writes:

... many of the most highly inspired even of their chief hierophants, theologians and prophets, who were celebrated for this kind of theosophy, not only in former times but also recently in our own day, under cruel tortures before the Roman courts declared that the whole delusion was produced by human frauds, and confessed that it was all an artfully contrived imposture; and they had the whole character of the system and the methods of their evil practices registered in the words uttered by them in public records.[30]

---

[26] A parallel might be seen in Julian (*Or.* 11.152d–153a), where Rome is named a Greek city because of its participation in the establishment and spread of Greek religious institutions.

[27] *PE* 4.1.8. for similar criticisms, see e.g., Origen, *C. Cels.* 3.36; 7.9.

[28] *PE* 4.1.8.   [29] *PE* 4.2.1–3.   [30] *PE* 4.2.10.

Who are these individuals who have admitted their deceptive behaviour? Eusebius reveals that they are the magistrates of Antioch, 'who indeed in the time of our persecution prided themselves especially on their outrages against us',[31] and a certain philosopher and prophet who received punishment at Miletus.[32] The anonymous philosopher is otherwise unknown.[33] But Eusebius devotes much attention to the events at Antioch in the ninth book of his *HE*, where he describes the establishment of a cult to Jupiter Philius by the curator of the city, Theotecnus, 'a violent and wicked man, who was an impostor, and whose character was foreign to his name'.[34] In league with the emperor Maximinus Daia, Theotecnus set up a priesthood at Antioch for the cult of Jupiter Philius:

and after inventing unholy forms of initiation and ill-omened mysteries in connection with it, and abominable means of purification, he exhibited his jugglery, by oracles which he pretended to utter, even to the emperor; and through a flattery which was pleasing to the ruler he aroused the daemon against the Christians and said that the god had given command to expel the Christians as his enemies beyond the confines of the city and the neighbouring districts.[35]

When Licinius defeated Maximinus Daia, he held an inquest into the cultic activities at Antioch. Theotecnus and his coterie of priests were tortured and executed for practising deception.[36] It is difficult to determine exactly why they were prosecuted. Eusebius sees it, of course, as punishment for the persecution of Christians by means of false oracular utterances. And, in fact, the punishment is mentioned as one instance, among others, of Licinius' treatment of persecutors in the East.[37] But it is clear that these persecutors were all supporters of Maximinus, whose executions were conducted along with those of Maximinus' children as part of Licinius' eastern purges.[38]

However, Eusebius' representation of the whole series of events is meant to cloud the issue. Anti-Christian activity is portrayed as the

---

[31] *PE* 4.2.11.

[32] For the importance of this passage for determinations of the date of the *PE*, see Sirinelli's discussion at Sirinelli and Des Places, *Eusèbe de Césarée. La Préparation Évangélique*, 8–14.

[33] See O. Zink and E. Des Places, *Eusèbe de Césarée. La Préparation Évangélique, Livres IV–V, 1–17*, SC 262 (Paris: Les Éditions du Cerf, 1979), 94 n. 4.

[34] *HE* 9.2.2. See Laurin, *Orientations maitresses des apologistes chrétiens*, 84–8; Sirinelli, *Les vues historiques d'Eusèbe de Césarée*, 439–45.

[35] *HE* 9.3; translation from A. C. McGiffert in the *NPNF* series.

[36] *HE* 9.11.6.   [37] *HE* 9.11.3–5.   [38] *HE* 9.11.7.

reason for the trial of Theotecnus and his priests, while support for Maximinus as a political allegiance is downplayed.[39] Of course, the authorities behind the persecution of Christians would obviously be only those whom Maximinus had himself put in positions of power such as magistracies, consulships, or governorships (Theotecnus, after all, had been granted a governorship just before Maximinus' defeat).[40] But Eusebius' description of the trial shows it as centred on the deceptive oracular utterances forged by Theotecnus to promote the persecution of Christians. Eusebius glosses over the political connection between Theotecnus and a now-defeated emperor, while his own religious interpretation, with its theological assumptions, is presented as definitive.

This brief digression on Theotecnus' activities is important, for it illuminates the context (interpreted in religious terms) that Eusebius has in mind as he writes about political theology in the *Praeparatio*. This nexus of cultic activity at local city level,[41] with the imperial persecution of Christians, provides insight into his motivations and concerns in denouncing Greek political theology. Eusebius can also employ the Theotecnus episode as hard 'proof' of the argument for oracular fraud.

At the same time, it must be kept in mind that Eusebius does not consider the fraud argument to be his own particular critique of the political theology. He merely refers to the fact that 'someone' might raise this sort of accusation. 'These arguments then, and yet more than these, one might bring together to assert that the authors of the oracles are not gods nor yet daemons, but the delusion and deceit of human impostors.'[42] He then quotes from the otherwise lost work of Diogenianus against impostors, after which he claims that he wants to introduce his own second form of argument against the political theology of the Greeks: the argument about daemonology.

---

[39] Of course, Maximinus' politics ought not be separated from his religious position; see Grant, 'The Religion of Maximin Daia', 4.143–166, esp. 159.

[40] *HE* 9.11.5.

[41] Even though Eusebius takes pains to show the wickedness of the emperor, in his narrative at *HE* 9, the persecutions are always worked out on city level, and the oracular cult at Antioch is, of course, rooted in the affairs of the *polis*. On the importance of the *polis* for Maximinus, see H. Castritius, *Studien zu Maximinus Daia*, Frankfurter althistorische Studien, 2 (Kallmunz: Michael Lassleben, 1969), 48–51.

[42] *PE* 4.2.12.

Oracular Daemons

Eusebius had earlier noted that 'the assistants of the oracles we must in plain truth declare to be evil daemons'.[43] Now he elaborates upon this notion by placing it within the context of the Greek doctrine of theological hierarchy.[44] A 'different kind' (*heteron tropon*) of Greek theology than that he had already mentioned (presumably the tripartite theology with its mythical, physical, and political branches) divides the subject into four classes (*genē*): the Supreme God, gods, daemons, and heroes.[45] Under these is a fifth class of wicked daemons who rule lower nature.[46] The first four are to receive worship (*therapeuein*) according to their rank, while the fifth is only to receive propitiation (*apomeilissesthai*) to keep them from doing wrong to humans.[47] Eusebius turns this back upon the Greeks, however, claiming that this classification 'distinguishes in word, but confuses in deed all these things'.[48] The Greeks are, according to Eusebius, enslaved by wicked daemons, who use the distinction between worship and propitiation as a cover for receiving what is actually worship from their superstitious adherents. Not only this, but all daemons should be considered wicked because of the true etymology of their name: 'daemon' comes from *deimainein* ('to fear and cause fear'), not *deēmonas* ('knowing'), as the Greeks presume.[49] And, since there is only one God, not many, the 'gods' should rather be given the name 'angels', as the Christian Scriptures teach.

Eusebius then seeks to buttress these criticisms he has made against Greek theology by quoting from Porphyry and others. For even Porphyry had asserted in his *De Abstinentia*[50] that it was not fitting to offer

---

[43] *PE* 3.17.1. Cp. Origen, *C. Cels.* 7.69; 8.7–9, *passim.* Coggan has suggested that we should distinguish the Christian conception of 'daemons' from the pagan conception of 'daemons' ('Pandaemonia: A Study of Eusebius' Recasting of Plutarch's Story of the "Death of Great Pan"', [Ph.D. dissertation, Syracuse University, 1992]). To do so, however, fails to grapple with the complexity of Eusebius' argument, which quotes from and responds to, Greek sources on daemonology. For further reflection, see Martin, *Inventing Superstition,* x–xi.

[44] There is general agreement that the Greek source for this theological hierarchy is Porphyry, but there is debate as to which work of that author Eusebius is here relying on. See O. Zink in Zink and Des Places, *Eusèbe de Césarée,* 7–8; H. Lewy, *Chaldaean Oracles and Theurgy* (Paris: Études Augustiniennes, 1978), 509–12; J. Bidez and F. Cumont, *Les Mages Hellénisés* (Paris: Société d'Éditions 'Les Belles Lettres', 1938), 2.275–282. For general context, see Martin, *Inventing Superstition,* 187–206.

[45] *PE* 4.5.1.

[46] For a somewhat different theological classification, see *PE* 5.3.2–8.

[47] *PE* 4.5.2.   [48] *PE* 4.5.3.   [49] *PE* 4.5.4.   [50] Quoted at *PE* 4.11.

animal (let alone, human) sacrifices to the gods (thus contradicting his message in the *Philosophia ex Oraculis*).[51] Hence, the divine powers that worked through the oracles and required sacrifices from those who sought oracles must be daemons not gods, and wicked not good.[52] According to Eusebius' reading of Porphyry, 'Apollo is a daemon and not a god; and not Apollo only but also all those who have been regarded as gods among all the nations, those to whom whole peoples, both rulers and ruled, in cities and in country districts, offer animal sacrifices. For these we ought to believe to be nothing else than daemons.'[53] He continues:

> How then, if indeed bloody sacrifice was unholy and abominable and hurtful, could those who were pleased with such things as these be good? And if they should also be shown to delight not only in such sacrifices as these, but, with an excess of cruelty and inhumanity, in the slaughter of men and in human sacrifices, how can they be other than utterly blood-guilty, and friends of all cruelty and inhumanity, and nothing else than wicked daemons?[54]

This passage stands as a bold statement of the major thrust of Eusebius' argument from daemonology against the political theology of the Greek oracle cults. It centres upon 'the name as well as the character' of the divine powers operating the oracles.[55] These are shown to be, according to Eusebius, wicked daemons and not good gods.[56] They call for sacrifices that any good being would not require. To give these daemons the appellation of gods is to degrade the name of the one true God. The one Supreme God would never accept the sacrifices that the daemons ask for, but instead seek a spiritual sacrifice. The evangelic teaching proposes that we 'bring with us no earthy or dead offering, nor gore and blood, nor anything of corruptible and material substance, but with a mind purified from all wickedness, and with a body clothed with the

---

[51] Quoted at *PE* 4.9; for the possibility of a coherent theology behind both texts, see A. Smith, 'Porphyry and Pagan Religious Practice', in J. J. Cleary (ed.), *The Perennial Tradition of Neoplatonism* (Louvain: Louvain University Press, 1997), 29–35.

[52] Cp. Origen, *C. Cels.* 3.2, 37; 4.29; 7.65, 69; 8.3. For discussion, see Coggan, 'Pandaemonia'; Rives, 'Human Sacrifice among Pagans and Christians', 80–3.

[53] *PE* 4.10.3.

[54] *PE* 4.10.4.

[55] *PE* 4.5.5. ὥσπερ οὖν τοῦ τρόπου, οὑτωσὶ δὲ καὶ τῆς προσηγορίας The idea, though not the exact wording, is the same as that expressed at 7.6.1 regarding the Hebrews who were so 'in name and in character' as well (ὁμοῦ τῇ προσηγορίᾳ καὶ τὸν τρόπον).

[56] At *PE* 7.2.4, the cult celebrations of the *poleis* are seen to be manifestations of worship of the daemon Pleasure.

ornament of purity and temperance which is brighter than any raiment, and with right doctrines worthy of God....'[57]

This idea of spiritual sacrifice, contrasted with physical sacrifices,[58] had been proposed already by Porphyry himself (as the quotation from *De Abstinentia* at 4.11 makes clear)[59] and Apollonius of Tyana (whose *De Sacrificiis* is quoted at 4.13).[60] Eusebius is primarily concerned to highlight the contradictions within Porphyry's thought on cult sacrifices,[61] and to show the irrational and wrong-headed superstition of adherents to the cults and the wickedness of the daemons behind the cults. Rather than desiring a spiritual form of sacrifice, daemons required sacrifices of physical bodies, be they animal or human. They are said 'to delight not only in slaughter and sacrifices of irrational animals, but also in manslaughter and human sacrifices'.[62] Those superstitious people who are dedicated to these cult centres 'pass at length beyond nature's limits, being so utterly driven frantic and possessed by the destroying spirits, as even to suppose that they propitiate the bloodthirsty powers by the blood of their dearest friends and countless other human sacrifices'.[63] The daemons lead their adherents on to sexually immoral behaviour. 'For they say that men ought to practise adulteries, and seductions, and other unlawful kinds of intercourse, in honour of the gods, as a sort of debt due to them.'[64] Furthermore, even the fraud and deceit performed by the prophets at the oracles is inspired by daemons, who 'were the first instructors in this evil art of imposture'.[65]

---

[57] *PE* 4.10.6; see also *Proph. Ecl.* 3.29 (*PG* 22.1156B); 3.36 (*PG* 22.1164D–1165A).

[58] Cp. Origen, *C. Cels.* 8.21. On the distinction, see S. Bradbury, 'Julian's Pagan Revival and the Decline of Blood Sacrifice', *Phoenix* 49 (1995), 332–41; E. Ferguson, 'Spiritual Sacrifice in Early Christianity and its Environment', *ANRW* (1980), 23.2.1151–1189. On the general decline of animal sacrifices in late antiquity, see M. Nilsson, 'Pagan Divine Service in Late Antiquity', *HTR* 38 (1945), 63–9.

[59] Porphyry will later be quoted as explicitly rejecting the polis-wide sacrifices to daemons in favour of spiritual sacrifice at *PE* 4.18.

[60] This excerpt from Apollonius of Tyana is repeated at *DE* 3.3 (105b–d). The fact that Eusebius quotes Apollonius in a favourable manner seems to match his statement at *C. Hier.* 5 (if Eusebius is, in fact, the author), where he avers that it is only the false representations of Apollonius by Damis and Philostratus that deserve criticism; Apollonius himself was a wise man. T. Hägg, 'Hierocles the Lover of Truth and Eusebius the Sophist', *SO* 67 (1992), 138–50, has argued against its authenticity, but his argument needs to be supplemented by further stylistic analysis.

[61] Quotations from Porphyry's *Phil. ex Or.* had favoured sacrifices, while his *De Abst.* opposed them; see A. Smith, 'Porphyry and Pagan Religious Practice', 29–35.

[62] *PE* 4.15.4.   [63] *PE* 4.15.7. Cp. Tatian, *Or.* 29; Athanasius, *C. Gent.* 25.

[64] *PE* 4.17.22.   [65] *PE* 5.10.12.

This representation of both the immorality and the spiritual and theological status of the beings working through oracular cults is also put within a narrative framework that attempts to show the origins and fall of daemonic control in the history of other nations. Eusebius' discussion of the origins of daemons does not come until later, in his exposition of Hebrew theology, but it is appropriate for the present discussion to include it here. At 7.16.1, he declares that the Hebrew oracles contain teachings on the origins of daemons. The angels had been created below the Holy Spirit as attendants on God. Some, however, turned away from God in rebellion and wanted to receive the title and worship that was fitting for God alone.[66] These became a 'different race' (*allo genos*) from the angels.[67] Their 'apostasy' was conducted under the leadership of Satan, 'whom the Scripture is wont to call dragon and serpent, and black and creeping, an engenderer of deadly poison, a wild beast, and a lion devouring mankind, and the adder among reptiles'.[68]

For their arrogance they were cast into Tartarus, except for a small part of them who were left on earth or in the lunar regions 'to exercise the athletes of piety'.[69] Thus they became the 'joint cause of the polytheistic delusion'.[70] This claim regarding their joint causation is clarified by an illuminating note at 5.2.1. There Eusebius writes: '[The daemons] and their rulers, who are certain powers of the air, or of the nether-world, having observed that the human race was grovelling low about the deification of dead men, and spending its labour very zealously upon sacrifices and savours which were to them most grateful, were ready at hand as supporters and helpers of this delusion.'[71] It seems that, for Eusebius, the daemons knew a good thing when they saw it, so to speak, and manipulated the already superstitious worship of deified mortals for their own advantage. Hence, euhemerism blended into daemonism; the worship of dead men made a smooth transition into worship of daemons.[72]

The *Demonstratio* adds further details of Eusebius' conception of the origins of daemons and their special connection with the nations of the world. Angels had been assigned by God to the ancient nations 'to be their leaders and governors like herdsmen and shepherds'.[73] Eusebius

---

[66] *PE* 7.16.10. Cp. Athenagoras, *Leg.* 24–5.   [67] *PE* 7.16.7.   [68] *PE* 7.16.3.
[69] *PE* 7.16.8.   [70] *PE* 7.16.8.   [71] *PE* 5.2.1.
[72] See Sirinelli, *Les vues historiques d'Eusèbe de Césarée*, 201–02; cp. Athenagoras, *Leg.* 26.
[73] *DE* 4.6 [155d]. Cp. Eusebius, *CI* 59 (Ziegler 76.12–13); 69 (Ziegler 104.9–17); 70 (Ziegler 108.33–109.3); and also, Origen, *C. Cels.* 1.24; 3.35; 5.26–32, 46; 7.68, 70. On the notion of angels of nations, see F. Cumont, 'Les anges du paganisme', *Revue de l'histoire des*

finds evidence for this view in Deuteronomy 32: 8, which states: 'When the most High divided the nations, when he distributed the sons of Adam, he set the bounds of the nations according to the number of the angels of God. His people, Jacob, became the portion of the Lord; Israel was the line of his inheritance.'[74] The Hebrews, therefore, had no angel allotted to them, for they had the Logos as their guide.[75] The angels of other nations allowed them to worship astral phenomena because they were too weak and ignorant to worship the creator of the stars, sun, and moon.[76] Eusebius had already said early in the *Praeparatio* that 'visible luminaries were assigned to all the nations'.[77] And elsewhere Eusebius had equated stars and other luminaries with angels and spiritual powers.[78] Deuteronomy 32: 8 had even been quoted (though only for comparison with a sentiment of Plato).[79]

What is most interesting about the *Demonstratio's* account of angels of nations is the way in which Eusebius works daemons into the narrative of decline. Satan and his daemons plotted against the angels of the nations, desiring the worship allowed to the stars for themselves. The national guardian angels were unable to defend their peoples against the onslaught of wicked powers and retreated to other parts of the universe.[80] The daemons went even further and attacked the nation of Israel and seduced it. The evil daemons, 'in invisible leadership of the nations mentioned [Assyrians, Egyptians, *et al.*], in days of old laid siege to the souls of Israel, involved them in various passions, seducing them and enslaving them to a life like that of the other nations'.[81] In these passages, we see from a different angle the narrative of decline from astralism to daemonism. Interestingly, the *Demonstratio* claims that the angels of nations have finally been restored with the coming of Christ, who drove

---

religions 72 (1915), 159–82; J. Danielou, 'Les sources juives de la doctrine des anges des nations chez Origène', *Recherches de science religieuse* 38 (1951), 132–7; E. Peterson, *Das Buch von den Engeln. Stellung und Bedeutung der heiligen Engeln im Kultus* (Munich: Kösel-Verlag, 1955); idem, 'Das Problem des Nationalismus im alten Christentum'; Chesnut, *The First Christian Histories*, 69; Kofsky, *Eusebius of Caesarea Against the Pagans*, 133 n. 141.

[74] Quoted at *DE* 4.7 [156b–c].

[75] *Pace* Farina, *L'Impero e l'imperatore cristiano in Eusebio di Cesarea*, 118, who claims the Logos maintained rule only over heaven, allotting government of all earthly nations to angels.

[76] *DE* 4.8 [157c–158b].

[77] *PE* 1.9.15. Cp. Origen, *C. Cels.* 5.10–13.

[78] 7.15.15 and 7.16.1.

[79] 11.26.8.

[80] *DE* 4.10 [161a–b].

[81] *DE* 2.3 [175d–176a].

out the wicked daemons from among the nations.[82] 'At last the Saviour
and Physician of the universe came down himself to men, bringing
reinforcement to his angels for the salvation of men, since the Father
had promised him that he would give him [the nations] as an inheritance.'[83] This raises the issue of the daemons' demise.

Even more important than Eusebius' treatment of the origins of
daemons is his account of their fall. At 4.15.6, and again at 4.17.4, he
claims that a date can be given to the destruction of daemonic power
in the reign of Hadrian, 'at which time the teaching of salvation began to
flourish among all mankind'.[84] Until the coming of Christ, the nations
had been bound by the superstitious fetters of daemonic powers. Since
that time, daemonic bondage had been broken. 'Nobody except our Lord
and Saviour the Christ of God has provided a way of escape for all men,
by preaching to all alike, Greeks and barbarians, a cure for their ancestral
malady, and deliverance from their bitter and inveterate bondage.'[85]

It is not merely a case of weakening the daemons, since, according to
Eusebius, the daemons have actually died. Churches and Christian
schools arose all across the *oikoumenē* after Christ's death and resurrection, 'while all the oracles and divinations of daemons are dead'.[86] At
5.5.4 and 5.16.4, Eusebius states that citations from Plutarch's *De Defectu
Oraculorum* prove that daemons were subject to death. His weightiest
piece of evidence in this regard is Plutarch's account of Pan's death.[87]
Plutarch had reported the story of an Egyptian steersman's experience of
hearing a ghostly voice while at sea, telling him to proclaim: 'The great
Pan is dead.'[88] He calls out that Pan is dead at a designated place in his
voyage, at which loud lamentation is made by unseen mourners. Later,
even the Emperor Tiberius investigated the matter.[89] After quoting this
story, Eusebius explains that, 'it was in the time of Tiberius, in which our

---

[82] *Pace* Farina, *L'Impero e l'imperatore cristiano in Eusebio di Cesarea*, 118.

[83] *DE* 4.10 [162d].

[84] *PE* 4.17.4. Incidentally, Clement drew the opposite conclusion regarding the reign of
Hadrian, claiming that it was during his reign that heresies first arose; see *Strom.* 7.17.

[85] *PE* 4.21.2; cp. *CI* 1.75 (Ziegler 130.23–34), where the gods Isis, Osiris, Typhon, and
the other 'races of gods, heroes and dead people' could not even foretell their own
destruction, which occurred when Christ visited Egypt as an infant.

[86] *PE* 5.1.7.

[87] See Coggan, 'Pandaemonia: A Study of Eusebius' Recasting of Plutarch's Story of the
"Death of Great Pan" '. For the connection of Plutarch's narrative to Plato's *Phaedrus*, see
S. Dusanic, 'Plato and Plutarch's Fictional Techniques: The Death of the Great Pan', *RM* 139
(1996), 276–94.

[88] *PE* 5.17.8.   [89] *PE* 5.17.9.

Saviour, making his sojourn among men is recorded to have been ridding human life from daemons of every kind'.[90]

It is not entirely clear why Eusebius pinpoints the defeat of daemons during the reign of Hadrian, especially since he possesses evidence such as this that fits his argument more closely. The most likely cause for settling on Hadrian's reign lies in the documentation of human sacrifice among the nations quoted from Porphyry's *De Abstinentia* 2.56.[91] There, Porphyry notes the claim of Pallas that human sacrifice had been abolished in nearly all the nations.[92] Pallas, Porphyry adds, 'compiled material on the mysteries of Mithras under the reign of Hadrian'.[93] Eusebius thus equates the report of the abolition of human sacrifice in Pallas with the emperor under whom Pallas wrote.[94] What is important at this point, however, is that the spiritual forces behind the cultic activity that was the subject of Greek political theology are no longer taken as a valid form of religious practice. Its operation was declared to be in the hands of wicked daemons, not good gods. Its character, typified in sexual indecency and sacrifices, was shown to be immoral and abhorrent; its power, which was fundamentally deceptive anyhow, was shown to be irretrievably broken with the deaths of daemons.

Eusebius' political theology must start here, with his attack against Greek civic theology. For him, Christianity was political in that it shattered the *polis*-based workings of daemons and usurped their role in guiding the lives of the *polis'* inhabitants.[95] Christ's teachings spread

---

[90] *PE* 5.17.13. Eusebius makes no mention of the episode in his *Chronicon*, though his remarks on the life of Christ are fairly vague, only mentioning that he preached the way of salvation and performed miracles (see the entries for the years 15–18 of Tiberius' reign).

[91] Quoted at *PE* 4.16.7.

[92] Cassius Dio reports the rumour of Hadrian himself practising human sacrifice on Antinöos (69.11.2–3); noted by D. Hughes, *Human Sacrifice in Ancient Greece* (London and New York: Routledge, 1991), 239 n.169.

[93] At *PE* 4.16.7. See Hughes, *Human Sacrifice in Ancient Greece*, 129–30, for discussion of this passage.

[94] Interestingly, Lactantius (without reference to Pallas) records that Hadrian abolished human sacrifice on Cyprus (*Div. Inst.* 1.21). Eusebius repeats the claim for the abolition of human sacrifice under Hadrian at *SC* 16.10. The *Chronicon* neglects such a record on the prohibition of human sacrifice for Hadrian (or any other emperor). The *HE*'s treatment of the reign of Hadrian (in 4.3–9) is concerned primarily with the fall of the Jews and the emperor's relative tolerance for Christians—two points which Eusebius could have employed as well in backing his claim for the end of daemonic influence during the reign of Hadrian in the *PE*, although he failed to do so. Like the *HE*, the *CI* emphasizes Hadrian's role in the fall of the Jews; see *CI* 1.35 (Ziegler 32) and 1.42 (Ziegler 43).

[95] On the overall impact of Christianity on the demise of *polis* identity, see Maas, ' "Delivered from Their Ancient Customs" '.

from *polis* to *polis*, driving out daemonic darkness and establishing the light of friendship with God. It must be said, then, that at least in the *Praeparatio*, Eusebius' political theology does not focus on Rome and its emperor. Rather, his political theology is a sustained overturning of Greek political theology, which has not one centre but many, dispersed throughout the *poleis* and country districts of all nations, Greek and barbarian.

DISCONNECTING NATIONS: EUSEBIUS' CONSTRUCTION OF BOUNDARIES

I have addressed above the issue of Eusebius' portrayal of Rome as one among the many nations and cities embraced by the political theology that he castigates as daemonic. I want to raise again Eusebius' representation of Rome, this time to consider the drawing of boundaries between nations and to question the firmness or weakness of these modes of distinction. Ethnic and national identities must be framed through the construction, maintenance and alteration of boundaries.[96] But our analysis requires more than the mere recognition of the boundaries that Eusebius lays in the *Praeparatio*. For boundaries can be made more or less permeable as the social or polemical situation dictates. Furthermore, in the multinational context portrayed in Eusebius' *Praeparatio*, an identity more complex than a simple binary opposition can be fashioned for 'us' against a multiplicity of 'them'.[97]

The boundaries created between 'us' and one of the groups of 'them' may bring out particular traits of differentiation and uniqueness, while the boundaries on the other side of 'us' (so to speak) may differentiate another group of 'them' in different ways, highlighting another set of distinctive features that mark out identity. Or, that particular boundary may be left undeveloped, in order to bring into sharper contrast, to draw with darker lines, the boundary between 'us' and the first group of 'them'. To conceive of these relationships as a hierarchy insufficiently accounts for the boundary-forming mechanisms that go into the construction of any identity. Identity is constructed just as much—even more—through the heralding of differences between 'us' and 'them' as

---

[96] See Barth, 'Introduction', 9–38.
[97] *Pace* Lieu, 'The Forging of Christian Identity', 81.

through the building of identity based upon the content—the cultural, religious, or hereditary 'stuff'—of a given people ('us') in isolation from others. Also, a purely hierarchical conception of rival identities cannot adequately explain the reconstrual of boundaries over time between a variety of different groups of others.

Already, we have seen the sharp boundary lines between Christians and Hebrews on the one side and Phoenicians, Egyptians, Greeks, and Jews on the other sides. It is now necessary to see where the boundaries fall for the Romans—to determine on which sides these boundaries will be painted with dark shades and imposing barriers, and on which sides they will be left blurred and obscure under the pen of Eusebius. The passages so far raised have left the boundary between Rome and the other daemonically controlled nations fairly thin in the area of cultic practices, while consequently marking a firm boundary between Rome and the Christians.

However, a highly important passage crops up somewhat anomalously within the context of Eusebius' attack against the allegorists. Unlike those Greeks who had been embarrassed at their ancestral stories and sought a way to explain them away as referring to physical phenomena, the Romans had rejected both the stories and their allegorical interpretations altogether. Eusebius writes: 'So it is that I admire the ancient Romans for the manner in which, when they perceived that all the physiological theories of the Greeks concerning the gods were absurd and unprofitable, or rather were forced and inconsistent, they excluded them, legends and all, from their own theology.'[98] Then Eusebius introduces Dionysius of Halicarnassus as evidence of Romulus' wisdom, who, 'among his other good deeds', rejected the Greek myths.[99] The quotation

---

[98] *PE* 2.7.9. Another positive note on one of the founding fathers of the Romans is provided in Clement's assertion (at 9.6.3–4) that Romulus' successor, Numa, had adopted an iconoclastic policy from the teachings of Moses: 'But Numa the king of the Romans, though he was a Pythagorean, received benefit from the teaching of Moses, and forbade the Romans to make an image of God in the shape of man or any animal. So in the first 170 years, though they built themselves temples, they made no image, neither in sculpture nor yet in painting.' A straightforward connection between Hebrews and Romans is here forged through the mouth of an author with whom Eusebius surely agreed. On Eusebius' citations from Clement, see J. Coman, 'Utilisation des Stromates de Clément d'Alexandrie par Eusèbe de Césarée dans la Préparation Evangélique', in *Uberlieferungsgeschichtlche Untersuchungen*, (=*TU* 125; 1981), 115–34.

[99] For discussion of Dionysius' account of the founding of Rome compared with Josephus' account of the origins of the Jewish nation, see D. Balch, 'Two Apologetic Encomia. Dionysius on Rome and Josephus on the Jews', *Journal for the Study of Judaism*, 13 (1982), 102–22.

from Dionysius describes the absence among the Romans of any story of the escapades of Kronos and Zeus, the rape of Persephone, or the sufferings of Dionysus.[100] Furthermore, Rome is said to have maintained a strong policy against adoption of foreign rites and religious customs, despite the massive influx of foreigners within its walls. In relation to the Greeks, Dionysius writes: 'I am nevertheless cautiously disposed towards them, and I prefer to accept the theology of the Romans, considering that the benefits derived from Greek legends are small, and not capable of benefiting many, but only those who have searched out the purposes for which they are made.'[101] Following the excerpt from Dionysius, Eusebius comments that the quotation has provided the opinions of 'the ancient and earliest men of the Roman empire concerning Greek [physical] theology'.[102]

This quotation and Eusebius' introductory and concluding statements are crucial, if complicating, in understanding Rome's place among the different nations. Dionysius mentions Rome's concern for proper worship of 'gods and daemons', and Romulus' establishment of 'temples, precincts, altars, and the erection of statues . . . , and festivals of all such kinds as ought to be kept in honour of each god or daemon, and sacrifices wherewith they delight to be honoured by men'.[103] However, Eusebius seems to pay these comments little attention. Instead, what is important for him is the proof that the Romans were wise enough to reject Greek myths about the gods and even their allegorical interpretations. He introduces the citation by placing Romulus' religious legislation within the series of 'his other good deeds'.[104]

This passage stands out from its context, in which Eusebius has laid out the abhorrent character of the Greeks and now begins to turn his attack against their physicalist allegorizing. Through his citation of Dionysius, Eusebius adds weight to his argument against the Greeks— for even the Romans have rejected the things of the Greeks. Eusebius' placement of Dionysius' discussion within his argument against the Greeks, as a sharp contrast to those Greeks, creates at the same time an important boundary between Romans and Greeks. And while the polytheistic customs and theology of the Romans are mentioned, Eusebius never dwells on these in his own words. Instead, his focus is

---

[100] *PE* 2.8.4–5.   [101] *PE* 2.8.11–12.

[102] *PE* 2.8.13. Gifford's rendering of *prōtois* in this passage as 'most eminent' is misleading; I have taken it in its temporal sense ('the earliest' or 'first in time').

[103] *PE* 4.8.2.   [104] *PE* 2.7.9.

aimed at pitting Romans against Greeks. This also weakens the boundary separating Romans from Christians; the Romans lack an element that had proved a serious part of the boundary between Christians and Greeks. Eusebius has simultaneously highlighted the boundary between Romans and Greeks and opened up a chink in the boundary that walls off Romans from Christians.

Acknowledgement of these boundary negotiations is vital for our understanding of Eusebius' 'theology of Rome'. Yet, one must be careful to avoid unduly emphasizing Eusebius' reference to the 'other good deeds' of Romulus, as well as his pretence of admiration for the ancient Romans.[105] First of all, *katorthōmata* may merely carry the sense of 'reforms' rather than 'good deeds'. Secondly, Eusebius' expression of admiration (*thaumazein*) for the Romans finds parallels in other such expressions for individuals or groups whom he nevertheless proceeds to criticize. For example, he sarcastically calls the Greeks 'all-wise' (*pansophoi*)[106] and the Egyptians 'wise' (*sophoi*);[107] the Greek allegorizers are labelled 'noble' (*gennaioi*)[108] and their physiological interpretations are 'marvellous' (*thaumastē*)[109] and 'noble' (*gennaia*);[110] Porphyry is 'the marvellous philosopher' (*thaumastos philosophos*)[111] and 'most wise' (*sophōtatos*);[112] Plato is named 'excellent' (*aristos*),[113] 'marvellous' (*thaumasios*)[114] and 'all-wise' (*pansophos*)[115] at points where the philosopher's attainment of truth is put in question. Eusebius even denies any pleasure in pointing out the faults of Plato, since he of all the Greeks was most nearly a 'friend' and held in honour.[116] These examples of Eusebius' generous (if not sarcastic) language for his opponents put paid to any attempt to claim his expression of admiration for the Romans as openly favouring them. Without more clues we must withhold judgement on how Eusebius' introduction of the Dionysius passage is to be taken.[117] This cautionary note aside, however, we can clearly see the manipulation of boundaries at work in this portion of the *Praeparatio*. The Romans are marked off from the Greeks, and as such are located

---

[105] *Pace* Farina, *L'Impero e l'imperatore cristiano in Eusebio di Cesarea*, 138–9.

[106] *PE* 1.8.13.   [107] *PE* 3.5.1.   [108] *PE* 2.6.21.   [109] *PE* 3.2.1.

[110] *PE* 3.3.21; 3.5.1.   [111] *PE* 3.7.5.   [112] *PE* 3.13.8.   [113] *PE* 2.6.23.

[114] *PE* 2.6.23; 13.14.3.   [115] *PE* 13.14.4; see also 13.20.8.

[116] *PE* 13.18.17; see also 13.21.14; 14.1.2; compare with his statements regarding Aristotle, 15.1.13.

[117] Other remarks on Rome made in the *PE* (at 6.10.23–4 [a quotation from Bardesanes], and 10.14.6 [a chronological calculation putting the reign of Romulus in the same period as the reign of Hezekiah, king of the Jews]) have only a marginal bearing on Eusebius' distinction between the Romans and Greeks.

more closely to the Christians. The possibility for at least some amount of openness bridging the Christian–Roman boundary must be allowed from our reading of this passage.

In the Dionysius excerpt, we thus detect the modes of Eusebius' boundary construction in action. His affirmation of the religious activity of Rome's early founders produces a more solid, impenetrable wall of difference between Romans and Greeks, on the one side, and a somewhat permeable and less imposing border between Romans and Christians on the other. Yet we must keep in mind what has been noted in the analysis of his criticism of Greek political theology. Rome was there implicated in the practices (even if not in the theological framework) of immoral and cruel cultic ritual. Eusebius' comments on the Dionysius excerpt thus exonerate Rome on two fronts of the tripartite division of theology (the mythical/historical and the physical), but not on the third (the political).

It might seem at first that the synchronism of Augustus and Christ, to which I turn next, would push the balance further in Rome's favour— that the boundary between Christians and Romans would fundamentally be broken by the equation of the rule of Augustus with the life of Christ. However, through a closer reading of the Augustus–Christ synchronism within its context, combined with some highly noteworthy statements in the *Demonstratio*, I hope to offer a fresh evaluation of Eusebius' synchronism within his political thought.

THE AUGUSTUS–CHRIST SYNCHRONISM

Eusebius' correlation of the work of Augustus in conquering the many disconnected nations, or polyarchy, and the work of Christ in conquering the daemons operating within those nations, or polytheism, has been considered one of the most important issues for delineating Eusebius' political theology among modern scholars.[118] I will argue

[118] See Sirinelli, *Les vues historiques d'Eusèbe de Césarée*, 388–411; R. A. Markus, 'The Roman Empire in Early Christian Historiography', *Downside Review* 81 (1963), 340–53; Chesnut, *The First Christian Histories*, 76–8; Kofsky, *Eusebius of Caesarea against the Pagans*, 215–19; Farina, *L'Impero e l'imperatore cristiano in Eusebio di Cesarea*, 143–54; H. Inglebert, *Les Romains Chrétiens face à l'Histoire de Rome* (Paris: Institut d'Études Augustiniennes, 1996), 165–67; E. Peterson, *Der Monotheismus als politisches Problem*, in E. Peterson, *Theologische Traktate* (Munich: Hochland Bücherei, 1951), 86–93.

here that the Augustus–Christ synchronism needs to be located within its proper context as ethnic argumentation, that is as part of the remaking of national identities and national histories in the defence of Christianity. If the synchronism is seen as part of Eusebius' attack against the Greek political theology of daemonic cult sites, it will become evident that the Roman emperor receives much less attention in Eusebius' *Praeparatio* than he does in modern treatments.

Augustus is mentioned by name only twice in the entirety of this work. In Eusebius' chronological argument in Book 10, Augustus is mentioned only to clarify the date of Plato: the philosopher lived near the end of the reign of the king of the Persians, a little before Alexander of Macedon, and roughly four hundred years before Augustus.[119] No significance need be attached to this remark, since Eusebius' only concern is the proper chronological determination for Plato.

The second passage is that of the synchronism itself, which occurs in a central passage of the *Praeparatio*'s prologue. Eusebius states: 'Immediately all the multitude of rulers among the Romans began to be abolished, when Augustus became sole ruler (*monarchēsantos*) at the time of our Saviour's appearance.'[120] At the very outset, Eusebius' heralding of one man's rule over the rule of many would have sounded a less felicitous tone in years that saw Rome divided between multiple rulers (Constantine, Licinius, and their sons).[121] There was no monarchy at the time Eusebius penned the *Praeparatio*: the only threat to the tetrarchic arrangement created under Diocletian was the imposition of the dynastic principle under his successors—there was no threat to the multiplicity of emperors across the Roman world. We should recall that the only questioning of the multiplicity of rulers came, in fact, from the ranks of the Christians. When commanded by the governor to offer libations to the tetrarchs, Procopius of Scythopolis responded with a quotation from Homer: 'The rule of many (*polykoiraniē*) is not good, let there be one ruler and one king.'[122] Procopius met a swift execution for these treasonable words and became the first of the martyrs in Palestine under the so-called Great Persecution. Eusebius' denunciation of polyarchy as

---

[119] *PE* 10.14.17.

[120] *PE* 1.4.4. πᾶσα μὲν αὐτίκα περῃρεῖτο πολυαρχία Ῥωμαίων, Αὐγούστου κατὰ τὸ αὐτὸ τῇ τοῦ σωτῆρος ἡμῶν ἐπιφανείᾳ μοναρχήσαντος. Such a synchronism was not new; see Hippolytus, *Comm. Dan.* 4.9.2–3; Origen, *C. Cels.* 2.30.20, 27; Melito, *Apol.* (*ap.* Eusebius, *HE* 4.26.7–8); cp. Gregory Nazianzenus, *Or.* 4.37.

[121] For the situation, see T. D. Barnes, *Constantine and Eusebius*, 66–8.

[122] Homer, *Il.* 2.204–205; cited at Eusebius, *Mart. Pal.* (shorter) 1.1.

connected to the polytheism of daemonic delusion and his declaration in favour of monarchy with the sole rule of Christ over those daemons must be seen in this sort of political context. The synchronism of Augustus and Christ could thus carry its own subversive message. This point has been ubiquitously ignored by scholars and so deserves full articulation here. If we turn to the preoccupations of earlier scholarship, however, even apart from the imperial political context, the passage does not embrace Roman rule to the extent claimed by others.

The issue for many has been to determine the nature of Augustus' connection to Christ. Was it a matter only of historical simultaneity (both dependent on a common Providence), or was the work of one dependent on the work of the other?[123] These questions can only be properly answered in the light of Eusebius' attack on Greek political theology. Eusebius is clear that his remarks on the Roman emperor are dedicated to opposing the daemonic control of the nations. An analysis of the passage as a whole will provide the proper perspective.

Eusebius had made the bold claim that Christianity was proven not only in words but in deeds as well. 'All words are superfluous, when the works are more manifest and plain than words—works which the divine and heavenly power of our Saviour distinctly exhibits even now.'[124] The works of the Saviour consisted of the spread of Christianity throughout all the nations and its endurance and strength despite persecution by invisible daemons and visible rulers.[125] The continued existence and spread of Christianity against all odds is, for Eusebius, its own defence.[126] This state of affairs could not obtain without the help of a truly divine power. The stress in this passage is upon the work of Christ seen in the spread of Christianity to all nations. Roman rulers are even given oblique reference as persecutors under the guidance of invisible daemons ('after these many years of persecution both by the invisible daemons and by the visible rulers of each age').[127]

Eusebius introduces the Augustus–Christ synchronism thus: 'For it must have been of a divine and secret power, that immediately at his word, and with the doctrine which he put forth concerning the sole sovereignty of the One God who is over all, at once the human race was set free from the delusive working of daemons, at once also from the

---

[123] See Chesnut, *The First Christian Histories*, 77; Sirinelli, *Les vues historiques d'Eusèbe de Césarée*, 388–411; Farina, *L'Impero e l'imperatore cristiano in Eusebio di Cesarea*, 147, 160–1; Inglebert, *Les Romains Chrétiens face à l'Histoire de Rome*, 165–7.

[124] *PE* 1.3.7.   [125] *PE* 1.4.1.   [126] See below, Chapter 7.   [127] *PE* 1.4.1.

multitude of rulers (*polyarchia*) among the nations.'[128] The repeated phrase, 'at once' is echoed in the statement referring to Augustus: 'Immediately (*autika*) all the multitude of rulers (*polyarchia*) among the Romans began to be abolished'.[129] But, additional material is inserted both as a parenthesis between these two proclamations of the immediate consequences of Christ's victory over daemons, and again following the reference to Augustus. Both offer a vivid description of the incessant strife directly caused by daemonic involvement in the affairs of the nations. The first runs:

of old in each nation numberless kings and local governors held power, and in different cities some were governed by a democracy, and some by tyrants, and some by a multitude of rulers, and hence wars of all kinds naturally arose, nations clashing against nations, and constantly rising up against their neighbours, ravaging and being ravaged, and making war in their sieges one against another, so that from these causes the whole population, both of dwellers in the cities, and labourers in the fields, from mere childhood were taught warlike exercises, and always wore swords both in the highways and in villages and fields...[130]

The second description evokes the daemonic activity connected to the war and strife of nations. It reads:

Surely there is good cause, when one considers it, to wonder why of old, when the daemons were tyrants over all the nations, and men paid them much worship, they were goaded by the gods themselves into furious wars against each other—so that now Greeks were at war with Greeks, and now Egyptians with Egyptians, and Syrians with Syrians, and Romans with Romans, and made slaves of each other and wore each other out with sieges, as in fact the histories of the ancients on these matters show...[131]

I have quoted these statements *in extenso* in order to develop a deeper sense of the Augustus–Christ synchronism within the overall context of the passage. Regarding this passage, F. E. Cranz had claimed that 'Eusebius tends to make Augustus the key figure.'[132] My reading of the passage points away from this assessment, however. Far from being

[128] *PE* 1.4.2; for the motif of Rome's ending the polyarchy of nations (a theme borrowed from Latin sources by the Greeks), see the sources cited at Sherwin-White, *The Roman Citizenship*, 429–30.
[129] *PE* 1.4.4.
[130] *PE* 1.4.3.
[131] *PE* 1.4.5; see *CI* 1.75 (Ziegler 125.22 ff).
[132] Cranz, 'Kingdom and Polity in Eusebius of Caesarea', 55.

the centre of a political theology in which Eusebius confers sacred status upon the Roman emperor as an earthly image of the heavenly mon- arch,[133] the passage firmly emphasizes Christ's victory over the many daemons who control many nations and produce many wars between those nations.[134] The historical fact of Augustus' rise to power over other Roman strong men (or even more, over the Hellenistic kingdoms)[135] functions as a proof of Christ's conquering of the warring daemons, and does not render explicit sacralization to the imperial office; we do an injustice to the passage to see that sort of imperial ideology here.

This point is consistent with, and even strengthened by, references to Augustus in the *Demonstratio*. In fact, the *Demonstratio* contains scat- tered comments about Augustus and Rome that are largely misread, ignored, or at best seen as anomalies in treatments of Eusebius' political thought.[136] At 3.7 (139d–141a), the synchronism of Augustus and Christ is raised in a manner that may at first be taken as a very positive depiction of Rome.[137] Augustus, as 'the supreme ruler over most of the nations',[138] subdues the Jews, Syrians, Cappadocians, Macedonians, Bithynians, Greeks, and others. This happened so that Christianity could easily spread throughout the nations under a unified empire.[139] Eusebius says that 'this was the work of God who is over all'.[140]

So far, one might reasonably take this as the sort of Christianization of imperial ideology that Eusebius has come to be known for. However, Eusebius adds an interesting caveat: 'And, moreover, that it might not be

---

[133] Eusebius will raise the notion of the earthly monarch as image of the heavenly monarch in later works such as the *VC* and *LC* (but see next footnote). For the beginning steps towards this ideology, see *PE* 7.13.

[134] Similarly, Drake, *Constantine and the Bishops. The Politics of Intolerance*, 360, noted in regard to the *HE* that, 'the events of the Roman Empire are peripheral, important only to the extent that they affect the people of the church'. See also, Cameron, 'Eusebius of Caesarea and the Rethinking of History', 78.

[135] See, e.g. *CI* 1.75 (126.28–127.16, esp. 127.1, 8–9); 1.77 (135.16–136.18, esp. 135.25–28); 1.72 (113.21–115.16).

[136] For example, Kofsky, *Eusebius of Caesarea against the Pagans*, 133 n. 141, refers to *DE* 4.9 as 'an uncharacteristic passage' in which Rome's unifying empire is seen as part of Satan's work in the world. It should be remembered that the passage never explicitly refers to Rome at all; but the assertion that a negative portrayal of Rome is uncharacteristic of Eusebius' *DE* needs to be questioned based upon the evidence discussed here.

[137] For other synchronisms, see 6.20 (299c–d) and 7.2 (345a–b).

[138] Αὐγούστου τῶν πλείστων ἐθνῶν μοναρχήσαντος.

[139] 140a–b. In this, Eusebius echoes Origen, *C. Cels.* 2.30.20, 27. Farina, *L'Impero e l'imperatore cristiano in Eusebio di Cesarea*, 151, supposes Christianity is therefore in a dependent relationship to Rome.

[140] 140c.

thought to prosper through the leniency of rulers, if some of them under the sway of evil designed to oppose the Word of Christ, he allowed them to do what was in their hearts, both that the athletes might display their holiness, and also that it might be made evident to all that the triumph of the Word was not of the counsel of men, but of the power of God.'[141] This oblique reference to the persecuting emperors is further established by the reminder of the horrid deaths of these men. 'The enemies of holiness paid their fitting penalty, driven mad with divine scourges, afflicted with terrible and vile diseases in their whole body, so that at last they were forced to confess their impiety against Christ.'[142] The depiction of the deaths of the persecutors is reminiscent of Eusebius' account of the deaths of Galerius and Maximinus Daia in the *HE*.[143] The former account even makes it clear that Galerius' 'palinode' was not the result of human agency, but was the result of God's working in human affairs.[144]

What is important for the present enquiry is the distance Eusebius attempts to put here between the Roman emperors and the spread of Christ's teachings. Rome, though producing an environment conducive to the spread of Christianity through its political unification of the *oikoumenē*, nonetheless plays the role of the enemy of piety and overtly attacks the Church. There is a sharp distinction between Christians and the forces of Rome, even in the very act of synchronizing the rule of Augustus with the reign of Christ. This can hardly be a sacralization of the imperial office.

Another reference to the persecuting emperors (again in an oblique fashion) occurs at *Demonstratio* 7.1 (334d). Eusebius had earlier declared that the appellation of Assyrians in the writings of the prophets (in this case Isaiah 7: 18–25) signified the Romans: 'For I believe that under the name of Assyrians he means the rule of the nations that gain empire at each period of history, because Assyrians in Hebrew means rulers. And the Romans are now such rulers.'[145] Now, Eusebius asserts that the 'king of the Assyrians' enslaved those Jews who did not follow Christ's teachings. But as for the Jews who became disciples of Christ, God 'girded them with intellectual and rational weapons, against the face of the said king of the Assyrians, and made them into heavy-armed ['hoplite'] soldiers, as his own army'.[146] Hence, a parallel is drawn between Rome's conquest of Jerusalem and its persecution of Christians.

---

[141] 140d.   [142] 140d.   [143] *HE* 8.16–17 and 9.10.14.   [144] *HE* 8.16.2.
[145] *DE* 7.1 [322a]. See also [331b].   [146] Ibid.

And even while Eusebius expends much effort in drawing out the implications of the defeat of the Jews by the Romans, he does not here (or ever, to my mind) exalt the Romans for this accomplishment.[147] Rather, the Romans in this case are merely God's instrument of punishment against the Jews, just as the Assyrians were in the days of Isaiah the prophet. The fact that Eusebius sees them as part of God's plan does not mean that the Romans, any more than Assyria or Babylonia, must have a close relationship with the Church.[148] And again, as in the passage on the Augustus–Christ synchronism above, Eusebius widens the gulf between Christians and Romans by raising the issue of persecution. In this case, the imagery used is that of warfare between the disciples of Christ as hoplite soldiers and the persecuting emperors. The boundary between these nations is marked by violence and battles, rather than peace and cooperation. Eusebius' imagery here is not readily conducive to the sort of religious legitimation that is often attributed to his 'political theology'.

A further element from the broader context of this passage needs to be added. It is normally assumed that Rome is responsible for the conquest of other nations, and this is supposed to mirror the spiritual conquest of daemons on the non-physical plane.[149] However, in *Demonstratio* 7.1, it is Christ who conquers the nations of the Eastern Mediterranean. Seeing Isaiah 8: 4 ('Wherefore before the child knows how to call his father or mother, he will take the power of Damascus and the spoils of Samaria against the king of Assyria', or as Aquila renders it, 'before the face of the king of Assyria')[150] as a prophecy of Christ, Eusebius draws the conclusion that Christ, not the emperor of Rome, is responsible for their subjugation. Eusebius writes:

As then, the king of the Assyrians is connected with the appearing of our Saviour, it is probable that here also the Roman Empire is intended, through their being directed by God to subject the nations to themselves. It is therefore prophesied that the child that is born will take the power of Damascus, and the spoils of Samaria, and will deliver them against the face of the Assyrians, and before the eyes of those ruled by God, and that he will do this at the time of his birth, directing the fate of humanity with secret divine power, while physically still a baby.[151]

---

[147] For later treatments of the Roman victory over the Jews, see below.

[148] *Pace* Farina, *L'Impero e l'imperatore cristiano in Eusebio di Cesarea*, 136, who claims Rome is different from these kingdoms since it will be transformed into the kingdom of heaven.

[149] Chesnut, *The First Christian Histories*, 77.

[150] Quoted at *DE* 7.1 [328d].

[151] *DE* 7.1 [331c]. Cp. *CI* 48 (Ziegler 55.4–56.6); Justin, *Dial.* 77–8.

This representation of the conquest of Near Eastern nations is repeated later: Christ 'has also literally by secret and divine power delivered the kingly power of both Damascus and all Syria and the spoils of Samaria, according to my interpretation, into the hands of the Roman Empire'.[152] Although Eusebius notes that the Roman Empire was to subjugate the nations, the true agency of the conquest is claimed to rest with Christ. Rome is not pictured here as the active conqueror, but as a passive beneficiary of the effects wrought by Christ.[153]

This puts an important twist upon our understanding of Eusebius' complex use of the imperial unification of the Roman Empire. Not only is any positive interpretation of Rome dissolved by Eusebius' equation of Rome with Assyria (in other words, just another conquering nation used temporarily by God), but even Rome's might and power is diminished through the representation of Christ as the agent of conquest.

This understanding sheds new light on a few comments that might be considered as positive assessments of Rome. For example, at 7.1 (322d), Romans are described as the rulers under God's rule; and at 7.1 (333c), the Roman army is said to be under God's direction. Such statements should not be taken as evidence of a high view of Rome, however. They only convey the assumption that God utilizes 'the powers that be' in his punishment of the Jewish people. The Jews had to receive, according to Eusebius, the penalty of rejecting and crucifying Christ. Christians, living lives of peace and detachment from the physical life, were not the ones to perform this task. Hence, the Romans became the instruments of God's punishment, not through any possible connection with the friends of God and holy nation, but as the dominant earthly kingdom at that time.

Elsewhere, there are other scarcely veiled statements made in reference to Rome that carry a negative tone. Rome's subjugation of Egypt is said to fulfil the prophecy from Isaiah 19: 4 that Egypt would fall into the hands of 'harsh masters'.[154] In a discussion of the Roman conquest of Jerusalem, the Jews are said to be conquered by 'foreigners and idolaters'.[155] These comments may seem slight, but nonetheless their effect is

---

[152] *DE* 7.1 (334d).

[153] An interesting parallel, albeit from a later work, is found at *CI* 40 (Ziegler 35): 'all these things happened to them from the assault of the enemies – which they did not make on their own, but God led them, all but dragging and pulling them to the siege of the accused'.

[154] *DE* 6.20 (299c–d).

[155] *DE* 7.1 (324d); and again at 7.1 (327a–b).

cumulative. More striking is Eusebius' passing reference to Rome as Gog, a nation that received harsh indictments from the prophet Ezekiel (and continues to exercise the eschatological imaginations of millennialists).[156] It was Jesus, Eusebius writes,

whom the prophecy foretold, in whose time the kingdom of Gog should be exalted concurrently with the growth of Christ's power. It is said that by this figure the Hebrews spoke enigmatically of the Roman Empire, which grew concurrently with the teaching of Christ.... [Ezekiel] says that Gog, the ruler of all of them [that is, the city of Rome, Mysia and Iberia] will be exalted at the coming of the Christ prophesied.[157]

While Eusebius does not mention the impending judgements against Gog heralded by Ezekiel, he surely had them in mind as he wrote. His equation of Rome with Ezekiel's Gog must be seen as nothing less than an implicit anti-Roman sentiment.[158] This is a startling conclusion to reach from the writings of the so-called founder of 'caesaropapism', but receives further confirmation from three other passages.

At one point, Eusebius offers an interesting claim regarding the disguised references to Rome that he finds in the biblical prophecies. The only reason the prophets abstain from naming the Romans openly is that the teaching of Christ spread throughout the Roman world and the books of the prophets circulated throughout the empire and in the city of Rome itself. 'It was therefore to prevent any offence being taken by the rulers of the empire from a too clear reference to them, that the prophecy was cloaked in riddles, in many contexts, notably in the visions of Daniel, just as in the prophecy we are considering, in which it calls them Assyrians, meaning rulers.'[159]

[156] *DE* 8.3 (424a–b). Rome received a similar comparison with Babylon in Augustine, *CD* 18.2 (*Babylon quasi prima Roma – Roma quasi secunda Babylonia*). For discussion of the parallel, see H. Bellen, 'Baylon und Rom – Orosius und Augustinus', in P. Kneissl and V. Losemann (eds), *Imperium Romanum*, Festschrift Karl Christ (Stuttgart: Franz Steiner Verlag, 1998), 51–60. For a discussion of contemporary applications of Gog in rabbinic eschatalogical thought, see R. Wilken, 'The Restoration of Israel in Biblical Prophecy: Christian and Jewish Responses in the Early Byzantine Period', in J. Neusner and E. Frerichs, (eds), *To See Ourselves as Others See Us* (Chico: Scholars Press, 1985), 459–60.
[157] *DE* 8.3 (424a–b).
[158] Commenting on Num. 24.7, where the LXX reads Gog for the Hebrew Agag, Eusebius reports in his *Proph. Ecl.* (1069C) that some suppose this to be a reference to the Romans, but others interpret it figuratively as the 'heavenly *politeia*' and the contemplation of intellectual dogmas (since Gog means 'dogmas'). This is surely an interesting passage, but one that has no firm bearing on the *DE*'s interpretation of the prophecies against Gog in Ezekiel.
[159] *DE* 7.1 (323a–b).

In other words, the prophecies about Rome had to be put in hidden terms so that they would find a wide audience and so offer 'proof' of Christ's life and work as a fulfilment of the prophetic oracles. In a similar manner, Eusebius had earlier stated that the Jews would have kept the prophecies hidden if it were not for the providential work of God in bringing about their translation under Ptolemy II Philadelphus (at *PE* 8.1.7). Thus, God foiled the Jews, on the one hand, who would have preferred to keep the secrets of prophecy from being broadcast; while God in turn tricked the Romans, who failed to realize they were the objects of devastating prophecies.

But what could be displeasing to Rome in the prophecies that would potentially cause them to want to eradicate the Scriptures? I have already mentioned the prophecies against Gog in Ezekiel. But here, Eusebius mentions the visions of Daniel. We are fortunate to have as one of the few remaining fragments of the latter half of the *Demonstratio* a passage from the fifteenth book that offers an interpretation of Daniel's report of the vision of Nebuchadnezzar, the king of Babylon, of a statue made of four metals, gold, silver, bronze, and iron. Eusebius emphasizes that the vision was that of the king and so represented a this-worldly perspective of power, whereas Daniel's own vision of beasts in the sea represented the divinely inspired perspective. As Eusebius writes: 'It was natural for the king, deceived as he was by the outward appearances of life, and admiring the beauty of the visible world like colours in a picture, to liken the life of all men to a great image, whereas the prophet was rather led to compare the vast and mighty surge of life to a great sea.'[160] Then, explaining that the four metals of the king's vision represented the great empires of the Assyrians (gold), the Persians (silver), the Macedonians (bronze), and the Romans (iron), Eusebius asserts that the stone, which smashed the entire image in the king's vision, was in fact the kingdom of God. 'And after these four, the kingdom of God was presented as a stone that destroyed the whole image. And the prophet agrees with this in not seeing the final triumph of the Kingdom of the God of the universe before he has described the course of the four world-powers under the similitude of the four beasts.'[161] Eusebius had just before noted that the final smashing of the image was to serve as a

---

[160] *DE* 15.fr.1, Heikel 493 l. 27–494 l. 4.

[161] *DE* Heikel 495, ll. 21–5. Farina's attempt to see the smashing of Rome as its transformation into a Christian Empire verges on the disingenuous (*L'Impero e l'imperatore cristiano in Eusebio di Cesarea*, 157).

chastisement to the king's arrogance and his myopic assumption that worldly things could last. Eusebius claims, 'the mutability of human things is revealed, and the end of earthly kingdoms, to purify [the king] of his pride, and to make him realize the instability of human things, or at least the final universal kingdom of God'.[162]

Eusebius' treatment of the prophetic visions recounted by Daniel, his application of the kingdom of iron to Rome and the iconoclastic stone to the Church, further highlights the boundary between Rome and Christianity that we saw emerging in the other passages discussed.[163] Again the imagery is violent: the kingdom of God clashes with the empire of Rome and gains a shattering success. The ephemeral nature of earthly kingdoms such as Rome is thus vividly portrayed. The sharp distinction between Romans and Christians is accented. Eusebius' theology of Rome must be seen in this new light.[164]

---

[162] *DE* Heikel 495, ll. 11–14. For the broader context of Eusebius' eschatology, see F. S. Thielman, 'Another Look at the Eschatology of Eusebius', *VC* 41 (1987), 226–37, though he fails to capitalize on the fragments from *DE* 15, which would have greatly increased the force of his argument.

[163] It is interesting to contrast Eusebius' treatment of the vision with Josephus at *AJ* 10.205–210 where he purposely omits an explanation of the kingdom of iron or of the stone that smashes the image. See F. F. Bruce, 'The Romans through Jewish Eyes', in M. Simon (ed.), *Paganisme, Judaïsme, Christianisme*, Mélanges offerts à Marcel Simon (Paris: Éditions E. de Boccard, 1978), 2–12; Sterling, *Historiography and Self-Definition*, 292–3; (on Josephus' eschatology more generally, see M. de Jonge, 'Josephus und die Zukunftserwartungen seines Volkes', in O. Betz, K. Haacker, and M. Hengel (eds), *Josephus-Studien: Untersuchungen zu Josephus, dem antiken Judentum und dem Neuen Testament* [Göttingen: Vandenhoeck and Ruprecht, 1974], 205–19; U. Fischer, *Eschatologie und Jenseitserwartung im hellenistischen Diasporajudentum* [Berlin and New York: Walter de Gruyter, 1978], 144–83). In fact, Eusebius may have closer parallels with contemporary rabbinic thought on Daniel's four kingdoms; e.g. Genesis Rabbah 16.4 (trans. H. Freedman and M. Simon, *Midrash Rabbah. Genesis* [London: Soncino Press, 1951], 1.128–30). For discussion, see J. Maier, *Jüdische Auseinandersetzung mit dem Christentum in der Antike* (Darmstadt: Wissenschaftliche Buchgesellschaft,1982), 200–5; G. Stemberger, *Jews and Christians in the Holy Land. Palestine in the Fourth Century*, trans. R. Tuschling (Edinburgh: T&T Clark, 2000), 284–9.

[164] I have not included *DE* 4.9 (159a), where Satan is said to have attempted to overcome the God-assigned national boundaries and implement a forced unity by driving out the angels of the nations, because Eusebius does not clearly place this satanic disruption of natural nationalities within the context of the unification of the *oikoumenē* under Rome. *Pace* Kofsky, *Eusebius of Caesarea against the Pagans*, 133 n. 141, where he claims, 'the Roman Empire emerges as part of Satan's program to oppose the ancient divine system of guardian angels'. Eusebius may have considered Rome as being under the control of Satan, as a manifestation of Gog or the iron kingdom from Daniel, but at least here at 4.9, Eusebius gives us no hints that Rome is to be understood.

Now that we have analysed the relevant passages from the *Demon-stratio*, let us return to the passage at *Praeparatio* 1.4. Instead of quickly equating the proclamations of peace (the beating of swords into plough-shares) with the Roman Empire itself, it may be more consistent with what we have seen to recognize the emphasis upon Christ and the spread of his teachings within Eusebius' statements. The focus is not upon Augustus in the synchronism: it is the spread of Christ's teaching throughout the world, not the conquest of Rome that causes the profound changes in customs and ways of life that Eusebius depicts. 'The cleansing from polytheistic error was accomplished', Eusebius writes, 'at the same time as the most pious and most peaceful teaching of our Saviour.'[165] Then Eusebius provides a series of examples of the good effects of the spread of the Gospel throughout the world. Rome is not mentioned again. The 'civilizing' changes are wrought by conver-sion to Christianity, not inclusion in the Roman Empire. Benefit 'pro-ceeds visibly from his [Christ's] doctrines', and it is 'only from his utterances, and from his teaching diffused throughout the whole world, [that] the customs of all nations are now set aright, even those customs which before were savage and barbarous; so that Persians who have become his disciples no longer marry their mothers, nor Scythians feed on human flesh, because of Christ's word which has come even unto them ...'.[166]

Eusebius later repeats the notion that it is Christ's teaching *alone* that produces these changes: 'the salutary law of the power of the Gospel having alone abolished the savage and inhuman disease of all these'.[167] Again, it is 'solely through the evangelic teaching of our Saviour', that Greeks and barbarians can attain to such a high point of philosophy as they now do among the Christians.[168] Eusebius has to emphasize the singularity and distinctiveness of Christian teachings; to do otherwise would dissolve the force of his defence of Christianity. If Rome is responsible for the 'civilizing' developments that Eusebius makes so much of, then Christianity would not be necessary, and Christians would still need to explain their rejection of ancestral customs in favour of the teachings of Christ.

---

[165] *PE* 1.4.5.   [166] *PE* 1.4.6. See Chapter 7 for discussion.
[167] *PE* 1.4.8.   [168] *PE* 1.4.9.

ROME IN THE LATER WORKS OF EUSEBIUS

Eusebius' monumental two-part apology, whose view of Rome was subsumed within the context of his critique of Greek civic theology and was far from obsequious, was completed while Constantine and Licinius uneasily shared control of the Roman world. By AD 315, the apologist had obtained reports of the former's message (ambiguous though it was) inscribed on his triumphal arch in the city of Rome[169] and seen a copy of the so-called Edict of Milan, which offered a felicitous, if short-lived, period of respite to the weary Church in the East. Licinius' renewal of persecution, as tension with Constantine failed to be adequately addressed following their military confrontations near Cibalae and Adrianople (AD 316), may have provided additional impetus for including less than favourable sentiments towards Rome in the *Praeparatio* and especially the *Demonstratio*.[170]

The following decade would see the victory of Constantine over Licinius, imperial involvement in ecclesiastical controversies that were close to home for Eusebius, and imperial attention and benefaction to churches in Palestine itself.[171] How did these drastic changes affect Eusebius' attitude to Rome? At the very outset, the experimentation with genres new to Eusebius' oeuvre—a panegyric for the emperor (the *LC*) and what may be the earliest full-scale hagiography (the *VC*)—is indicative of his attempt to grapple with (or take advantage of) the changed situation. However, the mimetic model of kingship (one ruler on earth models the one Ruler in heaven) and the fawning tone of the *VC*, which seem obvious to modern readers, should not be allowed to obscure the more sophisticated ideological and ecclesiastical moves that Eusebius was attempting in the later years of his life. The following considerations are meant only to offer a cursory and suggestive sketch of how we might approach his later works more fruitfully, especially in light of the conclusions I have drawn regarding Eusebius' vision of Rome

[169] See *HE* 10.4.16 (which is a quotation from his speech at Tyre delivered in AD 315).

[170] On the battles between Licinius and Constantine, see T. D. Barnes, *Constantine and Eusebius*, 67; on Licinius' religious policies (esp. as reflected in Eusebius' *DE*), see ibid., 70–2.

[171] For Constantine's series of conflicts with Licinius, see T. D. Barnes, *Constantine and Eusebius*, 62–77; for Constantine's ecclesiastical involvement, see Drake, *Constantine and the Bishops*; for Constantine's (or rather Helena's) Holy Land programme, see *VC* 3.25–47.3, with the commentary of A. Cameron and S. G. Hall, *Eusebius. Life of Constantine* (Oxford: Clarendon Press, 1999), *ad loc.*

in the *Praeparatio* and *Demonstratio*. I offer a brief discussion of the Augustus–Christ synchronism as it appears in his later works before turning to broader considerations of Eusebius' later theology of Rome.

Oration on the Church of the Holy Sepulchre (*SC*)

Consideration of the later occurrence of themes that occurred in the *Praeparatio* and *Demonstratio* highlight the consistency in Eusebius' approach over the years of transition from a climate of persecution to one of favour and beneficence. The Augustus–Christ synchronism is an example of a motif that recurs in his later works with much the same effect as his earlier ones. At the end of a narrative of historical decline among the nations of the world, Eusebius' oration on the Church of the Holy Sepulchre, addressed to a non-Christian audience in Constantine's court in AD 336, claims to offer proof of the Logos' ability to put an end to that daemonically driven decline. Amidst 'toparchies and polyarchies, tyrannies and democracies', the doctrine of one God was proclaimed, 'and at the same time the one kingdom of the Romans flowered every-where'.[172] Even more pointedly, Eusebius adds: 'as if from a single divine will, two beneficial shoots were produced for mankind: the empire of the Romans and the teachings of true worship'.[173] Here, at least at first, Eusebius comes closest to diminishing the causal relationship between Christ's defeat of daemons and Augustus' defeat of other nations as portrayed in the *Praeparatio*. 'The two great powers ... as if from a single starting post ... blossomed together at the same time and in the same manner as each other.'[174]

Surely, the relaxed climate of the 330s must have allowed Eusebius to feel more comfortable about using the language of harmony between Christianity and empire, which may have been more difficult to elicit under the antagonistic policies of Licinius 20 years earlier. Yet, at the same time that Eusebius seems to adopt a more amicable stance to the Roman Empire, he nonetheless maintains the causal relationship between Christ's work and Augustus' monarchy envisioned in his earlier work. Even as he declares that Church and empire have 'blossomed together', he notes that it was 'the power of our Saviour' that 'destroyed

---

172 *SC* 16.4; note the allusion to Melito *ap.* Eusebius, *HE* 4.26.7.
173 Ibid., (Drake's translation).
174 *SC* 16.5; note the allusion to Melito *ap.* Eusebius, *HE* 4.26.8.

the polyarchy and polytheism of daemons, announcing a single kingdom of God to all humanity, both Greeks and barbarians, and those at
the edges of the earth'.[175] This kingdom of God is distinct from the
kingdom of Rome, since Eusebius continues, 'once the sources of polyarchy were destroyed beforehand, Roman rule defeated the visible
[forms of polyarchy]'.[176] Once again, therefore, Eusebius manifests his
earlier conception of Rome's monarchy as totally dependent upon the
victory of Christ over daemonic forces. This point is further substantiated by the role to which the Augustus–Christ synchronism is put
within the broader context of the *SC*. The oration is, in a way, an
abbreviated articulation of Eusebius' vision of world history offered in
the *Praeparatio*: a narrative of historical decline in piety and wisdom
finds cessation only in the incarnation of the Logos and the spread of his
teachings, in spite of persecution, throughout all the nations of the
earth. The synchronism of Christ's work with Augustus' reign was only
the mundane proof for the Incarnation and Christ's victory over daemons and death through the resurrection—'if the truth of these things
needs proof'.[177] Indeed, there was 'an abundance of other proofs' that
Christ alone had filled the world with his name and his teaching;[178] no
one else had ever 'put an end to the barbarous and savage habits of
barbarian peoples by his most philanthropic laws, so that no longer do
his disciples among the Scythians practise cannibalism, nor those
among the Persians wed their mothers', and so on.[179] Any victory was
thus effectively removed from Augustus' hands and attributed solely to
Christ. In Eusebius' eyes, the Roman monarch merely stood as a proof of
the more important and far-reaching events effected by Christ.

The Commentaries

Further instances of the synchronism exhibit additional ambivalence
towards Rome in Eusebius' often neglected commentary on the Book of
Isaiah,[180] written sometime after AD 325.[181] The context is now quite

---

[175] Ibid.; on the spread of Christ's kingdom throughout all nations, see below Chapter 7.
[176] Ibid.   [177] *SC* 16.1.   [178] *SC* 16.8.
[179] *SC* 16.9 (translation adapted from Drake); note the similarity to *PE* 1.4, discussed in
Chapter 7.
[180] Its neglect is no doubt due to the lack of a translation in any modern language; see,
however, the admirable treatment of Hollerich (*Eusebius of Caesarea's* Commentary on Isaiah).
[181] For considerations of date, see ibid., 19–26.

different from the other instances of the synchronism we have seen in the *Praeparatio* or the *SC*, which formed integral parts of arguments for Christ's victory over the daemons. Here, he aims at the explication of biblical prophecies especially as these can be turned against the Jewish people. The Romans figure most prominently throughout the commentary as the agents of God's just punishment against the Jews for their disbelief,[182] so that the Roman siege of Jerusalem could be named 'the war of God against them',[183] and the Roman army could be given the appellation of 'the hand of the Lord'.[184] The emperors deemed most significant, and hence mentioned by name most often, are accordingly Vespasian and Hadrian—victorious generals in anti-Jewish military conflicts.[185] Constantine is never mentioned by name, Augustus only once.[186]

Because of the biblical prophetic focus of the commentary, Eusebius' manipulation of the Augustus–Christ synchronism is developed to meet ends different from those considered above. Instead, the synchronism is employed as a proof that the proper fulfilment of the prophetic passage under consideration occurred with the coming of Christ and not at any other time. So, in the first instance, Eusebius refers to the synchronism as a 'most clear sign (*sēmeion*)' of the fulfilment of a prophecy proclaiming the calling of foreign nations to become a 'new mountain and a house of God' (Is. 2: 1–4).[187] This sign was the peace and cessation of 'regional rule (*toparchias*) and polyarchy', and of strife between nations and even 'cities within nations fighting and waging war against each other'.[188] Nobody could see such peace and stability in former times 'as

---

[182] See, e.g., *CI* 1.11 (Ziegler 6.17); 1.18 (Ziegler 10.18); 1.25 (Ziegler 14.15); 1.27–8 (Ziegler 18.26–19.2); 1.35 (Ziegler 31.35–32.3); 1.42 (Ziegler 42.32–43.2); 1.42 (Ziegler 43.16–19); 2.8 (Ziegler 224.24–26); 2.48 (Ziegler 366.36). Cp. *Comm. Ps.* 58.7 (*PG* 23.541B); 58.13 (*PG* 23.545C); 54.24 (*PG* 23.492A); 68.25 (*PG* 23.753A); 74 (*PG* 23.824B); 79 (*PG* 23.829C–D); 74.1 (*PG* 23.852A–C; 853A–B); 74.9 (*PG* 23.860A); 78.1 (*PG* 23.941B); 79.14 (*PG* 23.964D–965B); 82.6, 8, 9 (*PG* 23.996C–997A); 82.12 (*PG* 23.1000A); 89.3–7 (*PG* 23.1133D).

[183] *CI* 2.48 (Ziegler 366.36).

[184] *CI* 1.76 (Ziegler 132.7–15); though Eusebius makes it clear that 'the hand of the Lord' in this passage, as referring to the Roman power, is different from other occurrences of 'the hand of the Lord' in Isaiah (see Ziegler 132.8).

[185] See *CI* 1.35 (Ziegler 31.35–32.3); 1.42 (Ziegler 42.32–43.2; 43.16–19); oddly, Titus' name is omitted from the *CI*, though he does appear in similarly argued passages from the *Comm. Ps.* (see *PG* 23.829D; 853B; 1133D).

[186] See *CI* 1.75 (Ziegler 127.5–7); see discussion below.

[187] *CI* 1.26 (Ziegler 14.26–15.1).

[188] Ibid., (Ziegler 15.1–4); see Farina, *L'Impero e l'imperatore cristiano in Eusebio di Cesarea*, 134.

we see with our eyes under Roman rule after the times of our Saviour, as there is a mingling (*epimixias*) of nations and a peace everywhere throughout the fields and cities'.[189] And yet the lines surrounding this avowal prohibit us from seeing this as a bright proclamation of the *pax Romana*. The empire was only a sign for those who otherwise might not believe the fulfilment of a prophecy that announced the concord and peace (a 'new law') of those who turned from their 'paternal gods'[190] and the 'ancient practices of fashioning swords and the tools of war'[191] and had adopted the new teaching of the Gospel, whose beginning was not in Rome, but on the contrary, 'was making its beginning from the land of the Jews and from Sion itself and entered the world unchecked and filled all the nations'.[192] Roman rule was secondary and came manifestly after the peace-making work of Christ.[193] Indeed, Augustus is not even mentioned in the passage—an omission that highlights Eusebius' Christocentric emphasis here (as elsewhere).

Let us turn to the single explicit mention of the first Roman emperor. Addressing a prophecy that Egypt would be handed over to cruel kings (Is. 19: 4), Eusebius asserts that the passage indicates a change of kingship that would occur 'in the time of the Lord's arrival in Egypt'.[194] 'Who would not be amazed', he asks, 'comparing the times of the saving proclamation of the Logos and along with it the destruction of the kingdom that was in Egypt, since from that time even until now the former rulers—I mean the Ptolemies—no longer rule them, but the Romans are declared to be their masters'.[195] Then, opting for the singular 'king' of Aquila, Symmachus and Theodotion over the plural 'kings' of the LXX in the second line of the prophecy, Eusebius sees further confirmation for his interpretation of the prophecy. The king was none other than Augustus, who 'was sole ruler (*monarchēsanta*) at the time of the birth of our Saviour' and 'destroyed the succession of the Ptolemies ruling among them, which had prevailed for a long time'.[196] The comments following this synchronism echo his ascription of cruelty

---

[189] Ibid., (Ziegler 15.8–11); cp. *Comm. Ps.* 71.6–8 (*PG* 23.804A).

[190] Ibid., (Ziegler 14.30–31).　　　[191] Ibid., (Ziegler 15.5–7).

[192] Ibid., (Ziegler 15.12–14).

[193] Ibid., (Ziegler 15.7–8, 10); *pace* Farina, *L'Impero e l'imperatore cristiano in Eusebio di Cesarea*, 80 (citing *Comm. Ps.* 71.6–8 [*PG* 23.801D], where the phrase 'the events before his parousia' refers to the widespread polyarchy and war, not to the *pax Romana*, as Farina would have it).

[194] *CI* 1.75 (Ziegler 126.31–32); for Christ's visit to Egypt while still a baby, see Matt. 2: 13–15.

[195] Ibid. (Ziegler 126.28–127.2).　　　[196] Ibid. (Ziegler 127.5–9).

to the Romans in the *Demonstratio* noted earlier. The Roman emperors (*autokratores*) who came afterwards, as 'strong kings—or rather "harsh" according to the Seventy—enslaved the *ethnos* of the Egyptians, by whom were sent at that time military generals ruling Egypt who treated them more harshly'.[197]

The commentary continues with further prophetic details regarding Roman dominion over Egypt. But the point is sufficiently clear; Eusebius saw Roman control of Egypt as the fulfilment of Isaiah's prophecy and as concurrent with Christ's own sojourn in Egypt. His intention is to prove the broader prophecy's applicability to Christ, and the Augustan victory over the last of the Ptolemies nicely confirms this interpretation for him. His statement on the cruelty of the later military generals preserves his earlier emphasis in the *Demonstratio* on Romans as the objects of 'cruel master' prophecies.

The description of the Romans as harsh rulers may be supplemented with a detail that evinces further reserve on Eusebius' part with respect to the Romans. While Eusebius was clearly impressed at the sight of Roman authorities in church 'bending the knee' and offering material support to Christianity,[198] and while he clearly finds the defeat of the Jews under Vespasian and Hadrian to be deserved,[199] the wealth accrued from the Roman siege of Jerusalem brought its own critique. When Isaiah spoke of the wealth of those who attacked Mount Sion as 'being a thing in a dream' (Is. 29: 7), the object of his prophecy was, according to Eusebius, none other than 'the Roman rulers' enjoyment of luxury in this life; for these were the ones attacking Jerusalem in the last siege'.[200] This passage needs to be given due weight, since it introduces an important caveat to those who would too easily see Eusebius' attitude to the Roman destruction of Jerusalem as an entirely positive event. As noted above, the Romans, as the instruments of God's judgement against the faithless Jews, were considered no more godly, righteous, or good than were the Babylonians or Assyrians whom God had earlier used to mete out well-deserved punishment on the Jews.

This point is confirmed by other passages marked by ambivalence toward Roman rule in his commentary. According to one prophecy of Jerusalem's destruction (Is. 2: 5–9), the idolatry of the Jews would only be replaced by the idolatry of those from foreign nations who came in to

---

[197] Ibid. (Ziegler 127.10–13).   [198] *CI* 2.36 (Ziegler 316.18).
[199] *CI* 1.35 (Ziegler 32.1); 1.42 (Ziegler 42.32–43.19).
[200] *CI* 1.95 (Ziegler 189.19–21).

inhabit the land. The prophecy indicated, according to Eusebius, the men of the Roman army,[201] who were 'the nations of foreigners and idolaters about to dwell in Jerusalem itself and the Judean land'; these ones 'filled the land full of abominable works of their hands ... and worshipped those [idols] made by their own fingers'.[202] In fact, when the prophet addresses God, 'Do not forgive them' (Is. 2: 9), the invocation does not pertain to the Jews, 'for the prophet would not pray against his own people (*tou idiou laou*)'.[203] Instead, Isaiah has declared these things with reference to 'those fighting against Jerusalem and being full of military power and all idolatry'. The fact that the Jews deserved their punishment did not, therefore, protect the Romans from moral and religious culpability, in Eusebius' eyes.

An image from his commentary on the Psalms, which received its final form at roughly the same time as the *CI*, may be added to our discussion.[204] The psalmist laments the desolation of the land: 'A pig from the woods grazed in it.'[205] Eusebius comments that this 'prophecy' carried a double fulfilment, first through Nebuchadnezzar the Babylonian king, then through the Roman army, which 'arriving after the coming of our Saviour, grazed in it'.[206] The image of Rome as the prophetic pig was far from flattering. Combined with the other passages on Rome's cruelty, idolatry, and luxury, Eusebius' remarks in the *Commentaria in Psalmos* exhibit a consistent detachment from, and even disapproval of, the Romans as a collectivity. The commentator of biblical prophecy was able to see the imperialistic might of the Roman army as the object of prophecy while simultaneously robbing it of real agency. The power to pacify the strife-ridden ways of the nations resided with Christ and the spread of his teachings throughout the world. The inclusion of Rome in his explication of biblical prophecy was meant to serve only as a sign or proof that Christ was the object of prophecy or to further highlight what had been affected through the work of Christ. This independent stance can even be detected in Eusebius' works devoted to the first Christian emperor.

---

[201] *CI* 1.27 (Ziegler 18.16).   [202] Ibid., (Ziegler 18.17–23).

[203] Ibid., (Ziegler 18.34–35).

[204] Lacking a critical edition or translation into any modern language, the *Comm. Ps.* has received scant scholarly attention. For considerations of date, see M.-J. Rondeau, *Les commentaires patristiques du psautier* (Rome: Pontifical Institute of Oriental Studies, 1982), 1.66–69. For issues of authenticity, see E. Schwartz, 'Eusebios', 1435–6; M.-J. Rondeau, 'Eusèbe de Césarée. Le Commentaire sur les psaumes', in M.-J. Rondeau and J. Kirchmeyer, *Dictionnaire de spiritualité* (Paris: Beauchesnes, 1961), IV.2.1687–1690.

[205] Ps. 79: 14 LXX (=80.13).   [206] *Comm. Ps.* 79.14 (*PG* 23.964D–965A).

The Constantinian Writings

The years of persecution, combined with Licinius' sour turn towards Christianity following his initial policy of tolerance during the years in which Eusebius was completing his apologetic double work, may have had far more of an impact on the bishop of Caesarea than might be allowed in the caricatures that show him as an ingratiating court theologian to Constantine. In fact, in all Eusebius' works dealing directly with Constantine, one senses a cautious manipulation of the imperial image and the imperial relationship to the Church that seems largely consistent with the independent stance outlined above. Throughout these works, Eusebius evinces a heightened concern to map out the place of the newly converted emperor in a world in which the Church was triumphing and the Logos was ruling, themes which were already prominent in his earlier works.[207] It was the Church that deserved allegiance and that was changing the lives of people from all social and ethnic categories; if the emperor joined himself to the Church, so much the better. A strong sense of ecclesiastical autonomy, I would argue, is felt even in his seemingly most panegyrical moments.[208]

Eusebius' adoption of the mimetic model of the imperial image did not preclude criticism or even outright rejection of some earthly rulers. In his oration delivered in honour of Constantine's 30 years as emperor (the *LC*), Eusebius details a narrative of historical decline under the influence of foul and violent daemons that reached a nadir in the impious superstition of the persecuting emperors. These men, driven to an insane frenzy by the daemons, led 'the armies of polytheism' as 'the enemies of God and opponents of humanity's salvation, being worse than savage barbarians'.[209] The persecuted Church, deemed 'the soldiers of God' and 'his personal army',[210] remained faithful until God rescued them from further violence through his 'attendant' (*theraponta*), Constantine.[211]

The rule of the tyrants whom Constantine defeated was emphatically not modelled upon the rule of the Logos in heaven. One of the most

---

[207] See Chapter 7.

[208] See Hollerich, 'Religion and Politics in the Writings of Eusebius', *CH* 59 (1990), 309–25.

[209] *LC* 7.8; translation adapted from Drake, *In Praise of Constantine*, 96.

[210] *LC* 7.7, 10.

[211] *LC* 7.12; see Drake, *In Praise of Constantine*, 166 n.11, for the issues surrounding the translation of *theraponta*.

important tasks of the oration is to develop an image of the legitimate emperor as one who participates in the activity of the Logos and hence can be named God's friend,[212] in distinction from images of illegitimate rule of 'tyrants'. As Eusebius declares:

For he who would bear the title of sovereign with true reason has patterned regal virtues in his soul after the model (*to mimēma*) of that distant kingdom. But one who has alienated himself from these virtues and who has denied the Universal Sovereign, who has neither acknowledged the Heavenly Father of souls nor adopted a decorum proper to a sovereign, but who has instead taken into his soul the chaotic and shameful and traded for regal kindness the spirit of a wild beast; one in whom exists [vices instead of virtues] ... one who has surrendered himself to these, though he should sometimes be considered to rule with the force of a tyrant, at no time will he hold the title of sovereign with true reason.[213]

Eusebius concludes: 'For how could one bear the likeness (*to mimēma*) of monarchical authority who has formed (*tetupōmenos*) in his soul a myriad of falsely depicted images (*epseudographēmenas ... eikonas*) of daemons?'[214] The panegyric's portrayal of the ideal ruler as embodying all of the virtues under the guidance of the Logos not only flatters the listening emperor, who admits to being a friend of God, but more importantly establishes the contours of Christian rule within a definable set of parameters. Certainly, Eusebius does adopt the mimetic model of kingship from an earlier Hellenistic discourse on monarchy; but what is important is the new and distinctively Christian context into which this is placed, as well as the usurpation by a bishop of the authority to define the imperial position.

The mimetic model of the imperial office was thus meant, not as a blanket acceptance or legitimation of the Roman ruler, but rather as a means of asserting moral and spiritual authority over the ruler. Such a model provided a means of constraining the emperor's activity and image of himself while providing a criterion by which to invalidate imperial rule when it diverged from this model. This attempt at

---

[212] *LC* 5.1. Here (as frequently in the *VC*), the epithet of 'friend of God' should probably be seen more as Eusebius' invoking of Hebrew and Christian models of friendship with God (as seen in e.g. *PE* 7; see above, Chapter 4) rather than the adoption of pagan conceptions of the emperor's divine *comes* (on which, see A. D. Nock, 'The Emperor's Divine *Comes*', *JRS* 37 [1947], 102–16).

[213] *LC* 5.2 (translation adapted from Drake).

[214] *LC* 5.3 (Drake's translation); note the use of the artistic metaphor for portraying an individual's virtues or vices (on which, see Johnson, 'Ancestors as Icons'; and above, Chapter 4).

developing mechanisms for defining the imperial role is just as true of Eusebius' hagiographical biography of Constantine as of his panegyric for the emperor's tricennial celebrations.

The most fruitful approach to the *VC* has been to read it within the generic assumptions of a 'mirror for princes' (*Fürstenspiegel*), that is, as an idealized portrait of Constantine as a model of good (Christian) rule for his sons who inherited the empire.[215] Here again, Eusebius sought to depict the emperor so as to articulate the virtues of a Christian ruler as well as to set limits for imperial rule, especially in relation to ecclesiastical matters. The pious emperor was to aim at the unity of the Church, while remaining circumspect during the proceedings of the gathered bishops and to submit to the will of the ecumenical body. Eusebius' report of Constantine's assumption of the title and task of 'the bishop of those outside the Church' is indicative of this project of maintaining a relative autonomy for Christian leaders of the Church at a time when a Christian held the imperial office.[216] What Constantine may have intended by the use of this title matters little; instead, the importance here is the weight that could be attached to it by the bishop writing a 'mirror for princes', which sought in effect to delimit and control the duties and character of a Christian emperor. The emperor was to do the work of God in the political, legal, and military spheres (as represented in his letter to Shapur, for instance),[217] while the 'bishops of those within' the Church were to control ecclesiastical affairs. We see here not so much the sacralization of the imperial office (though that may have been what Constantine intended), but an expression of the doctrine of the separation of Church and State.

These reflections focus on the person of Constantine, whose position as a uniquely Christian emperor stimulated Eusebius in his innovatory attempts at imperial hagiography and panegyric. I do not deny Eusebius' excitement at the advent of a Christian ruler; nor do I deny that his adoption of the mimetic model of imperial rule had the effect of legitimating monarchic rule, or that his representation of the fall of Jerusalem in his commentaries justified Roman military imperialism. The caricature of Eusebius as a blithering panegyrist and imperial

---

[215] See Chesnut, *The First Christian Histories*, 124.

[216] The episode is recorded at *VC* 4.24; W. Seston, denies the *VC*'s authenticity on these grounds ('Constantine as Bishop', *JRS* 37 [1947], 127–31).

[217] Quoted at *VC* 4.9–13; for discussion, see Miriam R. Vivian, *A Letter to Shapur: The Effect of Constantine's Conversion on Roman-Persian Relations* (Ph.D. dissertation University of California, Santa Barbara, 1987).

theologian must, however, be rejected in the face of this broader, more nuanced, view of his later works.[218] What results is a picture of a consistent and careful thinker through years of dramatic transformation and upheaval in Roman religious and cultural history.

CONCLUSIONS

The picture that emerges of Eusebius' theology of Rome as developed in the pages of the *Praeparatio* and *Demonstratio* (as well as later works) is by no means simple. I have attempted to delineate the contours of his complex thinking about the empire of the Romans and the emperor himself. Within the scope of ethnic argumentation, the national boundaries between Rome and the other nations were carefully forged during a period in which imperial favour towards Christianity was by no means certain. On the one hand, Rome was marked out as different from the other nations (especially the Greeks); the Romans practised polytheism but had not fallen to the same depths of superstition as the Greeks. Romulus, the founder of Rome, received a favourable assessment: Eusebius' primary concern was to mount a formidable attack against Greek political theology. Hence, his discussion focused on the level of the *polis* rather than the empire. He was keen to show the powerful effects of the spread of Christianity throughout the cities and country districts of the world. Christ is represented as the victor over the wicked daemons who had earlier driven out the guardian angels of the nations.

Within the context of this argument against the daemonic nature of Greek political theology and *polis* religious activity, the Augustus–Christ synchronism was carefully delineated. But it was, if my reading is correct, only meant as a sort of proof that Christ really had driven the daemons out of the *polis* cult centres. The dramatic changes that Eusebius depicted were all rooted in, and centred around, Christ. Augustus becomes but a bystander. All agency, force, and historical importance are taken from the Roman emperor and attributed to Christ and the spread of Christianity. Even the subjugation of certain nations

---

[218] For similarly nuanced views, see Ruhbach 'Die politische Theologie Eusebs von Caesarea', 236–58; Hollerich, 'Religion and Politics in the Writings of Eusebius'; Cameron, 'Eusebius of Caesarea and the Rethinking of History', 71–88.

(Damascus and Samaria, if not Judaea itself) were brought about by Christ while yet a baby, and handed over to the passive Augustus.

Eusebius' 'political theology' is located in the displacement of Greek political theology. His theology of Rome is subsumed within this larger project of the polemical representation of civic religions as loci of daemonic activity, which had been subsequently sundered by a victorious Christ and his expanding Church. Christ, not Augustus—the Church, not Rome—are the pivotal players and determining forces in Eusebius' political theology.

7

The Church as Apologetic: Eusebius' Legitimation of Christianity

INTRODUCTION

We have seen that Eusebius' defence of Christianity is rooted in the construction and manipulation of ethnic boundaries, the framing of connections and divisions between nations, and the ascription of particular markers of ethnic difference in the portrayal of national character. If Christianity's others have all been identified in ethnic terms and his apologetic rests fundamentally upon representing these ethnic others, then it becomes imperative to make a sustained enquiry into Eusebius' construction of Christian identity from this angle. Often, the assumption that Christianity is a universalizing religion, transcending (or attempting to transcend) all ethnic differences, colours the vision of modern readings of early Christian texts. Christianity is seen as superseding ethnic and national barriers by turning believers away from the ephemeral identities of bodily life towards a primarily spiritual identity.[1] Contemporary study of early Christianity suffers, however, when it employs a framework that may have more in common with modern ways of defining Christianity. But early Christian identity may have been more complex than we would like to admit. Emphasizing the 'universalism' that we find in (or bring to) early Christian texts is hardly

---

[1] See, for example, E. Peterson, *Das Buch von den Engeln. Stellung und Bedeutung der heiligen Engeln im Kultus* (Munich: Kösel-Verlag, 1955), 11–12; H. C. Kee, 'From Jesus Movement toward Institutional Church', in R. Hefner (ed.), *Conversion to Christianity: Historical and Anthropological Perspectives on a Great Transformation* (Berkeley and Los Angeles: University of California Press, 1993), 47–64; idem, *Who Are the People of God? Early Christian Models of Community* (New Haven and London: Yale University Press, 1995); even Martin's 'universal *ethnos*' perpetuates this (*Inventing Superstition*, 213–14).

adequate for the complex ways that early believers constructed their own identities and imagined their world.

Part of the reason that 'ethnic argumentation' as a means of writing apologetics seems so strange to modern sensibilities is that it rests upon an understanding of Christian identity that is (at least partly) incommensurate with some of our dominant paradigms of charting religious identity today.[2] 'Religion' and 'ethnicity' are often seen as easily separable categories, an assumption that can lead us to misconstrue ancient perceptions of such things, where 'religious practices were a defining feature of an *ethnos*'.[3] Caution has been advised: 'We should not be too insistent on separating "religion" from "ethnicity" in antiquity, when the ancients had a much more organic conception of these matters than do we'.[4] The present chapter seeks to analyse Eusebius' construction of Christian identity within the scope of his ethnic argumentation and further explore the world of nations onto which he mapped Christianity. First, I want to focus on the recurrent theme of Christianity as constituting a people drawn from all nations, epitomized in the label 'the Church from the nations'. A discussion of the ethnographical sections of the *Praeparatio* (so far, mentioned only in passing) will emphasize Eusebius' method of legitimizing Christianity as the disruption of the ethnic identities of its converts. His conception of Christian *philanthrōpia* will be shown as persistently implicated in the Greekness he eschews, as he defines Christian conversion as rejection of

---

[2] I refer here to notions of 'religion' as a system of beliefs, often with emphasis upon the individual as a free religious agent interacting or experiencing the divine. Paul Tillich, *Theology of Culture* (Oxford: Oxford University Press, 1983), provides a classic example, considering religion as one's 'ultimate concern'. The definition of E. Durkheim, *The Elementary Forms of Religious Life* (New York: Free Press, 1965), 62, remains limited as well ('A religion is a unified system of beliefs and practices relative to sacred things'). For a survey of modern definitions of religion, see Brian C. Wilson, 'From the Lexical to the Polythetic: A Brief History of the Definition of Religion', in T. Idinopolus and B. Wilson (eds), *What Is Religion?* (Leiden: Brill, 1998), 141–62. For a critique of the modernist category of religion, see C. Winquist, 'Thinking Religion', in Idinopolus and Wilson (eds), *What Is Religion?*, 163–71.

[3] See the excellent criticisms offered by Olster, 'Classical Ethnography and Early Christianity', 9–31, who castigates continued influence of Harnack's assumptions on Christianity as a *sui generis* religion in conflict with the pagan and Jewish religions. More recently, see Kimber Buell, 'Rethinking the Relevance of Race for Early Christian Self-Definition', 451–3, 456–8; eadem, *Why This New Race*. The quotation here is from Rives, 'Human Sacrifice among Pagans and Christians', 85. For the classical conceptualizations of religion, see Sourvinou-Inwood, 'What is *Polis* Religion?', 13–37; eadem, 'Further Aspects of *Polis* Religion', in 38–55.

[4] S. Cohen, *The Beginnings of Jewishness*, 138.

various barbarian practices. This first section will attend to Eusebius'
representation of Christian identity by means of his portrayal of who
Christians were before their conversion to Christianity: they were 'out of
all nations', but especially out of the Greek nation. The negative side of
Christian identity, that is, who Christians are not (any longer), will be
the focus. The second section of the present chapter will turn specifically
to his more positive conception of Christian identity, one that seeks
to connect Christians with ancient Hebrews. Passages from the
Demonstratio will illuminate this conceptualization of Christian identity
since Eusebius does not offer a sustained discussion of this topic in the
Praeparatio, a work devoted more to narrating the national descent of
others than explaining the existence of a 'new people'.

   Christian identity in the *Praeparatio* involves the transgression of
national boundaries and the rupturing of ethnic identities, in creating
a new people who exhibit the restoration of the ancient Hebrews.
Christianity's 'universalism' will be shown to mask particularity and to
come at the cost of reinscribing traditional Greek representations of
barbarian others.[5] Far from overlooking or superseding national barriers, Eusebius' legitimation of Christianity stands upon a consistent
delegitimation and rejection of the national other.

THE CHURCH FROM THE NATIONS

A salient feature of Eusebius' construction of Christian identity within
the overall project of ethnic argumentation (both in the *Praeparatio* and
Demonstratio) revolves around the appellation 'Church from the
nations'. I want to examine this conceptualization in the programmatic
prologue to the *Praeparatio* at 1.2–5. The discussion will cover the
importance of recent historical events (as depicted by Eusebius) for his
apologetic method, his use of traditional ethnographic assumptions
in charting and legitimizing Christian conversion, and his manipulation

---

   [5] So G. Stroumsa, *Barbarian Philosophy: The Religious Revolution of Early Christianity*
(Tübingen: Mohr [Siebeck], 1999), 25: 'Ecumenical inclusiveness entails the illegitimiza-
tion of the other's existence, and hence generates tensions and violent intolerance.' In
another context, J. M. Lieu surmised that the label Christian, 'serves as a total and ultimate,
an exclusive act of definition and so of redefinition; it affirms a new, all-encompassing,
non-negotiable, and even non-communicable identity' ('Martyrdom and the Beginning of
"Christian" Identity', in *Neither Jew Nor Greek* [New York: T&T Clark, 2002], 215).

of the topos of *philanthrōpia* in his delineation of the spread of Christianity. Throughout, I will emphasize Eusebius' representation of who Christians were before their conversion as a strategy of legitimation deployed for his own apologetic ends.

In deeds rather than words

Eusebius' prologue addresses primarily the continued accusation that Christians were characteristically irrational and driven by blind faith. It might be objected, Eusebius surmises, that Christians exhibited the height of wickedness by choosing 'with unreasoning and unquestioning faith the doctrines of the impious enemies of all nations'.[6] Earlier, Eusebius had noted that,

Some have supposed that Christianity has no reason to support it, but that those who desire the name confirm their opinion by an unreasoning faith and an assent without examination; and they assert that no one is able by clear demonstration to furnish evidence of the truth of the things promised, but that they require their converts to adhere to faith only, and therefore they are called 'the faithful,' because of their uncritical and untested faith.[7]

Eusebius rejoins that 'they were false accusers who declared that we can establish nothing by demonstration, but hold to an unreasoning faith'.[8] It is easy to recognize the relationship between this anti-Christian

---

[6] *PE* 1.2.4. U. Willamowitz-Moellendorf, 'Ein Bruchstück aus der Schrift des Porphyrius gegen die Christen' *ZNW* 1 (1900), 101–05, followed by von Harnack, *Porphyrios, 'Gegen die Christen'*, argued that this passage was an unacknowledged quotation (or at least epitome) of Porphyry's lost *Contra Christianos*. This assumption has been left unquestioned by later scholars, even in the corrective to Harnack raised by T. D. Barnes, 'Porphyry *Against the Christians*: Date and the Attribution of Fragments', *JTS* 24 (1973), 424–42. For the possibility that it belongs to Porphyry's *Philosophy from Oracles*, see R. Wilken, 'Pagan Criticism of Christianity: Greek Religion and Christian Faith', in W. R. Schoedel and R. L. Wilken (eds) *Early Christian Literature and the Classical Intellectual Tradition*, in honorem R. M. Grant (Paris: Éditions Beauchesne, 1979), 117–34; and E. D. Digeser, 'Lactantius, Porphyry, and the Debate over Religious Toleration', *JRS* 88 (1998), 129–46.

[7] *PE* 1.1.11. One should note the difference in vocabulary used here to describe the accusers' characterizations of the Christian faith (*alogos pistis*) to that used in the *Contra Hieroclem* (*euchereia kai kouphotēs*; e.g. at 4 and 19). *Alogos pistis* does not occur in the *C. Hier.*; nor does *euchereia kai kouphotēs* occur in the *PE*. Such differences only highlight Eusebius' tendency to employ the language of his interlocutors (see e.g. *alogos pistis* at Porphyry, *Ad Marc.* 23); they need not negate Eusebius' authorship of the *C. Hier.* (so Hägg, 'Hierocles the Lover of Truth and Eusebius the Sophist', 138–50). The charge of irrational faith was not new; see Origen, *C. Cels.* 1.9, 27; 3.44, 50, 55, 59, 74–5; 6.12–14.

[8] *PE* 1.3.1.

objection and matters of identity. Eusebius would be at great pains throughout the *Praeparatio* to show the reasonableness of Christianity, that Christians were a rational people in contrast to the other irrational peoples. But what is interesting here, at 1.3–4, is the way in which Eusebius claims he will overcome this objection: he makes the bold claim that he will offer a new approach to defending the reasonableness of Christianity that his apologetic forebears had not made. Whereas those before Eusebius had 'diligently pursued many other modes of treatment, at one time by composing refutations and contradictions of the arguments opposed to us, at another time by interpreting the inspired and sacred Scriptures by exegetical commentaries, and homilies on particular points, or again by advocating our doctrines in a more controversial manner',[9] he declared that he would work out the subject in his own particular way (*idiōs*).[10]

While scholars disagree as to what this brief claim for novelty could mean,[11] it may be best to take the lines immediately following it as providing the basis for understanding Eusebius' intention.[12] These consist of quotations from Paul that distinguish, in various ways, words from deeds and favour the latter as more representative of God's power.[13] For instance, the quotation from I Corinthians 2: 4

---

[9] *PE* 1.3.4.

[10] *PE* 1.3.5. For similar claims to novelty, see *HE* 1.1.3; *Chron.* 2.praef.

[11] According to Laurin, *Orientations maitresses des apologistes chrétiens* 355, Eusebius' innovation is to give more attention to the criticism of unreasoning faith. Sirinelli and Des Places, *Eusèbe de Césarée*, 234–5, suppose the newness to lie in his combination of the various genres (refutations of particular adversaries, exegetical commentaries, and polemical works of apologetics) of his predecessors within a single work. L. Perrone, 'Eusebius of Caesarea as a Christian Writer', 527, and Kofsky, *Eusebius of Caesarea against the Pagans*, 243–4 (in spite of his earlier denial, 79), argue that his novelty lies in his extensive citation of outside sources.

[12] See W. J. Ferrar, *The Proof of the Gospel* (Grand Rapids: Baker Book House, 1981), xv–xvi; Lyman, *Christology and Cosmology: Models of Divine Activity in Origen, Eusebius and Athanasius*, 86–8; Johnson, 'Eusebius' *Praeparatio Evangelica* as Literary Experiment'.

[13] On the distinction between words and deeds in early Christian discourse, see R. Lim, ' "By Word or by Deed?": Two Modes of Religious Persuasion in Late Antiquity', in M. Dillon (ed.), *Religion in the Ancient World* (Amsterdam: Hakkert, 1996), 257–69. The *locus classicus* of such a distinction is Thucydides 1.20–22, on which see F. M. Cornford, *Thucydides Mythistoricus* (Philadelphia: University of Pennsylvania Press, 1971), 52–3. On the opposition in Plutarch, see A. E. Wardman, 'Plutarch and Alexander', *CQ* 5 (1955), 96–107. Themistius refers to the need for *logos* not to be separated from deeds and 'proofs from deeds' at *Or.* 17.214a (on which see L. J. Daly, 'The Mandarin and the Barbarian: The Response of Themistius to the Gothic Challenge', *Historia* 21 (1972), 352–4). The word-deed opposition is thus a commonplace, though a powerful one.

reads: 'Our speech and our preaching were not in persuasive words of wisdom, but in the demonstration of the Spirit and power.'[14] Other Christian apologists had responded to opposition with defensces in the form of commentaries (*hupomnēmata*) or 'philological demonstrations' (*grammikais apodeixesi*),[15] but in light of the assertions quoted from Paul,[16] 'all words are superfluous, when the works are more manifest and plain than words—works which the divine and heavenly power of our Saviour distinctly exhibits even now, while preaching good tidings of the divine and heavenly life to all men'.[17] This emphasis upon facts or actions, and not upon words, is, I would argue, at the heart of Eusebius' new approach. If this is the case, the self-proclaimed particularity of Eusebius' apologetic rests not in his extensive citation—in fact, just the opposite. Despite the massive bulk of words used in the *Praeparatio*, Eusebius' self-declared novel approach to defending Christianity lies in an emphasis upon deeds, upon actual historical fact, upon real occurrences in the multi-national world that he portrays.[18]

These historical events, which display for Eusebius the activity of God in the world, centre upon the rise of Christianity within a distinctively ethnic milieu. The facts that make words so superfluous are the spread of Christianity among the nations, or as Eusebius later identifies it, the 'calling of the nations' (*tēn tōn ethnōn klēsin*).[19] Christ had prophesied that his teachings would spread throughout the whole world as a 'witness to all nations' (*eis marturion pasi tois ethnesin*), and he declared:

that the Church, which was afterwards gathered by his own power out of all nations, though not yet seen nor established in the times when he was living as man among men, should be invincible and undismayed, and should never be conquered by death, but stand and abide unshaken, settled and rooted upon his own power as upon a rock that cannot be shaken or broken.[20]

[14] *PE* 1.3.5.
[15] *PE* 1.3.6.
[16] *Pace* Sirinelli and Des Places, *Eusèbe de Césarée*, 235, who claim that 'Saint Paul's citation, drawn from the *First Epistle to the Corinthians*, is not very well adapted to the subject'.
[17] *PE* 1.3.7.
[18] In fact, Eusebius' approach in this regard was not novel at all. Origen had already asserted the priority of deeds over words in his own apologetic; see *C. Cels.* 1.26, 47, 67; 2.42, 79; 3.33, 68; 5.62; 7.17, 19, 26; 8.43. Eusebius would maintain the theme in his later writings; see e.g., *SC* 16.8; 17.15.
[19] *PE* 1.3.14.
[20] *PE* 1.4.8; for the notion of the Church from the nations, see Rom. 16: 4. Compare with *DE* 3.7 (138a–141b).

These historical facts—the victory of the Church and its spread throughout all the nations—were superior to any defence of Christianity based
upon words or ideas: 'the facts so manifestly all but cry out'.[21] The spread
of Christianity could only be possible with the power of God and words
were insufficient and paled in significance beside the radical changes
wrought by God's hand among the inhabitants of the nations.[22]

A little later, Eusebius heralds the endurance of even women and
children in persecution to the point of martyrdom as a proof of
the power of God, 'that shows by deeds rather than by words that the
doctrine of the immortality of the soul is true'.[23] Hence, the opposition
between words and deeds is maintained in the individual actions of
Christians and in their manner of life, as well as in the broader sweep of
Christianity throughout the nations. This marks an important caveat:
Eusebius should not be taken here as claiming that the nations of the
world have been 'Christianized' in their entirety. His emphasis is rather
upon the conversion of members of the nations who have rejected the
ancestral customs and way of life of those nations. Had he wanted to
make the claim that whole nations had converted to Christianity, he
might have recalled such evidence as he had included in the *HE* on the
conversion of Abgar, the king of Edessa.[24] In the *Praeparatio*, it is
enough—in fact it is his main point—to show the fulfilment of Christ's
words that Christianity would 'in no way be vanquished or subjected by
his enemies, no, [it would] yield not even to the gates of death, because
of that one speech uttered by himself, saying: "Upon this rock I will
build my Church, and the gates of Hades shall not prevail against it." '[25]

This is all part of the cluster of ideas surrounding Eusebius' attack on
Greek political theology and his conception of Rome and Augustus
discussed in earlier chapters. The daemons were conquered as a
result of Christ's salvific word in the times of Augustus (or Hadrian).
Polytheism was routed as former devotees, who had maintained the cult
of daemons among the *poleis* of the nations of the world, converted to

[21] *PE* 1.3.9; cp. *PE* 3.3.15; *DE* 3.2 (95b); *SC* 18.15; the phrase seems to be a topos
originating with Demosthenes, *Olynth.* 1.2 (see Carriker, *The Library of Eusebius*, 138);
cp. Cicero, *Cael.* 20.47.

[22] See Lyman, *Christology and Cosmology*, 104–06.

[23] *PE* 1.4.14. Similarly, see *PE* 6.6.71; Athenagoras, *Leg.* 11.

[24] *HE* 1.13; 2.1.6–7. For discussion of this episode in the *HE*, see S. Brock, 'Eusebius and
Syriac Christianity', in Attridge and Hata (eds), *Eusebius, Christianity and Judaism*, 212–34.

[25] *PE* 1.3.11, citing Matt. 16: 18; the metaphor may derive from non-Christian literature, see Homer, *Il.* 9.312 (with Lucian, *Fug.* 30; Philostrratus, *VS* 542); see also, Eusebius,
CI 2.28 (Ziegler 293); *Comm. Ps.* 90.1, 2 (*PG* 23.1145B).

Christianity with eyes opened to the radiance flowing from Christ's true teachings. These converts rejected the customs of their forefathers and the ancestral way of life of the nations and became members of a people drawn from all nations. Their new identity was integrally centred upon this fact—the rejection of their previous national ways of life. By calling Christianity the 'Church out of the nations' Eusebius was not primarily concerned to highlight that Christians were, as might be termed today, a 'multicultural' group of people (though he sometimes makes this point when he uses such phrases as, 'both Greeks and barbarians').[26] Instead, the emphasis in such an epithet is that new members of the Church have rejected their previous allegiances and identities as members of particular nations and adopted a new identity that runs counter to everything that was considered customary and characteristic of those nations.

Ethnographies of Conversion

I want to return now to an interesting feature of Eusebius' portrayal of Christianity as a 'Church from the nations'. As part of his proof that Christianity has spread through all the nations of the world and as evidence that conversion to Christianity has resulted from the over-powering of daemonic powers, Eusebius includes brief ethnographical sketches describing the life of members of various nations and their change upon conversion. My analysis of these 'ethnographies of conversion' (as I call them) will attempt to show how Eusebius inherits traditional Greek ethnographic categories and manipulates them for his apologetic aims of legitimating Christianity.

After the time of Christ, Christianity had, for Eusebius, shown a remarkable rapidity in its spread throughout the nations. The teaching of Christ had 'run through' all nations: 'The fame of his gospel has filled the whole world on which the sun looks down; and the proclamations concerning him ran through all nations, and are now still increasing and advancing . . .'.[27] Members of all nations had turned away from their paternal customs and ancestral superstition to follow the teaching of Christ. Their conversion to Christianity affected their identity as members of particular *ethnē*. The peoples from any given nation

---

[26] e.g., *PE* 1.1.6; 1.2.3; 1.4.11; 1.4.14; 6.6.71; 12.32.7; 14.3.4.
[27] *PE* 1.3.10. See also 1.3.13.

possessed a character representative of that nation. This character was depicted by Eusebius in starkly negative tones, as superstition, impiety, irrationality. Upon turning to Christianity, members of these nations gave up their ancestral character and adopted the ways of Christ, characterized by piety, rationality, and truth. Becoming more specific in 1.4, Eusebius narrows in on certain barbarian nations to show the effects of conversion upon their peculiar national character.

> Only from his utterances, and from his teaching diffused throughout the whole world, the customs of all nations (*ethnōn*) are now set aright, even those customs which before were savage and barbarous; so that Persians who have become his disciples no longer marry their mothers (*mētrogamein*),[28] nor Scythians feed on human flesh (*anthrōpoborein*),[29] because of Christ's word which has come even unto them, nor other races (*genē*) of barbarians have incestuous union with daughters and sisters, nor do men madly lust after men and pursue unnatural pleasures,[30] nor do those, whose practice it formerly was, now expose their dead kindred to dogs and birds, nor strangle the aged, as they did formerly, nor according to their ancient custom do they feast on the flesh (*anthrōpothutein*)[31]

[28] This is the earliest occurrence of this verb, which otherwise remains in Christian literature after Eusebius (Gregory of Nyssa, *C. Fatum*, PG 45.169B; Ps.-Clement, *Rec.* 9.20, 25). It should be kept in mind that Diocletian had recently issued an edict (AD 295) prohibiting incest, possibly aimed at inhabitants of newly acquired lands in Mesopotamia (*Collatio* 6.4; *CJ* 5.4.17). For discussion, see H. Chadwick, 'The Relativity of Moral Codes: Rome and Persia in Late Antiquity', in Schoedel and Wilken (eds), *Early Christian Literature and the Classical Intellectual Tradition*, esp. 145–53. On similar edicts issued in a later century, see A. D. Lee, 'Close-Kin Marriage in Late Antique Mesopotamia', *GRBS* 29 (1988), 403–14.

[29] The attribution of cannibalism to the Scythians appears as early as Herodotus (see 4.62–65). The verb *anthrōpoborein* seems to occur outside of Christian literature only in Philo of Alexandria (*Praem. et Poen.* 90 and 92, *V. Contemp.* 9, and *Provid.* fr. 2.65 [cited at *PE* 8.14] where it is applied in each case to animals such as crocodiles and hippopotami). The attestations at Zeno, *SVF* 1.fr. 254.3 and Chrysippus, *SVF* 3.frs. 746.5 and 750.3 should not be taken as direct quotations of either author's exact words. Significantly, these 'fragments' are contained in the works of Christian apologists (the first and last are both from Theophilus, *Autol.* 3.5; the middle fragment is from Epiphanius, *Panarion* 3.39). It may be of some interest to note that the term occurs in Eusebius' corpus almost double the amount of total occurrences elsewhere (*PE* 7.16.3 ['the devil as a lion eats humans']; *HE* 1.2.19; 8.7.1; 8.7.2; *DE* 1.6.55 [21a]; 4.10.2 [161b]; 5.praef.11 [204d]; 5.praef.14 [205b]; *CI* 2.14 [Ziegler 244.8]; *LC* 16.9 [Heikel 251.32]). For Roman attribution of such behaviour to barbarians, see B. Powell, 'What Juvenal Saw: Egyptian Religion and Anthropophagy in *Satire* 15', *RM* 122 (1979), 185–9.

[30] The terminology here is probably an allusion to Romans 1.26–27. A broad characterization of 'the ancient nations' that contains reference to similar behaviour occurs at 7.2.6.

[31] The only other use of this verb in Greek literature that I can find is at Strabo 11.4.7, on the Albanians.

of their dearest friends when dead, nor like the ancients offer human sacrifices to the daemons as to gods, nor slaughter their dearest friends and think it piety.[32]

Eusebius then moves into an unacknowledged quotation from Porphyry's *De Abstinentia* 4.21, which verifies his more generic statements regarding funerary practices at the end of the above citation. The Massagetae[33] and Derbices sacrificed and killed their elderly relatives. The Tibareni cast their relatives from a precipice; the Hyrcanians and Bactrians exposed their relatives to dogs and birds while still alive, the Caspians, when they were dead; the Scythians buried them alive and sacrificed their spouses on funeral pyres.[34] Eusebius has the Scythians practising cannibalism, while Porphyry has them practising live burials and human sacrifices.[35]

The accuracy of these ethnographic reports is, of course, not at issue.[36] Descriptions of cannibalism (or other strange eating habits), incest (or other 'unnatural' sexual practices), and horrifying customs regarding death and dying were common in ancient accounts of unknown or marginalized peoples.[37] Strabo's account of the inhabitants of Ireland is a striking example of this. 'The inhabitants are more savage than the Britons, since they are man-eaters as well as grass-eaters, and since, further, they count it an honorable thing, when their fathers die, to devour them, and publicly to have intercourse, not only with the other women, but also with their mothers and sisters.... As for the matter of man-eating, that is said to be a custom of the Scythians also...'.[38] Such immoral and grotesque practices as drinking blood,

---

[32] *PE* 1.4.6; the passage is adapted later at *SC* 16.9; *Theoph.* 3.7; 5.17.

[33] See Herodotus 1.216. For similar ascription to the Indians of eating the elderly, see Herodotus 3.38.

[34] *PE* 1.4.7. For a similar ascription of inhuman practices towards the elderly, see Diodorus 3.33.2–6.

[35] See also the similar ethnographic descriptions by other authors quoted by Eusebius: Bardesanes, *Liber legum regionum* (6.10; the work is also transmitted in Rufinus' Latin translation of Ps.-Clement, *Recognitio* 9.19–29); Porphyry, *De Abst.* (4.16.1–10); Clement, *Strom.* (10.6.1–14).

[36] On the historical reality of Persian incest (though for a later period), see Lee, 'Close-Kin Marriage in Late Antique Mesopotomia', 403–14.

[37] See T. E. J. Wiedemann, 'Between Men and Beasts: Barbarians in Ammianus Marcellinus', in I. S. Moxon, J. D. Smart and A. J. Woodman (eds), *Past Perspectives: Studies in Greek and Roman Historical Writing* (Cambridge: Cambridge University Press, 1986), 189–201.

[38] *PE* 4.5.4. The translation is adapted from that of H. L. Jones in the LCL edition; I have taken the variant ποηφάγοι for πολυφάγοι, following Wiedemann, 'Between Men and Beasts', 190.

sacrifice of infants, or nocturnal orgies could also be imputed to members of 'fringe' (especially religious) groups in order to legitimize exclusion or oppression.[39]

Significantly, incest and cannibalism had been prominent accusations cast against the Christians, causing no little concern among earlier apologists.[40] Eusebius implicitly counters these accusations and, in fact, reverses the charges by claiming that Christianity produces the opposite effect, the cessation of cannibalism and incest. Although Eusebius never mentions these anti-Christian slanders,[41] this passage is surely an attempt to put such practices back where they belong, among barbarian peoples.[42] Thus, he deftly exonerates Christians from such moral depravity. At the same time, he nonetheless perpetuates and reinscribes the negative representations of the barbarian 'other' that were prominent features of Greek ethnographical descriptions.

The persistence of the typically Greek bias against barbarians will receive further attention below; but it may be beneficial to pause briefly and consider the prominence of Greekness as a sort of default identity to which Eusebius often falls. The Greeks are the object of attack throughout most of the *Praeparatio*. But the Greeks are attacked not as an entirely 'other' nation, but as one from which the Christians, with whom Eusebius most identifies himself, have come. The Christian 'we' of the *Praeparatio* is most often represented as a collectivity of those who once were Greeks but have now left their Greek identity behind for a new Christian one. While there was occasion to refer to Christians as once having been Phoenicians or Egyptians,[43] the vast number of first person collective identifications in the *Praeparatio* is made with reference to

[39] See Sallust *Cat.* 22; Livy 39.8, 10; Diodorus 22.5.1; Epiphanius *Panarion* 26.4–5. For discussion, see Wiedemann, 'Between Men and Beasts'; Rives, 'Human Sacrifice among Pagans and Christians'.

[40] See Justin, *II Apol.* 12; Athenagoras, *Leg.* 3.1; 31.1; Minucius Felix, *Oct.* 9.5–6; Origen, *C. Cels.* 6.40; Cyril of Jerusalem, *Cat.* 16.8; Salvian, *Gub. Dei* 4.17. For discussion, see A. Henrichs, 'Pagan Ritual and the Alleged Crime of the Early Christians: A Reconsideration', in P. Granfield and J. Jungmann (eds), *Kyriakon*, Festschrift Johannes Quasten (Münster: Verlag Aschendorff, 1970), 1. 18–35; S. Benko, 'Pagan Criticism of Christianity during the First Two Centuries A. D.', *ANRW* (1980), 23.2.1055–1118; R. Wilken, *The Christians as the Romans Saw Them* (New Haven: Yale University Press, 1984), 17–21; Rives, 'Human Sacrifice among Pagans and Christians'.

[41] These slanders are mentioned explicitly at *HE* 4.7.10–11; 5.1.14.

[42] This is a variant of what has been called the 'retorsion argument' (from *retorqueo*); see Rives, 'Human Sacrifice among Pagans and Christians', 74–7.

[43] See *PE* 1.10.54 (within a paragraph that is repeated verbatim at 2.praef.1–2); 2.praef.4; 2.1.51.

Greeks. Furthermore, these identifications with Greeks are more pronounced and more evocative of an ethnic context than those referring to other *ethnē*. A significant example of this occurs at 1.5. One of our opponents, Eusebius considers, might question us, 'Since, being Greeks by birth (*genos*) and having the mind of the Greeks, being gathered out of many kinds of nations (*ethnōn*), like chosen men in a newly enlisted army, we have become deserters of our paternal superstition.'[44] This statement contains the ethnic features of biological kinship (*genos*), mental character (or 'culture'), and a shared ancestral ('paternal') religious element.

Elsewhere, he would state that, 'we, being Greeks (*hēmin... Hellēsin ousin*)' have borrowed the ways of Moses.[45] This statement raises an interesting point that Eusebius made in his narrative of Greek theft of arts and wisdom from barbarian nations. His aim, he wrote, was to demonstrate 'that the wise men of the Greeks have been zealous imitators of Hebrew doctrines, so that our calumniators can no longer reasonably find fault with us, if we ourselves, admiring the like doctrines with their philosophers, have determined to hold the Hebrew oracles in honour'.[46] These declarations clearly indicate the image of Christian identity that Eusebius is attempting to convey. They had once been Greeks, just like the ancient philosophers, and had gone in search of the source of the true wisdom, located among the barbarians (in particular, the Hebrews). The reason that Christians could not maintain their Greekness, even after Greek philosophers had long ago found barbarian wisdom, was because the Greeks had imperfectly transmitted it and then had quickly fallen into discord. Hence, the dominant paradigm of pre-Christian identity with which Eusebius identifies himself and those Christians whom he represents is that of the Greeks and follows the example of the early Greek philosophers.

To return to the Scythians and Persians of the ethnographic reports discussed above, one could say that Eusebius' maintenance of the alterity of the barbarians was the residue of a personal history steeped in Greek identity. Eusebius portrays Christians, including himself, as those who have come from the tradition and identity of Greekness. In spite of this residual, or latent, Greekness in his outlook on barbarians, Eusebius considers himself no longer a Greek. The driving force of his apologetic methodology, of ethnic argumentation, is that Christians are no longer

---

[44] *PE* 1.5.10; see also, 1.5.11, 13.   [45] *PE* 13.praef.1.
[46] *PE* 10.14.19; see also 10.8.17.

to be identified with any of the other nations, not even the Greeks. They are a 'Church from the nations', a new *ethnos*—or rather, the restored Hebrew *ethnos*—and embody in the corporate identity a new way of life (*politeia*).[47] Although Eusebius and the Christians he represents were once Greeks, conversion to Christianity has marked a rupture of ethnic identity. They are now a new people.

We see, therefore, in Eusebius' ethnographic remarks the attempt to discard the Christians' former identity as Greeks while nonetheless preserving one of the most standard features of such an identity, the Greek–barbarian polarity. Indeed, this polarity is intimately tied to his argument that Christianity is true and supported by a divine power since the actions and events of history (not merely words) have shown the remarkable success of Christianity as prevailing throughout the nations. The rejection of the barbaric practices of cannibalism, incest, and killing of the elderly by members of the stereotypically barbarian nations produced a proof in deeds, not words, for Christianity's validity. As Eusebius concluded: 'These were the customs of a former age, and are now no longer practised in the same manner, the salutary law of the power of the Gospel having alone abolished the savage and inhuman plague of all these evils.'[48]

Philanthrōpia and the Spread of Christianity

The term Eusebius uses for 'inhuman' (*apanthrōpon*) in this statement raises an interesting issue. Often in the *Praeparatio*, the work of daemons through the *polis* cult centres is described as *apanthrōpon*,[49] especially in the case of their desire for human sacrifices. For instance, when showing that only daemonic powers could be the agents active in oracular cults, Eusebius claims that daemons have driven their devotees 'beyond the limits of nature' to sacrifice their dearest friends.[50]

Sometimes a father sacrificed his only son to the daemon, and a mother her beloved daughter, and the dearest friends would slay their relatives as readily as any irrational and strange animal, and to the so-called gods in every city and country they used to offer their friends and fellow citizens, having sharpened their philanthropic (*philanthrōpon*) and sympathetic nature into a merciless

---

[47] See below.   [48] *PE* 1.4.8.
[49] Or *misanthrōpon*: see e.g., *PE* 5.1.8.   [50] *PE* 4.15.7.

and inhuman (*apanthrōpon*) cruelty, and exhibiting a frantic and truly daemonic disposition.[51]

The language used here is reminiscent of Eusebius' ethnographic description at 1.4.7. The 'dearest relatives' (*hoi philtatoi*) are sacrificed (*katasphattein*) to daemons as to gods, in a 'beastly' (*thēriōdēs*)[52] and barbaric manner. The sentiment is essentially one of *philanthrōpia* being replaced by *apanthrōpia*.[53]

The ethnographical report at 1.4 is at pains, therefore, to show a reversal of this trend. As a direct result of the coming of Christ, the decline into *apanthrōpia* wrought by daemons among the nations is put to an end; *philanthrōpia* is restored.[54] Eusebius declares:

Since all are not of such [learning], and since the Word is philanthropic and turns nobody at all away but heals every man by remedies suitable for him and invites the unlearned and simple to the amendment of their ways, naturally in the introductory teaching of those who are beginning with the simpler elements, women and children and the common herd, we lead them on gently to the religious life, and adopt the sound faith to serve as a remedy, and instil into them right opinions of God's providence, and the immortality of the soul, and the life of virtue.[55]

Philanthrōpia is here exhibited in the inclusion of, and concern for, marginal groups such as women, children, and the uneducated. Along with the ethnographic declarations, it is an articulation of the general thrust of Eusebius' argument in *Praeparatio* 1.1–5 and his portrayal of Christian identity. For Eusebius, Christianity severs social barriers based upon gender, age, education, and former ethnicity.

Such philanthropic claims of inclusion recur throughout the *Praeparatio*. At 1.1.6, Eusebius declares that friendship with God is preached to all: 'Greeks along with barbarians, men as well as women and children, poor and wealthy, wise and uneducated, not even despising the class

---

[51] *PE* 4.15.8.

[52] On other representations of animal-like behaviour among humans, see B. Shaw, ' "Eaters of Flesh—Drinkers of Milk". The Ancient Mediterranean Ideology of the Pastoral Nomad', *Ancient Society* 13–14 (1982/83), 5–31; Wiedemann, 'Between Men and Beasts', 196–201.

[53] The contrast between the two terms occurs on numerous other occasions in the *PE*: e.g. 2.4.2; 5.18.3; 13.21.13.

[54] It should be noted that, in contrast to the general decline into *apanthrōpia*, Moses' legislation was termed 'noble and philanthropic' (*semna kai philanthrōpa*) at *PE* 13.21.13.

[55] *PE* 1.5.3.

(*genos*) of slaves from the calling.'[56] Later, Eusebius remarks that whole myriads of disciples have accepted Christ's teaching: 'men, women and children, slaves and free persons, humble and distinguished, barbarians along with Greeks as well, in every place and city and region, in all the nations under the sun'.[57] Again, 'Our Word, then, reasonably receives every race[58]—not only of men, but of women also, not only of free persons and slaves, but of barbarians and Greeks—towards godly education (*paideia*) and philosophy.'[59] The boundaries of the ancient world are ignored by Christians as they learned 'to honour each person as of the same race (*homogenē*) and to recognize as a dearest friend and brother the one who was considered a stranger, as if by a law of nature'.[60]

These claims to inclusion are part of a broader tradition. *Philanthrō-pia* was an important feature of encomia of cities or peoples in Roman imperial times. According to D. Balch, *philanthrōpia* involved a twofold pattern when applied to cities: 'to receive unfortunate strangers or exiles who are fleeing calamities elsewhere and to "send out" settlers who colonize, hellenize, spread one's way of life'.[61] The notion of

---

[56] *PE* 1.1.6; cp. Clement, *Strom.* 4.8.58.

[57] *PE* 1.4.11. See also 1.4.14; 5.1.7–8; for discussion of such phrases within the scope of Roman identity, see Sherwin-White, *The Roman Citizenship*, 437–44.

[58] Gifford, *ad loc.*, wrongly translates this as 'the entire race' as if it refers to the human race; in fact, it cannot be translated this way, and must refer to 'the race of men', 'the race of women', and so on.

[59] *PE* 12.32.7.

[60] *PE* 1.4.11.

[61] Balch, 'Two Apologetic Encomia. Dionysius on Rome and Josephus on the Jews', *Journal for the Study of Judaism* 13 (1982), 111. See Josephus, *Ap.* 2.282, 284: 'there is not one city of the Greeks nor any barbarian one, nor a single nation where [our laws] have not proceeded … Just as God walks throughout the whole universe, so our law proceeds throughout all mankind'; or also, Aristides, *Or.* 1.324: 'zeal for your [the Athenians'] wisdom and way of life has gone out to every land by a certain divine fortune'; and *Or.* 1.325,326: 'Every nation both in the cities and the country-districts' have adopted the Greek language, having 'left behind their paternal languages'. Further examples of *philanthrōpia* within national encomia are noted by Balch at 111, 118–19; cp. Diodorus, 3.8.2. On Aristides' *Panathenaic Oration*, see J. Oliver, 'The Civilizing Power', *Transactions of the American Philosophical Society* 58 (1968), 1–223, esp. 13–14. For the concept in the forth century, see A. D. Nock, 'The Praises of Antioch', *JEA* 40 (1954), 76–82; G. Downey, 'Philanthropia in Religion and Statecraft in the Fourth Century after Christ', *Historia* 4 (1955), 199–208; L. J. Daly, 'Themistius' Plea for Religious Toleration', *GRBS* 12 (1971), 65–79; ibid., 'The Mandarin and the Barbarian: The Response of Themistius to the Gothic Challenge', *Historia* 21 (1972), 351–79; ibid., 'Themistius' Concept of *Philanthropia*', *Byzantion* 45 (1975), 22–40; C. Ando, 'Pagan Apologetics and Christian Intolerance in the Ages of Themistius and Augustine', *JECS* 4 (1996), 171–207; P. Heather and D. Moncur, *Politics, Philosophy, and Empire in the Fourth Century. Select Orations of Themistius* (Liverpool: Liverpool University Press, 2001), 66–7. This characteristic also occurs at Diodorus 3.8.2.

inclusivity, which is central to *philanthrōpia,* is thus supplemented with that of active dispersion of a communal way of life that is seen as beneficent and morally superior. Acceptance of otherwise marginalized individuals (women, slaves, barbarians) by the community is combined with dynamic outreach to those individuals. Both of these facets of *philanthrōpia* are manifest in Eusebius' description of Christianity.

Eusebius' language both of openness to all nations and of the spread of Christianity to all nations can be seen to echo these earlier sentiments. The representation of Christianity as spreading through all nations and producing the good effects of virtuous living and true philosophy can thus be seen as part of a tradition of 'apologetic encomia' of cities and *ethnē,* or rather in the case of the *Praeparatio,* 'encomiastic apology'. This conclusion further accentuates the need for taking seriously the construction of Christian identity within a distinctly ethnic context. Eusebius' defence of Christianity rests upon such identity construction. On the one hand, the other nations are represented in ways that invalidate them by their very representation; on the other, Christianity receives legitimation by its very representation, in so far as the representation is granted by the reader. The virtue of *philanthrōpia* is embodied in the Logos which runs throughout all nations, neglecting no one—men and women, barbarians and Greeks, slaves, and free persons—crossing national boundaries—Greek, Persian, Scythian—and creating a new people who are a 'Church from the nations'. Thus, since Christianity is constructed as bearing such a historically momentous role, its position is legitimated in historical actions, not words. *Philanthrōpia,* as the transgression of ethnic (and other) boundaries, lies at the heart of Eusebius' conception of a defensible Christian identity.

Philanthrōpia and the Limits of Openness

Eusebius' ethnic argumentation is supported by his conception of Christianity as a transnational identity with a central aim of including people from all social categories among its ranks. Along with its roots in ancient Hebrew past, this *philanthrōpia* of Christianity is a key element in his defence of the faith. Not only did Eusebius admit to the openness of the Church to all nations and to all levels of society, he made it an integral feature of Christian identity and made it a recurrent theme of the *Praeparatio*.[62]

Philanthrōpia must not, however, be mistaken for universalism or inclusivism in the modern senses of those words. Something similar to modern religious universalism might seem to lie in the remarks of Porphyry regarding an oracle delivered by Apollo and recorded in his *Philosophia ex Oraculis*.[63] But even here, Porphyry's assertion that other religious approaches are allowable (even laudable), certainly does not imply modern values of tolerance and pluralism. The oracle reads:

> Steep is the road and rough that leads to heaven,
> Entered at first through portals bound with brass.
> Within are found innumerable paths,
> Which for the endless good of all mankind
> They first revealed, who Nile's sweet waters drink.
> From them the heavenward paths Phoenicians learned,
> Assyrians, Lydians and the Hebrew race.[64]

Eusebius then provides Porphyry's own comments on the oracle. 'For the road to the gods is bound with brass, and both steep and rough;[65] the barbarians discovered many paths thereof, but the Greeks went astray, and those who already held it even perverted it. The discovery was ascribed by the god to the Egyptians, Phoenicians, Chaldaeans (for these were Assyrians), Lydians and Hebrews.'[66] One recalls the words later to be written by Symmachus: 'It is not possible to arrive at so great a secret by a single path.'[67]

---

[62] D. Mendels, *The Media Revolution of Early Christianity: An Essay on Eusebius' Ecclesiastical History* (Grand Rapids: Eerdmans Publishing Co., 1999), 148–9.

[63] One might also consider Maximus of Tyre, *Dissert.* 2.10: 'Let them know the divine race, only let them know. If Pheidias' art rouses the Greeks towards memory of God, and the honour of animals rouses Egyptians, and a river some, and fire others, I do not denigrate their disharmony. Only let them know, only let them love, only let them remember [God].' For discussion, see A. H. Armstrong, 'The Way and the Ways: Religious Tolerance and Intolerance in the Fourth Century A. D.', *VC* 38 (1984), 10 (where he attributes the passage in question to *Dissert.* 8, end).

[64] *PE* 9.10.2.

[65] Cp. Porphyry, *Ad Marc.* 7.

[66] *PE* 9.10.3.

[67] *Non uno itinere perveniri potest ad tam grande secretum* (*Rel.* 3.10). Cp. Constantine's letter to Alexander and Arius *ap.* Eusebius, *VC* 2.69.3; see also Themistius, *Or.* 5.68d–69a; Augustine, *Ep.* 16. For general discussion of the tenor of pagan expressions of religious tolerance in a 'Christianized' world, see Armstrong, 'The Way and the Ways'; Drake, *Constantine and the Bishops*, 247–50; idem, 'Constantinian Echoes in Themistius', *SP* 34 (2001), 44–50; Ando, 'Pagan Apologetics and Christian Intolerance'.

These sentiments ought not to be conflated with tolerance of all religious positions or practices (indeed, the latter is seeking only tolerance of Symmachus' own minority religious position); nor should Eusebius' *philanthrōpia*. The acceptance of all races within the embrace of the 'Church from the nations' was contingent upon the converts' rejection of their ancestral ways. The ethnographical descriptions of Persian and Scythian conversions at 1.4.6 make a clear separation of 'before' and 'after'. Certain behaviours that were characteristic of being Scythian (e.g. cannibalism) or of being Persian (e.g. incest) were to be left behind as baggage from one's ethnic past as one took on a new ethnic identity. Eusebius stresses the language of change with 'before' (*prin*), 'previously' (*proteron*), 'according to ancient custom' (*kata to palaion ethos*), and 'as those long ago [did]' (*kata tous palaious*). This is contrasted with 'no longer' (*mēketi*), the repetition of 'nor [this] . . . nor [that]' (*mēde . . . mēde*), and 'no longer now' (*nun ouketh'*). The before/ after image of conversion is further produced by the language of rejection and renunciation of previous customs and identity: *apostantes*;[68] *apostraphentas*;[69] *pheugein*;[70] *apophugē*;[71] *anachōrēsis/anachōrein*;[72] *metathesthai*;[73] and *metalēpsis* (as 'substitution').[74]

The practices, customs, and theologies of the nations are considered 'beastly and barbaric' (*thēriōdē kai barbara*)[75] or 'beastly and inhuman' (*thēriōdē kai apanthrōpon*).[76] Later, Eusebius says, 'Not only Greeks but the most savage barbarians and those dwelling at the uttermost ends of the earth restrain their irrational beastliness (*thēriōdias*) and received the doctrines of philosophy.'[77] It is significant that the only two places in the *Praeparatio* where the terms *thēriōdē* and *thēriōdia* are joined with a form of *barbaros*[78] are both here in 1.4, in a discussion on the openness of Christianity to members of all nations.[79] This point cautions us from too readily applying notions of ethnic pluralism to what we might today want to regard as a 'multicultural' Christianity. Instead, the

---

[68] *PE* 1.2.2; 1.5.10.   [69] *PE* 1.2.3; 1.3.15.   [70] *PE* 1.10.54; 2.praef.1.
[71] *PE* 3.13.25.   [72] *PE* 2.praef.4; 2.1.51; 2.4.4.   [73] *PE* 1.2.4.
[74] *PE* 7.1.3.   [75] *PE* 1.4.6.   [76] *PE* 1.4.8.

[77] *PE* 1.4.13. On the use of the phrase 'edges of the earth' in classical literature, see J. S. Romm, *The Edges of the Earth in Ancient Thought* (Princeton: Princeton University Press, 1992), 38–41.

[78] The joining of beastliness with barbarianness is at least as early as Aristotle, *EN* 1145a30. For the joining of the two terms in the thought of Plutarch, see A. Nikolaidis-Rethymnon, 'Ἑλληνικός—βαρβαρικός: Plutarch on Greek and Barbarian Characteristics', *WS* 20 (1986), 241–2.

[79] Other occurrences of *thēriōdēs* and its cognates are: 2.4.3; 2.5.3–4; 3.5.2; 7.2.6.

philanthrōpia and openness of Christianity represented in the *Praeparatio* work simultaneously with notions of exclusivity and traditional ethnic biases.

What one scholar concluded in reference to Clement of Alexandria could be aptly applied to Eusebius: 'By presenting Christianity in a universalizing, aggregative manner, [he] masks the particularity of his version of Christianness.'[80] Eusebius constructs a vision of Christianity that is premised upon a rejection of ancestral ethnic customs by Christians. The openness is towards all who are willing to apostasize from their paternal way of life, as depicted by Eusebius. In other words, he represents a particular people whose membership is open to other particular peoples in so far as they reject the identity of their ancestral peoplehood and adopt a new identity by becoming part of a new people.

The theme of *philanthrōpia* as religious pluralism valued by many moderns is quite different, then, from the *philanthrōpia* of the gospel heralded by Eusebius. The particularizing openness of Christianity's *philanthrōpia* functions as a mechanism driving Eusebius' argument for the superiority of Christianity. Of course, the sort of rejection of ancestral barbarian customs, which inclusion in the Christian community entailed, would have appealed to a Greek audience. Since, even while including members of barbarian and savage nations, the teaching of the Logos displaced the identity that seemed characteristic of barbarian peoples and rendered barbarian character rational, pious, and philosophically ascetic. In other words, Eusebius believed Christian *philanthrōpia* could do what Greek *paideia* had claimed as its function: foster a philosophic ('civilized') life.[81]

Eusebius' ethnic argumentation, however, was squarely aimed at dismantling such Hellenocentrism. According to Eusebius, when the personified Philosophy came to the Greeks, she had to look elsewhere for wisdom since the Greeks were naked and bereft of all wisdom.[82] They had been narrated into a history which put them in second place; they had been forced to borrow or steal wisdom and the beneficial arts from barbarian nations. The Second Sophistic had produced the dominating claims that *paideia*, virtue, and civilization were the property of the

---

[80] Kimber Buell, 'Race and Universalism in Early Christianity', 450. See now, eadem, *Why This New Race*, 21–9, 138–65.

[81] On the notion of *philanthrōpia* as a distinctively Greek feature in the works of Plutarch, see Nikolaidis-Rethymnon, 'Ἑλληνικός—βαρβαρικός', 239–41; he cites R. Hirzel, 'philanthropy ... is a genuine Greek character trait' (239 n. 45).

[82] *PE* 10.4.8–10.

Greeks, open to others only in so far as they left behind their previous ethnic identities in adopting Greekness as it was variously defined.[83] Eusebius countered such claims with his own narrative of the history and placement of nations, and his counter-assertions that it was Christianity alone that could provide for the implementation of the philosophic life among barbarian and savage nations.

Christianity, in the *Praeparatio*, had usurped the philanthropic and civilizing role that had formerly been regarded as characteristic of Greekness. Now, according to Eusebius, the Greeks stood in need of the same saving Logos as the barbarians. In fact, it had been a barbarian *ethnos*— the Hebrews—that had been the Logos' special possession as the friends of God. A striking claim of this subversion of Greek superiority can be found at 14.10.11, where Eusebius writes: 'And [true reason] will show myriads of Panhellenes and myriad races of barbarians also, of whom the former with the help of the already mentioned sciences recognized neither God, nor virtuous life, nor anything at all that is excellent and profitable, while the latter without all these sciences have been eminent in piety and philosophy.' The 'races of barbarians' can only refer to the Hebrews whom Eusebius has been discussing in the previous context. But what is interesting in this passage is his use of the title 'Panhellenes' to refer to the Greeks who boasted of exclusive claims to various fields of knowledge such as astronomy, arithmetic, geometry, and music.[84] The Panhellenion, a league of 33 cities founded in AD 131 under Hadrian, claimed direct descent from ancient Greek ancestors.[85] Its establishment marked the significance placed upon Greekness under the Roman Empire. Eusebius' jibe against its members here emphasizes the broader context of hegemonic Greek discourse against which we ought to see his displacement of Greekness in preference to a barbarian race.

Like Tatian, who had gleefully bandied the epithet of 'barbarian' in the faces of his Greek opponents,[86] Eusebius had asserted that the Hebrews

[83] See, e.g., Aristides, *Or.* 1.326.

[84] *PE* 14.10.10. The appellation had already occurred in a quotation from Clement's *Protrepticus* at 2.6.10.

[85] For varying views on its origins and motivations, see Jones, 'The Panhellenion', 29–56; Spawforth, 'The Panhellenion Again', 339–52; idem, 'Shades of Greekness', in Malkin (ed.), *Ancient Perceptions of Greek Ethnicity*, 375–400; Romeo, 'The Panhellenion and Ethnic Identity', 21–40.

[86] See, for instance, his bold proclamations at *Or.* 42 (cited at *PE* 10.11.35): 'These things [his chronological proofs], O Greeks, I have arranged for you, I Tatian, practising philosophy in accordance with the barbarians, having been born in the land of Assyria, but educated first in your teachings and then in those which I now claim to announce to you.'

were to be counted as barbarians.[87] Furthermore, his displacement of Greeks from their lofty position elevated the barbarians collectively, even if his main purpose was to show the Greek philosophical dependence upon Hebrew wisdom. The barbarians possessed or had discovered things beneficial for life, which the Greeks transferred to themselves.[88] The Christians, therefore, could not be blamed for their adoption of what was beneficial from the barbarian Hebrews.[89]

At the same time, Eusebius' 'ethnography of conversion' offered at 1.4 perpetuates polemical or negative representations of the barbarian 'other' that were commonplace in Greek and Hellenizing literature.[90] His call for rejection of ancestral ways maintains this long-standing marginalization of barbarian others, even as he heralds their inclusion into Christianity. Eusebius must keep a category of extreme otherness—displayed in the practices of cannibalism, incest, and horrifying funerary practices—in order to heighten the dramatic effects of the spread of Christianity within his narrative.

A NEW—AND YET THE OLDEST—PEOPLE

Eusebius had begun the *Praeparatio* with the telling words, 'Christianity, whatever it is . . .'.[91] He quickly followed it up with the assertion that it was fitting to define (*diarthrōsai*) the word 'gospel' (*euangelion*), which, according to him, was the proclamation of true piety and friendship with God that shone throughout the world from the word of God.[92] Then, he

---

[87] *PE* 7.18.11; 10.8.18; 11.6.1–2; 11.18.26; 11.19.2.

[88] *PE* 10.1.1–8; 10.3.26; 10.4.9; 10.6.15; 10.8.17; 11.6.39; 14.10.10.

[89] *PE* 7.1.3; 10.4.32; 11.praef.5; 13.13.66; 14.1.4; 15.1.12.

[90] Plutarch, an important thinker within Eusebius' gambit of reading, is a noteworthy example of the perpetuation of the Greek-barbarian antithesis more recent to Eusebius' time. For a discussion, see Nikolaidis-Rethymnon, Ἑλληνικος—βαρβαρικος'.

[91] *PE* 1.1.1. Τὸν χριστιανισμόν, ὅ τι ποτέ ἐστιν ... The use of *Christianismos* first occurred in the letters of Ignatius of Antioch, *Magn.* 10.1, 3; Rom. 3: 3; Phil. 6: 1; cp. *Mart. Poly.* 10.1; see Lieu, 'The New Testament and Early Christian Identity', 192–3; eadem, 'Martyrdom and the Beginning of "Christian" Identity', 216–17.

[92] 1.1.2–5. At *CI* 1.77 (Ziegler 134.4 ff), Eusebius had given the opposite side of this coin, claiming that the Gospel (in the form of the texts of the evangelists) defined Christianity. Origen had commenced his *Comm. Iohann.* with the issue of defining 'gospel', as well. For discussion of such questions in isagogic literature, see Johnson, 'Eusebius' *Praeparatio Evangelica* as Literary Experiment'.

commenced the second chapter with the proposal that he would explain who 'we' are to those who might enquire into the nature of Christianity. 'Are we Greeks or barbarians? Or what is intermediate to these? And what do we claim to be, not in regard to name, because this is manifest to all, but in the manner and purpose of our life?'[93]

Matters of self-definition and identity were at the heart of his apologetic project from its very inception. Yet, the *Praeparatio* seems more concerned with the identity of Christianity's others, particularly in light of the extensive attention to Greek identity and descent. The greater part of the *Praeparatio* is focused upon the Greeks and their historical relation to the other nations, or the connections of Jews and Greeks to the ancient Hebrews. No doubt Eusebius' conception of Christian identity supports and motivates his construction of Greek or Jewish (or other) ethnic identities. And likewise his portrayal of the other nations will inform his construction of Christian identity, adding emphasis to certain characteristics that distinguish the one from the others. When he asks, 'What might Christianity legitimately be called, since it is neither Hellenism nor Judaism?'[94] he recognizes the necessity of defining Christianity by defining its others.

This question of the positive identification of Christianity is only partly answered by his concept of the 'Church from the nations', which is prevalent in the *Praeparatio*'s prologue. Eusebius' sustained portrayal of the others' identities has forced him to postpone serious treatment of Christian identity until the first books of the *Demonstratio*. He even asserts as much later in the *Demonstratio*: 'As I have treated of the manner of our Saviour's teaching and legislation in the beginning of this work [the *Demonstratio*], when I explained *what Christianity is*, I will now refer my readers to that exposition.'[95] A striking example of this focus on Christian identity in the first part of the *Demonstratio* occurs at 1.6 (24c): when the Logos gave his teachings 'to all men both Greeks and barbarians to keep, he clearly revealed what Christianity is (*ti pote estin ho Christianismos*), who we are, and the nature of the Teacher of the words and instruction, our Lord and Saviour the Christ of God

---

[93] *PE* 1.2.1. τίνες ὄντες ... πότερον Ἕλληνες ἢ βάρβαροι, ἢ τί ἂν γένοιτο τούτων μέσον, καὶ τίνας ἑαυτοὺς εἶναί φαμεν, οὐ τὴν προσηγορίαν, ὅτι καὶ τοῖς πᾶσιν ἔκδηλος αὕτη, ἀλλὰ τὸν τρόπον καὶ τὴν προαίρεσιν τοῦ βίου.

[94] *PE* 1.5.12.

[95] *DE* 9.11 (444c); the words italicized here are identical to the very first words of the *PE*: ton Christianismon ho ti pote estin.

himself'.[96] For this reason, it is imperative that the *Demonstratio*'s statements illuminate our discussion of Christian identity.

The remainder of this chapter will seek to analyse the theme of Christians as forming a distinct nation or people.[97] Previously we have attended to the notion of the 'Church from the nations', in which the pre-Christian identity of Christians was emphasized. Now we turn to the more positive portrayal of Christian identity. Just as Christianity's others were represented as particular nations, so also Christian identity is presented in national terms. In what follows, I will first offer a survey of ethnically loaded appellations for Christianity, that is, terms that are already used to signify other nations (e.g. *ethnos*, *politeia*, or *politeuma*, as well as the addition of *laos* in the *Demonstratio*).[98] These will then be considered as part of his crucially important project of exhibiting Christianity as a restoration of the ancient Hebrew *ethnos*. This last point is often made in studies of the *Praeparatio*; but rarely, if ever, is this restoration of the Hebrews viewed within an *ethnic* context and analysed for its effects upon Christian identity as a distinctly *ethnic* identity. Instead, the image of Eusebius' Christianity is usually limited to that of a religious or theological category of monotheism, or Hebrew *religion*.[99]

The Christian Nation

Focus upon Christianity as a corporate entity carried with it a cluster of metaphors of peoplehood. Eusebius could claim that the Christians are

---

[96] *DE* 1.6.(24c). ἃ καὶ πᾶσιν ἀνθρώποις Ἕλλησί τε καὶ βαρβάροις φυλάττειν παραδιδούς, σαφῶς τί ποτέ ἐστιν ὁ Χριστιανισμὸς ἐξέφηνεν, τίνες θ᾽ ἡμεῖς καὶ ὁποῖος ὁ τῶν τοιῶνδε λόγων τε καὶ μαθημάτων διδάσκαλος, αὐτὸς ὁ σωτὴρ καὶ κύριος ἡμῶν Ἰησοῦς ὁ Χριστὸς τοῦ θεοῦ.... See Hollerich, 'Hebrews, Jews, and Christians: Eusebius of Caesarea on the Biblical Basis of the Two States of the Christian Life', 172–84.

[97] For the metaphor of Christians as a nation in earlier Christian literature, see Olster, 'Classical Ethnography and Early Christianity', 9–31; Kimber Buell, 'Rethinking the Relevance of Race for Early Christian Self-Definition', 449–76; eadem, 'Race and Universalism in Early Christianity', 429–68; Lieu, *Christian Identity in the Jewish and Graeco-Roman World*, 239–68.

[98] On Eusebius' use of these terms, see Chapter 2.

[99] e.g. Inglebert, *Les Romains Chrétiens face à l'Histoire de Rome*, 161; Martin, *Inventing Superstition*, 214; Ulrich, *Euseb von Caesarea und die Juden*, 110–21, especially 113 where he claims that Christianity is a 'Revitalisierung jener ältesten und ehrwürdigsten hebräischen Religion'. While admirable in many ways, Ulrich does not want to push any ethnic element of Eusebius' apologetic method.

like 'the chosen men (*logades*) of a newly enlisted army'.[100] Or, alternatively, he could refer to them as a 'school' (*didaskaleion*) which taught particular doctrines and practised a particular manner of life.[101] Such an appellation fits nicely within the contemporary habit of seeing Christianity as a religious or philosophical entity that is concerned with making propositional truth-claims about God and the world. It has been my contention that this is to unduly distort Eusebius' project and aims, his construction and deployment of identities, and his articulation of boundaries.

Eusebius is well practised in the strategic application of metaphor, and the metaphors of school and army represent valuable angles by which Eusebius formulates and manipulates Christian identity. These metaphors are, however, only a small part of the complex conceptualization of Christian identity in the *Praeparatio*. In fact, I would maintain that Eusebius' use of such terms to describe Christianity always lies within a matrix of nations and national ways of life and ways of thinking. For instance, the portrayal of Christians as a newly enlisted army at 1.5.10 is placed firmly within the context of the 'Church from the nations' discussion of *Praeparatio* 1.2–5. At 12.33.3, where the metaphor of school is used, Christians are at the same time given the appellation of a 'pious citizen-body' (*politeuma*), within the very same sentence.[102] Furthermore, the brief chapter to which this sentence belonged was headed by a reference to the 'whole *ethnos* [of the Christians]'.[103] This chapter heading is the only straightforward occurrence of the term *ethnos* in reference to Christians in the *Praeparatio*. Given the limited attention to Christian identity in the *Praeparatio*, this need not surprise us, even if it is disappointing.

It will remain for the *Demonstratio* to fill out our picture. Christians are entitled an *ethnos* in the context of Eusebius' argument against those who suppose Jesus to be an enchanter in *Demonstratio* 3. Christ could not have belonged to such a class of individuals, Eusebius argues, for

---

[100] *PE* 1.5.10; see also, *LC* 7.6–8, 10, 13.

[101] *PE* 14.3.4; see also 4.4.1; 12.33.3.

[102] Numenius was later to be quoted as saying that 'the school of the Epicureans is like a certain true citizenship (*politeia*)', at 14.5.3.

[103] *OTI MH XPHN EK TWN OY KATA ΛΟΓΟΝ ΠΑΡ᾽ ΗΜΙΝ ΒΙΟΥΝΤWΝ ΤΟ ΠΑΝ ΕΘΝΟΣ ΔΙΑΒΑΛΛΕΣΘΑΙ*. That the chapter headings of the *PE* were composed by Eusebius, and not by a later hand, has been convincingly shown by Mras, *Eusebius Werke VIII. Die Praeparatio Evangelica*, VIII–IX; on chapter headings in Eusebius' works generally, see T. D. Barnes, 'Constantine's Good Friday Sermon', *JTS* 27 (1976), 418–21.

'which enchanter ever took it into his head to establish a new nation (*ethnos*) called after his own name?'[104] Similarly, at *Demonstratio* 4.16, Eusebius asserts that Christ 'has filled the world with his virtue and his name, establishing the race (*genos*) of Christians, named after him, among all nations'.[105]

Even familial notions are applied to the Christian *ethnos* at *Demonstratio* 1.9 (32d), where he attempts to explain the prolific progeny of the ancient Hebrews against the renunciation of sexual behaviour, even for procreation, among Christians. Eusebius argues that, whereas the ancient Hebrews needed to procreate to pass on their way of life in isolation from the wicked nations, Christians adopted numerous children in a spiritual sense. 'In our day these men are necessarily devoted to celibacy that they may have leisure for higher things; they have undertaken to bring up not one or two children, but a prodigious number, and to educate them in godliness, and to care for their life generally.'[106] Another instance of kinship language is found at *Praeparatio* 1.4.11. Here, Eusebius describes the philanthropic message of the Gospel as exhorting Christians 'to welcome every person as of the same race (*homogenēs*) and to recognize the one considered a stranger as closest of kin and a brother by the law of nature'.[107] Thus, even the biological element of ethnicity, in its parent-to-child and brother-to-brother (and presumably sister) relationships, is metaphorically applied to Christians by Eusebius.[108]

The notion of Christians as a 'people founded by Christ' recurs in numerous passages.[109] An excellent example is found at *Demonstratio* 10.8 (510cd), which is worth quoting in full.

And the peroration of the whole prophecy [from Psalms] crowning all ('The generation that comes shall be announced to the Lord, and they shall announce his righteousness to a people (*laos*) that shall be born, whom the Lord

---

[104] *DE* 3.6 (131cd); cp. Origen, *C. Cels.* 1.45; 2.78; 3.8; 4.42; 8.75.

[105] *DE* 4.16 (194a).

[106] *DE* 1.9 (32d); cp. Josephus, *BJ* 2.120; Porphyry, *Ad Marc.* 1.

[107] *PE* 1.4.11; cp. Themistius, *Or.* 6.77a–78b.

[108] In this, he is following the precedent of Jesus at Matt. 12: 48, and Paul at Gal. 4: 26. For excellent recent discussion on the conception of the biological and spiritual family in early Christian discourse, see A. S. Jacobs, '"Let Him Guard *Pietas*": Early Christian Exegesis and the Ascetic Family', *JECS* 11 (2003), 265–81; R. Krawiec, '"From the Womb of the Church": Monastic Families', *JECS* 11 (2003), 283–307; and A. S. Jacobs and R. Krawiec, 'Fathers Know Best? Christian Families in the Age of Asceticism', *JECS* 11 (2003), 257–63; Kimber Buell, *Making Christians*.

[109] See e.g., *DE* 1.1 (7); 2.3 (61cd, 83a); 10.3 (477a).

has made) specifically foretells the Church from the nations, and the generation established on the earth, through our Saviour Jesus Christ. For what could this people (*laos*) be which, it is here said, will be born for God after these things, which did not exist of old, and did not appear among men, but will hereafter? What was the generation, which was not then, but which it is said will come, but the Church established by our Saviour in all the world, and the new people (*laos*) from the nations, of which the Holy Spirit wonderfully spoke through Isaiah saying, 'Who has heard such things, and who has seen them thus? The earth was in travail for one day and a nation (*ethnos*) was born at once'.[110]

Eusebius has effectively allowed the biblical prophecy to shape his vision of Christian identity while at the same time legitimizing Christianity through the scriptural citation. A passage from *Demonstratio* 2.3 (76d) reiterates: the Christians are 'a people (*laos*) who from the four corners of the earth even now is welded together by the power of Christ'.[111] Such passages concisely exhibit the fusion of his two primary images of Christian identity: the Church from the nations and the Church as a nation.[112] Christians are a nation out of the nations, a people made up of many peoples.[113]

Such a conception may seem odd, especially if we maintain the traditional approach of ethnic identity as biologically fixed. In that case, it would be incorrect to speak of ethnic identities that can be rejected for a new one. Yet, such an essentialist approach to ethnicity is not only shown to be misleading in light of the discursive approach to ethnic identity noted earlier,[114] it is also an inadequate approach to understanding Eusebius' own conceptual framework. As will be shown below, Christians as a nation drawn out of the nations were modelled on the ancient Hebrews, who were no less gathered from other nations. But first, the Christian possession, or rather, embodiment, of a *politeia/ politeuma* should be assessed. As noted in an earlier chapter,[115] the

---

[110] *DE* 10.8 (510cd). The passage from Isaiah is quoted to similar effect at *HE* 1.4.3 and *CI* 2.57 (Ziegler 402–03).

[111] *DE* 2.3 (76d); *laos* seems to be favoured in the *VC* as well, see e.g. 2.61.3; 2.63.

[112] The previous discussion on 'the Church from the nations' was dedicated to relevant passages in the *PE*. The phrase, however, occurs repeatedly throughout the *DE* as well. See, *DE* 3.2 (101d); 5.2 (219b); 6.7 (265c); 6.17 (283d); 6.21 (301a); 7.1 (326d); 7.3 (355b); 9.6 (431d); 9.17 (457c); 9.18 (460a); 10.8 (509c, 510c).

[113] The image occurs in later works as well; see, e.g. *CI* 2.38 (Ziegler 322.31). Further references (especially from Eusebius' *Comm. Psalm.*) are noted at Farina, *L'Impero e l'imperatore cristiano in Eusebio di Cesarea*, 282–7.

[114] See Chapter 1.

[115] See Chapter 2.

terms *politeia* and *politeuma* pertained to a key element (whether as a way of life or the particular conduct prescribed by a nation's legal code) of Eusebius' conception of *ethnos*.

Reference to Christians' *politeuma* was employed in the passage discussed, which identified Christianity as a school (*PE* 12.33.3). The fact that this passage is in close proximity to a remark on the Christian *ethnos* (12.33's chapter heading) should not be forgotten. For here we have the concurrence of two important terms of ethnicity being applied to Christianity. Eusebius would repeat his use of *politeuma* to signify Christians in an important passage at the beginning of the *Demonstratio*. There he remarks that 'Christianity is neither any Hellenism or Judaism, but the most ancient *politeuma* of piety, [which is] between these two.'[116]

The occurrence of the Christians' *politeia* arises at *Praeparatio* 15.61.12, where Eusebius writes: 'We cling solely to piety towards God the creator of all things, and by a life of temperance and a different godly *politeia* of virtue strive to live in a manner pleasing to him who is God over all.'[117] Elsewhere in the *Praeparatio*, authors who are cited by Eusebius will also employ *politeia* in reference to Christianity. Tatian refers to 'our *politeia*, and the history of our laws'.[118] Clement mentions those who interpret the three natures discussed by Plato (*Rep.* 3.415A) as signifying three forms of *politeiai*: those of the Jews, the Greeks, and the Christians.[119] No difference in meaning can be detected between the use of *politeuma* and *politeia* in these passages; they all denote the organization and manner of life (often prescribed in laws) on the social, collective level.[120]

The idea of the Christian *politeia/politeuma* is abundant in the *Demonstratio*. Much space in Eusebius' discussions of the person of Jesus are devoted to his foundation of a polity and way of life for the new nation.[121] Strikingly, Eusebius claims that the city and *politeia* of Christ has replaced the cities and *politeiai* of the nations, through the conversion to Christianity of members of those nations.[122]

---

[116] *DE* 1.2 (14). ὁ χριστιανισμός, οὔτε ἑλληνισμός τις ὢν οὔτε ἰουδαισμός, ἀλλὰ τὸ μεταξὺ τούτων παλαιότατον εὐσεβείας πολίτευμα....

[117] *PE* 15.61.12.

[118] Quoted at *PE* 10.11.26. τῆς καθ᾽ ἡμᾶς πολιτείας ἱστορίας τε τῆς κατὰ τοὺς ἡμετέρους νόμους.... The *politeia* and history that Tatian mentions are those of the Hebrews and the Christians simultaneously, since there is such a degree of fluidity and continuity between the two in his thinking.

[119] At *PE* 13.13.19.

[120] See Chapter 2.

[121] See, *DE* 1.2 (14); 4.12 (167b); 4.17 (196a); 5.4 (225b); 7.1 (326a).

[122] *DE* 6.20 (298d).

Elsewhere, he writes: 'In all battles [Christ] triumphed over the devil, and all the unseen enemies and foes led by him, and made us who were slaves [to the devil] his own, and built of us, as of living stones, the house of God, and the citizenship (*politeuma*) of piety.'[123]

The employment of *politeia/politeuma* to convey the legislative element of the *ethnos* is prominent. In fact, one of the most important—if not the most important—activities of Jesus was his institution of a new law code. The dominant role of Christ, as represented in the *Demonstratio*, is that of legislator.[124] As a lawgiver, he was like Moses; but whereas the latter instituted an imperfect and limited *politeia*, Christ revived through his legislation the way of life of the ancient Hebrews.[125]

The dominant conception of Christian identity in the *Praeparatio* and *Demonstratio* was thus clearly centred on the collective identity of an *ethnos* or *laos* with its attendant communal way of life (*politeia/politeuma*).[126] And Christ, from whom it derived its name, was its founder and lawgiver. Such identity construction, it should be noted, was not limited to Eusebius' apologetic project. During the same decade in which the *Praeparatio* was composed, Eusebius issued an edition of the *HE* with the prologue as we now have it.[127] Here, Eusebius programmatically stated:

It is admitted that, when in recent times the appearance of our Saviour Jesus Christ had become known to all men, there immediately made its appearance a new nation (*ethnos*); a nation confessedly not small, and not dwelling in some corner of the earth, but the most numerous and pious of all nations, indestructible and unconquerable, because it always receives assistance from God. This nation, thus suddenly appearing at the time appointed by the

---

[123] *DE* 4.17 (199b). Note the allusion to I Peter 2.5, 9–10; cp. *Proph. Ecl.*, *PG* 22.1077B; 1081B; 1157B; *CI* 2.43 [Ziegler 342–344]; in contrast to Plotinus, *Enn.* 2.9.18.

[124] See, *DE* 1.4 (7bc); 1.6 (24c); 1.7 (25b, 26d, 27a, *passim*); 3.2 (90c, 91bc, 102a); 3.6 (131cd); 4.13 (169a); 9.11 (443c). This motif is apparent in the *PE* as well, see *PE* 4.1.5; 7.8.40. See Hollerich, 'Religion and Politics in the Writings of Eusebius', 318; Farina, *L'Impero e l'imperatore cristiano in Eusebio di Cesarea*, 104–05.

[125] See J. E. Bruns, 'The Agreement of Moses and Jesus in the *Demonstratio Evangelica* of Eusebius', *VC* 31 (1977), 117–25.

[126] This point was noticed (all too briefly) in Gallagher, 'Piety and Polity': 2.139; Kofsky, *Eusebius of Caesarea against the Pagans*, 100; Sirinelli, *Les vues historiques d'Eusèbe de Césarée*, 136–7.

[127] For a helpful survey of the history of scholarship on the *HE*'s various editions and dates, see Beggs, 'From Kingdom to Nation: The Transformation of a Metaphor in Eusebius' Historia Ecclesiastica', 53–89; see also, A. Louth, 'The Date of Eusebius' *Historia Ecclesiastica*', *JTS* 41 (1990), 111–23.

inscrutable counsel of God, is the one which has been honoured by all with the name of Christ.[128]

The whole *HE* was meant to supply this nation with a history and consequently with an identity. Hence, the major themes that often receive attention among scholars of the *HE* (namely, a concern for the succession and continuity of the Church's leadership, the struggle with outsiders [literally, 'the wars waged by the nations against the divine Word'],[129] the identification of heretics, and the contours of scriptural canon)[130] should be understood as part of this larger project.[131] Eusebius' panegyric on the completion of the church at Tyre delivered c. AD 315, included in the tenth book of the *HE*, confirms this emphasis. By way of a rhetorical question, he proclaims:

Who has founded a nation (*ethnos*) which of old was not even heard of, but which now is not concealed in some corner of the earth, but is spread abroad everywhere under the sun...? What king prevails to such an extent, and even after death leads on his soldiers, and sets up trophies over his enemies, and fills every place, country and city, Greek and barbarian, with his royal dwellings....[132]

References to Christians as a race elsewhere in the *HE* evinced a similar portrayal of the communal identity of the Christians.[133] Eusebius' historical account of the early Church was, therefore, driven by the desire to explore and advocate an ethnic conceptualization of Christianity.

The metaphor persisted in Eusebius' later writings as well; I close this section with a striking quotation from his commentary on the Psalms, which probably received its final form around AD 325.[134] His declaration

[128] *HE* 1.4.2.

[129] *HE* 1.1.2 (translation adapted from T. D. Barnes, *Constantine and Eusebius*, 129).

[130] This is an abbreviated list of the six (or seven) themes of the *HE* identified by scholars. See, especially R. M. Grant, *Eusebius as Church Historian* (Oxford: Clarendon Press, 1980); but also, T. D. Barnes, *Constantine and Eusebius*, 129–40.

[131] A. Momigliano, 'Pagan and Christian Historiography in the Fourth Century', in idem (ed), *The Conflict between Paganism and Christianity in the Fourth Century* (Oxford: Clarendon Press, 1963), 79–99; Chesnut, *The First Christian Histories*, 130–1, and A. Droge, 'The Apologetic Dimensions of the *Ecclesiastical History*', in Attridge and Hata (eds), *Eusebius, Christianity and Judaism*, 492–509, had noted the importance of identifying Christianity as an *ethnos* for the *HE*, but Beggs, 'From Kingdom to Nation', is the only one to have offered an extensive study of how such a conception of Christianity provided the framework and direction for the *HE* as a whole.

[132] *HE* 10.4.19, 20.

[133] See e.g. *HE* 4.7.10; 4.15.6; 5.1.20–1.

[134] See Rondeau, *Les commentaires patristiques du psautier*, 1.66–69. For issues of authenticity, see E. Schwartz, 'Eusebios', 1435–6; Rondeau, 'Eusèbe de Césarée. Le Commentaire sur les psaumes', IV.2.1687–1690.

in this commentary expresses the force that ethnicity carried in his conception of Christian identity.

Therefore, the enemies of God did not want there to be a nation (*ethnos*) of God among humans; on the contrary, they were eager to wipe out even the name of Israel. But God, ever restoring a nation (*ethnos*) for himself upon the earth, established, after the fall of the former people (*laos*) [the Jews], the Church out of the nations, even the new and novel nation (*ethnos*), which was established throughout the whole world from a selection (*eklogē*) of the nations.[135]

Christians as Hebrews

The relationship between the ancient Hebrews and the more recent Christians is the fundamental area in which this identification is played out. For Eusebius, Christianity was a restoration of the ancient Hebrew way of life and theology. Once pure and unsullied by ignorance and moral weakness, the Hebrews had originally led a life that embodied friendship with God. As a result of Egyptianizing processes after their sojourn in Egypt, the Hebrews devolved into the bastardized nation of the Jews.[136] Moses had given them a legislation that had been prefaced by a memorial to the lives of their Hebrew forefathers. And, taken allegorically, his law code still represented the high standards of life and character practised by the Hebrews. Taken literally, the law could still at least minimally restrain the Jews from becoming like the other nations in character, theology, and way of life, but it fell far below the original Hebrew purity. Hence, according to Eusebius, only a few individuals maintained the high theological and moral level of the ancient Hebrews and thus received their name. However, Christ's appearance on earth radically changed all this and fundamentally altered the national landscape. Through the activity and teaching of Christ, the ancient Hebrew *ethnos* found national restoration in the form of Christianity. The Christians formed a new people, drawn out from the nations to form themselves around the way of life and theological clear-sightedness of the ancient friends of God.[137] The ways in which Eusebius connected the newcomers on the historical stage, the

---

[135] *Comm. Ps.* 82.4, 5 (*PG* 23.993D–996A).

[136] See *PE* 7.8.37–40, discussed in Chapter 4.

[137] Unfortunately, the otherwise illuminating discussions of this theme by Ulrich, *Euseb von Caesarea und die Juden*, 66, 113–16, and, too a lesser extent, Gallagher, 'Piety and Polity', and 'Eusebius the Apologist' 251–60, see Christianity only as a restoration of Hebrew 'religion', thus neglecting the ethnic identity construction of Eusebius.

Christians, with the ancient Hebrews are significant for understanding his ethnic legitimation of Christianity.

At various places, Eusebius explicitly gives individual Christians the appellation of 'Hebrew'. For instance, Paul is called a 'Hebrew theologian'.[138] And Eusebius even claims that John the Evangelist was a 'Hebrew of Hebrews'.[139] Eusebius generalizes: 'the apostles and disciples of our Saviour are Hebrews'.[140] In a significant passage, he clarifies his meaning of the term 'Hebrew doctrines': 'And by "doctrines of the Hebrews" I mean not only the oracles of Moses, but also those of all the other godly men after Moses, whether prophets or apostles of our Saviour, whose consent in doctrines must reasonably make them worthy of one and the same title.'[141] This avowal is indicative of Eusebius' habit, especially throughout his 'proof' that Plato borrowed ideas from the writings of the Hebrews, of conflating the Hebrews with 'us'.[142] Eusebius fluidly moves from third-person pronouns for the ancient Hebrews to first-person pronouns of Christians of the apostolic era and later. For instance, on the topic of the use of songs for the education of the young, he seems to be concerned with the ancient Hebrews of Moses' writings or David's psalms.[143] In fact, Eusebius explicitly claims that it was the 'Hebrews of old times' who judged songs for their moral worth.[144] But then after quoting from Plato's *Laws* 2.671a–d, he shifts his reference to the traditional practice of composing songs and hymns to God, which 'has been handed down among *us*'.[145]

Alongside such shifts in pronoun, texts from the Hebrew scriptures often alternate with texts from the New Testament, though both are generically referred to as 'the writings [or the oracles] of the Hebrews'.[146] Hence, Eusebius' need to make the statements cited above, that the New

---

[138] *PE* 11.19.4.

[139] *PE* 11.19.2. Joseph (7.8.36) and Moses (7.7.1) had already received the appellation of 'Hebrew of Hebrews' in the *PE*; and even Josephus receives the title at *DE* 6.18 (291b). The phrase recalls Paul's statement that he was a 'Hebrew of Hebrews' at Phil. 3: 5.

[140] *PE* 11.23.11.

[141] *PE* 12.52.35.

[142] On this sort of identification in earlier Christian authors, see Lieu, *Christian Identity in the Jewish and Graeco-Roman World*, 78–9.

[143] *PE* 12.22.2.

[144] *PE* 12.23.4.

[145] *PE* 12.24.5. This is probably an allusion to Col. 3: 16, where Paul exhorts his readers to sing 'psalms, hymns and spiritual songs to God'.

[146] See e.g. *PE* 11.13.7 (I Thess. 4: 6); 11.13.8 (James 4: 6); 11.18.13 (John 15: 1, 5); 11.18.25 (John 5: 19); 11.19.4 (Col. 1: 15–17); 11.23.10 (I Cor. 1: 30); 11.26.7 (Eph. 6: 12); 11.32.1 (I Cor. 7: 31); 11.36.2 (Gal. 4: 26); 11.38.7 (I Cor. 2: 9, John 14: 2); 12.6.23 (II Cor. 5: 10); 12.6.24 (Rom. 2: 16, 6); 12.19.1 (Heb. 8: 5); etc.

Testament authors were Hebrews.[147] It does not seem to bother him that this employment of New Testament authors seems to make incoherent his concern to show that Plato is dependent upon the Hebrews for his wisdom. It may be that, since Eusebius sees Christianity and hence the New Testament writings as seamlessly contiguous with Hebrew thought, he considers their witness to be exactly on a par with the writings of Moses as representative of doctrines of the Hebrews to such a degree that they can be cited as being predecessors to Plato's own thinking. If this is the case, a considerable depth must be seen in Eusebius' conception of Hebrew–Christian continuity.

The continuity from the one people to the other receives its most succinct and transparent form in Eusebius' criticism of Greek disunity after Plato. He offers the unity characteristic of Hebrew history as an antithesis to the incessant discord that marks the Greek record of philosophical history. Beginning with the ancient Hebrews, Eusebius writes: 'The Hebrews on their part from long time of old and, so to say, from the very first origin of man, having found the true and religious philosophy have carefully preserved this undefiled to succeeding generations, son from sire having received and guarded a treasure of true doctrines.'[148] This declaration affirms the antiquity and pristine unity of the Hebrews. Such unity, Eusebius then declares, remained unbroken through Moses (who never 'thought of disturbing and changing any of the doctrines held by his forefathers')[149] and the prophets (who never 'ventured to utter a word of discord either against each other or against the opinions held by Moses and the more ancient friends of God').[150] Eusebius locates Christianity in a direct line with both these pre-Mosaic and post-Mosaic Hebrews thus: 'Not even has our school, which has arisen from there [the ancient friends of God] ... introduced anything at variance with the earlier doctrines; or perhaps one should rather say that we pass on in word and in manner of life the same course as the God-beloved Hebrews before Moses.'[151]

Hence, Eusebius glosses over the great discontinuity in time and thought of each group of people designated Hebrews, those before Moses, those after Moses, and the Christians. An unbroken and seamless continuity and unity of thought and way of life replaces the disjunctions of chronological separation and doctrinal disharmony that

---

[147] This point is explicitly made at *PE* 11.19.3 (John 1: 1–4, 14).
[148] *PE* 14.3.1.   [149] *PE* 14.3.2.
[150] *PE* 14.3.3.   [151] *PE* 14.3.4.

anti-Christian polemicists might (and did) raise (e.g. Celsus, Porphyry, and later Julian).[152] His emphasis is further enhanced in the following statement: 'Our doctrines ... testified to by all [our] authors, first, middle and last, with one mind and one voice, confirm with unanimous vote the certainty of that which is both the true piety and philosophy.'[153]

The significance of identifying Christianity as a renewal of the Hebrew way of life is thus already clear in the relevant passages from the *Praeparatio* alone. The first books of the *Demonstratio*, however, offer Eusebius' most sustained argument for this supposition. The *Demonstratio's* depiction of Christ as the founder and lawgiver of the Christian *ethnos* capitalizes upon the claim that Christ had been

the only one to revive the life (*bios*) of the old Hebrew saints, long perished from amongst men, and to have spread it not among a paltry few but through the whole world; from which it is possible to show that in crowds men through all the world [are following the way] of those holy men of Abraham's day, and that there are innumerable lovers of their godly manner of life (*politeia*) from barbarians as well as Greeks.[154]

Christianity was neither Hellenism nor Judaism, but 'the most ancient *politeuma* for holiness', an 'intermediate law and way of life preached by the godly and holy men of old time, which our Lord and Saviour has raised up anew after its long sleep'.[155]

The theme of Christianity as the 'true Israel' complements this portrayal.[156] Alternatively, the Hebrews were called the first Christians.[157] Abraham and Job, in particular, were designated with this title.[158] Eusebius had similarly argued that Hebrews were 'Christians before Christ' at *HE* 1.4.[159] Unlike Justin Martyr, who had asserted that

[152] As seen above, Eusebius himself used the argument from disagreement against the Greek philosophers with some effect; see Chapter 5.

[153] *PE* 14.3.5.

[154] *DE* 3.3 (103bc).

[155] *DE* 1.2 (14). See also, 1.5 (9d); 1.6 (20d, 22b–23a); 1.7 (28b); 2.3 (86a); 3.3 (103d, 104bc, 107b); 4.13 (169a); 5.praef (208a–c).

[156] See *DE* 2.3 (64c, 76d); 7.3 (358d, 359b).

[157] *DE* 1.5 (12ab); 4.10 (164d); 4.15 (174d–176b).

[158] Abraham: 'who lived as a Christian, not as a Jew' (*DE* 1.6 [13b]); Job: 'he was such a good Christian in his life' (*DE* 1.6 [15c]).

[159] For a discussion of the 'Christians before Christ' concept, see Ulrich, *Euseb von Caesarea und die Juden*, 113–115. 'kann [Euseb] rückprojizierend auch solche Menschen Christen nennen, die sich vor der Offenbarung Christi im Fleisch durch ihre besondere Gottesbeziehung ausgezeichnet und die sich auf diese Weise gleichsam als "Christen vor Christus" bewährt haben—eben die "alten Hebräer"' (114).

'all who lived with *logos* were Christians',[160] Eusebius was attempting to reconstruct the history of nations, in which a particular people were depicted as living according to reason on a corporate, national level. As this unfolded over the course of history, Eusebius needed to incorporate Christianity into the history of the earlier people. It was in this way that he sought to legitimize Christianity. The argument that Hebrews were actually Christians highlights the fact that he is constructing his portrait of the Hebrews in Christianity's own image. This was especially true of Eusebius' construal of the ancient Hebrew theology as Logos theology.[161] It is also worked out in another way in some passing remarks of the *Demonstratio*.

While the kinship connections of ancient Hebrews was treated at *Demonstratio* 1.9, in the cases of Abraham and Job Eusebius stresses that they were drawn into the Hebrew *ethnos* from other nations. Job, according to Eusebius, did 'not at all belong to the race of the Jews'.[162] Abraham had been a foreigner (*alloethnos*) to Hebrew piety until he 'rejected his ancestral superstition and left his home and kindred and fathers' customs, and the manner of life in which he was born and reared'.[163] These remarks hint at a picture of the ancient Hebrews as a people drawn from the nations in the same way that the Christians were drawn from the nations. Those who converted to Christianity could be said merely to have followed the example of ancient saints like Abraham and Job.

In any case, Eusebius fundamentally crafts strategic connections between the Christians and ancient Hebrews. This motif finds its most exquisite expression in the statement:

I have, abundantly proved that the Word of God announced to all nations the ancient form of their ancestors' piety, as the new covenant does not differ from the form of holiness, which was very ancient even in the time of Moses, so that *it is at the same time both old and new*. It is, as I have shown, very, very old; and, on the other hand, it is new through having been as it were hidden away from men through a long period between, and now come to life again by the Saviour's teaching.[164]

---

[160] *I Apol.* 46.3. For discussion, see B. Seeberg, 'Die Geschichtstheologie Justins des Märtyrers', *ZKG* 58 (1939), 37–8.

[161] See *PE* 7.12–15, as noted in Chapter 4.

[162] *PE* 7.8.30. Eusebius contradicts this when he writes in the *DE* that Job was in the fifth generation of the line of Abraham (1.6 [14d]).

[163] *DE* 1.3 (16).

[164] *DE* 1.6 (16d); cf. the assertions of Constantine at *VC* 2.57. Cp. Gregory Nazianzenus, *Or.* 4.67, 110.

Such assertions to continuity were critical to Eusebius' apologetic project. His portrayal of the Greeks and Jews as late and dependent upon others, and as exemplifying an impious and irrational national character is entirely negative. Christianity, to be shown superior over these other nations, was represented as identical to the Hebrews as possible. For, by stressing the continuity of Christianity with the ancient Hebrews, Eusebius could claim for the Christians all the marks of superiority allotted to the Hebrews. The antiquity, purity, rationality, piety and other distinctive features of ethnic difference that character-ized the ancient Hebrews were thus attributed to the newly formed Christian people. Greeks and Jews were displaced from the ranks of cultural and historical preeminence; while Christians, because of their identification with the Hebrews, were relocated from being a recent, derivative and immature people to the position of the most ancient and most pious *ethnos*. Ethnic identity construction is at the heart of Eusebius' apologetic method. Though Christianity is named 'a school of true philosophy' in the *Praeparatio*, it should not detract from this ethnic configuration that lies at the heart of Eusebius' methodology. It is through the connections and characterizations of nations that Eusebius conceives his defence of Christianity.

CONCLUSIONS

This chapter has argued that Eusebius' defence of Christianity is achieved through a representation of Christians as both 'the Church from the nations' and as a nation reviving the Hebrew *politeia*. Such an identity intrinsically entails, and even boasts, the transgression of national boundaries. Christians have, according to Eusebius, left behind previous identities and now operate under a new ethnic identity and have adopted a new way of life. While Christians are primarily pictured as apostates from Greekness in the *Praeparatio*, Eusebius' manipulation of ethnographic accounts of Persian and Scythian immor-ality exemplifies his construction of Christian *philanthrōpia*. At the same time, it perpetuates traditional Greek biases against barbarian otherness.

Apologetics, as performed by Eusebius, is a thoroughgoing and sustained construction of Christian ethnic identity. Many elements that are easily subsumed by moderns into a category of 'religion' are deeply embedded within an ethnic framework. The defence of theological doctrines is only offered in the context of a historical narrative of the ancient Hebrews. The defence of the person and work of Christ in the *Demonstratio* emphasizes his role as the founder and law-giver of a new nation. Christian identity is articulated in ethnic terms; its legitimation rests upon its connectedness to the ancient Hebrew *ethnos*. Eusebius' Christianity was not merely a 'religion', nor were its others. Christianity was a nation whose members had been drawn from all other nations.

APPENDIX 1:

The Structure of the *Praeparatio*

Eusebius' *Praeparatio* exhibits a concern for order unlike the work of any previous apologist. Apart from periodic statements alerting the reader of the place in the overall arrangement of the argument, he offers two general statements declaring the basic structure of his argument, one in the first (which, however, covers only the first six books), the other in the last book of the *Praeparatio*.

At 1.6.5, he provides the following schema (into which I have inserted references to the sections referred to):

First, therefore, let us inquire how [the Greeks] have judged concerning the first creation of the world (1.6.1–1.8.19); then consider their opinions about the first and most ancient superstition found in human life (1.9.1–18); and, thirdly, the opinions of the Phoenicians (1.9.19–2.praef.3); fourthly, those of the Egyptians (2.praef.4–2.1.53); after which, fifthly, making a distinction in the opinions of the Greeks, we will first examine their ancient and more mythical delusion (2.1.52–2.8.13), and then their more serious and, as they say, more physical philosophy concerning the gods (3.1.1–3.17.3); and after this we will travel over the account of their admired oracles (4.1.1–5.36.5); after which we will also take a survey of the serious doctrines (viz., Fate) of the noble philosophy of the Greeks (6.1.1–6.11.83).

Elsewhere, he refers to his treatment of oracles (and also of the notion of Fate undergirding the oracles) as 'political philosophy', which had been preceded by the branches of 'historical, which they call mythical, theology' and 'physical theology' (4.1.2).

In the fullest account, Eusebius describes the arrangement of the *Praeparatio*'s argument at 15.praef.1–7 in the following manner:

Since I wanted to refute the polytheistic error of all the nations at the beginning of the *Praeparatio Evangelica* as a recommendation and a defence of our departure from them, I investigated first of all in the first three books not only the tales, which the children of their theologians and poets treated comically about their native gods, but also their solemn and indeed unspeakable physical theories, transferred above perhaps to heaven and the parts of the universe by their noble philosophy.... Moreover, in three other books after the first three [Books 4–6] I also laid bare with brilliant refutations the account of their famed oracles and the false opinion about Fate, which is celebrated by the many, making use not only of our own works but also the words especially of the philosophers themselves among the Greeks. And from there, I moved on to the oracles of the Hebrews, and in an equal-numbered arrangement of books [Books 7–9] again I presented the reasonings for the dogmatic theology embraced by them and their whole history attested even by the Greeks themselves. Next [Book 10] I refuted the Hellenic character, how they had derived the benefit of all things from barbarians and contributed no serious teaching of their own, and when I had brought into the light the comparison of the times during which those renowned among the Greeks and the prophets of the Hebrews were born, forthwith in the three books after these [Books 11–13] I exhibited the concurrence of the philosophers honoured by the Greeks with the opinions of the Hebrews.... In the book before this one [Book 14], I detected those of the Greek philosophers who thought differently from us as thinking differently not only in relation to us, but to their own kinsmen, and as being overturned by their own acquaintances.... Continuing this even now in the last book, being the fifteenth of the present treatise, I will give what remains to the things being described, dragging into the light yet even now the solemnities of the noble philosophy of the Greeks and laying bare the lack of useful learning in them.

As argued in earlier chapters, the triadic structuring described by Eusebius in this passage is best seen in light of the two main sections of the *Praeparatio* in Books 1–6 and 7–15; for even the second phase of the narrative of the Greeks at 9–15 is directly connected to the narrative of the Hebrews in 7–8. The following outline appropriately renders the structure of the work:

A. Prologue (1.1.1–1.5.14)
B. The narrative of Greek descent (Books 1–6)
　1. Greek account of cosmogony (1.6.1–1.8.19)
　2. Greek account of primitive theology (1.9.1–18)
　3. The ancient Phoenicians (1.9.19–2.praef.3)
　　a. Cosmological reflections—first principles (1.10.1–6)
　　b. Forefathers of the Phoenicians (1.10.7–44)
　　c. Worship of animals—the serpent god (1.10.45–53)
　4. The ancient Egyptians (2.praef.4–2.1.53)
　　a. Forefathers of the Egyptians (2.1.1–32)
　　b. Worship of animals (2.1.33–51)
　5. The ancient Greeks (2.1.52–6.11.83)
　　a. Ancestors of the Greeks: 'the mythical, or rather historical, theology' (2.1.52–2.8.13)
　　b. 'Physical theology' (3.1.1–3.17.3)
　　c. 'Political theology' based upon oracles (4.1.1–5.36.5)
　　d. Serious doctrines of the Greeks—Fate (6.1.1–6.11.83)
C. The narrative of Hebrew descent (Books 7–8)
　1. Reformulation of theory of decline among the nations (7.2)
　2. The ancient Hebrews (7.3–8.14)

    a. Progress in earliest times (7.3–5)
    b. Difference between Hebrews and Jews (7.6)
    c. Hebrew forefathers (7.7–8)
    d. Hebrew theology (7.9–8.14)
D. Second phase of the narrative of Greek descent (Books 9–15)
    1. Greek accounts of Hebrew stories (9.1–42)
    2. The Greeks as plagiarizers (10.1–14)
    3. Platonic borrowings from the Hebrews (11.1–13.13)
    4. Platonic divergence from the Hebrews (13.14–21)
    5. Discord among the Greeks (14.1–15.62)
    6. The discord of the Greeks before and after Plato (14.3.6–14.16.13)
        a. Plato on his predecessors (14.3.6–14.4.12)
        b. Numenius on Plato's successors (14.4.13–14.9.3)
        c. Dissension because of conjectural nature of Greek philosophy (14.9.4–14.13.9)
        d. Dissension of Greek philosophers on God and first principles (14.14.1–14.16.13)
    7. Criticisms of philosophical schools and their founders (14.17.1–15.32.8)
        a. Scepticism (14.17.1–14.18.30)
        b. Aristippus and the Cyrenaics (14.18.31–14.19.7)
        c. 'Empiricists' such as Protagoras and Metrodorus (14.19.8–14.20.12)
        d. Epicurus (14.20.13–14.21.7)
        e. Aristotle (15.2.1–15.13.5)
        f. Stoics (15.13.6–15.22.67)
        g. Physical philosophers in general (15.22.68–15.32.8)
    8. Discord of physical philosophers on cosmogonical doctrines (15.32.9–15.52.17)

APPENDIX 2:

The Concept of Progress in Eusebius

An important element in Eusebius' portrayal of ancient peoples is the motif of moral and religious decline. Important expressions of this theme occur at numerous points in his argument.[1] In these instances, Eusebius characterizes the historical development of the nations as following a trend from less irrational and impious beliefs to completely mindless and wicked practices and doctrines. An original astral polytheism gradually gave way to the worship of elements or fruits of the earth, the principle of pleasure or the sources thereof, humans, and even animals. Sacrificial cult developed from offerings of plants or incense to animals and humans.

Nevertheless, some Eusebian scholars have asserted that Eusebius was a proponent of a 'theory of progress' in world history.[2] Chesnut, for example, claims that Eusebius held 'a rather optimistic view of the world, seeing real, continuous progress in all areas—civilization, culture, morality, and religion', and 'rejected the basic premise of romantic primitivism, which held that civilization was necessarily evil and corrupting in itself'.[3] The starting point of such assertions is Eusebius' HE 1.2.17–23, which is a supposedly unmistakable declaration of progress theory. A primitive state of ignorance and lawlessness, when humans lived like wild beasts,[4] was followed by a later stage of mildness and peacefulness in human relations.[5] Unlike other formulations of progress in the ancient world (e.g. that of Diodorus), however, Eusebius' account includes intermediate stages between the earlier chaotic beastliness and the later orderliness that significantly delimits his narrative of historical progress. As a result of early humanity's violence and impiety, God chastened them by sending disasters

---

[1] See, e.g., PE 1.9.13–14, 16–19; 2.5.4–5; 2.6.11–15; 7.2.1–6; cp. Eusebius, SC 13.16; Athanasius C. Gentes 3–11 (especially 9). See, König-Ockenfels, 'Christliche Deutung der Weltgeschichte bei Eusebs von Cäsarea', 354–8.

[2] See, Droge, Homer or Moses, 168–93; R. Grant, 'Civilization as a Preparation for Christianity in the Thought of Eusebius', 62–70; Chesnut, The First Christian Histories, 66–95; Kofsky, Eusebius of Caesarea Against the Pagans, 135–6 (despite the fact that Kofsky earlier had described a theory of decline in the PE); and W. Kinzig, Novitas Christiana Die Idee des Fortschritts in der Alten kirche bis Eusebius (Gottingen: Vandenhoeck & Ruprecht, 1994), 517–53.

[3] Chesnut, The First Christian Histories, 66, 93.

[4] HE 1.2.18–19.

[5] HE 1.2.23.

of various kinds, plagues and wars.[6] This manner of divine discipline seems to have failed, however, as humanity sunk further into immorality and impiety, 'like a deep fit of drunkenness'.[7] This historical stage, marked by decline in religion and morals, troubles any attempt to see this as a straightforward account of progress. Furthermore, the state of wickedness to which human life had sunk only began to be remedied when the divine Word, induced by philanthropy, began to offer manifestations of himself to members of the Hebrew nation.[8] Significantly, the transformation to peace and orderliness among all peoples occurred only as a result of the spread of the Hebrew teachings and legislation.[9] Any account of Eusebius' theory of progress must be nuanced by these two features: the initial decline among other nations, and the progress of the early Hebrews as a result of theophanic encounters. Historical progress was a nation-specific affair.

A similarly nuanced reading is required in the case of a comparable passage at *Demonstratio* 8.praef.5–12. Early humans are again portrayed as having lived a beastly existence, without cities, constitutions or laws. Here, Eusebius adds that innate conceptions of the existence of God only became muddled as to the nature of that God, unable to transcend the limits of the visible world. Hence, these primitive humans deified other humans and animals.[10] Divine Justice chastised their immorality with disasters and wars.[11] To only a few holy men did Justice (to be equated, of course, with the Word of the *HE*) reveal herself in oracles and theophanies. The legislation and teachings of these ancient Hebrews eventually spread throughout the other nations, pacifying them and bringing about the establishment of laws and constitutions.[12] Then the Incarnation, the fullest theophany, took place. As with the passage from the *HE*, progress made its advance along national trajectories. The other nations' decline was arrested and progress achieved only in connection with the Hebrews.

Hence, any apparent contradiction between the themes of historical decline (as in the *Praeparatio*) and progress (as in the *HE* and *Demonstratio*) in the works of Eusebius is alleviated, at least to some degree, by attending to the declarations of decline within his supposed narratives of progress and by focusing more closely on the national dimensions of progress.[13] Decline and progress are not monolithic historical forces for Eusebius; rather, they exist simultaneously in human history emerging distinctly only within the fabric of particular nations' historical narratives.

An important discussion from a later work, the *Theophania*, which some have supposed to be merely a summation of his earlier arguments in both the

---

[6] *HE* 1.2.20.   [7] *HE* 1.2.21.   [8] *HE* 1.2.21–22.
[9] *HE* 1.2.23.   [10] *DE* 8.praef. [364ab].   [11] *DE* 8.praef. [364cd].
[12] *DE* 8.praef. [364d–365a].

[13] Though he emphasizes progress, Farina has argued that Eusebius' claims to decline and to progress are not contradictory; see *L'Impero e l'imperatore cristiano in Eusebio di Cesarea*, 77–8.

Demonstratio and *Praeparatio*,[14] remarkably exhibits the two opposing themes side by side. In the second book of the *Theophania*, Eusebius describes the decline from the worship of astral phenomena to the fruits of the earth, the rational faculties, the passions, humans, animals, idols, and finally daemons.[15] The discord of Greek philosophers also plays an important role in this narrative of decline.[16] Then, the narrative shifts dramatically to portray the steady historical advance of moral and spiritual progress as a result of Providence.[17] The life of humanity, Eusebius claims, was brought to a stage of peacefulness, and was prepared to receive the perfect doctrine of God (at the time of the Incarnation).[18] Yet, just as in the earlier cases, what seems to be a narrative of progress is simultaneously marked by decline among the non-Hebrew nations. In fact, elements of decline are more noticeable here than in the *HE* and *Demonstratio*. God is described as giving instruction, through the Word, only to the Hebrews—'men who were worthy';[19] and it was through the Hebrew prophets that the seeds of truth were sown among all peoples.[20] The other nations, in spite of the providential efforts of the Word, remained recalcitrant and unrestrained in their impious behaviour.[21] The Incarnation was necessary, avers Eusebius, since humans could not learn the truth on their own.[22]

As with the earlier narratives of progress, the histories of the other nations are characterized by decline, while progress remains reserved for the Hebrews. The other nations only partake of this progress in so far as they join themselves to the stream of Hebrew history. Eusebius' conception of the direction(s) of national history, while at first appearing contradictory, upon closer reading offers a more complex picture of the risings and fallings of national character, religion, and philosophical thought. The contrast between progress and decline in the writings of Eusebius is a contrast between nations. Because of the Word's manifestations to the Hebrews, they are able to make progress in wisdom and virtue. The other ancient nations, stained by impiety and marked by decline, are able to participate in such moral and intellectual progress only in so far as they are influenced by the Hebrews. This conception of progress and decline is closely aligned with his ethnic argumentation, both in the *Praeparatio* and elsewhere.

---

14 See, e.g. Kofsky, *Eusebius of Caesarea Against Paganism*, 276–82.
15 *Theoph.* 2.1–82.   16 See esp. *Theoph.* 2.47–52.   17 *Theoph.* 2.83–97.
18 *Theoph.* 2.93.   19 *Theoph.* 2.85.   20 *Theoph.* 2.96.
21 *Theoph.* 2.86.   22 *Theoph.* 2.94.

Select Bibliography

Editions

Gaisford, T., *Eclogae Propheticae*, PG 22 (Paris: J. –P. Migne, 1857).

Gressman, H., *Eusebius Werke III. Die Theophanie* (Leipzig: J. C. Hinrichs'sche Buchhandlung, 1904).

Heikel, I. A., *Eusebius Werke VI. Die Demonstratio Evangelica* (Berlin: Akademie-Verlag, 1913).

—— *Eusebius Werke I. Über Das Leben Constantins, Constantins Rede an die heilige Versammlung, Tricennatsrede an Constantin* (Leipzig: J. C. Hinrichs'sche Buchhandlung, 1902).

Helm, Rudolf, ed., *Eusebius Werke VII. Die Chronik des Hieronymus*, 3rd edn. (Berlin: Akademie-Verlag, 1984).

Klostermann, Erich, *Eusebius Werke IV. Gegen Marcell, Über Die Kirchliche Theologie*, GCS 14 (Leipzig: J. C. Hinrichs'sche Buchhandlung, 1906).

Montfaucon, B., *Commentaria in Psalmos*, PG 23 (Paris: J. –P. Migne, 1857).

Mras, K., *Eusebius Werke VIII. Die Praeparatio Evangelica* (Berlin: Akademie-Verlag, 1954, 1956).

Schwartz, E., *Eusebius Werke II. Die Kirchengeschichte* (Leipzig: J. C. Hinrichs'sche Buchhandlung, 1903, 1908).

Ziegler, Joseph, *Eusebius Werke IX. Der Jesajakommentar* (Berlin: Akademie-Verlag, 1975).

Translations*

Cameron, A., and Hall, S. G., *Eusebius. Life of Constantine* (Oxford: Clarendon Press, 1999).

Drake, H. A., *In Praise of Constantine*, University of California Publications: Classical Studies, 15 (Berkeley and Los Angeles: University of California Press, 1975).

Ferrar, W. J. (ed. and trans.), *The Proof of the Gospel* (Grand Rapids: Baker Book House, 1981).

Gifford, E. H., *Preparation for the Gospel*, 2 Vols (Grand Rapids: Baker Book House, 1981).

Lee, Samuel, *Eusebius Bishop of Caesarea on the Theophania* (Cambridge: The University Press, 1843).

McGiffert, A. C., *The Church History of Eusebius*, NPNF 1 (Grand Rapids: Eerdmans Publishing Co., 1952).

* My translations throughout have been adapted from the translations given here.

Secondary Sources

Adler, William, *Time Immemorial: Archaic History and its Sources in Christian Chronography from Julius Africanus to George Syncellus* (Washington, DC: Dumbarton Oaks, 1989).

——, 'Eusebius' *Chronicle* and its Legacy', in Harold W. Attridge and Gohei Hata (eds), *Eusebius, Christianity and Judaism* (Detroit: Wayne State University Press, 1992), 467–91.

Ahrweiler, H., 'Eusebius of Caesarea and the Imperial Christian Idea', in Avner Raban and Kenneth Holum (eds), *Caesarea Maritima: A Retrospective after Two Millenia* (Leiden: E. J. Brill, 1996), 541–6.

Albright, W. F., 'Neglected Factors in the Greek Intellectual Revolution', *Proceedings of the American Philosophical Society* 116 (1972), 225–42.

Anderson, Benedict, *Imagined Communities: Reflections on the Origins and Spread of Nationalism* (London: Verso, 1983).

Ando, Clifford, 'Pagan Apologetics and Christian Intolerance in the Ages of Themistius and Augustine', *JECS* 4 (1996), 171–207.

Arazy, Abraham, *The Appellations of the Jews (Ioudaios, Hebraios, Israel) in the Literature from Alexander to Justinian*, 2 Vols (Ph.D. dissertation New York University, 1977).

Armstrong, A. H., 'The Way and the Ways: Religious Tolerance and Intolerance in the Fourth Century A. D.', *VC* 38 (1984) 1–17.

Armstrong, J. A., *Nations Before Nationalism* (Chapel Hill: University of North Carolina Press, 1981).

Atherton, Patrick, 'The City in Ancient Religious Experience', in A. H. Armstrong (ed.), *Classical Mediterranean Spirituality* (London: Routledge & Kegan Paul, 1986), 314–36.

Attridge, Harold W. and Hata, Gohei (eds), *Eusebius, Christianity and Judaism* (Detroit: Wayne State University Press, 1992).

Balch, D. L., 'Two Apologetic Encomia. Dionysius on Rome and Josephus on the Jews', *Journal for the Study of Judaism in the Persian, Hellenistic and Roman Period*, 13 (1982), 102–22.

Banks, Marcus, *Ethnicity: Anthropological Constructions* (New York: Routledge, 1996).

Barnes, Jonathan, *Porphyry. Introduction* (Oxford: Oxford University Press, 2004).

Barnes, T. D., 'Porphyry *Against the Christians*: Date and the Attribution of Fragments', *JTS* 24 (1973), 424–42.

——, 'Constantine's Good Friday Sermon', *JTS* 27 (1976), 414–23.

——, *Constantine and Eusebius* (Cambridge: Harvard University Press, 1981).

Barr, James, 'Philo of Byblos and his "Phoenician History" ', *Bulletin of the John Rylands Library* 57 (1974–5) 17–68.

Barth, F., 'Introduction', in *Ethnic Groups and Boundaries: The Social Organization of Culture Difference* (Boston: Little, Brown and Co., 1969), 9–38.

Baskin, Judith, *Pharaoh's Counsellors: Job, Jethro and Balaam* (Chico: Scholars Press, 1983).

Baumann, Gerd, *The Multicultural Riddle: Rethinking National, Ethnic, and Religious Identities* (New York: Routledge, 1999).

Baumgarten, A. I., *The Phoenician History of Philo of Byblos* (Leiden: Brill, 1983).

Baynes, Norman H., 'Eusebius and the Christian Empire', *Annuaire de l'institut de philologie et d'histoire orientales* 2 (1933), 13–18; reprinted in idem, *Byzantine Studies and Other Essays* (London: Athlone Press, 1955), 168–72.

Beare, F. W., *The First Epistle of Peter* (Oxford: Blackwell, 1958).

Beggs, M. R., 'From Kingdom to Nation: The Transformation of a Metaphor in Eusebius' *Historia Ecclesiastica*' (Ph.D. dissertation, University of Notre Dame, 1998).

Bellen, Heinz, 'Baylon und Rom–Orosius und Augustinus', in P. Kneissl and V. Losemann (eds), *Imperium Romanum*, Festschrift Karl Christ (Stuttgart: Franz Steiner Verlag, 1998), 51–60.

Benko, Stephen, 'Pagan Criticism of Christianity during the First Two Centuries A. D.', *ANRW* (1980), 23.2.1055–1118.

Bertram, G., 'ἔθνος. People and Peoples in the LXX', in Gerhard Kittel (ed.), G. W. Bromiley (trans.), *TDNT* (Grand Rapids: Eerdmans Publishing Co., 1964), 364–9.

Bickerman, E. J., 'Origenes gentium', *CP* 47 (1952), 65–81.

Bidez, J. and Cumont, F., *Les Mages Hellénisés* (Paris: Société d'Éditions 'Les Belles Lettres', 1938).

Bilde, Per *et al.* (eds), *Ethnicity in Hellenistic Egypt* (Aarhus: Aarhus University Press, 1922).

Billig, M., *Banal Nationalism* (London: Sage, 1995).

Bladel, Kevin van, 'New Light on the Religious Background of Elegabalus, Aramaean Emperor of Rome', American Philological Association 2003 Annual Meeting, unpublished.

Borgen, Peder, 'Philo and the Jews', in Per Bilde *et al.*, (eds), *Ethnicity in Hellenistic Egypt* (Aarhus: Aarhus University Press, 1992), 122–38.

Bounoure, Gilles, 'Eusèbe citateur de Diodore', *REG* 95 (1982), 433–9.

Bowersock, Glen W., *Hellenism in Late Antiquity* (Ann Arbor: University of Michigan Press, 1990).

——, 'Jacoby's Fragments and Two Greek Historians of Pre-Islamic Arabia', in G. Most (ed.), *Collecting Fragments* (Göttingen: Vandenhoeck & Ruprecht, 1997), 173–85.

Bowie, E. L., 'Greeks and their Past in the Second Sophistic', in *Studies in Ancient Society, P&P,* Moses Finley (ed.) (London: Routledge, 1974), 166–209.

——, 'Hellenes and Hellenism in Writers of the Early Second Sophistic', in S. Said (ed.), *ΕΛΛΗΝΙΣΜΟΣ. Quelques jalons pour une histoire de l'identité Grecque* (Leiden: Brill, 1991), 183–204.

Boys-Stones, G. R., *Post-Hellenistic Philosophy* (Oxford: Oxford University Press, 2001).

Bradbury, S., 'Julian's Pagan Revival and the Decline of Blood Sacrifice', *Phoenix* 49 (1995), 331–56.

Brock, Sebastian, 'Eusebius and Syriac Christianity', in Attridge and Hata (eds), *Eusebius, Christianity and Judaism*, 212–34.

Brown, Truesdell, 'Euhemerus and the Historians', *HTR* 39 (1946), 259–74.

Brubaker, Rogers, 'Civic and Ethnic Nations in France and Germany', in J. Hutchinson and A. D. Smith (eds), *Ethnicity* (Oxford: Oxford University Press, 1996), 168–73.

Bruce, F. F., 'The Romans through Jewish Eyes', in *Paganisme, Judaïsme, Christianisme*, Mélanges offerts à Marcel Simon (Paris: Éditions E. de Boccard, 1978), 2–12.

Bruns, J. Edgar, 'The Agreement of Moses and Jesus in the *Demonstratio Evangelica* of Eusebius', *VC* 31 (1977), 117–25.

Buell, Denise Kimber, *Making Christians: Clement of Alexandria and the Rhetoric of Legitimacy* (Princeton: Princeton University Press, 1999).

——, 'Ethnicity and Religion in Mediterranean Antiquity and Beyond', *Religious Studies Review* 26 (2000), 243–9.

——, 'Rethinking the Relevance of Race for Early Christian Self-Definition', *HTR* 94 (2001), 449–76.

——, 'Race and Universalism in Early Christianity', *JECS* 10 (2002), 429–68.

——, *Why This New Race: Ethnic Reasoning in Early Christianity* (New York: Columbia University Press, 2005).

Byron, Gay, *Symbolic Blackness and Ethnic Difference in Early Christian Literature* (New York: Routledge, 2002).

Cameron, Averil, 'Eusebius of Caesarea and the Rethinking of History', in E. Gabba (ed.), *Tria Corda: Scritti in onore di Arnaldo Momigliano* (Como: Edizioni New Press, 1983), 71–88.

——, *Christianity and the Rhetoric of Empire* (Berkeley and Los Angeles: University of California Press, 1991).

——, 'Apologetics in the Roman Empire—A Genre of Intolerance?': '*Humana Sapit:*' *Études d'Antiquité tardive offertes à Lellia Cracco Ruggini. L'Antiquité Tardive* 3 (2002), 219–27.

—— and Stuart G. Hall, *Eusebius. Life of Constantine* (Oxford: Clarendon Press, 1999).

Canivet, Pierre and Leroy-Molinghen, Alice, *Théodoret de Cyr. Histoire des moines de Syrie*, SC 234 and 257 (Paris: Les Éditions du Cerf, 1977, 1979).

Carriker, A. J., 'Some Uses of Aristocles and Numenius in Eusebius' *Praeparatio Evangelica*', *JTS* 47 (1996), 543–9.

——, *The Library of Eusebius of Caesarea* (Leiden: Brill, 2003).

Castritius, Helmut, *Studien zu Maximinus Daia*, Frankfurter althistorische Studien, 2 (Kallmunz: Michael Lassleben, 1969).

Certeau, M. de, *The Practice of Everyday Life* (Berkeley: University of California Press, 1988).

Chadwick, Henry, 'The Relativity of Moral Codes: Rome and Persia in Late Antiquity', in W. R. Schoedel and R. L. Wilken (eds), *Early Christian Literature and the Classical Intellectual Tradition*, in honorem R. M. Grant (Paris: Beauchesne, 1979), 135–53.

Chatterjee, P., *The Nation and its Fragments* (Princeton: Princeton University Press, 1993).

Chesnut, Glenn, 'The Ruler and the Logos in Neo-pythagorean, Middle Platonic, and Late Stoic Political Philosophy', *ANRW* 2.16.2 (1978), 1310–32.

—— , *The First Christian Histories: Eusebius, Socrates, Sozomen, Theodoret, and Evagrius* (Macon: Mercer University Press, 1986).

Christensen, Torben, 'The So-Called Edict of Milan', *C&M* 35 (1984), 129–76.

Chroust, Anton-Hermann, 'Charges of Philosophical Plagiarism in Greek Antiquity', *The Modern Schoolman* 38 (1961), 219–37.

Coggan, Sharon Lynn, 'Pandaemonia: A Study of Eusebius' Recasting of Plutarch's Story of the "Death of Great Pan"', (Ph.D. dissertation Syracuse University, 1992).

Cohen, Edward, *The Athenian Nation* (Princeton: Princeton University Press, 2000).

Cohen, Shaye, 'Religion, Ethnicity and Hellenism in the Emergence of Jewish Identity in Maccabean Palestine', in *Religion and Religious Practice in the Seleucid Kingdom*, Per Bilde *et al.* (eds), (Aarhus: Aarhus University Press, 1990), 204–23.

—— , '*Ioudaios to genos* and Related Expressions in Josephus', in *Josephus and the History of the Greco-Roman Period: Essays in Memory of Morton Smith*, Fausto Parente and Joseph Sievers (eds), (Leiden: E. J. Brill, 1994), 23–38.

—— , *The Beginnings of Jewishness: Boundaries, Varieties, Uncertainties* (Berkeley and Los Angeles: University of California Press, 1999).

Collins, John J., *Between Athens and Jerusalem: Jewish Identity in the Hellenistic Diaspora* (New York: Crossroads, 1983).

Coman, J., 'Utilisation des Stromates de Clément d'Alexandrie par Eusèbe de Césarée dans la Préparation Evangélique', in *Uberlieferungsgeschichtliche Untersuchungen* (=*TU* 125; 1981), 115–34.

Connor, Walker, 'A Nation Is a Nation, Is a State, Is an Ethnic Group, Is a . . .', *Ethnic and Racial Studies* 1 (1978), 377–400.

Cornford, F. M., *Thucydides Mythistoricus* (Philadelphia: University of Pennsylvania Press, 1971).

Cox Miller, Patricia, 'Strategies of Representation in Collective Biography: Constructing the Subject as Holy', in T. Hägg and P. Rousseau (eds), *Greek Biography and Panegyric in Late Antiquity* (Berkeley and Los Angeles: University of California Press, 2000), 209–54.

——, 'Visceral Seeing: The Holy Body in Late Ancient Christianity', *JECS* 12 (2004), 391–411.

Cranz, F. E., 'Kingdom and Polity in Eusebius of Caesarea', *HTR* 45 (1952), 47–66.

Cumont, F., 'Les anges du paganisme', *Revue de l'histoire des religions* 72 (1915), 159–82.

Daly, L. J., 'Themistius' Plea for Religious Toleration', *GRBS* 12 (1971), 65–79.

——, 'The Mandarin and the Barbarian: The Response of Themistius to the Gothic Challenge', *Historia* 21 (1972), 351–79.

——, 'Themistius' Concept of *Philanthropia*', *Byzantion* 45 (1975), 22–40.

Danielou, J., 'Les sources juives de la doctrine des anges des nations chez Origène', *Recherches de science religieuse* 38 (1951), 132–7.

Davis, Kathleen, 'National Writing in the Ninth Century: A Reminder for Postcolonial Thinking about the Nation', *Journal of Medieval and Early Modern Studies* 28 (1998), 611–37.

Dawisha, Adeed, 'Nation and Nationalism: Historical Antecedents to Contemporary Debates', *International Studies Review* 4 (2002), 3–22.

Decharme, P., 'Note sur un fragment des "Daedala" de Plutarque', in *Mélanges Henri Weil: Recueil de mémoires concernant l'histoire et la littérature grecques dédié à Henri Weil* (Paris: Thorin, 1898), 111–17.

De Jonge, Marianus, 'Josephus und die Zukunftserwartungen seines Volkes', in O. Betz, K. Haacker, and M. Hengel (eds), *Josephus-Studien: Untersuchungen zu Josephus, dem antiken Judentum und dem Neuen Testament* (Göttingen: Vandenhoeck & Ruprecht, 1974), 205–19.

Dempf, Alois, *Der Platonismus des Eusebius, Victorinus, und Pseudo-Dionysius*. Sitzungsberichte der Bayerische Akademie der Wissenschaften, phil.-hist. Klasse 3 (Munich: Beck, 1962).

Denzey, Nicola, 'The Limits of Ethnic Categories', in A. Blasi, J. Duhaime and P.-A. Turcotte (eds), *Handbook of Early Christianity* (New York: Altamira Press, 2002), 489–507.

De Romilly, Jacqueline, *The Rise and Fall of States According to Greek Authors* (Ann Arbor: University of Michigan Press, 1977).

Des Places, Edouard, 'Eusèbe de Césarée juge de Platon dans la *Préparation Évangélique*', in *Mélanges de philosophie grecque offerts à Mgr. Dies* (Paris: Libraire Philosophique J. Vrin, 1956), 69–77.

——, *Numenius. Fragments* (Paris: Société d'Édition 'Les Belles Lettres', 1973).

——, 'Numenius et Eusèbe de Césarée', *SP* 13 (1975), 19–28, reprinted in *Études Platoniciennes. 1929–1979* (Leiden: Brill, 1981), 316–25.

Digeser, E. D., 'Lactantius, Porphyry, and the Debate over Religious Toleration', *JRS* 88 (1998), 129–46.

Dillon, John, 'Philosophy as a Profession in Late Antiquity', in S. Swain and M. Edwards (eds), *Approaching Late Antiquity* (Oxford: Oxford University Press, 2004), 401–18.

Doergens, Heinrich, 'Eusebius von Cäsarea als Darsteller der phönizischen Religion', *Forschungen zur christlicher Literatur- und Dogmengeschichte* [Paderborn] 12.5 (1915), 1–103.

——, 'Eusebius von Cäsarea als Darsteller der griechische Religion', *Forschungen zur christlicher Literatur- und Dogmengeschichte* [Paderborn] 14.3 (1922), 1–133.

Dörrie, Heinrich, 'Platons Reisen zu fernen Völkern: Zur Geschichte eines Motivs der Platon-Legende und zu seiner Neuwendung durch Lactanz', in W. Den Boer *et al.* (eds), *Romanitas et Christianitas* (Amsterdam: North-Holland, 1973), 99–118.

Downey, Glanville, 'Philanthropia in Religion and Statecraft in the Fourth Century after Christ', *Historia* 4 (1955), 199–208.

Drake, H. A., *In Praise of Constantine: A Historical Study and New Translation of Eusebius Tricennial Orations*, University of California Publications: Classical Studies 15 (Berkeley and Los Angeles: University of California Press, 1975).

——, *Constantine and the Bishops. The Politics of Intolerance* (Baltimore: Johns Hopkins University Press, 2000).

——, 'Constantinian Echoes in Themistius', *SP* 34 (2001), 44–50.

Droge, Arthur, *Homer or Moses? Early Christian Interpretations of the History of Culture*, Hermeneutische Untersuchungen zur Theologie 26 (Tübingen: Mohr [Siebeck], 1989).

——, 'The Apologetic Dimensions of the *Ecclesiastical History*', in Attridge and Hata (eds), *Eusebius, Christianity and Judaism*, 492–509.

——, 'Josephus Between Greeks and Barbarians', in L. H. Feldman and J. R. Levison (eds), *Josephus' Contra Apionem* (Leiden: Brill, 1996), 115–42.

Drucker, Johanna, *The Alphabetic Labyrinth* (London: Thames and Hudson, 1995).

Duara, Praesenjit, 'Historicizing National Identity, or Who Imagines What and When', in Geoff Eley and Ronald G. Suny (eds), *Becoming National* (Oxford: Oxford University Press, 1996), 151–77.

Durkheim, Emile, *The Elementary Forms of Religious Life* (New York: Free Press, 1965).

Dusanic, Slobodan, 'Plato and Plutarch's Fictional Techniques: The Death of the Great Pan', *RM* 139 (1996), 276–94.

Dvornik, Francis, *Early Christian and Byzantine Political Theology*, Vol. 2 (Washington DC: Dumbarton Oaks Center for Byzantine Studies, 1966).

Dyson, Stephen, 'Native Revolts in the Roman Empire', *Historia* 20 (1971), 239–74.

Eddy, Samuel K., *The King is Dead: Studies in Near Eastern Resistance to Hellenism* (Lincoln: University of Nebraska Press, 1961).

Edwards, Mark J., 'Philo or Sanchuniathon? A Phoenician Cosmogony', *CQ* 41 (1991), 213–20.

——, 'Pagan and Christian Monotheism in the Age of Constantine', in S. Swain and M. Edwards, *Approaching Late Antiquity* (Oxford: Oxford University Press, 2004), 211–34.

——, M. Goodman and S. Price (eds), *Apologetics in the Roman Empire* (Oxford: Oxford University Press, 1999).

Eissfeldt, Otto, *Taautos und Sanchunjaton. Sitzungsberichte der deutschen Akademie der Wissenschaften zu Berlin*, Klasse fur Sprachen, Literatur und Kunst, 1 (Berlin, 1952).

——, 'Art und Aufbau der phonizischen Geschichte des Philo von Byblos', *Syria* 33 (1956), 88–96; reprinted in *Kleine Schriften* 3 (Tübingen: Mohr [Siebeck], 1966), 398–406.

Elliott, John Hall, *The Elect and the Holy* (Leiden: Brill, 1966).

Farina, Raffaele, *L'Impero e l'imperatore cristiano in Eusebio di Cesarea* (Zurich: Pas Verlag, 1966).

Fears, J. Rufus, 'Optimus princeps—Salus generis humani: The Origins of Christian Political Theology', in E. Chrysos (ed.), *Studien zur Geschichte der Römischen Spätantike* (Athens: A. A. Fourlas—S. D. Basilopoulos Co., 1989), 88–105.

Feldman, Louis H. and Levison, John R. (eds), *Josephus' Contra Apionem* (Leiden: Brill, 1996).

Ferguson, E., 'Spiritual Sacrifice in Early Christianity and its Environment', *ANRW* (1980), 23.2.1151–1189.

Ferrar, W. J. (trans.), *The Proof of the Gospel* (Grand Rapids: Baker Book House, 1981).

Finley, Moses, *The Use and Abuse of Ancient History* (London: Hogarth Press, 1986).

Fischer, Ulrich, *Eschatologie und Jenseitserwartung im hellenistischen Diasporajudentum* (Berlin and New York: Walter de Gruyter, 1978).

Florovsky, George, 'Origen, Eusebius, and the Iconoclastic Controversy', *CH* 19 (1950), 77–96.

Foakes-Jackson, F. J., *Eusebius Pamphili, Bishop of Caesarea in Palestine and First Christian Historian: A Study of the Man and His Writings* (Cambridge: Heffers, 1933).

Francis, James, 'Living Icons: Tracing a Motif in Verbal and Visual Representation from the Second to Fourth Centuries C.E.', *AJP* 124 (2003), 575–600.

Frede, Michael, 'Celsus' Attack on the Christians', in J. Barnes and M. Griffin (eds), *Philosophia Togata II* (Oxford: Oxford University Press, 1997), 218–40.

——, 'Origen's Treatise *Against Celsus*', in M. J. Edwards, M. Goodman and S. Price (eds), *Apologetics in the Roman Empire* (Oxford: Oxford University Press, 1999), 131–56.

——, 'Eusebius' Apologetic Writings', in Edwards *et al.*, *Apologetics in the Roman Empire* 223–50.

Freudenthal, J., *Alexander Polyhistor und die von ihm erhaltenen Reste jüdischer und samaritanischer Geschichtswerke*, Hellenistische Studien I, II (Breslau: Skutsch, 1875).

Fritze, Ernst, *Beiträge zur sprachlich-stilistischen Würdigung des Eusebios* (Borna-Leipzig: Robert Noske, 1910).

Gagarin, Michael, *Antiphon the Athenian* (Austin: University of Texas Press, 2002).

Gager, J., *Moses in Greco-Roman Paganism* (Nashville: Abingdon Press, 1972).

Gallagher, Eugene, 'Piety and Polity: Eusebius' Defense of the Gospel', in Neusner *et al. Religious Writings and Religious Systems*, 2.139–55.

——, 'Eusebius the Apologist: The Evidence of the *Preparation* and the *Proof*', *SP* 26 (1993), 251–60.

Geffcken, Johannes, *The Last Days of Greco-Roman Paganism*, trans. S. MacCormack (Amsterdam: North-Holland Publishing Co., 1978).

Gellner, Ernst, *Nations and Nationalism* (Oxford: Blackwell, 1983).

George, J and Johnson, S. (eds), *Greek Literature in Late Antiquity* (Aldershot: Ashgate, forthcoming).

Gero, Stephen, 'The True Image of Christ: Eusebius' Letter to Constantia Reconsidered', *JTS* 32 (1981), 460–70.

Gifford, E. H. (trans.), *Preparation for the Gospel*, 2 Vols, (Grand Rapids: Baker Book House, 1981).

Goehring, James E., 'The Origins of Monasticism', in Attridge and Hata (eds), *Eusebius, Christianity and Judaism*, 235–55.

Goldhill, Simon (ed.), *Being Greek Under Rome: Culture, Identity, the Second Sophistic and the Development of Empire* (Cambridge: Cambridge University Press, 2001).

Goodenough, E. R., 'The Political Philosophy of Hellenistic Kingship', *YCS* 1 (1928), 55–102.

Goodman, Martin, 'Josephus' Treatise *Against Apion*', in Edwards, *et al.* (eds), *Apologetics in the Roman Empire* 45–58.

Gorman, Peter, 'Pythagoras Palaestinus', *Philologus* 127 (1983), 30–42.

Goudriaan, Koen, *Ethnicity in Ptolemaic Egypt* (Amsterdam: J. C. Gieben, 1988).

——, 'Ethnical Strategies in Graeco-Roman Egypt', in Per Bilde, *et al.* (eds), *Ethnicity in Hellenistic Egypt*, 74–99.

Grant, R. M., 'The Religion of Maximin Daia', in J. Neusner (ed.), *Christianity, Judaism and Other Greco-Roman Cults* (Leiden: Brill, 1975), 4.143–166.

——, 'Civilization as a Preparation for Christianity in the Thought of Eusebius', in F. F. Church and T. George (eds), *Continuity and Discontinuity in Church History: Essays Presented to G. H. Williams* (Leiden: Brill, 1979), 62–70.

——, *Eusebius as Church Historian* (Oxford: Clarendon Press, 1980).

Gruen, Erich S., 'Jewish Perspectives on Greek Culture and Ethnicity', in Irad Malkin (ed.), *Ancient Perceptions of Greek Ethnicity* (Cambridge: Harvard University Press, 2001), 347–74.

Gudeman, A., 'Herennius Philon von Byblos', *RE* 8 (Stuttgart: J. B. Metzlersche Buchhandlung, 1913), cols. 650–61.

Guthrie, W. K. C., *In the Beginning* (London: Methuen & Co. Ltd., 1957).

Guyot, Peter, 'Antinous als Eunuch: Zur christlichen Polemik gegen das Heidentum', *Historia* 30 (1981), 250–4.

Hadas, M., 'Nationalist Survival under Hellenistic and Roman Imperialism', *Journal for the History of Ideas* 11 (1950), 131–40.

Hägg, T., 'Hierocles the Lover of Truth and Eusebius the Sophist', *SO* 67 (1992), 138–50.

Hall, Jonathan, *Ethnic Identity in Greek Antiquity* (Cambridge: Cambridge University Press, 1997).

——, 'Discourse and Praxis: Ethnicity and Culture in Ancient Greece', *Cambridge Archaeological Journal* 8 (1998), 266–9.

——, *Hellenicity: Between Ethnicity and Culture* (Chicago: University of Chicago Press, 2002).

Hall, Stuart, 'Race: The Floating Signifier', videorecording (Northampton, MA: Media Education Foundation, 1996).

Hardie, P., 'Plutarch and the Interpretation of Myth', *ANRW* II.33.6 (1992), 4743–87.

Hardwick, Michael, *Josephus as an Historical Source in Patristic Literature Through Eusebius* (Atlanta: Scholar's Press, 1989).

——, '*Contra Apionem* and Christian Apologetics', in Feldman and Levison (eds), *Josephus' Contra Apionem*, 369–402.

Harl, K. W., 'Sacrifice and Pagan Belief in Fifth- and Sixth-Century Byzantium', *P&P* 128 (1990), 7–27.

Harnack, Adolf von, *Porphyrios, 'Gegen die Christen', 15 Bucher: Zeugnisse, Fragmente und Referate. Abhandlungen der koniglichen preussischen Akademie der Wissenschaften*, Philosophisch-historische Klasse, Nr. 1 (Berlin, 1916).

——, 'The Tidings of the New People and of the Third Race', in idem, *The Mission and Expansion of Christianity in the First Three Centuries*, trans. J. Moffat (New York: Harper and Bros., 1962), 240–78.

Harrison, V. E. F., 'Word as Icon in Greek Patristic Theology', *Sobornost* 10 (1988), 38–49.

Harvey, Graham, *The True Israel: Uses of the Names Jew, Hebrew and Israel in Ancient Jewish and Early Christian Literature* (Leiden: Brill, 1996).

Hastings, Adrian, *The Construction of Nationhood: Ethnicity, Religion and Nationalism* (Cambridge: Cambridge University Press, 1997).

Heather, Peter and Moncur, David, *Politics, Philosophy, and Empire in the Fourth Century. Select Orations of Themistius* (Liverpool: Liverpool University Press, 2001).

Hengel, Martin, *Judaism and Hellenism*, 2 Vols (Philadelphia: Fortress Press, 1974).

Henrichs, Albert, 'Pagan Ritual and the Alleged Crime of the Early Christians: A Reconsideration', in P. Granfield and J. Jungmann (eds), *Kyriakon*, Festschrift Johannes Quasten (Münster: Verlag Aschendorff, 1970), 1.18–35.

Hobsbawm, Eric, *Nations and Nationalism since 1780: Programme, Myth, Reality* (Cambridge: Cambridge University Press, 1990).

Hollerich, Michael, 'Religion and Politics in the Writings of Eusebius: Reassessing the First "Court Theologian" ', *CH* 59 (1990), 309–25.

—— , *Eusebius of Caesarea's Commentary on Isaiah* (Oxford: Clarendon Press, 1999).

—— , 'Hebrews, Jews, and Christians: Eusebius of Caesarea on the Biblical Basis of the Two States of the Christian Life', in P. M. Blowers *et al.* (eds), *In Dominico Eloquio (In Lordly Eloquence)*, Essays on Patristic Exegesis in honor of Robert Louis Wilken (Grand Rapids: Eerdmans Publishing Co., 2002), 172–84.

Hughes, Dennis D., *Human Sacrifice in Ancient Greece* (London and New York: Routledge, 1991).

Inglebert, Hervé, *Les Romains Chrétiens face à l'Histoire de Rome* (Paris: Institut d'Études Augustiniennes, 1996).

Isaac, Benjamin, 'Ethnic Groups in Judaea Under Roman Rule', in idem, *The Near East Under Roman Rule* (Leiden: E. J. Brill, 1998), 257–67.

—— , *The Invention of Racism in Classical Antiquity* (Princeton: Princeton University Press, 2004).

Jacobs, Andrew S., ' "Let Him Guard *Pietas*": Early Christian Exegesis and the Ascetic Family', *JECS* 11 (2003), 265–81.

—— and Krawiec, R., 'Fathers Know Best? Christian Families in the Age of Asceticism', *JECS* 11 (2003), 257–63.

—— , *The Remains of the Jews: The Holy Land and Christian Empire in Late Antiquity* (Stanford: Stanford University Press, 2004).

Jacobsen, J. P., *Les Mânes* (Paris: 1924).

Jacoby, Felix, 'Euemeros', *RE* 6 (Stuttgart: J. B. Metzlersche Buchhandlung, 1904), cols. 952–72.

—— , *Die Fragmente der Griechischen Historiker* (Leiden: Brill, 1958).

Jaeger, Werner, 'Greeks and Jews: The First Records of Jewish Religion and Civilization', *Journal of Religion* 18 (1938), 127–43.

Johnson, Aaron P., Review of G. R. Boys-Stones, *Post-Hellenistic Philosophy* (Oxford: Oxford University Press, 2001), *CJ* 99 (2004), 362–5.

—— , 'Identity, Descent and Polemic: Ethnic Argumentation in Eusebius' *Praeparatio Evangelica*', *JECS* 12 (2004), 23–56.

—— , 'Ancestors as Icons: The Lives of Hebrew Saints in Eusebius' *Praeparatio Evangelica*', *GRBS* 44 (2004), 245–64.

—— , 'Philonic Allusions in Eusebius, *PE* 7.7–8', *CQ* 56 (2006, forthcoming).

—— , Review of A. Kofsky, *Eusebius of Caesarea Against the Pagans* (Leiden: Brill, 2000), *VC* 59 (2006, forthcoming).

—— , 'Eusebius' *Praeparatio Evangelica* as Literary Experiment', in S. Johnson (ed.), *Greek Literature in Late Antiquity: Dynamism, Didacticism, Classicism* (Aldershot: Ashgate, 2006, forthcoming).

Jones, C. P., '$\check{\epsilon}\theta\nu o\varsigma$ and $\gamma\acute{\epsilon}\nu o\varsigma$ in Herodotus', *CQ* 46 (1996), 315–20.

—— , 'The Panhellenion', *Chiron* 26 (1996), 29–56.

Just, Robert, 'The History of Ethnicity', *Cambridge Archaeological Journal* 8 (1998), 277–9.

Kalligas, P. 'Traces of Longinus' Library in Eusebius' Praeparatio Evangelica' *CQ* 51 (2001), 584–98.

Kamtekar, Rachana, 'Distinction Without a Difference? Race and *Genos* in Plato', in J. Ward and T. Lott (eds), *Philosophers on Race* (Oxford: Blackwell, 2002), 1–13.

Kapelrud, Arvid, *The Ras Shamra Discoveries and the Old Testament* (Norman: University of Oklahoma Press, 1963).

Kasher, Aryeh, *The Jews in Hellenistic and Roman Egypt: The Struggle for Equal Rights*, Texte und Studien zum Antiken Judentum 7 (Tübingen: Mohr [Siebeck], 1985).

Kee, Howard Clark, 'From Jesus Movement toward Institutional Church', in R. Hefner (ed.), *Conversion to Christianity: Historical and Anthropological Perspectives on a Great Transformation* (Berkeley and Los Angeles: University of California Press, 1993), 47–64.

—— , *Who Are the People of God? Early Christian Models of Community* (New Haven and London: Yale University Press, 1995).

Kelly, J. N. D., Jerome: *His Life, Writings and Controversies* (London: Duckworth, 1975).

Kinzig, Wolfram, *Novitas Christiana. Die Idee des Fortschritts in der Alten Kirche bis Eusebius* (Göttingen: Vandenhoeck & Ruprecht, 1994).

Kofsky, Aryeh, 'Eusebius of Caesarea and the Christian-Jewish Polemic', in *Contra Iudaeos. Ancient and Medieval Polemics between Christians and Jews*, O. Limor and G. Stroumsa (eds), (Tübingen: Mohr [Siebeck], 1996), 59–83.

—— , *Eusebius of Caesarea Against the Pagans* (Leiden: Brill, 2000).

König-Ockenfels, D., 'Christliche Deutung der Weltgeschichte bei Eusebs von Cäsarea', *Saeculum* 27 (1976), 348–65.

Konstan, David, 'Defining Ancient Greek Ethnicity', *Diaspora* 6 (1997), 97–110.

Krawiec, Rebecca, ' "From the Womb of the Church": Monastic Families', *JECS* 11 (2003), 283–307.

Krueger, Derek, 'Typological Figuration in Theodoret of Cyrrhus's *Religious History* and the Art of Postbiblical Narrative', *JECS* 5 (1997), 393–419.

Lamberton, R., *Homer the Theologian: Neoplatonist Allegorical Reading and the Growth of the Epic Tradition* (Berkeley and Los Angeles: University of California Press, 1986).

Laurin, J. –R., *Orientations maitresses des apologistes chrétiens de 270 à 361*, Analecta Gregoriana 61 (Rome: Pontificia Universita Gregoriana, 1954).

Lenski, Noel, *Failure of Empire: Valens and the Roman State in the Fourth Century A.D.* (Berkeley: University of California Press, 2002).

Lee, A. D., 'Close-Kin Marriage in Late Antique Mesopotomia', *GRBS* 29 (1988), 403–14.

Levin, Saul, 'The Old Greek Oracles in Decline', *ANRW* 2.18.2 (1989), 1599–1649.

Levinson, Joshua, 'Bodies and Bo(a)rders: Emerging Fictions of Identity in Late Antiquity', *HTR* 93 (2000), 343–72.

Lewy, Hans, *Chaldaean Oracles and Theurgy* (Paris: Études Augustiniennes, 1978).

Liebert, G., 'Die "theologia tripertita" in Forschung und Bezeugung', *ANRW* I.4 (1973), 63–115.

Lieu, J. M., 'The Forging of Christian Identity', *Mediterranean Archaeology* 11 (1998), 71–82.

—— , 'The New Testament and Early Christian Identity', in eadem, *Neither Jew Nor Greek? Constructing Early Christianity* (New York: T&T Clark, 2002), 191–209.

—— , 'Martyrdom and the Beginning of "Christian" Identity', in eadem, *Neither Jew Nor Greek? Constructing Early Christianity* (New York: T&T Clark, 2002), 211–231.

—— , *Christian Identity in the Jewish and Graeco-Roman World* (Oxford: Oxford University Press, 2004).

Lightfoot, J. B., 'Eusebius of Caesarea', in W. Smith and H. Wace (eds), *A Dictionary of Christian Biography* (New York: AMS Press, 1967) 2.308–48.

Lim, Richard, ' "By Word or By Deed?", Two Modes of Religious Persuasion in Late Antiquity', in M. Dillon (ed.), *Religion in the Ancient World* (Amsterdam: Hakkert, 1996), 257–69.

Limor, O. and Stroumsa, G. (eds), *Contra Iudaeos. Ancient and Medieval Polemics between Christians and Jews* (Tübingen: Mohr [Siebeck], 1996).

Lintott, Andrew, *Imperium Romanum* (New York: Routledge, 1993).

Louth, A. 'The Date of Eusebius' Historia Ecclesiastica', *JTS* 41 (1990), 111–123.

Luderitz, Gert, 'What is the Politeuma?', in Jan W. Van Henten and Pieter W. Van der Horst (eds), *Studies in Early Jewish Epigraphy* (Leiden: Brill, 1994), 183–225.

Luibheid, Colm, *Eusebius of Caesarea and the Arian Crisis* (Dublin: Irish Academic Press, 1978).

Lyman, J. Rebecca, *Christology and Cosmology: Models of Divine Activity in Origen, Eusebius and Athanasius* (Oxford: Clarendon Press, 1993).

Maas, Michael, '*Mores et Moenia*: Ethnography and the Decline in Urban Constitutional Autonomy in Late Antiquity', in W. Pohl and M. Diesenberger (eds), *Integration und Herrschaft: Ethnische Identitäten und soziale Organisation im Frühmittelalter* (Vienna: Verlag der Österreichischen Akademie der Wissenschaften, 2002), 25–35.

—— , ' "Delivered from their Ancient Customs": Christianity and the Question of Cultural Change in Early Byzantine Ethnography', in K. Mills and A. Grafton (eds), *Conversion in Late Antiquity and the Early Middle Ages* (Rochester: University of Rochester Press, 2003), 152–88.

MacMullen, Ramsay, 'Tertullian and "National" Gods', *JTS* 26 (1975), 405–10.

Maier, J., *Jüdische Auseinandersetzung mit dem Christentum in der Antike* (Darmstadt: Wissenschaftliche Buchgesellschaft, 1982).

Malingrey, Anne-Marie, 'Le Personnage de Socrate chez Quelques Auteurs Chrétiens du IVe Siècle', in *Forma Futuri. Studi in Onore del Cardinale Michele Pellegrino* (Turin: Bottega d'Erasmo, 1975), 159–78.

Malkin, Irad, 'Introduction', in idem (ed.), *Ancient Perceptions of Greek Ethnicity* (Cambridge: Harvard University Press, 2001), 1–28.

Mann, Michael, 'Nation-states in Europe and other Continents: Diversifying, Developing, not Dying', *Daedalus* 122 (1993), 115–40.

Markus, R. A., 'The Roman Empire in Early Christian Historiography', *Downside Review* 81 (1963), 340–53.

Martin, Dale, *Inventing Superstition* (Cambridge: Harvard University Press, 2004).

Mason, Hugh J., *Greek Terms for Roman Institutions*, American Studies in Papyrology 13 (Toronto: Hakkert, 1974).

Mendels, Doron, *The Rise and Fall of Jewish Nationalism* (Grand Rapids: Eerdmans Publishing Co., 1997).

——, *Identity, Religion, Historiography* (Sheffield: Sheffield Academic Press, 1998).

——, *The Media Revolution of Early Christianity: An Essay on Eusebius' Ecclesiastical History* (Grand Rapids: Eerdmans Publishing Co., 1999).

Millar, Fergus, 'Paul of Samosata, Zenobia and Aurelian: The Church, Local Culture and Political Allegiance in Third-Century Syria', *JRS* 61 (1971), 1–17.

——, *The Roman Near East. 31 BC–AD 337* (Cambridge: Harvard University Press, 1993).

Mitchell, Stephen, 'Ethnicity, acculturation and empire in Roman and late Roman Asia Minor', in Stephen Mitchell and Geoffrey Greatrex (eds), *Ethnicity and Culture in Late Antiquity* (London: Duckworth, 2000), 117–50.

Moerman, M., 'Ethnic Identification in a Complex Civilization: Who are the Lue?' *American Anthropologist* 67 (1965), 1215–30.

Momigliano, Arnaldo, 'Pagan and Christian Historiography in the Fourth Century', in idem (ed.), *The Conflict Between Paganism and Christianity in the Fourth Century*, (Oxford: Clarendon Press, 1963), 79–99.

Moore, George F., 'Baetylia', *AJA* 7 (1903), 198–208.

Morgan, Catherine, 'Ethnicity and Early Greek States', *PCPS* 37 (1991), 131–63.

——, 'Ethnicity', in S. Hornblower and A. H. Spawforth (eds), *Oxford Classical Dictionary*, 3rd edn (Oxford: Oxford University Press, 1996), 558–9.

Mortley, Raoul, *The Idea of Universal History from Hellenistic Philosophy to Early Christian Historiography* (Lewiston: Edwin Mellen Press, 1996).

Mosshammer, A. A., *The Chronicle of Eusebius and the Greek Chronographic Tradition* (Lewisburg: Bucknell University Press, 1979).

Mras, Karl, *Eusebius Werke VIII. Die Praeparatio Evangelica*, GCS 43.1–2 (Berlin: Akademie-Verlag, 1954, 1956).

Murray, C., 'Art in the Early Church', *JTS* 28 (1977), 303–45.

Murray, Oswynn, 'Hecataeus of Abdera and Pharaonic Kingship', *JEA* 56 (1970), 141–70.

Nautin, Pierre, 'Sanchuniathon chez Philon de Byblos et chez Porphyre', *Revue Biblique* 56 (1949), 259–73.

Nautin, Pierre, 'La Valeur Documentaire de l'Histoire Phenicienne', *Revue Biblique* 56 (1949), 573–8.

Nikolaidis-Rethymnon, Anastasios G., 'Ἑλληνικος—βαρβαρικος: Plutarch on Greek and Barbarian Characteristics', *WS* 20 (1986), 229–44.

Nilsson, M., 'Pagan Divine Service in Late Antiquity', *HTR* 38 (1945), 63–9.

Nock, A. D., 'The Emperor's Divine *Comes*', *JRS* 37 (1947), 102–16.

—— , 'The Praises of Antioch', *JEA* 40 (1954), 76–82.

Oden, R. A., 'Philo of Byblos and Hellenistic Historiography', *PEQ* 110 (1978), 115–26.

Oliver, James H., 'The Civilizing Power', *Transactions of the American Philosophical Society* 58 (1968), 1–223.

Olster, David, 'Classical Ethnography and Early Christianity', in K. Free (ed.), *The Formulation of Christianity by Conflict through the Ages* (Lewiston: E. Mellen Press, 1995), 9–31.

O'Meara, Dominic J., *Pythagoras Revived: Mathematics and Philosophy in Late Antiquity* (Oxford: Clarendon Press, 1989).

Palm, J. *Rom, Römertum und Imperium in der griechischen Literatur der Kaiserzeit* (Lund: Reg. Societas Humaniorum Litterarum Lundensis, 1959).

Parker, Holt N., 'The Teratogenic Grid', in J. P. Hallett and M. B. Skinner (eds), *Roman Sexualities* (Princeton: Princeton University Press, 1997), 47–65.

Parker, Robert, 'Greek States and Greek Oracles', in R. Buxton (ed.), *Oxford Readings in Greek Religion* (Oxford: Oxford University Press, 2000), 76–108; originally published in P. A. Cartledge and F. D. Harvey (eds), *Crux: Essays Presented to G. E. M. de Ste Croix on his 75th Birthday* (Exeter: Imprint Academic, 1985), 298–326.

Parkes, James, 'Jews and Christians in the Constantinian Empire', *SCH* 1 (1964), 69–79.

Pepin, J., 'La théologie tripartite de Varron', *REA* 2 (1956), 265–94.

Perrone, L., 'Eusebius of Caesarea as a Christian Writer', in Avner Raban and Kenneth Holum, (eds), *Caesarea Maritima: A Retrospective After Two Millenia* (Leiden: Brill, 1996), 515–530.

Peterson, Erik, *Der Monotheismus als politisches Problem. Ein Beitrag zur Geschichte der politischen Theologie im Imperium Romanum*, in *Theologische Traktate* (Munich: Hochland Bücherei, 1951), 45–147.

—— , *Das Buch von den Engeln. Stellung und Bedeutung der heiligen Engeln im Kultus* (Munich: Kösel-Verlag, 1955).

—— , 'Das Problem des Nationalismus im alten Christentum', in idem, *Frühkirche, Judentum und Gnosis* (Freiburg: Herder, 1959), 51–63.

Pilhofer, Peter, *Presbyteron Kreitton. Der Altersbeweis der jüdischen und christlichen Apologeten und seine Vorgeschichte* (Tübingen: Mohr [Siebeck], 1990).

Poole, Ross, *Nation and Identity* (New York: Routledge, 1999).

Pouderon, Bernard, *et al.*, *Aristide. Apologie*, SC 470 (Paris: Les Éditions du Cerf, 2003).

Powell, Barry, 'What Juvenal Saw: Egyptian Religion and Anthropophagy in *Satire* 15', *RM* 122 (1979), 185–9.

Preez, du P. *The Politics of Identity: Ideology and the Human Image* (New York: St Martin's Press, 1980).

Puech, Aimé, *Histoire de la littérature grecque chrétienne* (Paris: Société d'Édition 'Les Belles Lettres', 1930).

Rad, Gerhard von, 'Israel, Judah and Hebrews in the Old Testament', in Gerhard Kittel (ed.), G. W. Bromiley (trans.), *Theological Dictionary of the New Testament* (Grand Rapids: Eerdmans Publishing Co., 1964), 356–9.

Riaud, J., 'Les Thérapeutes d'Alexandrie dans la tradition et dans la recherche critique jusque'aux découvertes de Qumran', *ANRW* II.20.2 (1987), 1189–295.

Richter, Daniel, *Ethnography, archaism, and identity in the Early Roman Empire* (Ph.D. dissertation University of Chicago, 2001).

——, 'Plutarch on Isis and Osiris: Text, Cult, and Cultural Appropriation', *TAPA* 131 (2001), 191–216.

Ricken, F., 'Die Logoslehre des Eusebios von Caesarea und der Mittelplatonismus', *Theologie und Philosophie* 42 (1967), 341–58.

Ridings, Daniel, *The Attic Moses: The Dependency Theme in Some Early Christian Writers* (Göteborg: Acta Universitatis Gothoburgensis, 1995).

Riedweg, Christoph, *Ps.-Justin (Markell von Ankyra?), Ad Graecos de vera religione (bisher 'Cohortatio ad Graecos'). Einleitung und Kommentar* (Basel: F. Reinhardt, 1994).

Rives, James B., 'Human Sacrifice among Pagans and Christians', *JRS* 85 (1995), 65–85.

Romeo, Ilaria, 'The Panhellenion and Ethnic Identity', *CP* 97 (2002), 21–40.

Romm, J. S., *The Edges of the Earth in Ancient Thought* (Princeton: Princeton University Press, 1992).

Rondeau, M. –J., *Les commentaires patristiques du psautier* (Rome: Pontifical Institute of Oriental Studies, 1982).

——, 'Eusèbe de Césarée. Le Commentaire sur les psaumes', in M. –J. Rondeau and J. Kirchmeyer, *Dictionnaire de spiritualité* (Paris: Beauchesnes, 1961), IV.2.1687–90.

Rose, H. J., 'De Iove Latiari', *Mnemosyne* 55 (1927), 273–9.

Roth, Norman, 'The "Theft of Philosophy" by the Greeks from the Jews', *Classical Folia* 32 (1978), 53–67.

Rubin, Milka, 'The Language of Creation or the Primordial Language: A Case of Cultural Polemics in Antiquity', *Journal of Jewish Studies* 49 (1998), 306–33.

Ruhbach, Gerhard, 'Die politische Theologie Eusebs von Caesarea', in idem (ed.), *Die Kirche angesichts der konstantinischen Wende* (Darmstadt: Wissenschaftliche Buchgesellschaft, 1976), 236–58.

Ruppel, Walter, 'Politeuma. Bedeutungsgeschichte eines staatsrechtlichen Terminus', *Philologus* 82 (1927), 268–312, 434–54.

Sacks, Kenneth S., *Diodorus Siculus and the First Century* (Princeton: Princeton University Press, 1990).

Schmidt, Karl L., 'ἔθνος in the New Testament', in Gerhard Kittel, (ed.), G. W. Bromiley, (trans.), *TDNT* (Grand Rapids: Eerdmans Publishing Co., 1964), 369–372.

—— , 'ἐθνικός', in Kittel, (ed.), G. W. Bromiley, (trans.), *TDNT* (Grand Rapids: Eerdmans Publishing Co., 1964), 372.

Schoedel W. R. and Wilken, R. L. (eds), *Early Christian Literature and the Classical Intellectual Tradition*, in honorem R. M. Grant (Paris: Éditions Beauchesne, 1979).

Schreckenberg, Heinz, 'Text, Überlieferung und Textkritik von *Contra Apionem*', in L. H. Feldman and John Levison, (eds.), *Josephus' Contra Apionem* (Leiden: Brill, 1996), 250–70.

Schroeder, Guy, and Des Places, E., *Eusèbe de Césarée. La Préparation Évangélique, Livre VII*, SC 215 (Paris: Les Éditions du Cerf, 1975).

Schwartz, E., 'Eusebios von Caesarea', *RE* 11 (Stuttgart: J. B. Metzlersche Buchhandlung 1909), cols. 1370–439.

Schwartz, Seth, 'Language, Power and Identity in Ancient Palestine', *P&P* 148 (1995), 3–47.

Seeberg, Bengt, 'Die Geschichtstheologie Justins des Märtyrers', *ZKG* 58 (1939), 1–81.

Seeck, Otto, 'Das sogenannte Edikt von Mailand', *ZKG* 12 (1891), 381–6.

Seston, W., 'Constantine as Bishop', *JRS* 37 (1947), 127–31.

Setton, Kenneth M., *The Christian Attitude Toward the Emperor in the Fourth Century* (New York: Columbia University Press, 1941).

Shaw, B., ' "Eaters of Flesh–Drinkers of Milk". The Ancient Mediterranean Ideology of the Pastoral Nomad', *Ancient Society* 13–14 (1982–3), 5–31.

Sherwin-White, A. N., *The Roman Citizenship* (Oxford: Clarendon Press, 1973).

Sirinelli, Jean, *Les vues historiques d'Eusèbe de Césarée durant la période prénicéene*, Faculté des Lettres et Sciences Humaines, Publications de la Section de Langues et Litteratures 10 (Dakar: Universite de Dakar, 1961).

Sirinelli, Jean and Des Places, E., *Eusèbe de Césarée. La Préparation Évangélique, Livre I*, SC 206 (Paris: Les Éditions du Cerf, 1974).

Smelik, K. A. D., and Hemelrijk, E. A., 'Who Knows Not What Monsters Demented Egypt Worships?' *ANRW* 2.17.4 (1984), 1852–2000.

Smith, Andrew, 'Porphyry and Pagan Religious Practice', in J. J. Cleary, (ed.), *The Perennial Tradition of Neoplatonism* (Louvain: Louvain University Press, 1997), 29–35.

Smith, Anthony D., *The Ethnic Origins of Nations* (Oxford: Blackwell, 1986).

—— , *The Antiquity of Nations* (Cambridge: Polity Press, 2004).

Smith, M. 'A Hidden Use of Porphyry's History of Philosophy in Eusebius' Praeparatio Evangelica', *JTS* 39 (1988), 494–504.

Sourvinou-Inwood, Christiane, 'What is *Polis* Religion?', in R. Buxton (ed.), *Oxford Readings in Greek Religion* (Oxford: Oxford University Press, 2000), 13–37; originally published in O. Murray and S. Price (eds), *The Greek City From Homer to Alexander* (Oxford: Oxford University Press, 1990), 295–322.

—— , 'Further Aspects of *Polis* Religion', in R. Buxton (ed.), *Oxford Readings in Greek Religion* (Oxford: Oxford University Press, 2000), 38–55; originally published in *Annali dell' Istituto Universitario Orientale di Napoli, Sezione di Archeologia e Storia Antica* 10 (1988), 259–74.

Spawforth, A. J., 'The Panhellenion Again', *Chiron* 29 (1999), 339–52.

—— , 'Shades of Greekness', in I. Malkin (ed.), *Ancient Perceptions of Greek Ethnicity* (Cambridge: Harvard University Press, 2001), 375–400.

Stemberger, G., *Jews and Christians in the Holy Land. Palestine in the Fourth Century*, trans. R. Tuschling (Edinburgh: T&T Clark, 2000).

Sterling, Gregory, *Historiography and Self-Definition* (Leiden: Brill, 1992).

Stowers, Stanley K., 'Greeks Who Sacrifice and Those Who Do Not: Toward an Anthropology of Greek Religion', in L. M. White and O. L. Yarbarough (eds), *The Social World of the First Christians. Essays in Honor of Wayne A. Meeks* (Minneapolis: Fortress Press, 1995), 293–333.

Stroumsa, Guy G., *Barbarian Philosophy: The Religious Revolution of Early Christianity* (Tübingen: Mohr [Siebeck], 1999).

Swain, Simon, *Hellenism and Empire: Language, Classicism, and Power in the Greek World AD 50–250* (Oxford: Clarendon Press, 1996).

Swain S. and Edwards M. (eds), *Approaching Late Antiquity* (Oxford: Oxford University Press, 2004).

Swift Riginos, A., *Platonica: The Anecdotes concerning the Life and Writings of Plato*, Columbia Studies in the Classical Tradition 3 (Leiden: Brill, 1976).

Teixidor, J., *The Pagan God: Popular Religion in the Ancient Near East* (Princeton: Princeton University Press, 1977).

Thielman, F.S., 'Another Look at the Eschatology of Eusebius', *VC* 41 (1987), 226–37.

Thompson, Dorothy, 'Ethnê, taxes and administrative geography in early Ptolemaic Egypt', in I. Andorlini *et al.* (eds), *Atti del XXII Congresso Internazionale di Papirologia* (Firenze: Istituto Papirologico 'G. Vitelli', 2001), 2.1255–63.

Tillich, Paul, *Theology of Culture* (Oxford: Oxford University Press, 1983).

Ulrich, Jorg, *Euseb von Caesarea und die Juden. Studien zur Rolle der Juden in der Theologie des Eusebius von Casarea* (Berlin and New York: Walter de Gruyter, 1999).

Unger, G. F., 'Die Blüthezeit des Alexander Polyhistor', *Philologus* 47 (1889), 177–83.

Vivian, Miriam R., *A Letter to Shapur: The Effect of Constantine's Converions on Roman-Persian Relations*, (Ph.D. dissertation University of California, Santa Barbara, 1987).

Walbank, F. W., 'The Problem of Greek Nationality', *Phoenix* 5 (1951), 41–60; reprinted in T. Harrison (ed.) *Greeks and Barbarians* (New York: Routledge, 2002), 234–56.

——, 'Nationality as a Factor in Roman History', *HSCP* 76 (1972), 145–68.

Wallace-Hadrill, D. S., *Eusebius of Caesarea* (London: A. R. Mowbray & Co., Ltd., 1960).

——, 'Eusebius of Caesarea's *Commentary on Luke*: Its Origin and Early History', *HTR* 67 (1974), 55–63.

Ward, Julia K., '*Ethnos* in the *Politics*: Aristotle and Race', in J. Ward and T. Lott (eds), *Philosophers on Race* (Oxford: Blackwell, 2002), 14–37.

Wardman, A. E., 'Plutarch and Alexander', *CQ* 5 (1955), 96–107.

Whitmarsh, Tim, *Greek Literature and the Roman Empire: The Politics of Imitation* (Oxford: Oxford University Press, 2001).

——, 'Alexander's Hellenism and Plutarch's Textualism', *CQ* 52 (2002), 174–92.

Wiedemann, T. E. J., 'Between Men and Beasts: Barbarians in Ammianus Marcellinus', in I. S. Moxon, J. D. Smart and A. J. Woodman (eds), *Past Perspectives: Studies in Greek and Roman Historical Writing* (Cambridge: Cambridge University Press, 1986), 189–201.

Wilken, Robert L., 'Pagan Criticism of Christianity: Greek Religion and Christian Faith', in *Early Christian Literature and the Classical Intellectual Tradition*, W. Schoedel and R. Wilken (eds) (Paris: Editions Beauchesne, 1979), 117–34.

——, *The Christians as the Romans Saw Them* (New Haven: Yale University Press, 1984).

——, 'The Restoration of Israel in Biblical Prophecy: Christian and Jewish Responses in the Early Byzantine Period', in J. Neusner and E. Frerichs, (eds.), *'To See Ourselves As Others See Us'* (Chico: Scholars Press, 1985), 443–72.

Willamowitz-Moellendorf, U., 'Ein Bruchstück aus der Schrift des Porphyrius gegen die Christen', *ZNW* 1 (1900), 101–05.

Wilson, Brian C., 'From the Lexical to the Polythetic: A Brief History of the Definition of Religion', in Thomas Idinopolus and Brian Wilson (eds), *What Is Religion?* (Leiden: Brill, 1998), 141–62.

Winquist, Charles E., 'Thinking Religion', in Thomas Idinopolus and Brian Wilson, *What Is Religion?* (Leiden: Brill, 1998), 163–71.

Young, Frances, 'Greek Apologists of the Second Century', in Edwards *et al.*, *Apologetics in the Roman Empire*, 81–104.

Zanker, G., 'Enargeia in Ancient Criticism of Poetry', *RM* 124 (1981), 297–311.

Zernatto, G., 'Nation: The History of a Word', *Review of Politics* 6 (1944), 351–66.

Zink, Odile, and Des Places, E., *Eusèbe de Césarée. La Préparation Évangélique, Livres IV–V, 1–17*, SC 262 (Paris: Les Éditions du Cerf, 1979).

Zucker, F., 'Euhemeros und seine *Hiera Anagraphe* bei den christlichen Schriftstellern', *Philologus* 64 (1905), 465–72.

Zuntz, G., 'Baitylos and Bethel', *Classica et Mediaevalia* 8 (1945), 169–219.

General Index

Abraham 104–5
allegory 58, 68–9, 85–8, 122–3, 157,
    171–2
angels 64 n. 34, 163, 166–8
Apollo 63, 71, 75, 164, 214
Aristides, the Apologist 6, 9–10
asceticism 110, 122–4, 140
Augustus 154, 156, 174–80, 185,
    187–91, 196–7, 204

baetylia 90

Cadmus 20, 58, 77–80, 134
cannibalism 188, 206–8, 218
Celsus 8–9
chronology 74, 135–6, 150, 175
circumcision 71, 105, 116–17
Clement of Alexandria 7–8, 60, 78, 86
Constantine 11–12, 22, 153–4,
    186–17, 189, 193–5
conversion 185, 204–10, 215–18, 231
cosmogeny 59–64, 70, 96, 234–6

daemons 36, 91–2, 98–9, 158, 163–70,
    172, 176–8, 180, 187–8, 193,
    204, 210–11
decline, narrative of 64, 72–3, 97–9,
    107–9, 110, 167, 187–8, 193,
    237–9
Dio Chrysostom 132–3

Egyptians 20–1, 62–3, 81–5, 89,
    74–7, 106–9, 118–19, 134,
    137–8, 141, 173, 190–1, 208,
    214, 227, 234–5
  animal worship of 76, 235
ethnicity 5–10, 17, 19, 24, 25–54,
    124–5, 220

origin of term 26
boundaries of 5, 27–8, 51–4,
    170–80, 184, 232
elements of
  language 43–4, 48
  narrative of descent 19–21, 26,
    29–30, 55–7, *passim*
  skin colour 48
  territory 27, 29, 48, 90–1
  religion 9–10, 44–5, 88,
    199–200, 209, 220, 232–3
theory of 25–33
see also nation, race
ethnography 7, 23, 205–8,
    209–11, 215
euhemerism 67, 69–73, 75–6, 78,
    80–5, 159, 166

Fate 122, 234–5

Gog 182
Greeks 4, 15–16, 19–21, 50–3,
    57–64, 68, 77–80, 126–52,
    155–60, 162–4, 171–4,
    208–10, 216–18, 232,
    234–5
  alphabet of 134–5
  as thieves 52, 81, 130–6, 150–1,
    209
  Greek philosophers
    discord of 61–2, 128, 142–9,
     229, 239
    lateness of 6, 84–5, 135–6, 137,
     150–1
  Seven Sages 7, 132–4, 136

Hadrian 4, 65, 90 n. 173, 159, 168–9,
    189, 191, 204

hagiography 111–14
Hebrews 19–21, 37–9, 43–4, 49, 64,
    73, 94–125, 134–45, 149–50,
    167, 209, 214, 217–18,
    222, 225, 227–33, 235–6,
    238–9
  alphabet of 134–5
  distinct from Jews 100, 106–9, 111,
    114–19, 227, 236
  from Heber 114–15
  Patriarchs 103–7, 112–13, 118,
    230–11
Hellenocentrism 65, 140, 216–17
Hesiod 68, 71
historiography, Hellenistic 2–4,
    66–7, 106, 128–9

incest 71, 188, 206–8, 218
Introduction (*eisagoge*) 14–15, 61,
    117–19
Isis 63, 75–6

Jews 3–4, 8, 15–16, 37–9, 42–3, 49,
    53, 105, 107–9, 128, 179–81,
    189–92, 232
  distinct from Hebrews 20–1,
    100, 106–9, 111, 114–19,
    227, 236
  as race of philosophers 38–9, 52,
    122
Josephus 3–4, 106, 114–15, 124,
    128–9
Justin Martyr 230–1

Kronos 63, 71, 75, 83, 89

Licinius 11–12, 161, 186–7,
    193
Logos 113, 117–18, 121, 124,
    139–40, 153, 167, 188,
    193–4, 213, 216–17, 219,
    231, 238–9
Lucian 4 n. 15, 38 n. 61, 132–3

Maximinus Daia 11, 15 n. 68, 161–2,
    179
monotheism 17, 108, 130, 133, 149,
    176, 220
Moses 21, 107–9, 110–13,
    117–21, 124, 136, 138–41,
    144
  Law of 45–6, 111–12, 116–17, 118,
    120, 123, 141, 227

nation (*ethnos*) 3, 5–10, 17, 19, 22,
    25–33, 40–51
nation-state 31–3
Numenius 129, 145–7

oracles 91–2, 133, 160–6,
    234–5
Origen 9–10
Orpheus 20, 58, 77–80, 132
Osiris 63, 75–6, 79, 83

paganism, *see* Egyptians, Greeks,
    Phoenicians, etc.
Panhellenion 4, 217
Persians 23, 134, 185, 188, 206,
    207 n. 36, 215
philanthropia 199, 210–18
Philo, of Alexandria 95 n. 2, 101–2,
    104, 112, 115, 124
Philo, of Byblos 65–72, 81, 86, 89
philosophy 132, 142, 145–9
  Pre-socratics (physical
    philosophers) 145, 147–8,
    236
  Academics 145–7, 236
  Peripatetics 147
  Stoics 147
  Epicureans 97–8, 146–7
  Cynics 132
  Skeptics 147
Phoenicians 62, 64–74, 81, 83–5,
    90–1, 134, 208, 214, 234–5
  alphabet of 44, 84 n. 141, 134

animal worship of 72, 235
Plato 20–1, 99, 126–7, 137–43,
        145–7, 151, 173, 228–9,
        236
Plutarch 61–2, 65, 85, 86, 92, 111–12,
        148, 168
politeia (or *politeuma*) 46–8, 50
political (or civic) theology 21, 90,
        153–60, 162, 169–70, 178, 180,
        204, 234
Porphyry 15 n. 68, 65, 86–7, 159,
        163–5, 169, 173, 207, 214
Pythagoras 52, 133–4, 148–9

race (*genos*) 6, 10, 17, 19, 25–30,
        35–40, 48–51, 166, 163, 209,
        212, 222
religion, *see* ethnicity
Rome 12, 21–2, 153–6, 158–60,
        170–5, 178–97, 204

sacrifice
    ancient practice 63–4, 237
    animal sacrifice 63 n. 32, 164–5, 237

human sacrifice 155, 159, 165, 169,
        207, 210–11
    spiritual sacrifice 164–5
Scythians 23, 132, 155, 185, 188,
        206–7, 215
Second Sophistic 4, 7
Septuagint 32, 41–2, 45, 122, 183,
        190–1
Socrates 62, 104, 149

Tatian 7, 47, 217, 224
theology
    astral 61–4, 69–70, 96–7, 148,
        167, 237
    hierarchy 163
    of animals 72, 76, 89,
        237
    of the Hebrews 121–3, 144,
        149–50, 166, 228, 235–6
    tripartite division 58, 156–8, 163,
        174, 234

universalism 17, 53, 198–200, 211–13,
        214–16